THE UNTOLD STORY OF THE WORLD'S LEADING ENVIRONMENTAL INSTITUTION

One Planet

Sikina Jinnah and Simon Nicholson, series editors

Peter Dauvergne, *AI in the Wild: Sustainability in the Age of Artificial Intelligence*

Vincent Ialenti, *Deep Time Reckoning: How Future Thinking Can Help Earth Now*

Maria Ivanova, *The Untold Story of the World's Leading Environmental Institution: UNEP at Fifty*

THE UNTOLD STORY OF THE WORLD'S LEADING ENVIRONMENTAL INSTITUTION

UNEP AT FIFTY

MARIA IVANOVA

FOREWORD BY JOHN W. McDONALD

THE MIT PRESS CAMBRIDGE, MASSACHUSETTS LONDON, ENGLAND

This book was set in ITC Stone Serif, Stone Sans, and Avenir by Westchester Publishing Services. Printed and bound in the United States of America.

Library of Congress Cataloging-in-Publication Data

Names: Ivanova, Maria (Maria H.), author.
Title: The untold story of the world's leading environmental institution : UNEP at fifty / Maria Ivanova ; foreword by John W. McDonald
Description: Cambridge, Massachusetts : The MIT Press, [2021] | Series: One planet | Includes bibliographical references and index.
Identifiers: LCCN 2020015014 | ISBN 9780262542104 (paperback)
Subjects: LCSH: United Nations Environment Programme—History. | Environmental protection—International cooperation—History.
Classification: LCC TD169 .I86 2021 | DDC 363.7/056—dc23
LC record available at https://lccn.loc.gov/2020015014

10 9 8 7 6 5 4 3 2 1

In memory of the women and men who have passed and who, with imagination and courage, created the system of global environmental governance.

CONTENTS

SERIES FOREWORD

This is at once an odd and exhilarating time to be alive. Our species, *Homo sapiens,* has had roughly 350,000 years on the planet. For most of that time our ancestors barely registered as a quiet voice in a teeming chorus. No more. Now, a human cacophony threatens the ecological foundations upon which all life rests, even as technological wonders point the way toward accelerating expansion. We find ourselves at a moment of reckoning. The next handful of decades will determine whether humanity has the capacity, will, and wisdom to manufacture forms of collective life compatible with long-term ecological realities, or whether, instead, there is an expiration date on the grand human experiment.

The One Planet book series has been created to showcase insightful, hope-fueled accounts of the planetary condition and the social and political features upon which that condition now depends. Most environmental books are shackled by a pessimistic reading of the present moment or by academic conventions that stifle a writer's voice. We have asked One Planet authors to produce a different kind of scholarship. This series is designed to give established and emerging authors a chance to put their best, most astute ideas on display. These are works crafted to show a new path through the complex and overwhelming subject matters that characterize life on our New Earth.

The books in this series are not formulaic. Nor are they Pollyannaish. The hope we have asked for from our authors comes not from overly optimistic accounts of ways forward, but rather from hard-headed and clear-eyed accounts of the actions we need to take in the face of sometimes overwhelming odds. One Planet books are unified by deep scholarly engagement brought to life through vivid writing by authors freed to write from the heart.

Thanks to our friends at the MIT Press, especially to Beth Clevenger, for guiding the One Planet series into existence, and to the contributing authors for their extraordinary work. The authors, the Press, and we, the series editors, invite engagement. The best books do more than convey interesting ideas: they spark interesting conversations. Please write to us to let us know how you are using One Planet books or to tell us about the kinds of themes you would like to see the series address.

Finally, our thanks to you for picking up and diving into this book. We hope that you find it a useful addition to your own thinking about life on our One Planet.

Sikina Jinnah and Simon Nicholson

FOREWORD

Ambassador John W. McDonald

The only way to solve a conflict at any level of society is to sit down face to face and talk about it.

—Ambassador John W. McDonald (1922–2019)[1]

I am delighted that Dr. Maria Ivanova took the initiative to share with younger generations the actions taken by the members of the United Nations at the UN Conference on the Environment in 1972 in Stockholm and which led, in the fall of 1972, at the UN General Assembly in New York, to the establishment of the United Nations Environment Programme (UNEP), located in Kenya.

This is a timely and much-needed book in which Dr. Ivanova rediscovers and captures the beginnings of UNEP trying to grow as fast as possible to fulfill the expectations of the global community, but soon also experiencing the effects of a fast-changing world. Confidence and mistrust, successful implementation and misinterpretations of UNEP's mission have alternated over the years. As governments change and national interests are redefined, facts are forgotten or transformed, alternative narratives set in, and conventional "wisdom" takes the place of historical accounts. The creation of the United Nations Environment Programme is just that kind of historical occurrence that has lost its vivid color and has been replaced by a "deficiency by design" narrative that is simply incorrect.

Dr. Ivanova has an exceptional understanding of the ideals, hopes and urgent needs regarding the protection of the global environment ever since they rose into the conscience of world leaders in the late 1960s. She guides us through a complex reality over half a century to gain a better understanding of UNEP's creation as well as its efforts, activities, and changes, as well as governments' responsiveness, or lack and manipulation thereof, to UNEP's needs.

When I look back in time, only a few people around the world in the mid-1960s had begun to realize that something was going on in our global climate that required attention. I am appreciative of the United Nations and the members of its General Assembly for their understanding and taking the first steps toward action to protect the environment. I am grateful to the Swedish government for inviting governments to come to Stockholm in 1972. It was an astonishing gathering of developed and developing countries which agreed at the end of the Stockholm Conference on the creation of a new international environmental institution.

This new institution was based on a plan that I had been able to get through the United States bureaucracy over two years of preparation with all interested US Agencies and which was even supported by a forward-thinking Nixon White House. As Secretary of the US delegation at the Conference in Stockholm, I shared with half a dozen delegates from other countries my four draft resolutions for the creation of a new international environmental institution. The participants of the conference recognized the need for long-term global action and brought the same kind of strong desire and superb ideas to the negotiation table. In a spirit of positive cooperation, a plan of action to establish an environmental institution emerged and was accepted by the whole conference—with enthusiasm and by acclamation.

The UN had 132 members in 1972. No one imagined a UN with 193 members in forty-five years; no one could possibly imagine that UNEP would have to deal with immense political changes after the fall of the Berlin Wall, with erratic global economic, social, and financial growth, and with increasingly fast-developing technology. Small differences between countries became bigger, new and totally unexpected environmental issues arose globally and kept growing, ignoring political borders. The result is that our global environment began to show the grave ravages of our daily sins. All this imposed incredible challenges on UNEP in the following decades. Yes, forecasts and future plans multiplied, but no one would dream of saying in 1972 or even in the 1980s that "climate change is the most pressing global challenge, constituting an existential threat to humanity." Yet, that is what participants at COP24 in December 2018 concluded.

With a stroke of genius, Dr. Maria Ivanova convened for the first and only time in 2009 all five executive directors of UNEP along with eighty leaders in global environmental governance from around the world, across sectors, and spanning four generations. We met in Glion, Switzerland—face to face—to understand the past and to create a better and more efficient future with and for UNEP. I was eighty-seven years old at that time, and the experience moved me, inspired me, encouraged me, and empowered me. And it still gives me hope.

No institution, large or small, ever changes by itself. People are afraid of change, of what it might do to their job, their turf, their security. When change is proposed—as it must be again and again to save our global environment and ourselves—the most typical reaction is to sit tight and do nothing. Sometimes, however, a small shift does take place because of pressure and ideas from an outside source. This book, with its extraordinary rigor of analysis, depth of understanding, and scale of vision, is that source!

January 27, 2019
Arlington, VA

PREFACE

Anniversaries offer opportunities to reflect on the past and imagine the future. In 2022, the United Nations Environment Programme (UNEP) turns fifty and has a chance to reinvent itself. Created to "divert operating agencies into environmental ways, to color their programs environmental," how has UNEP done so far, and what should it do differently?[1] Who can cause that change, and how can they do so? These questions have defined my work as a student and a scholar for over twenty years.

I entered the field of global environmental governance at the very start of the reform process of international environmental governance, in 1997. A graduate student at Yale University pursuing master's degrees in international relations and environmental policy (because international environmental policy did not exist as a field at the time), I became an advocate for a global environmental organization. My advisor, Professor Daniel Esty, had received a grant from the MacArthur Foundation to launch a debate about the institutional design for global environmental policy. He asked me to assist.

Born and raised in Bulgaria, I had arrived in the United States only five years earlier, in 1992, to study at Mount Holyoke College. My role was therefore that of an apprentice—learning the substance, managing the process, running the logistics. Yet, Dan Esty gave me the opportunity and responsibility to co-create the first Global Environmental Governance

Dialogue. We brought together many of the founders and leaders in the global environmental governance system itself—Maurice Strong, Peter Thacher, Alicia Bárcena, Julia Marton-Lefèvre, Alvaro Umaña, Michael Gusovsky, and Makarim Wibisono, among others. The discussions were thought-provoking and invigorating, and we saw potential for a sustained and expanding dialogue. We managed to deliver the event at half the projected cost, which allowed us to launch the Global Environmental Governance Project and to host annual dialogues. Dan Esty joked for a long time that it was my Eastern European background that made this initiative of bringing rigorous academic analysis into policy sustainable.

We argued explicitly for the creation of a Global Environmental Organization to address failed collective action on environmental concerns and to overcome institutional fragmentation. Such an organization, we contended, would have greater authority and legitimacy and thus function more effectively than UNEP. As political debates intensified in the run-up to the 2002 Johannesburg Summit on Sustainable Development, we produced a co-edited volume, *Global Environmental Governance: Options and Opportunities*, which featured scholars and practitioners from around the world.[2] Arguments for and against a World Environment Organization were becoming more heated, and since I had begun a PhD program at Yale, I decided to explore why we did not have such an organization. Why was UNEP created as a subsidiary body, a programme, in 1972? What was the original vision? Did the founders of UNEP miss this important detail, or was the programme deliberately designed, as some scholars argued, in order to incapacitate it? Having engaged with many of the people who were present at the programme's creation, I simply was not convinced by the theory of deliberate deficiency.

I therefore ventured into the UN archives and the offices and living rooms of many of the people who had created the major institutions for environmental governance. I pieced together a story that was quite different from what I had read in my textbooks. And as I continued to engage in policy discussions, I witnessed policymakers grappling with the same questions the founders of UNEP had tackled in the 1970s: What are the key functions of an environmental governance system at the global level? Can existing institutions be improved to address these functions, or is a new body required? What is the best institutional design, and how can we ensure that it will work? What is the relationship between environmental and development goals, and how should the institution be governed? Over time, as I unearthed the story of UNEP's creation and operation, my argument changed.

UNEP, I found, was not deficient by design, and its limiting factor was not its structure. Transforming it into a specialized agency, a World or Global Environmental Organization, therefore, would not address the underlying problems. I had proven myself wrong and identified the flaws in the proposals of several governments. I set out to discover how and why UNEP had performed the way it did through empirical and engaged research.

In 2004, as a doctoral student, I co-taught a class about UNEP with Mohamed El-Ashry of the Global Environment Facility and Professor Gordon Geballe, at the request of Gus Speth, who was then the dean of the Yale School of Forestry & Environmental Studies. We undertook the first university-led evaluation of UNEP, and I am grateful to the many UNEP staff who made our analysis possible. Jacob Duer was our UNEP focal point, Kati Autere ensured we had what we needed, and Deputy Executive Director Shafqat Kakakhel engaged with the students and encouraged our thinking. In 2005, thanks to the generosity of Yale alumnus Jim Leitner, the entire class traveled to Kenya to present our evaluation to environment ministers at the UNEP Governing Council. Executive Director Klaus Töpfer hosted us and welcomed the analysis. Our report, *Can the Anchor Hold? Rethinking the UN Environment Programme for the 21st Century*,[3] was possible because of the assistance of numerous UNEP officials who would continue to support my analysis for many years to come.

Understanding the richness and complexity of UNEP's Nairobi location would not have been possible without the hospitality and generosity of Professor Wangari Maathai and the Green Belt Movement, one of the most prominent grassroots women's organizations in the world. Wangari had just learned that she was the recipient of the 2004 Nobel Peace Prize, the first environmentalist to receive this honor, and yet she found the time to work with us and inspire us. We spent a week with a local community learning about life in Kenya. Transcending the realities of high-level politics, this local work inspired us all and launched many environmental careers. Subsequently, I organized similar trips as a faculty at the College of

William & Mary and the University of Massachusetts Boston. The opportunity to be both "environmentalists in heels" and "environmentalists in Birkenstocks," my students reflected, shaped their future trajectories. I continued to convene, reflect, write, and engage, and when the environmental governance reform process rekindled in 2006, the Global Environmental Governance Project had become a trusted partner. A few years later, it transformed into the Center for Governance and Sustainability at UMass Boston when I joined the faculty of the John W. McCormack Graduate School of Policy and Global Studies at the university.

History is made of stories about the influence of individuals and institutions. This book is a tribute to the collective wisdom of the women and men committed to solving environmental problems and working through international institutions to do so. Professor Oran Young's suggestion to explore the leadership of UNEP as an explanatory variable sparked the idea to convene all of UNEP's executive directors with whom I had interacted since the start of the reform process. They had never before been in the same room discussing the past, present, and potential of the organization. With generous support from the UN Foundation, thanks to Mohamed El-Ashry, from the governments of Switzerland (thanks to Ambassador Franz Perrez), Germany (thanks to Stephan Contius), the Horn of Africa Regional Environment Centre and Network in Ethiopia (thanks to Professor Araya Asfaw), and the UN Institute for Training and Research (thanks to Carlos Lopes), in 2009, we convened a rare gathering, the Global Environmental Governance Forum in Glion, Switzerland. The Forum brought together for the first and only time all five consecutive executive directors of UNEP until that date: Maurice Strong, Mostafa Tolba, Elizabeth Dowdeswell, Klaus Töpfer, and Achim Steiner. Eighty global environmental leaders, including founders and directors of key international institutions and emerging young leaders, gathered to reflect on the past and envision the future. I am grateful to Julia Marton-Lefèvre, who hosted an elegant celebration of Maurice Strong's eightieth birthday back-to-back with the Forum, thus providing a compelling reason for many dignitaries to engage in both events.

Ambassador John W. McDonald's narrative of the original vision for a new international environmental organization and his account of the

0.1 Ambassador John W. McDonald (left) with Ambassador Lumumba Di-Aping (right) and emerging leaders at the 2009 Global Environmental Governance Forum in Glion, Switzerland.

decisions on UNEP's location in Nairobi struck us all. The stories of Bill Ruckelshaus, the first Administrator of the US Environmental Protection Agency; of Ambassador Lars-Göran Engfeldt who was Sweden's Liaison Officer at the 1972 Stockholm Conference; of Jim MacNeill, the Secretary General of the 1987 Brundtland Commission; of Michael Zammit Cutajar, the first Executive Secretary of the UN Framework Convention on Climate Change (UNFCCC); of Yolanda Kakabadse, President of the International Union for Conservation of Nature (IUCN) and later of the World Wide Fund for Nature (WWF); of Ambassador Peter Maurer, Co-chair of the UN General Assembly's environmental governance reform process; and of Ambassador Lumumba Di-Aping, Chair of the G-77, who would become Co-chair of the Copenhagen climate COP a few months later, painted a complex picture of ambitious vision, limited capacity, strained connectivity, and missed opportunities. The dialogue in Glion broke boundaries and forged lasting connections. It led to national dialogues on global environmental governance in Argentina, China, Nepal, Ethiopia, and Uganda hosted by young emerging leaders.

In so many ways, Ambassador John W. McDonald is at the core of this book. The Glion forum was a manifestation of his credo—"sit down face to face and talk"—and his insights reminded us all that individuals imagine institutions, create, and change them. Collaboration with Ambassador McDonald and his wife Christel McDonald, former European civil servant and a historical researcher in conflict resolution, continued much beyond the forum. Every year at UMass Boston, we bestow the Ambassador John W. McDonald award for leadership and innovation in global governance and conflict resolution. The graduate students who receive the award will continue the spirit and ambition of Ambassador McDonald as they grow their leadership potential.

Through the leadership profiles of the executive directors, this book brings the individual into the institutional analysis and highlights the challenges and opportunities during their era. I am grateful to Christiana Figueres, who inspired the work on the leadership profiles, and to Ehsan Masood, who encouraged me to interview the bosses' bosses—the UN Secretaries-General. My thoughtful conversations with Kofi Annan, Ban Ki-moon, and Deputy Secretary-General Amina Mohammed, who is responsible for the sustainable development agenda for UN Secretary-General António Guterres, deepened the analysis.

I am thankful to the nearly two hundred individuals, current and former UNEP staff members, government representatives, intergovernmental organization officials, and civil society representatives for the formal interviews and countless informal dialogues that contribute to this book's rich empirical depiction of the past fifty years of UNEP's history. Many agreed to be quoted in the book, for which I am grateful. The Cast of Characters section provides an overview of the women and men whose voices appear several times throughout the narrative and illustrates their relationship to and perspective on UNEP. For others, identities remain protected and a random three-digit reference is used in place of a name. Many are not quoted directly, but their input informed the narrative. My insights from participation in UNEP's Governing Council since 2001 and in the UN Environment Assembly sessions complement the interviews. In collaboration with the Federal Office for the Environment of Switzerland, the Nordic Council of Ministers, and the government of Finland, our team has continued to convene and engage policymakers. Through the Global Environmental Dialogues over the past twenty years, we have created a powerful network of committed individuals whose encouragement has been indispensable.

I am also thankful to the institutions that enabled and supported my work throughout the years. First, I would like to express my deepest gratitude to Mount Holyoke College. In 1991, inspiring each other to do the impossible, a number of us high-school seniors in Bulgaria applied to college in the Unites States. Against impossible odds, I received a full scholarship to Mount Holyoke College and had the freedom to pursue any scholarly endeavor I could imagine. Having interviewed so many luminaries, I have noticed a pattern in personal stories. "How did you become interested in this field of study?" I would ask. And the answer, 80 percent of the time, points to a professor in college. My story is no different. In the spring semester of 1993, my interest in international environmental policy was sparked in a course on Scandinavian government and politics that I took with Professor Eric Einhorn at the University of Massachusetts Amherst. And, over the years, my professors—Penny Gill and Catherine LeGouis at Mount Holyoke College; Jim Cathey, Erik Einhorn, and Peter Haas at UMass Amherst; and Katarina Eckerberg at Umeå University in Sweden—reinforced the drive to learn more, do better, and make an impact.

Second, at Yale University, my desire to bridge science and policy blossomed and faculty and staff enabled me to engage meaningfully at the intersection of the two. I am grateful to Yale for opening an unimaginable breadth of opportunities, and to my mentors there—Dan Esty, Ben Cashore, Gus Speth, Gordon Geballe, Marian Chertow, Brad Gentry, and John Wargo—for helping me go the extra mile. The Rev. Albert P. Nielson Environmental Ethics Award and the Teresa Heinz Scholarship for Environmental Research supported my work as a master's student. The Yale Center for the Study of Globalization Dissertation Research Award, the Globalization and Self-Determination Project Dissertation Fellowship, and the Academic Council for the UN System Dissertation Award supported much of my doctoral research work.

In 2005, when I joined the Department of Government at the College of William & Mary, I joined a community of scholars who engaged actively with theory and practice. The Woodrow Wilson Center Fellowship in 2009–2010 was critical to the convening of the 2009 Global Environmental Governance Forum and the analysis of the outcomes that constitute an important part of this book. The 2015 Andrew Carnegie Fellowship was instrumental to finalizing the manuscript.

At UMass Boston, I have found an institutional home supportive of scholarship with impact, and I am grateful to my colleagues in the Department of Conflict Resolution, Human Security, and Global Governance and the McCormack Graduate School of Policy and Global Studies. Craig Murphy's work on the history of the UN Development Programme had been an inspiration since I was a graduate student and working with him to create a new PhD program in global governance and human security was truly an honor and a privilege. Provost Winston Langley, Dean Steve Crosby, Dean Ira Jackson, and Dean David Cash encouraged and supported my work at the science-policy interface and stood up for me when political interests challenged some academic findings. The Center for Collective Intelligence at MIT provided the institutional home where I could complete the manuscript, and I am grateful to its Director, Professor Tom Malone, and its Executive Director, Kathleen Kennedy, for continuing to engage me as a visiting scholar.

This book has taken several different forms and its completion involved the artistry of many people. The dissertation that I defended in 2006 bears little resemblance to what is now in your hands, but it sparked my passion for UNEP. My dissertation committee members, Professors Daniel Esty, Benjamin Cashore, Frances Rosenbluth, and Paul Wapner, guided the work that still continues to inspire me. I am grateful for the care and encouragement from my friends Anne Rademacher, Arman Grigorian, Carolyn Deere Birkbeck, Christiane Ehringhaus, Irina Faion, Marina Campos, Melissa Goodall, Monica Araya, Niko Urho, Pia Kohler, Rita Lipson, Trista Patterson, and Seth Cook. Special thanks to Reggie Talbert for building up my strength and stamina. Annabell Waititu, Joe Ageyo, Philip Osano, and Wanjira Mathai offered insight and inspiration every time I was in Nairobi since 2001, and have become part of my family there. Joe Ageyo and I began producing short films that became what some called the white papers on global environmental governance in images.[4] I am grateful to Joe for locating and procuring the images in this book that bring the founding of UNEP in Nairobi to life.

Much of my work has developed alongside my teaching, and my students at Yale, the College of William & Mary, and UMass Boston have informed and inspired me. We explored history, pondered over performance, and imagined new institutional design scenarios. I am particularly grateful to Susanah Stoessel, who co-created with me the Environmental History Project, and preserved and analyzed precious archival material. The research team at the Center for Governance and Sustainability at UMass Boston helped me build a robust empirical baseline. Natalia Escobar-Pemberthy was the force behind the creation of the massive financial database of UNEP's resources. We now have a unique tool that allows us to track UNEP's finances since its creation. The research assistance from Anna Dubrova, Candace Famiglietti, James Whitacre, Andrew Fasullo, Gabriela Bueno Gibbs, Judit Senarriaga, Jungwoo Chun, and Michael Cole was critical in understanding UNEP and visualizing parts of its operations, but, most importantly, it spurred important conversations about the past, present, and potential of global environmental governance. We continue this work in new ways in collaboration with UNEP where, with the Law Division, we are working on the Environmental Conventions Index, which assesses the extent to which countries implement their obligations under the international environmental agreements. I am particularly grateful to the Honorable Vincent Biruta, former minister of environment (and currently minister of foreign affairs) of Rwanda, and to Juliet Kabera, director general of the Rwanda Environment Management Authority, both of whom have taken up the Index as the basis for pan-African collaboration on improving environmental performance.

Writing the untold story of the world's leading environmental institution is a challenging and rather risky task. There are many embedded beliefs about the United Nations and about UNEP and its place in the world. Unearthing these stories, checking them against the historical record and against the narratives of the historical figures present at creation, and displaying the different layers demanded a lot of empirical work and multiple tests of the narrative. There will likely be scholars, staff, and politicians who take issue with some of the narrative despite my efforts at objectivity, integrity, and intellectual honesty. As this book is the first full-length study of UNEP, I hope it will invite more scholarship and more open debate. The engagement of Ambassador Macharia Kamau, the Permanent Representative of Kenya to the United Nations, with the precursor analysis for this book strengthened the narrative as well as my conviction and passion for this subject. It also confirmed the political relevance of this inquiry and, opening a discussion in the United Nations, contributed to the opportunity to serve on the UN Scientific Advisory Board to UN Secretary-General Ban Ki-moon.

My thanks go to Beth Clevenger for believing in this book and prompting me (multiple times!) to make it better, and to Sikina Jinnah and Simon Nicholson for their guidance and for launching the One Planet series with the goal of bringing science and policy into direct dialogue. I am also grateful to the three anonymous reviewers whose comments and suggestions improved my argument, and to John Matuszak, whose open review of the manuscript helped identify gaps and omissions and pushed it to the next level. This narrative has also been improved by expert editing throughout its various permutations. I thank Melissa Goodall, Ehsan Masood, and Pia Kohler for their careful reading and constructive suggestions, for engaging with the manuscript's substance and style. All mistakes, of course, remain mine.

As we approach the fiftieth anniversary of UNEP, I look back at the twenty years during which I have engaged with the organization and realize that, to my family, this has seemed like a never-ending journey. I am deeply grateful to my parents, Rumiana Jeleva and Hristo Ivanov, for their support of my choices in life. The path I took seems inevitable in retrospect but was unprecedented and impossible to imagine at the start. Thank you for being there for me every step of the way! I wish I could be closer. My husband, Alexander Gritsinin, has been the staunchest supporter of my work and the source of intellectual inspiration. We met when I was just beginning the PhD program at Yale, and he saw me through the trials and tribulations of a dissertation and two new jobs. Thank you for always being on my side and for making me sing along with *Hamilton*, "I am not throwing away my shot!" Thanks also to our sons, Gleb and Aleksandr Gritsinin, for creating an amazing family that I am so grateful to be a part of.

This work builds on the efforts of so many people who created international institutions and labored tirelessly to ensure that they function well. I feel privileged to have had the opportunity to meet the founders, the leaders, and the operatives of the global environmental governance system. Many of them have passed and, in these pages, I offer the story of their legacy. And I hope to inspire others who will continue it.

January 31, 2020
Boston, Massachusetts

CAST OF CHARACTERS

The thirty-nine people in this section appear throughout the book with insights about UNEP and the system of global environmental governance. I have had the privilege to speak with all but three of them (Ambassador Dr. Kipyego Cheluget, Ambassador Joseph Odero-Jowi, and Barbara Ward) and am grateful for their ideas and encouragement. A dagger (†) following a name indicates that the person is deceased.

INGER ANDERSEN

Inger Andersen is Under-Secretary-General of the United Nations and Executive Director of the United Nations Environment Programme (UNEP). Between 2015 and 2019, Ms. Andersen was the Director General of the International Union for Conservation of Nature (IUCN). Ms. Andersen brings a passion for conservation and sustainable development with more than thirty years of experience in international development economics, environmental sustainability and policy making, as well as in designing and implementing projects and generating on-the-ground impact. She has played a key role in supporting riparian countries on international water management and hydro-diplomacy. Ms. Andersen also held various leadership roles at the World Bank for fifteen years, including as Vice President of the Middle East and North Africa and as Vice President for

Sustainable Development; and at the United Nations, starting in the UN Sudano-Sahelian Office working on drought and desertification issues.

KOFI ANNAN[†]

Kofi Annan was the seventh Secretary-General of the United Nations, serving two terms, from January 1997 to December 2006. During his tenure, he was instrumental in revitalizing the organization through a number of initiatives. One of his main goals was to comprehensively reform the United Nations to make it more effective; he championed a human-rights approach and established ties with a variety of stakeholders from civil society and the private sector. Mr. Annan was an avid advocate of the rule of law and the Millennium Development Goals. He strengthened UN peacekeeping operations, including establishing two intergovernmental bodies, the Human Rights Council and the Peacebuilding Commission. For this work, Mr. Annan and the United Nations received the Nobel Peace Prize in 2001. Born in Ghana, he was also a champion for Africa and the environment. He made the environment one of the ten core principles of the UN Global Compact (2000) and acted as founding Chairman of the Alliance for a Green Revolution in Africa (2012). After his work at the UN, Mr. Annan founded the Kofi Annan Foundation, whose mission is to catalyze the political will to address issues related to human rights, security, and development. He also acted as chairman of The Elders, an international organization created by Nelson Mandela.

BAN KI-MOON

Ban Ki-moon, the eighth Secretary-General of the United Nations, served for two terms, from 2007 to 2016. Previously, he was a diplomat in South Korea's Ministry of Foreign Affairs. Ban Ki-moon is well-known for his leadership on climate change and focus on peacekeeping. The Paris Agreement on climate change was a major accomplishment during his tenure, for which he was named one of *Foreign Policy*'s Top 100 Global Thinkers and featured on *Forbes*'s list of The World's Most Powerful People. In 2013, Ban Ki-moon established the Scientific Advisory Board to the UN Secretary-General; this board focused on science, technology, and innovation and comprised twenty-six scholars from around the world. He teaches at Yonsei University's Institute for Global Engagement and Empowerment in Seoul, South Korea.

AMBASSADOR DR. KIPYEGO CHELUGET

Ambassador Cheluget served as Assistant Secretary-General for Programmes at the Common Market for Eastern and Southern Africa (COMESA). He was appointed to the position by the Summit of Heads of State and Government, held in Kampala, Uganda, in November 2012. Before joining the COMESA Secretariat, Ambassador Cheluget served as Deputy High Commissioner of Kenya to New Delhi, India, as Kenya's High Commissioner to Zambia and Malawi, and as Permanent Representative to COMESA.

ARTHUR DAHL

Arthur Dahl joined UNEP in 1989 as Deputy to the Director of the Oceans and Coastal Areas Programme Activity Centre in Nairobi. Mr. Dahl later served as Deputy Assistant Executive Director in Geneva from 1996 to 1998 and as Director of the Coral Reef Unit from 2000 to 2002, in addition to coordinating the UN system-wide Earthwatch from 1992 to 2000. After retiring from UNEP, he has been a Visiting Professor at the University of Brighton (UK) and an international consultant on indicators of sustainability, environmental assessment and observing strategies, coral reefs, biodiversity, islands, environmental education, and social and economic development. In 2018, Mr. Dahl and colleagues received the New Shape Prize for global governance reform of the Global Challenges Foundation.

ELIZABETH DOWDESWELL

Elizabeth Dowdeswell served as UNEP Executive Director from 1993 to 1998. Before joining UNEP, she served as Canada's Assistant Deputy Minister of Environment, where she oversaw the Atmospheric Environment and Meteorological Service and negotiations for the UN Framework Convention on Climate Change. In 1996, Ms. Dowdeswell ranked sixty-six in the *New York Times Magazine*'s list of the one hundred most powerful women in the world. From 2002 to 2010, she served as founding president and CEO of the Nuclear Waste Management Organization in Canada. From 1998 to 2010, Ms. Dowdeswell was an adjunct professor at the McLaughlin-Rotman Centre for Global Health at the University of Toronto, and from 2010 until 2014 she served as President and CEO of the Council of Canadian Academies. In September 2014, Prime Minister Stephen Harper appointed Ms. Dowdeswell as Ontario's 29th Lieutenant Governor.

IDUNN EIDHEIM

Idunn Eidheim joined the Norwegian Ministry of Climate and Environment prior to the 1992 Rio Earth Summit and has served as chief negotiator, chair, and bureau member at many summits, international processes, and conferences related to environment and development. Ms. Eidheim served as Deputy Director General for International Cooperation at the ministry and has been responsible for environmental matters in the UN. She was involved in the creation of the Intergovernmental Platform on Biodiversity and Ecosystem Services (IPBES), and in advancing science-policy related initiatives and processes, including UNEP's Global Environment Outlook and the Global Chemicals Outlook, among others. She was instrumental in bringing the challenges of plastic pollution in the ocean to the international agenda.

MOHAMED EL-ASHRY

From 1994 to 2003, Dr. Mohamed El-Ashry served as CEO and Chairman of the Global Environment Facility (GEF), which he helped establish. Under his leadership, the GEF grew from a pilot program created in 1991 to the largest single source of funding for the global environment with 173 member states. Dr. El-Ashry served as Chief Environmental Adviser to the President and Director of the Environment Department at the World Bank, and as Senior Vice President of the World Resources Institute (WRI). He was a member of the UN Secretary-General's High-Level Panel on System-wide Coherence. In 2006, Dr. El-Ashry was honored with UNEP's Champions of the Earth Award for his policy leadership. He is currently a senior fellow at the UN Foundation.

AMBASSADOR LARS-GÖRAN ENGFELDT

Ambassador Lars-Göran Engfeldt served as a Liaison Officer for Sweden at the 1972 Stockholm Conference. He worked at the Swedish Mission to the United Nations in New York from 1968 to 1970 and was Assistant Under-Secretary for UN Affairs at the Ministry for Foreign Affairs from 1984 to 1988. In 1989, he was appointed Ambassador and served as the Permanent Representative to UNEP as well as the Chairman of the Friends of the Chair group for the 1997 Nairobi Declaration. He represented Sweden as Environment Ambassador on the Preparatory Committee to the 2002 World Summit on Sustainable Development. Ambassador Engfeldt also served as Deputy Permanent Representative of Sweden at the Permanent Mission in New York.

CHRISTIANA FIGUERES

Christiana Figueres served as Executive Secretary of the United Nations Framework Convention on Climate Change (UNFCCC) from 2010 to 2016. She led the UNFCCC to the successful 2015 Paris Climate Conference and Paris Agreement. Throughout her tenure, Ms. Figueres brought together national and sub national governments, corporations and activists, financial institutions and communities of faith, think tanks and technology providers, NGOs and parliamentarians, to jointly deliver the Paris Agreement. For this achievement, she has been credited with forging a new brand of collaborative diplomacy. Together with Tom Rivett-Carnac, she founded Global Optimism Ltd., a purpose-driven enterprise focused on social and environmental change. They are co-authors of the book *The Future We Choose* and produce the podcast *Outrage and Optimism.*

RICHARD GARDNER†

Richard Gardner was a longtime professor at Columbia Law School and an advisor to Maurice Strong during the preparatory process for the Stockholm Conference. Gardner had served as Deputy Assistant Secretary of State for international organization affairs under Presidents John F. Kennedy and Lyndon B. Johnson. He also served as US Ambassador to Italy and

Spain under Presidents Jimmy Carter and Bill Clinton, respectively, and as a senior advisor to the US Ambassador to the United Nations. A renowned scholar, Richard Gardner published numerous books and articles and shaped careers of generations of students. His popular seminar *Legal Aspects of US Foreign Economic Policy* run from 1955 to 2012 when Gardner retired, making it the longest-running course of its kind at Columbia Law School.

MARK HALLE

Mark Halle served as Executive Director of the International Institute for Sustainable Development (IISD-Europe) from 2002 until his retirement in 2016. From 1975 to 1980, he was a program officer at UNEP and engaged in the preparation and launch of the World Conservation Strategy. He joined WWF as Conservation Officer in 1980 and IUCN in 1983 where he served as Assistant, then Deputy Director, of the Conservation for Development Centre. He was responsible for all personnel and operations in the field, including IUCN's growing network of regional and country offices. Mr. Halle subsequently served as Director of Development and Director of IUCN's Global Policy Division.

CALESTOUS JUMA†

Professor Calestous Juma was an international authority in the application of science and technology to sustainable development. *New African* magazine recognized him as one of the most influential Africans in 2012, 2013, and 2014. He was Professor of the Practice of International Development at the Harvard Kennedy School. Born and raised in Kenya, Professor Juma founded the Africa Center for Technology Studies—Africa's first independent policy research institution on technology in development—in Nairobi in 1988. He was the first Executive Secretary of the Convention on Biological Diversity (1995–1998) and established the Permanent Secretariat in Montreal.

DONALD W. KANIARU

Donald W. Kaniaru served as an environmental lawyer in Kenya's Ministry of Foreign Affairs and later at UNEP from 1975 to 2003, where he was

Director of the Division on Environmental Policy Implementation as well as Director of the Division of Environmental Conventions. In the early 1970s, Mr. Kaniaru was Second Secretary at Kenya's Permanent Mission to the United Nations in New York and was known as Ambassador Odero-Jowi's "right-hand man" who helped get UNEP to Nairobi. Mr. Kaniaru is Managing Partner at Kaniaru & Kaniaru Advocates and was Chairman of the National Environment Tribunal of Kenya for nine years, until the end of 2013. He also served at the Center for International Environmental Law, based in Washington, DC, for over ten years.

WANGARI MAATHAI†

Wangari Maathai was the founder of the Green Belt Movement, an environmental organization that empowers communities, particularly women. In 2004, Maathai became the first African woman to receive the Nobel Peace Prize. Born in rural Nyeri, Kenya, she was also the first woman to receive a doctorate (1971) in East and Central Africa and to attain the position of Chair and Associate Professor of the Department of Veterinary Anatomy at the University of Nairobi. Professor Maathai served in Kenya's Parliament and as Assistant Minister for Environment and Natural Resources. She mobilized a social movement in Kenya and saved the Karura Forest from certain destruction in the 1990s.

JAMES "JIM" MACNEILL†

Jim MacNeill served as Director of Environment at the Organisation for Economic Co-operation and Development (OECD) in Paris from 1978 to 1984 and as Secretary General of the World Commission on Environment Development (1984), where he contributed as lead author to the *Our Common Future* report (1987). He was Special Advisor to Maurice Strong during his time as Secretary-General of the 1992 UN Conference on Environment and Development in Rio de Janeiro. In 1997, Mr. MacNeill became a member and, in 1999, Chairman of the World Bank's Inspection Panel. He served in several capacities with the Government of Canada, including at the Department of Energy, Mines, and Resources; as Acting Assistant Deputy Minister of Water and Renewable Resources;

and as Special Advisor on the Constitution and Environment in the Privy Council Office.

DANIEL "DAN" MAGRAW

Dan Magraw is President Emeritus of the Center for International Environmental Law (CIEL), which he led from 2002 to 2010. From 1992 to 2001, Mr. Magraw was Director of the International Environmental Law Office at the US Environmental Protection Agency. He served on numerous US delegations to international negotiations, co-chaired a White House assessment of regulation of GMOs, and served as Acting Principal Deputy Assistant Administrator of EPA's Office of International Activities. He taught at the University of Colorado and was a Visiting Scientist at the National Center for Atmospheric Research. He is Senior Fellow and Professorial Lecturer at the Foreign Policy Institute at Johns Hopkins' School of Advanced International Studies (SAIS).

WILLIAM "BILL" H. MANSFIELD III

Bill Mansfield served as Assistant Secretary-General at the United Nations and as UNEP Deputy Executive Director to Dr. Mostafa Tolba from 1986 to 1992. In 1993, Mr. Mansfield served as senior consultant to UNEP's Executive Director. From 1995 to 1996, he ran the Global Environment Facility (GEF) in Nairobi. From 2000 until his retirement in 2017, Mr. Mansfield was Senior Advisor to the Director of the UNEP regional office for North America in Washington, DC.

JULIA MARTON-LEFÈVRE

Julia Marton-Lefèvre served as Director General of the International Union for Conservation of Nature (IUCN) from 2007 to 2015. Prior positions included Rector of the UN-mandated University for Peace (UPEACE) in Costa Rica, Executive Director of LEAD (Leadership for Environment and Development) International, and Executive Director of the International Council for Science. She began her international career in a programme on environmental education at UNESCO. Ms. Marton-Lefèvre was Edward P. Bass Distinguished Visiting Scholar at Yale University. She chairs the Tyler Prize for Environmental Achievement and the Alliance of Biodiversity International and the International Center for Tropical Agriculture (CIAT). She is independent advisor to the Intergovernmental Science-Policy Platform on Biodiversity and Ecosystem Services (IPBES).

WANJIRA MATHAI

Wanjira Mathai is the Vice President and Regional Director for Africa at the World Resources Institute in Nairobi, Kenya. She is the Chair of the Wangari Maathai Foundation and the former Chair of the Green Belt Movement, the organization that her mother, Wangari Maathai founded in 1977. Ms. Mathai has led initiatives driving social and environmental change at both the local and global level. She has served in strategic and advocacy roles on climate change, youth leadership, sustainable energy, and landscape restoration at Women Entrepreneurs in Renewables (wPOWER) and the Green Belt Movement. Ms. Mathai is one of a few Six Seconds EQ Practitioners in Kenya and was named one of the 100 Most Influential Africans by *New African Magazine* in 2018.

JOHN MATUSZAK

John Matuszak served for thirty years with the US federal government at the State Department, USAID, and the US Department of Agriculture. He worked as Senior Policy Advisor and Division Chief for Sustainable Development and Multilateral Affairs with the State Department's Bureau of Oceans and International Environmental and Scientific Affairs. Mr. Matuszak was elected Vice President of the UN Environment Assembly (UNEA) Bureau for UNEA-2 in 2016 and UNEA-3 in 2017. He served on the High-Level Group advising UNEP's Global Environmental Outlook publications. Mr. Matuszak was Vice President of the Bureau of Rio+20 and served on the Bureau of the UN Economic Commission for Europe Committee on Environmental Policy. He represented the United States on the ministerial intergovernmental preparatory committee of the Group on Earth Observations (GEO).

AMBASSADOR JOHN W. MCDONALD†

Ambassador John W. McDonald served as an American diplomat in the fields of development and peacebuilding. As Director of Economic and Social Affairs at the Bureau of International Organization Affairs at the US State Department in the 1970s, he was instrumental in UNEP's creation, for which he received the State Department's Superior Honor Award. In 1974, he was appointed deputy director general of the International Labour Organization. Subsequently, he was appointed as Ambassador twice by President Jimmy Carter and twice by President Ronald Reagan to lead multilateral diplomatic efforts. Ambassador McDonald then joined the State Department's Center for the Study of Foreign Affairs and retired in 1987 after forty years of service. In 1992, he co-founded the Institute for Multi-Track Diplomacy, which addresses international ethnic conflicts and environmental conditions. He led the establishment of the Pakistan-India Kartarpur Peace Corridor, which gave Sikhs peaceful access to three of their religion's holy shrines.

AMINA MOHAMMED

Appointed in 2017, Amina Mohammed serves as Deputy Secretary-General of the United Nations. She was Nigeria's Federal Minister of Environment from November 2015 to December 2016. She worked for three successive administrations in Nigeria on the Millennium Development Goals and coordinated $1 billion annually in relevant interventions. Ms. Mohammed was instrumental in bringing about the 2030 Agenda for Sustainable Development, including the Sustainable Development Goals, while serving as Special Adviser to UN Secretary-General Ban Ki-moon on Post-2015 Development Planning. Ms. Mohammed teaches as Adjunct Professor in Development Practice at Columbia University and advises many international boards, including the Global Development Program of the Bill and Melinda Gates Foundation, the African Women's Millennium Initiative, and 2016 African Union Reform, among others.

AMBASSADOR JOSEPH ODERO-JOWI†

Ambassador Odero-Jowi was best known for bringing the United Nations Environment Programme (UNEP) Headquarters to Nairobi, Kenya. Dr. Odero-Jowi served as Minister for Economic Planning and Development in 1969, as Kenya's Ambassador to the United Nations, and as UN Development Programme chief advisor. An economist, author, and history teacher, he studied at Kagumo Teachers College and in India.

JANOS PASZTOR

Janos Pasztor is the Executive Director of C2G, the Carnegie Climate Governance Initiative. Previously, he served as Assistant Secretary-General in the Executive Office of UN Secretary-General Ban Ki-moon and as Senior Advisor to the UN Secretary-General on Climate Change from 2015 to 2016. He was Executive Secretary of the UN Secretary-General's High-Level Panel on Global Sustainability and Director of the Climate Support Team. Additionally, Mr. Pasztor served as the Director for the Environment Management Group (EMG), a core coordination initiative by UNEP. Early in his career, he was an energy program officer (1986–1989) at UNEP, which led him to the position of Senior Program Officer in the secretariat of the 1992 Rio Earth Summit.

AMBASSADOR FRANZ PERREZ

Ambassador Franz Perrez is the head of the International Affairs Division of Switzerland's Federal Office for the Environment. As Switzerland's environmental ambassador, Ambassador Perrez is the nation's lead negotiator on environmental issues such as climate change. He has also worked with the Department of Public International Law, the Swiss Department of Foreign Affairs, and the State Secretariat for Economic Affairs. Ambassador Perrez served as President of COP11 of the Basel Convention and of COP8 of the Rotterdam Convention, and was panelist in the WTO dispute on tuna-dolphin between Mexico and the United States. He lectures at the University of Bern School of Law on international environmental law.

MANUEL PULGAR-VIDAL

Manuel Pulgar-Vidal was Peru's Minister of Environment from 2011 to 2016 and President of COP20 of UNFCCC in Lima. He works as a lawyer on climate and energy issues and currently serves as Leader of Climate and Energy Practice at WWF International. He has held leadership positions such as Executive Director of the Peruvian Society for Environmental Law and President of the Interamerican Association for Environmental Defense. His expertise includes watershed conservation, agricultural research, mining, and natural resource management. Mr. Pulgar-Vidal is also a professor at the Pontifical Catholic University of Peru in the areas of environmental law, natural resource management and mining, and energy and environment.

JOHN SCANLON

John Scanlon is an international lawyer and Special Envoy for African Parks. From 2010 to 2018, he served as Secretary-General of CITES, the Convention on International Trade in Endangered Species of Wild Fauna and Flora. He was Principal Adviser on Policy and Programme, as well as Team Leader of the Strategic Implementation Team at UNEP. He also served as Director of the Environmental Law Centre and Head of the Environmental Law Programme at IUCN. Before that, Mr. Scanlon was Chief Executive of the Department of Environment, Heritage and Aboriginal Affairs in South Australia.

YOUBA SOKONA

Youba Sokona is special adviser for sustainable development at the South Centre. He has been engaged in energy, environment, and sustainable development in Africa for over thirty-five years. Mr. Sokona served as Vice-Chair of the Intergovernmental Panel on Climate Change (IPCC) and as co-chair of IPCC Working Group III on the mitigation of climate change for the Fifth Assessment Report after being lead author since 1990. Previously, Mr. Sokona served as Coordinator of the African Climate Policy Centre and Executive Secretary of the Sahara and the Sahel Observatory.

ERIK SOLHEIM

Erik Solheim was appointed as UNEP Executive Director in 2016 and resigned from the position in November 2018. Before joining UNEP, Solheim was head of the OECD Development Assistance Committee (DAC). He was leader of the Socialist Left Party in Norway and served in Parliament. He was special advisor to the Norwegian Ministry of Foreign Affairs in Sri Lanka, where he was the chief negotiator of the truce between the Sri Lankan government and the Tamil Tigers in 2002. Solheim has also been involved in peace processes in Nepal, Myanmar, and Sudan. In 2005, he became Minister of International Development, and in 2007 he was appointed Minister of the Environment and held both posts until 2012. During his tenure, Norwegian development aid rose to 1 percent. After resigning from UNEP, Mr. Solheim returned to Norway, where he joined the Green Party and the World Resources Institute as senior advisor. He is also convener of the Belt and Road International Green Development Coalition.

JAMES GUSTAVE "GUS" SPETH

James Gustave "Gus" Speth cofounded the Natural Resources Defense Council and subsequently the World Resources Institute and served on the Council on Environmental Quality in the Executive Office of US President Jimmy Carter. Mr. Speth was senior adviser to President Bill Clinton and guided a US environmental task force on international development and environmental security. From 1993 to 1999, he was Administrator of the UN Development Programme. He served as Special Coordinator for Economic and Social Affairs under UN Secretary-General Boutros Boutros-Ghali, piloted the UN Development Assistance Plan, and chaired the UN Development Group. From 1999 to 2009, Mr. Speth was Dean of the Yale School of the Environment and after his retirement, he continued teaching at Vermont Law School. He is author of several books on environment and development.

ACHIM STEINER

Achim Steiner served as Executive Director of the UN Environment Programme from 2006 to 2016 and, since 2017, as the Administrator of the

UN Development Programme. In the interim, he was the Director of the Oxford Martin School. Prior to joining the UN, Mr. Steiner served as Director General of the International Union for the Conservation of Nature (IUCN). He started his career at the Rural Regional Development Department, GIZ, in Germany and from 1991 to 1997 worked at IUCN in South Africa and in Washington, DC. He then became chief technical adviser of the Mekong River Commission and subsequently Secretary-General of the World Commission on Dams. Mr. Steiner was born in Brazil to a German farmer and has lived and worked in Africa, Asia, the Middle East, Europe, Latin America, and the United States.

MAURICE STRONG†

Maurice Strong was a Canadian businessman specializing in oil and mineral resources who also served as UN Under-Secretary-General and became UNEP's first Executive Director (1973–1975). By his early thirties, Mr. Strong was President of the Power Corporation of Canada. Later, he served as the head of PetroCanada, Canada's national oil company, as Chairman of the Canada Development Investment Corporation, and as Director of the American private conglomerate Tosco. He later worked as Deputy Minister for the Canadian International Development Agency (CIDA). In 1970, UN Secretary-General U Thant appointed Strong as Secretary-General of the 1972 Stockholm Conference. Mr. Strong also served as Secretary-General of the 1992 Rio Earth Summit, as President of the Council of the University of Peace from 1998 to 2006, and as an active honorary professor at Peking University.

IBRAHIM THIAW

Ibrahim Thiaw has been the Executive Secretary of the United Nations Convention to Combat Desertification since 2019. Prior to this position, in 2018, Mr. Thiaw was Special Adviser to the UN Secretary-General for the Sahel. He was UNEP's Deputy Executive Director and Assistant Secretary-General of the United Nations from 2013 to 2018, having previously served as Director of the Division for Environmental Policy Implementation at UNEP. Before joining the UN in 2007, Mr. Thiaw worked as

Regional Director for West Africa, and later as acting Director General at the International Union for Conservation of Nature (IUCN), and served in the Ministry of Rural Development in Mauritania for ten years.

MOSTAFA TOLBA†

Dr. Mostafa Tolba was the second and longest-serving UNEP Executive Director, from 1976 to 1992. Dr. Tolba led the Egyptian delegation to the 1972 Stockholm Conference and served as UNEP's Deputy Director during the mandate of Maurice Strong. Prior to joining UNEP, Dr. Tolba was on the faculty of sciences at Cairo University, where he established a department of microbiology. He was professor and head of the department of botany at the University of Baghdad from 1954 to 1959. Thereafter, he joined the Egyptian civil service as Undersecretary of State for Higher Education and Minister of Youth. He was the first president of the newly established Academy for Scientific Research and Technology in 1971. In 1994, upon his retirement from UNEP and return to Egypt, Dr. Tolba established the International Center for Environment and Development (ICED) a non-profit organization financing environmental projects.

KLAUS TÖPFER

Prof. Dr. Klaus Töpfer started his career in academia and later transitioned into politics. Dr. Töpfer became minister for the Environment and Health in the regional government of Rhineland-Palatinate in 1985. Subsequently, he served as Federal Minister of the Environment, Nature Conservation, and Nuclear Safety from 1987 to 1994 and as Federal Minister for Regional Planning, Civil Engineering, and Urban Development from 1994 to 1998. He was actively involved in the preparations for the 1992 Rio Earth Summit, and in December 1997, UN Secretary-General Kofi Annan appointed Dr. Töpfer as UNEP Executive Director. Dr. Töpfer also became Acting Executive Director of UN-Habitat and served in that role until 2000. In 2009, the German government appointed Dr. Töpfer as the founding Director of the Institute for Advanced Sustainability Studies in Potsdam.

ANNABELL WAITITU

Annabell Waititu is the Vice President for programs at Big Five Africa Ltd. She works in the water and environment sector in East Africa, particularly on water-sector reforms, climate-resilience integration, and gender-equality mainstreaming. She is an investment committee member of KIFFWA (Kenya Innovative Finance Facility for Water), board member at Sanivation, and associate of (WOCAN) Women Organizing for Change in Agriculture and Natural Resource Management. She has consulted on Water for Africa Cities, the Nile Basin Initiative, Kenya's water sector reforms, and the Water Supply and Sanitation Improvement Program of the World Bank/ WSP, Water and Sanitation projects of USAID, UNICEF, and the Dutch government. Ms. Waititu served at the Environment Liaison Centre International (ELCI) in Nairobi.

BARBARA MARY WARD, BARONESS JACKSON OF LODSWORTH†

Barbara Ward was an author, an economist, and a longtime champion of social and environmental justice. An early proponent of sustainable development, Ms. Ward was commissioned by Maurice Strong, Secretary-General of the UN Conference on the Human Environment, to write the *Only One Earth* report. In 1971, Ward founded the International Institute for Environment and Development (IIED) and served as President and Chair. She was active in the 1974 Cocoyoc Declaration, the UN Conference on Trade and Development, and the Vancouver Habitat Conference on Human Settlements. Ms. Ward also taught as a professor of economic development at Columbia University for five years.

MICHAEL ZAMMIT CUTAJAR

Michael Zammit Cutajar headed the UN Climate Change secretariat from 1991 to 2002, organizing the negotiations of the 1992 UN Framework Convention on Climate Change and serving as the Convention's Executive Secretary (1996–2002). As Malta's first Ambassador on Climate Change (2002–2011), he took part in and chaired negotiations under the

UN Framework Convention and its Kyoto Protocol. In 2015, he advised the French delegation in its Presidency of UNFCCC COP21, which adopted the Paris Agreement. Before his engagement in the climate change arena, Mr. Zammit Cutajar had worked in and around the UN on international trade, development, and environment questions, including on the start-up of UNEP (1971–1974).

LIST OF ABBREVIATIONS

ACC	Administrative Committee on Co-ordination
AMCEN	African Ministerial Conference on the Environment
ASG	Assistant Secretary-General
BRS	Basel, Rotterdam, and Stockholm Conventions Secretariat
CBD	Convention on Biological Diversity
CEB	United Nations System Chief Executives Board for Coordination
CFCs	Chlorofluorocarbons
CITES	Convention on International Trade in Endangered Species
CMS	Convention on Migratory Species
COP	Conference of the Parties
CPR	Committee of Permanent Representatives
DCPI	Division of Communication and Public Information (UN Environment Programme)
DDT	Dichlorodiphenyltrichloroethane
DELC	Division of Environmental Law and Conventions (UN Environment Programme)
DOEM	Designated Officials for Environmental Matters

DTIE	Division of Trade, Industry and Environment (UN Environment Programme)
EAC	East African Community
ECB	Environmental Coordination Board
ECE	Economic Commission for Europe
ECOSOC	United Nations Economic and Social Council
EMG	Environment Management Group
EU	European Union
EUROPOL	European Union's Law Enforcement Agency
FAO	Food and Agriculture Organization
G-77	Group of 77
GDP	Gross Domestic Product
GEF	Global Environment Facility
GEMS	Global Environment Monitoring System
GEO	*Global Environment Outlook*
GEO	Group on Earth Observations
GEOSS	Global Earth Observation System of Systems
GMEF	Global Ministerial Environment Forum
GRULAC	Group of Latin America and the Caribbean
HLPF	High-Level Political Forum
IACSD	Inter-Agency Committee on Sustainable Development
IAEA	International Atomic Energy Agency
IAEG	Inter-Agency Environment Management Group
IARC	International Agency for Research on Cancer
ICAO	International Civil Aviation Association
ICSC	International Civil Service Commission
ICSU	International Council for Science
IEA	International Energy Agency
IEG	International Environmental Governance
IGAD	Intergovernmental Authority on Development
ILO	International Labour Organization
IMCO	International Maritime Consultative Organization
IMO	International Maritime Organization
INTERPOL	International Criminal Police Organization
IPBES	Intergovernmental Science-Policy Platform on Biodiversity and Ecosystem Services

IPCC	Intergovernmental Panel on Climate Change
IRPTC	International Register of Potentially Toxic Chemicals
IUCN	International Union for the Conservation of Nature
MARPOL	International Convention for the Prevention of Pollution from Ships
MEA	Multilateral Environmental Agreement
NASA	National Aeronautics and Space Administration
NGO	Non-governmental Organization
NIEO	New International Economic Order
NRDC	Natural Resources Defense Council
OCA/PAC	Oceans and Coastal Areas Programme Activity Centre
OCHA	Office for Coordination of Humanitarian Affairs
OECD	Organisation for Economic Co-operation and Development
OHCHR	Office of the High Commissioner for Human Rights
PACD	United Nations Plan of Action to Combat Desertification
PCBs	Polychlorinated Biphenyls
SAICM	Strategic Approach to International Chemicals Management
SBSTTA	Subsidiary Body on Scientific, Technical and Technological Advice
SDGs	Sustainable Development Goals
SIDS	Small Island Developing States
SWMTEP	System-Wide Medium-Term Environment Programme
UK	United Kingdom of Great Britain and Northern Ireland
UN	United Nations
UN-HABITAT	UN Human Settlements Programme
UN-REDD	UN Programme on Reducing Emissions from Deforestation and Forest Degradation
UNCCD	United Nations Convention to Combat Desertification
UNCHE	United Nations Conference on the Human Environment
UNCTAD	United Nations Conference on Trade and Development
UNDP	United Nations Development Programme
UNEA	United Nations Environment Assembly
UNEP	United Nations Environment Programme

UNESCO	United Nations Educational, Scientific and Cultural Organization
UNFCCC	United Nations Framework Convention on Climate Change
UNFPA	United Nations Population Fund
UNHCR	Office of the United Nations High Commissioner for Refugees
UNICEF	United Nations International Children's Emergency Fund
UNIDO	United Nations Industrial Development Organization
UNODA	United Nations Office for Disarmament Affairs
UNODC	United Nations Office on Drugs and Crime
UNOG	United Nations Office at Geneva
UNON	United Nations Office at Nairobi
UNOV	United Nations Office at Vienna
US	United States
WCO	World Customs Organization
WFP	World Food Programme
WHO	World Health Organization
WMO	World Meteorological Organization
WTO	World Trade Organization

LIST OF FIGURES AND TABLES

1

UNEP: THE PAST AND POTENTIAL OF A GLOBAL ENVIRONMENTAL INSTITUTION

Adults keep saying: "We owe it to the young people to give them hope." But I don't want your hope. I don't want you to be hopeful. I want you to panic. I want you to feel the fear I feel every day. And then I want you to act. I want you to act as you would in a crisis. I want you to act as if our house is on fire. Because it is.

—Greta Thunberg, climate activist, at the 2019 World Economic Forum

Social movements and civil resistance groups mobilize populations to pressure governments to change policies. The civil rights movement of the 1950s and 1960s and the anti-war student protests during the Vietnam War era in the United States resulted in powerful political change. Strikes in Poland in the 1980s led to the fall of the iron curtain and the end of the Cold War.[1] In 2018, a sixteen-year-old Swedish activist, Greta Thunberg, protesting governmental inaction in confronting the existential climate crisis, launched a climate strike that has become a global phenomenon, spurring protests in 163 countries. "Our house is on fire. I am here to say, our house is on fire," Thunberg implored global leaders at the 2019 World Economic Forum in Davos, Switzerland.[2] And the world is literally burning. Fires have ravaged California, the Amazon, and Australia. In early 2020, Australia's fires obliterated 14.5 million acres, an area six times the size of the fires in the Amazon in 2019, and half a billion native animals perished in the blaze.[3] Fires engulfed cities and towns, lines of transport and communication were severed, and the air was thick with soot. This, however, was not the first time the situation had felt so dire.

"We had rivers that caught on fire," William D. Ruckelshaus, the first Administrator of the US Environmental Protection Agency, recalled. "The Cuyahoga River going through Cleveland burst into flames in 1969."[4] These unignorable pollution problems mobilized a US public already alarmed by the inextricable link between pollution and public and planetary health that Rachel Carson's 1962 *New York Times*–bestselling book *Silent Spring* had made so vivid. Twenty million concerned Americans, 10 percent of the population at the time, spilled into the streets on the first Earth Day on April 22, 1970, forcing environmental protection onto the national political agenda. This assertive environmental constituency catalyzed action from both President Nixon and the US Congress, marking a groundbreaking era in environmental policy and legislation. In Europe, sulfur and nitrogen oxide emitted by the burning of fossil fuels in the United Kingdom were carried by northerly winds for hundreds of miles before returning to earth in northern Europe as acid rain, fog, and snow. The resulting dying lakes and forests made it clear that pollution did not stop at national borders, and that countries could only pursue solutions through common effort.[5] Japan, the poster-child for the Western development model, had also come face-to-face with the alarming costs of unbridled industrialization. Neurological disorders, fetal deformations, and other fatal diseases had been traced to mercury, cadmium, and polychlorinated biphenyl (PCB) poisoning. These are some of the concerns that prompted the establishment, in 1972, of the first, and still arguably the premier, global environmental institution: the United Nations Environment Programme (UNEP).

In the decades since, while witnessing these distressing results, we have continued to exploit nature, the fundamental support for human existence. "Our house is burning down and we're blind to it," French President Jacques Chirac proclaimed passionately at the 2002 World Summit on Sustainable Development in Johannesburg, a call that Greta Thunberg would amplify seventeen years later, inspiring a global youth movement. "The earth and humankind are in danger, and we are all responsible," Chirac lamented.[6] "You have stolen my dreams and my childhood with your empty words," Thunberg reproached world leaders at the 2019 UN General Assembly. "We are in the beginning of a mass extinction, and all you can talk about is money and fairy tales of eternal economic growth.

How dare you!" Environmental problems persist, and global environmental governance has not delivered on its original promise.

Recognizing the impact of human activities on the environment, for the past five decades world leaders have convened at global summits to make collective decisions about how to take responsibility and tackle global environmental problems. In the run-up to these conferences, experts have observed and measured environmental problems, identified their causes and consequences, and developed plans of action. Governments have crafted agreements and mobilized resources and created a progressively larger number of institutions at the national and international levels to guide decisions and influence behavior. We have made significant progress in environmental information, institutions, and awareness. We have come close to resolving one major global environmental problem—depletion of the ozone layer—and have made progress on others. Many environmental problems endure, however; some are getting worse, and new challenges and crises are emerging. What has UNEP done, and what opportunities have been missed and why? And how do we move forward?

Creating UNEP was the most visible and enduring outcome of the first global summit on environmental issues, the 1972 Stockholm Conference on the Human Environment (see table 1.1 for an overview of global environmental summits). The mission of the new institution was to assess the state of the environment; to inform, inspire, and empower countries and the UN system; to promote a partnership among UN agencies; and to catalyze cooperation and encourage synergy. Designed as a nimble, fast, and flexible entity at the core of the UN system, UNEP was to be the world's ecological conscience and the center of gravity for environmental affairs, the anchor institution for the global environment. A normative institution, it was designed not to be a firefighter itself but to measure, envision, and craft a program, and let others carry it out. Fifty years later, UNEP remains unknown to many and is often misunderstood. How has it performed, and why, endure as important unanswered questions.

"Since 1972 UNEP has been the mothership for watching the horizon, identifying both emerging environmental challenges and solutions; and delivering the science for decision making," noted Inger Andersen, a Danish development economist who became UNEP's seventh executive director in 2019, adding that "it has played an important part in moving the environmental needle on a number of critical issues."[7] UNEP,

1.1 Environmental governance as perceived by NGOs in 1974. (Illustration from Stockholm Conference ECO newspaper, vol. IV (1), 2. In the author's possession.)

Table 1.1 Fifty years of environmental summits

Logo	Year	Conference Name	Location	Participation	Outcomes
	1972	UN Conference on the Human Environment (UNCHE), also known as ***the Stockholm Conference***	Stockholm, Sweden	113 states	• Creation of UNEP • Declaration of the United Nations Conference on the Human Environment, or Stockholm Declaration, with twenty-six principles • Action Plan for the Human Environment with 109 recommendations
IN OUR HANDS EARTH SUMMIT'92	1992	UN Conference on Environment and Development (UNCED), also known as ***the Rio Earth Summit***	Rio de Janeiro, Brazil	172 states	• Creation of the Commission on Sustainable Development • Rio Declaration on Environment and Development, or Rio Declaration, with 27 principles • Agenda 21
WORLD SUMMIT ON SUSTAINABLE DEVELOPMENT JOHANNESBURG 2002	2002	World Summit on Sustainable Development (WSSD), also known as ***the Johannesburg Summit***	Johannesburg, South Africa	191 states	• Johannesburg Declaration on Sustainable Development • Plan of Implementation of the World Summit on Sustainable Development
	2012	UN Conference on Sustainable Development, also known as ***Rio+20***	Rio de Janeiro, Brazil	188 states	• High-Level Political Forum established to replace Commission on Sustainable Development • *The Future We Want* outcome document • 2030 Agenda • Sustainable Development Goals (SDGs) process launched
Upcoming Summit	2022	*Planned commemoration of the creation of UNEP as per UN General Assembly Resolution 73/333*			

Source: Maria Ivanova, "Coloring the UN Environmental: The Catalytic Role of the UN Environment Programme," *Global Governance*, 26 (2020): 311.

as Andersen reflected, is also "an organization that has a tremendous load to carry in this time of environmental crisis which does not come easy in an economic system that is built on the relentless exploitation of nature."

This book is a biography of UNEP that explains its origin and formative years; elucidates its successes, crises, and turning points; explores the factors that shaped this trajectory; and presents an outlook for its future. In 2022, UNEP turns fifty, and this anniversary provides an opportunity to reflect and rethink, to forge a renewed identity for the United Nations Environment Programme. The chapters here track UNEP's place within a geopolitical context over time and among competing institutions. Recording previously untold stories, the narratives in the pages that follow correct misunderstandings and reveal the life within what is often considered a lifeless bureaucracy. Relating the promises and pitfalls of UNEP's history, this book presents the complexity of the institution and explains how its capacity, connectivity, and credibility have been shaped by politics, geography, and individuals. And it offers a vision for a more effective "anchor institution" for the global environment.

ANCHOR INSTITUTION FOR THE GLOBAL ENVIRONMENT

Anchor institutions are large place-bound and mission-based nonprofit organizations that are socially and economically intertwined with their local communities, play an integral role in their local economies, and have explicit social purposes.[8] Universities and hospitals are typical anchor institutions operating at the local or regional level. They operate as hubs with the requisite expertise, leadership, capacity, and connectivity. At the international level, anchor institutions are the primary, though not the only, institutions in a global issue area that collect and collate information, analyze data and policy options, develop and prescribe policy, and support the development of necessary capacity in terms of governance, human resources, or financial capabilities. They define the problems, develop new policy ideas and programs, manage crises, and set priorities for shared activities that would not otherwise exist.[9] Unlike businesses, anchor institutions cannot change locations even in the face of considerable hardship and thus are tied to, and shaped by, their locations. They are anchored in their local communities, which, ideally, provide them with a skilled labor force, secure and safe environment, and desirable quality of life as well as reliable infrastructure and telecommunication capabilities. They also anchor the local economy because they are a major employer and customer of goods and services. Much like universities, international organizations have created their own enclaves or campuses that operate as cities within a city, with their own planning, transportation, public safety, health care, and even education. They are contiguous, physically and operationally, with the city within which they exist and cannot operate in isolation. And they are there to stay.

Small, smart, and nimble, UNEP was created as the anchor institution for the global environment with a foundation in the capital of Kenya, Nairobi. Its raison d'être was coordination of the environmental activities in the UN system. It was also expected to produce scientific assessments of the state of the environment, provide sound technical and policy analysis, and catalyze environmental action within both the UN system and at the national level.[10] Created as what Robert Cox would call a forum organization,[11] UNEP was to be an explicitly normative body that offers a framework for member states to exchange information and views, develop and legitimize policies, and negotiate binding legal agreements. The intent was not for UNEP to be an operational, or a service, organization that conducts specific environmental activities on its own and provides common or individual services. UNEP was to be "a pinch of silver to energize mighty reactions," as Gordon Harrison of the Ford Foundation remarked in 1977.[12] Envisioned as the leading global environmental authority and advocate, UNEP had to find its place among the existing UN agencies, which were larger in terms of staff, resources, and infrastructure. Many of the existing UN agencies viewed UNEP with suspicion. They dubbed UNEP the "United Nations Everything Programme" and carefully guarded their turf.[13]

UNEP has grown considerably over the past five decades from a small entity in Nairobi to an organization of over 1,200 staff in forty-five duty stations in forty-three countries around the world. Over 60 percent of these duty stations, however, have fewer than five employees. UNEP is an international institution in which women have attained gender parity in professional staff positions and where senior management is over 60 percent female. As of 2019, both the executive director and the deputy executive director are women. Figures 1.2 and 1.3 provide a portrait of UNEP through its people and its presence in the world.[14]

The People of UNEP

1,242 staff: 748 (60%) professional and 494 (40%) general service
Of the 1,242 members, 328 (26%) are MEA* staff

Gender Parity for Professional Staff

Women	Men
297 (53%)	264 (47%)

Staff come from 115 countries around the world

Top 10 nationalities at professional level and above**

1. Kenya
2. USA
3. Germany
4. UK
5. France
6. Canada
7. China
8. Italy
9. Spain
10. Finland

45 duty stations in 43 countries

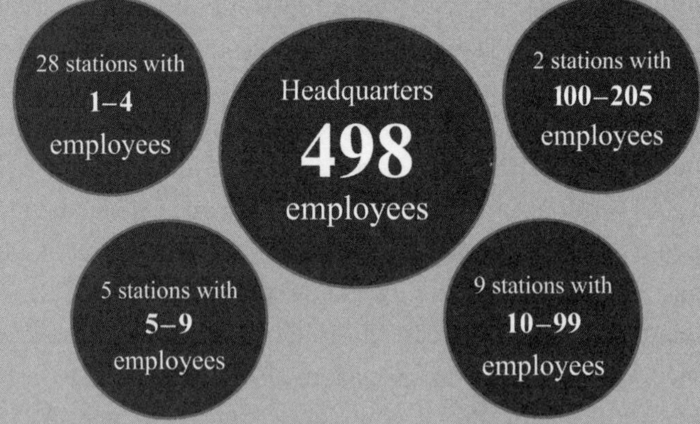

*MEA: Multilateral environmental agreement

**These staff numbers range from 23 for Finland to 51 for Kenya

1.2 The people of UNEP. Source: UNEP, "Human Resources Management Report," December 31, 2019.

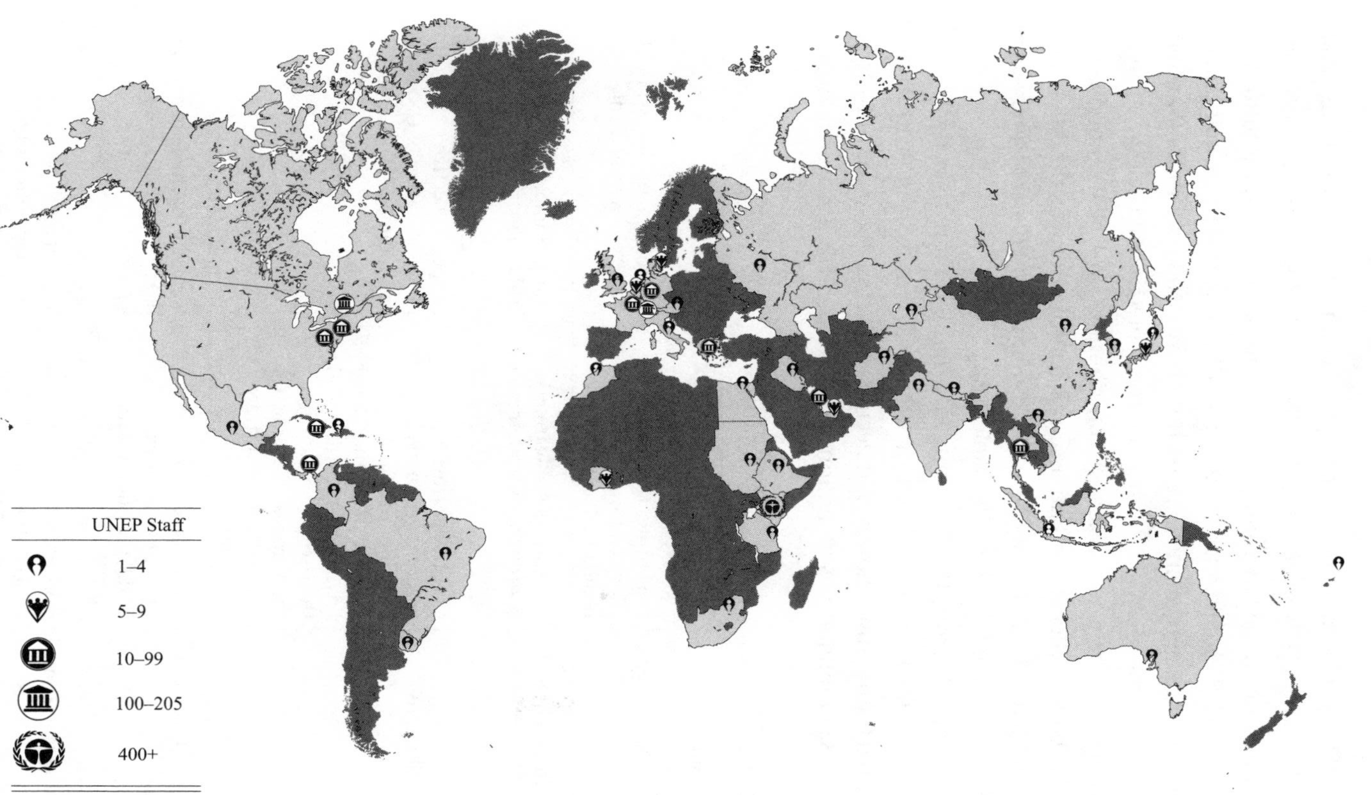

1.3 UNEP offices around the world. An interactive version of this map is available at https://www.environmentalgovernance.org/untold-story.

UNEP's financial resources comprise voluntary contributions from member states. They include regular UN budget allocations, member-state contributions to the Environment Fund, and earmarked contributions. In addition, UNEP's revenues include contributions to fifteen multilateral environmental agreements (MEAs) hosted by UNEP and to the Multilateral Fund of the Montreal Protocol on the Protection of the Ozone Layer, explained in chapter 4. Assessed contributions to UNEP comprise UN regular budget allocations and assessed contributions to the MEAs and the Multilateral Fund, whereas other funding elements are based solely on voluntary contributions (see table 1.2).

In nominal terms, the Environment Fund has more than doubled in forty years—from $31.5 million in 1979 to $70 million in 2019. When adjusted for inflation, however, it decreased by close to 40 percent—from almost $111 million to $70 million. And although UNEP's overall income

Table 1.2 Main sources of financing for UNEP

Categories	Description and Source	Focus
UN regular budget	Constitutes the share allocated from the UN regular budget to UNEP	Supports mainly the work of UNEP's governing bodies
Environment Fund	Constitutes non-earmarked contributions from member states	Supports implementation of UNEP's Programme of Work
Earmarked contributions	Constitutes trust funds and other earmarked contributions from member states, the Global Environment Facility (GEF), the Green Climate Fund, the European Commission, foundations, the private sector, and UN bodies	Supports selective implementation of UNEP's Programme of Work
Conventions and protocols	Constitutes trust funds for fifteen MEAs for which UNEP provides secretariat functions	Supports the implementation of MEAs administered by UNEP
Multilateral Fund	Constitutes assessed contributions from forty-nine member states	Supports the implementation of the Montreal Protocol

has grown to $570 million in 2018, the bulk of it, 87 percent, came from extrabudgetary, earmarked resources that respond primarily to donor preferences and limit the organization's initiative.

UNEP's mandate is explicitly normative; it serves as "the leading global environmental authority that sets the global environmental agenda, promotes the coherent implementation of the environmental dimension of sustainable development within the United Nations system, and serves as an authoritative advocate for the global environment."[15] UNEP, however, moved toward a more operational role as it experienced increasing demand for concrete technical assistance and support. Three main drivers account for this dynamic. As the first UN institution to be headquartered in the Global South, UNEP was at the forefront of environmental challenges and witnessed the tensions among a growing population, development demands, pressure on dwindling resources, degradation of ecosystems, and threats to human security. Staff, therefore, saw demand for technical assistance and felt a need to be more responsive to these demands. Second, concrete projects are noticeable, easy to showcase and report on, and attractive. Third, funders were sending contradictory signals when they demanded concrete results rather than broad policy reports, thus pushing the organization to engage on the ground in practice while also insisting that UNEP should remain exclusively normative.[16] Torn between a highly normative mandate to measure the state of the environment and to catalyze and coordinate action, and the pull to respond and act on concrete demands for immediate support, UNEP has struggled to find its place and its voice and define its institutional identity. The lack of clarity about UNEP's role and mandate has affected planning and implementation as well as the managerial and political will to make hard choices. Consequently, donor confidence has decreased, leading to fewer countries supporting UNEP and to further program reductions.

Through a rich diplomatic history of this understudied institution,[17] this book interrogates conventional wisdom about two conflicting identities: is UNEP, the anchor institution for global environmental governance, weak and inefficient or has it been an astounding success?[18] No scholarly or policy consensus exists about the performance of UNEP or the factors that have shaped it. Grounded in extensive empirical work, this book fills this gap. It offers a revisionist history of UNEP, one that does not grow out of theoretical assumptions but instead builds on historical research and first-hand accounts, including an examination of UN archives and documents, compilation and analysis of UNEP financial data since 1973, close to two hundred interviews, participation in international conferences and summits, convenings of policymakers and scholars, and countless conversations with leaders and officials in national and international institutions. It provides a roadmap of what has happened in the last fifty years and an outlook for what may happen in the next fifty and beyond. It narrates a journey through where we have been, where we are, and where we might go. It shows how the answers to the core questions that define an organization's identity—Who are we? What is our place in the world? Why is it important?—change over time. A nuanced analysis of UNEP's work, accomplishments, and difficulties since its creation builds a comprehensive history that provides the foundation for understanding UNEP's institutional identity.

THE CREATION CLAIMS OF DEFICIENCY BY DESIGN

Much of the global environmental governance literature assumes that UNEP was purposefully designed to be weak.[19] The odds of even convening a successful international conference on the environment were rather slim when the idea first came up in 1967.[20] Environmental protection evoked a range of conflicting connotations among countries. For developing countries it denoted protectionism, conditionality, and an obstacle to development. For Eastern Bloc countries, it conjured capitalist attempts to stunt economic and political progress in the race for military dominance and ideological supremacy. For many industrialized countries, it represented a potential tool for developing countries to pressure them for greater resource transfers. Yet, from June 5 to 16 in 1972, 131 governments gathered in Stockholm for the UN Conference on the Human Environment to consider "the need for a common outlook and for common principles to inspire and guide the peoples of the world in the preservation and enhancement of the human environment."[21] They deliberated intensely, sometimes acrimoniously, during the two-week conference, with heated arguments reflecting tensions between countries of the Global North and South, advocates for environment and those for development, and stakeholders concerned about effectiveness and equity.[22]

Many developing countries had only recently gained independence and considered economic growth a first priority in order to buttress their autonomy. In much of Africa, Asia, and Latin America, environmental problems were not the side effects of excessive industrialization, but often a symptom of inadequate development. "We didn't care in the developing countries about pollution at that time," remarked Dr. Mostafa Tolba, scientist and head of the Egyptian delegation to the Stockholm Conference, who would later become UNEP's longest serving executive director. "I come from a country where the illustration on our ten-pound notes was a chimney with smoke coming out. That represented industrialization, economic growth. We considered our industrialization a miracle."[23] Developing countries were anxious about the risk of sacrificing development objectives to a global environmental agenda and suspicious that industrialized countries were using the environment to impose controls on their population growth. The creation of a collective, comprehensive, and ambitious vision for the environment therefore seemed highly unlikely. An action plan and a new institution to implement that vision, even more so. Despite these deep differences, however, countries reached an unprecedented level of agreement on the problems at hand and possible paths forward, as chapter 2 explains. They established important core principles through a political declaration and created a new international environmental body within the United Nations: UNEP.

This process relied on the leadership of key individuals within and outside governments. The very idea of a planetary environmental conference was the brainchild of a few Swedish nationals who convinced their government, and subsequently the UN member states, to rally behind this effort.[24] Those governments that had already been pressured to protect and improve the environment took on a leadership position on the world stage. In Sweden, a public debate on mercury and its impacts on human health contributed to the creation of the Swedish Environmental Protection Agency in 1967 and the passing of the 1969 Environment Protection Act to prevent water and air pollution as well as other potential hazards to the environment and human health.[25] The United States had just undergone a flurry of institutional innovations and legal developments, including the 1970 National Environmental Policy Act (NEPA), which created the President's Council on Evironmetal Quality. The protests on Earth Day in April 1970 and broad concerns over environmental trends, were followed by the creation of the Environmental Protection Agency and the Clean Air, Clean Water, and Endangered Species Acts. This, in turn, led other governments to consider environmental issues more seriously. Having powerful countries as proponents of this first-of-its-kind venture also enabled Maurice Strong, the Canadian Secretary-General of the Stockholm Conference, to ensure its success.

The creation of UNEP was no easy task. Governments had convened in Stockholm with assurances that "no new machinery will be created," yet, the deliberations focused on the form, function, and financing of a new UN body.[26] A key assumption in the literature is that "[s]ome of the strongest states in the system … strongly opposed the creation of a strong and independent agency."[27] However, as John W. McDonald, then Director of Economic and Social Affairs at the Bureau of International Organization Affairs at the US State Department, explained, he had developed an idea for a new strong, independent institution for the environment. McDonald had been instrumental in the creation of several UN offices, including the UN Fund for Population Activities, UN Volunteers, and the post of UN Disaster Relief Coordinator, and was a proponent of a centralized structure for all environmental efforts. "I used the argument I had used earlier for the creation of the UN Population Fund," Ambassador McDonald recalled. Population had never been the focus of the UN system and was a critical issue that required a separate and distinct institution. "I said the same thing about the environment," he noted. "There is a growing movement across the world, particularly in the United States, and if we want anything to happen in this global system, we have to have a new agency. And that became my mantra—you had to have a new agency to actually make this happen."[28] The United States was in fact not simply a proponent but an active leader of the creation of what would become the UN Environment Programme.

The creation of UNEP as a subsidiary body, a programme under the UN General Assembly's oversight rather than a stand-alone, specialized agency, has led scholars to assume that UNEP was "designed for failure; or at least for something less than success."[29] The perception of UNEP's mandate as impossible and hopeless and its budget as dismal have prompted the conclusion that its institutional form is an insurmountable weakness.[30] Moreover, the assumption that UNEP was located in Nairobi to marginalize it has reinforced the "deficiency by design" narrative. The conclusion, therefore, is that if institutional design were to change, any deficiencies would disappear. The almost exclusive focus on UNEP's status as a subsidiary body as the root problem has led to repeated arguments in favor of a fundamental institutional redesign that would "upgrade" UNEP to a specialized agency. However, a careful analysis of UNEP's achievements and challenges shows that the vision for "upgrading" institutional design is based on faulty assumptions and needs to be recalibrated. Importantly, changing institutional form does not automatically improve performance. The transformation of the UN Industrial Development Organization (UNIDO) from a subsidiary body to a specialized agency in the 1970s, for example, has not produced evidence of a considerably stronger organization.[31]

This book debunks some of these long-standing myths about UNEP's creation by providing historical evidence and in-depth analysis of the institutional history of UNEP and the individuals who shaped it. Notably, this analysis demonstrates that UNEP is not deficient by design. It was created against the odds at a time when environmental concerns were just emerging. Establishing it as a programme rather than a specialized agency and providing it with voluntary financial resources were well-intentioned early choices. There is no indication that the performance or finances of subsidiary bodies such as the UN Development Programme, the World Food Programme, or the UN High Commissioner for Refugees are affected negatively because of their institutional form. In fact, their budgets are the largest in the UN system and much higher than the budgets of any specialized agency (see figure 1.4).[32]

Contrary to prevailing accounts, locating UNEP in Nairobi was neither a plot to marginalize the new institution nor a concession to developing countries to gain their support for its creation.[33] Rather, such a location was envisioned as a tool of greater equity in the distribution of international institutions around the world, and the final decision was the product of a contested vote in committee at the United Nations, as

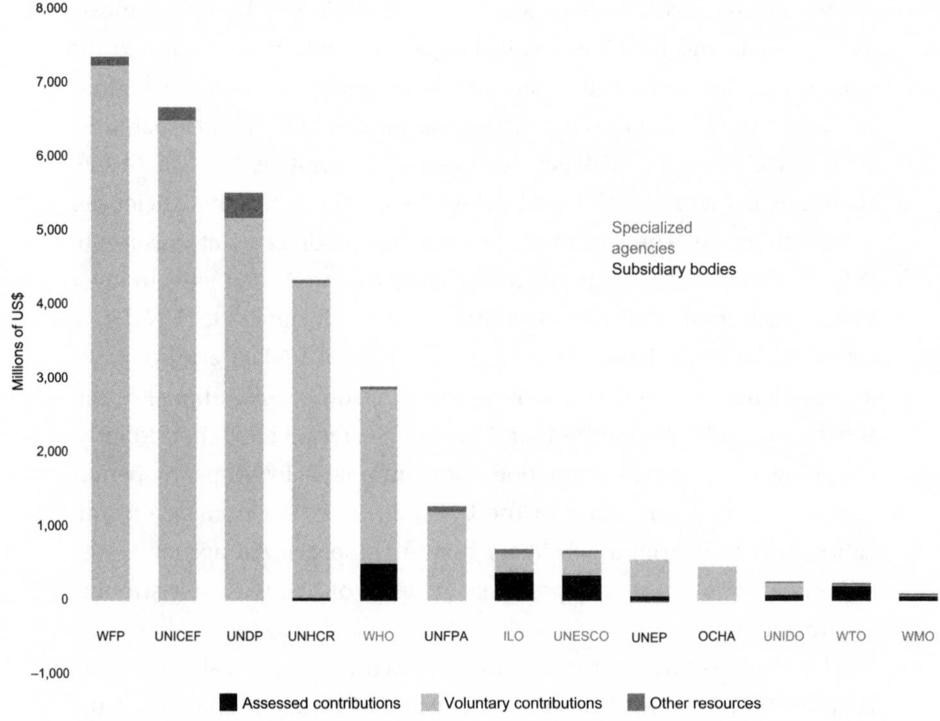

1.4 Annual income, in millions of USD, of select UN bodies in 2018.

chapter 2 recounts in detail.[34] Nevertheless, in practice, capacity constraints, the remoteness from the institutions that UNEP had to influence and coordinate, coupled with connectivity challenges in Nairobi and the uneven credibility of the agency, became important limiting factors to UNEP's performance. As John Scanlon, former Secretary-General of CITES and former senior policy advisor at UNEP, argued, "We need a smaller, smarter, better-connected institution."[35] This inquiry into UNEP's history and performance illustrates how the original institutional design remains a strong foundation for the UNEP we need in the twenty-first century.

GOAL ATTAINMENT AND PROBLEM RESOLUTION

Created to coordinate the environmental activities in the UN system, UNEP was also meant to provide reliable scientific assessments of the state of the environment and to develop the necessary policies and legal, institutional, and regulatory mechanisms. To what extent has it delivered on this mandate? Has it resolved environmental problems? Why or why not? These are the questions at the heart of this book. Understanding UNEP's accomplishments and challenges and the reasons behind them is critical to envisioning its future. Chapters 3 and 4 present an assessment of goal attainment (progress toward institutional goals as defined in the mandate) and of problem resolution (progress toward resolving the problems the institution was designed to address).[36]

Analysts have criticized UNEP as "weak, underfunded and ineffective in its core functions"[37] and largely deficient in its ability to galvanize more attention, respect, and urgency for the environmental agenda. Conversely, others have praised UNEP as "one of the most impressive UN organizations in terms of its actual achievements."[38] "Given its mandate, its resources, and its authority," wrote one scholar, UNEP is "a remarkable success."[39] Both assessments are grounded in the view that UNEP was deliberately designed as deficient. Poor performance was presumed as a natural outcome of this design, and any achievement was seen as an extraordinary feat for overcoming UNEP's allegedly flawed institutional form.

UNEP's performance, however, cannot be characterized simply as success or failure. Its track record is complex and nuanced, and it has evolved. Throughout its fifty-year history, UNEP has achieved success and has also stumbled. Chapter 3 examines how UNEP has performed in regards to its core mandated functions of coordination of environmental activities in the UN system, environmental assessment, and policy development and illustrates the tension between the normative and operational expectations of UNEP. Chapter 4 then examines its work in addressing major global environmental problems across a range of environmental issues including the resolution of the depletion of the ozone layer, regional seas pollution, regulation of chemicals and waste, and the climate change regime, as well as land degradation and the loss of species and forests. Despite some successes, however, UNEP has lost its sense of purpose and place in the international system. "We are guilty of trying to be all things to all people,"[40] one staff member remarked, and "go where funding comes from, not where knowledge has accumulated and action is necessary," noted another.[41]

UNEP has been eclipsed by the myriad other UN entities competing for funding and attention, a striking outcome considering UNEP's original mandate to coordinate UN institutions. Often, governments have set up new bodies for the problems UNEP had identified and, as these bodies gained operational independence, UNEP's influence has diminished, rendering coordination and collaboration more challenging and costly. With time, the multiplication of environmental organizations became a self-reinforcing pattern and the result, as Steven Charnovitz wrote, was "a nightmare scenario ... [a] crazy quilt pattern of environmental governance [that] is too complicated, and is getting worse each year."[42] Indeed, UNEP staff's perception of the organization's effectiveness deteriorated in the span of just four years, between 2012 and 2016. Over 60 percent of respondents to a UNEP staff survey in 2012 perceived the organization as effective but, in 2012, only 45 percent did. Moreover, one-third of respondents in 2016 took a neutral position.[43] These results show the optimism staff members felt in the run-up to the 2012 UN Conference on Sustainable Development, Rio+20, and the disappointment that followed. UNEP underwent a suite of reforms over its history, as chapter 7 explains, and the formal conclusion of the reform process took place at Rio+20. The impact of the reforms, however, has not been sufficiently felt throughout the organization in terms of internal functionality or of addressing environmental problems. "In effect we work in silos," a staff member noted in the 2016 internal UNEP staff survey, "and as such our communication to the world seems rather fragmented, same rhetoric year in year out and all global reports seem to indicate that the environment is in free-fall getting worse by the day. Clearly, we have not managed to change mind sets out there—whether through normative approaches or otherwise. We need a strategic and organizational rethink!!!!"[44]

In essence, UNEP's performance is characterized by a dichotomy: The organization remains highly relevant, its evolving mandate is ambitious and necessary, and it has increased the prominence of global environmental concerns. It has, however, failed in setting priorities, planning properly, making decisions, and efficiently using its resources. Reflecting this dual identity, staff express both exasperation and hope: "Although I am proud to work here," a staff member noted, "I feel frustrated because I do not think we have reached our potential ... But I still have hope in our organization!"[45] The competitive climate for financing and political attention demands successful projects, visible outcomes, and improvements.

However, as a 2019 evaluation of UNEP by the UN Office of Oversight Services notes, "lack of accountability, unclear roles and responsibilities, incomplete change management efforts, lack of support to knowledge management, uneven results-based management and inadequate support for policy implementation have hindered effectiveness."[46]

Against the odds of political, financial, and location challenges, UNEP has delivered on much, though not all, of its mandate. It resolved problems and launched important processes when it had the means to provide scientific evidence, the authority and political support to convene policy deliberations, and the courage and capacity to create and guide the necessary institutions to support implementation. Success eluded UNEP when it competed with other institutions and failed to renew its commitment, sustain its engagement, and provide continuity to projects, programs, and initiatives. Importantly, the institutional form of a subsidiary body, a programme in the UN system, did not determine its effectiveness. As this book explains, capacity, connectivity, and credibility are core elements of performance. The combination of design, including mandate and finances, leadership, and location, shape these factors and influence UNEP's performance.

CAPACITY, CONNECTIVITY, CREDIBILITY

"The environment is all-encompassing; it cuts across everything," Kofi Annan explained in our interview. "No institution can claim monopoly over the environment. Whether we like it or not, other agencies, other institutions will get engaged. What is important is for them to know when to coordinate their efforts, to pool their efforts, to pool their resources, and not work at cross purposes."[47] With a growing number of institutions with environmental mandates and activities, UNEP's clout as the anchor institution has been challenged. UNEP's institutional design—its mandate and financial mechanism—placed it *in authority* to take decisions and action. To be effective, it also has to be *an authority*, to have the requisite credibility and reputation to influence decisions.[48] At the time of its creation, governments provided UNEP with an ambitious mandate—and thus the legal authority and a financial mechanism—to serve as the anchor institution for the global environment. They expected that the new institution would grow to become *an authority*, indeed, *the authority*, in global environmental governance.

UNEP has undeniably made significant strides but is not duly recognized for its past and present achievements. It suffers from a lack of credibility, especially among developed countries, where not only the public but even environmental experts ignore or are not aware of UNEP's work. Many of its challenges are due to limited capacity, connectivity, and credibility (see figure 1.5). UNEP's capacity derives from its people and its resources—the staff it can recruit and the partners it can mobilize, as well as the funding and other contributions it can generate for its own work and for work on the issues under its purview. Communication technologies and infrastructure determine connectivity, the ability to connect to constituencies far and near and to be visible and accessible. Investment by the host government is indispensable to connectivity. The authority and influence of an institution determine its credibility, which derives from the quality of work by staff and partners, its visibility, and its reputation for delivering results. UNEP's success in raising awareness led to an increase in the prominence of the environmental agenda; but with a growing number of organizations in the field, UNEP lost in the competition for resources, financial and human.

While institutional form is undoubtedly important, it has not been the limiting factor of performance.[49] The anchor institution is fighting an inherent political constraint: the environment is not a priority for many member states. "Ultimately, the problem is not the structure," Bill Mansfield, UNEP's deputy executive director from 1986 to 1992, emphasized. "The problem is the priority that governments put on the environment.

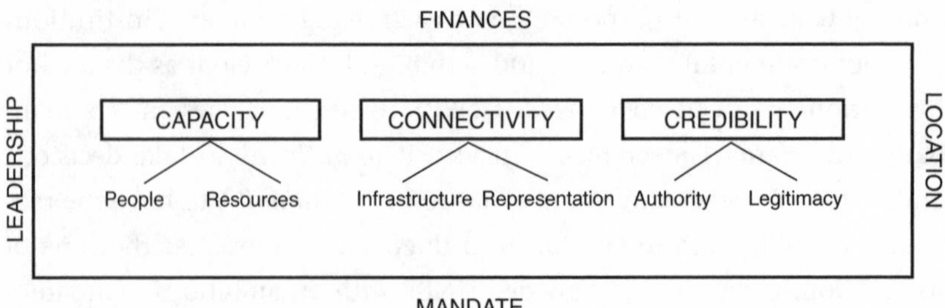

1.5 Performance analysis framework.

No matter how you structure [an organization], unless governments give it priority, it won't happen the way you want it to happen."[50] With limited capacity and connectivity, UNEP has not been sufficiently visible and convincing to both the governments in need of its support and to donors. Accordingly, the organization's finances are grossly inadequate to address its broad mandate, and while the amount of funding is not determined by UNEP's structure as a programme rather than a specialized agency, it has been simply insufficient for carrying out its core mission.

Leadership influences the vision, management, and culture of the organization, its sense of identity and purpose, and is critical to capacity and credibility. The narrative in chapter 6 traces the historical arc of UNEP's leadership from its first executive director, Maurice Strong, who assumed the post in 1973, to the seventh executive director, Inger Andersen, who took office in June 2019 after Erik Solheim stepped down unexpectedly in November 2018.[51] The in-depth profiles of each director explain their leadership styles and skills, the particular external and internal pressures within which they operated, and the direction in which they took the organization. Every executive director has left their indelible mark on the institution. Seeking to reshape the organization's identity, each has articulated a new narrative about UNEP's institutional priorities. In the first twenty years, only two executive directors, Maurice Strong and Mostafa Tolba, shaped UNEP. The institution evolved from an idea about a catalytic, collaborative, convincing entity that would inspire environmental action across a multitude of actors to an independent body that had to claim its rightful place at the UN table. In the two decades between the 1992 Rio Earth Summit and Rio+20, UNEP lost parts of its mandate to new institutions and much of its visibility and convening power. Elizabeth Dowdeswell, Klaus Töpfer, and Achim Steiner sought to insert UNEP into the new sustainable development narrative and government priorities. In 2018, only two years into his term, Erik Solheim, the sixth executive director, stepped down. He had initiated a sudden and unwelcome change of UNEP's name to UN Environment and had begun reforming the way the organization engaged with member states and business. Changing the organization's name overnight chipped away at UNEP's identity and caused unnecessary turmoil within and confusion among its constituencies. Greater enagement with China led to the tripling of the country's financial contributions to the Environment Fund and made it one of UNEP's top 15 contributors, as evidenced in chapter 6. When Inger Andersen took leadership, she reverted to using the United Nations Environment Programme and UNEP, making the case that she will lead an institution that "must get the job done."[52]

Operating in complex social-relational systems, each executive director has had to balance the demands to serve as technical expert, manager, politician, and visionary. They have had to promote the organization externally to ensure its financing stream and provide direction and vision internally to shape the organizational culture and values, the basis for organizational identity. And building on the foundation of their predecessors, each has left a lasting imprint on the organization.

UNEP's Nairobi location has shaped the evolution of the organization's substantive focus by influencing whom it can recruit and retain, how connected it is to its constituencies, and how accessible it is to existing and emerging partners.[53] Location, examined in detail in chapter 5, has been largely ignored in institutional investigations because it is seen as an issue that is too simple analytically and too difficult politically. Location should be viewed, however, not as binary (entirely either good or bad), but rather as more or less challenging or supportive of a particular mandate. Place matters because it shapes what an organization can reasonably be expected to deliver successfully. Institutions are likely to be more effective if they are located closer to the problems they are charged with addressing and the partners they need to work with. For an operational agency, this means being on the ground in the countries whose problems it seeks to address; for a normative agency like UNEP was intended to be, this means being close to the agencies that it was supposed to influence. The physical distance and lack of communication made UNEP's normative mandate, and its coordination task in particular, daunting. With its headquarters located far outside the dense "hotspots" of political activity, UNEP has been isolated from the UN agencies it is expected to work with closely. Even UNEP's headquarters in Nairobi, staff note, has been divorced from the rest of the organization, which is spread around the world with only a handful of staff in each office, as figure 1.3 illustrated.

The most important location dynamic is the serendipity of interactions with people at other organizations. It is such exchanges that lead to finding the specialists necessary for a particular project, receiving a referral for a distinguished candidate for an open post, or obtaining critical competitive intelligence.[54] Being present in the ecosystem of other similar institutions allows an organization to plug into a powerful information flow and to develop relationships with donors as well as with scientists, NGOs, and media. The downside of a location with a high concentration of similar institutions, however, is that they, too, are looking for talent. UNEP's limited face-to-face interaction with counterparts in other agencies and its inadequate long-distance communication technologies for the first three decades of its history has marginalized it. UNEP's offices in Paris, New York, and Geneva have tried to step into the liaison role but have been limited by the lack of headquarters status, the reluctance of headquarters to delegate necessary and appropriate responsibility, and scarce human and financial resources. UNEP's isolation from the political pressures of the UN system has, on the other hand, enabled it to carve out its own identity and retain staff for longer periods.

Systematic intergovernmental efforts to reform the system of international environmental governance began in 1997 at the Rio+5 conference in New York and concluded formally with the adoption of *The Future We Want* outcome document at the 2012 UN Conference on Sustainable Development, Rio+20. These extensive efforts are detailed in chapter 7. Rio+20 concluded an important discussion in which governments decided that UNEP's original mandate and design, and its form and function, were robust and thus required increased funding, visibility, and authority. We live in an era of outrage and optimism, Christiana Figueres, former head of the UN Framework Convention on Climate Change, contends, where collective action is imperative to create the future we choose.[55] Everything we need to survive and thrive on this planet depends, directly or indirectly, on the natural environment, and the anchor institution for the global environment holds a critical role. UNEP has the potential to serve as the knowledge hub and political platform in global environmental governance. Chapter 7 lays out an action agenda for transformation.

"UNEP has a tangible opportunity to frame the future," Manuel Pulgar-Vidal, environment minister of Peru from 2011 to 2016, remarked. "The UN Secretary-General is aligning the objectives of international instruments, and UNEP could play a significant role at the domestic level to enable countries to do what they have to do. However, it does not."[56] Why is that, and how can UNEP fulfill this potential? Everything that UNEP has done can be seen as a product of both an inspirational vision and an organizational obstacle course. Envisioning the future of UNEP must build on a solid understanding of its past, as well as the choices made over the course of its first five decades, and their consequences. UNEP has proven that it is a resilient institution able to bounce back, against the odds of its small size, limited resources, remote location, and inherent competition with the other UN agencies. With a new universal environmental assembly that can convene all 193 UN member states and initiate challenging political debates on the most pressing environmental issues, UNEP has officially positioned itself *in* authority to provide the political center of gravity for global environmental governance.

UNEP's fiftieth anniversary in 2022 provides a symbolic opportunity for a fundamental transformation into becoming *the* authority on the global environment. This commemoration moment can spur the necessary momentum and political will to launch such a transformation through integrated, ambitious solutions. UNEP could and should become the go-to institution for information on the state of the planet, for a normative vision of global environmental governance, and for support for domestic environmental agendas and for non-state actors. Indeed, UNEP could help create a guiding, totalizing vision for sustainable development, with environment as the foundation for planetary and public health and well-being.

2

DELIBERATE DESIGN: FORM, FUNCTION, FINANCES, AND LOCATION

[T]his Conference [is] itself a fresh expression of the spirit which created the United Nations—concern for the present and future welfare of humanity. It does not aim merely at securing limited agreements but at establishing peace and harmony in life—among all races and with Nature ... We are supposed to belong to the same family sharing common traits and impelled by the same basic desires, yet we inhabit a divided world. How can it be otherwise?
—Indira Gandhi, Speech at the 1972 Stockholm Conference

By the 1970s, "the environmental alarm clock buzzed in many ears, in many nations," noted Fitzhugh Green, one of the US delegates preparing the 1972 UN Conference on the Human Environment in Stockholm.[1] Environmental problems had created a crescendo of public concern in industrialized countries as the threats posed by toxic chemicals, the large-scale destruction of natural ecosystems, and the loss of species had become visible and were obviously linked to human activity. Pollution, it became clear, did not stop at border crossings, and solutions required common effort. The new scientific understanding of the causes and consequences of environmental degradation imposed new responsibilities across borders. Ready for more informed and systematic collective action, many governments summoned the political attention and will to design a new international institution to promote international cooperation on addressing environmental challenges.

On June 16, 1972, Maurice Strong closed the Stockholm Conference by declaring that while the tasks of the conference had seemed almost impossible, governments had faced up to the challenge with a determination to find solutions. "The Governments represented here," Strong stated, "fully mean what they have said. Their unanimous recommendation is for the establishment of the ongoing United Nations environmental machinery and the necessary initial funding."[2] After years of negotiation within the preparatory process, governments agreed on the form, functions, and finances of the new institution. The decisions about its name, governance, and location, however, were made in December 1972 in New York during the twenty-seventh session of the UN General Assembly.

At that session, governments adopted Resolution 2997 on *Institutional and Financial Arrangements for International Environmental Cooperation* creating the United Nations Environment Programme with four organs: a fifty-eight-member Governing Council for Environmental Programmes, an Environment Secretariat headed by an executive director, an Environment Fund, and an Environmental Coordination Board. This chapter lays out how countries reached this outcome and explains the intention behind UNEP's design. Why was the new environmental institution created as a programme, i.e. a subsidiary organ, and not a specialized agency? Was it designed to be weak? Why was its financing voluntary, and what have been the consequences? And why was it located in Nairobi? The answers to these questions explain the origins of UNEP as the anchor institution for the global environment and offer insights into institutional design changes that would or would not be possible or desirable.

OBSTACLE COURSE ON THE ROAD TO STOCKHOLM

Billed as the original landmark event in global environmental governance, the Stockholm Conference convened and succeeded in the face of multiple obstacles. Preparations for the conference had been slow under Jean Mussard, director of the Conference Secretariat, but gained momentum in the autumn of 1970, when Maurice Strong, a Canadian businessman with an avid interest for international affairs, development, and the United Nations, replaced Mussard. The UN General Assembly appointed Strong as Secretary-General of the Conference largely because of his skills as a leader and coordinator. While he was himself unfamiliar with the scientific underpinnings of environmental concerns, Strong understood their political and economic dimensions and had the capacity to persuade leaders from around the world that collective action was necessary. As Professor William Clark observed, Strong had "the vision of the astronaut; seeing planet earth as a globe without boundaries, cradled in its fragile life-supporting biosphere."[3] Sverker Åström, the Swedish Permanent Representative to the United Nations, recalled in his memoir that Strong's appointment was a stroke of luck. He was "perhaps the best example of a 'pragmatic idealist,'" Åström wrote. "His talent, experience, engagement, personal charm and ability to generate trust made him the ideal organizer of the large and incredibly complicated undertaking of a world conference."[4] Strong's vision of "only one earth" became the conference motto and he managed to bring together people across political divisions.

Convincing countries to send delegations to the Conference was only the first challenge. Developing countries were openly skeptical about the objectives and motives of the conference and felt that it was going to place substantial burdens on them, which, a senior US official remarked, "caused some concern, even paranoia in some places."[5] Strong's mission, therefore, was to reassure and engage, and he was quite good at it. According to Bill Reilly, Administrator of the US Environmental Protection Agency from 1989 to 1993, Strong was "very effective at involving developing countries, in going around and communicating to a number of governments."[6] His guiding formula was "the process is the policy," meaning that a functioning process of engagement with all actors was in itself an important outcome. "Everywhere I went," Strong wrote in his memoir, *Where on Earth are We Going*, "I conferred with presidents, prime ministers, business leaders and scientists, arguing, explaining, listening, learning, cajoling, coopting."[7] As Professor Adebayo Adedeji, Nigeria's Federal Commissioner for Economic Development and Reconstruction, remarked, "The concern of the industrialized nations with measures to curb pollution appeared to us as yet another obstacle in the already handicapped race for material progress." Maurice Strong, however, "soon made it clear that all of us, irrespective of the stage of our development, have a large stake in the matter."[8] Emphasizing the fact that environmental problems such as falling groundwater levels, eroding soil, desertification, and depleted fisheries could slow and even arrest economic development, Strong resourcefully and persuasively eased suspicions and fostered engagement.

Strong identified India and Brazil as countries critical to the success of the conference. India was "especially influential among developing countries," Strong noted, and one of his first official visits was to New Delhi, where he met with Prime Minister Indira Gandhi and convinced her to attend the conference.[9] Indira Gandhi had a deep interest in and knowledge of the environment, and Strong managed to get her attention by pointing to the political stakes. As he wrote in his memoir, he told Mrs. Gandhi, who was deeply sensitive to political concerns, that "If the developing countries sit out the conference, it would leave the issues in the hands of the industrialized countries." As expected, Strong recalled, "thereafter, India became one of the leading participants in preparations

2.1 Indira Gandhi, Prime Minister of India, greeted by Maurice F. Strong, Secretary General of the 1972 Stockholm Conference, upon her arrival at the Folkets Hus building to attend the Conference. Credit: UN Photo/Yutaka Nagata.

for the conference and a strong and effective proponent of the developing countries' position."[10] India's leadership was critical for gaining the support of the Global South and securing their commitment to engage in negotiations.

Indira Gandhi understood and successfully articulated both the need to protect the environment and to lift people out of poverty. She urged taking the longer perspective and achieving a higher standard of living in harmony with nature. Many developing-country governments, however, were suspicious of the environmental agenda, fearing neo-colonialism. Brazil, for example, rallied an electric countercurrent among developing countries with the idea that international environmental policies could impede economic progress. Bernardo de Azevedo Brito, Brazil's representative to the Stockholm Conference, argued that "the environment cannot be utilized ... to perpetuate policies of stagnation [and] only development can provide mankind at large with the kind of environment it deserves." He urged governments to "build a new world instead of contemplating an impossible and undesirable return to primeval conditions of life."[11] Strong understood these concerns and empathized with developing countries, but he emphasized that environment and development could not be separated, that they were intrinsically two sides of the same coin.[12]

In parallel with his work to engage the Global South, Strong recognized that many industrialized countries also needed convincing. The United States was an ardent proponent of the conference, capitalizing on a vibrant environmental movement at home and growing national environmental institutions. The United Kingdom and France, meanwhile, were far more skeptical. Wary of potential regulations that might hamper the fleet of the British-French supersonic Concorde jet airliners, which first flew in 1969 (and would be retired in 2003), they wanted to limit the potential reach of the conference.[13] Based on concerns of this nature, France and the UK teamed up with Germany, Italy, and Belgium to form the "Brussels Group," an alliance with the express goal of coordinating positions in advance of the conference and preventing the adoption of international standards regulating environmental quality or pollution.[14] The United States and the Netherlands were active supporters of the Stockholm Conference but also appeared on the membership list of the Brussels group.

Strong realized the critical need for intellectual leadership as the foundation for the Stockholm conference. He worked with Barbara Ward, a British economist and journalist who was known for her advocacy on behalf of developing countries, to assemble a team of 152 scientific and intellectual leaders from fifty-eight countries to serve as consultants for the conference agenda and produce the main background document. Strong's special advisors included renowned economic thinkers from the Global South such as Gamani Corea of Sri Lanka, Mahbub ul Haq of Pakistan, Enrique Iglesias of Uruguay, and Ignacy Sachs of Poland (who had also lived in India and Brazil). Their presence conveyed the clear message that Strong was listening to developing countries' concerns and was aware of their interests. "When we were asked to prepare a conceptual framework for the Stockholm Conference, we didn't get a conceptual framework," Barbara Ward stated in her opening speech to the Stockholm Conference. "What we got was something like standing under Niagara. This is a time when people's ideas about the planet they live in, about the way they have to live, about the way they can live, are changing in an absolutely monumental fashion … [P]eople are radically beginning to reconsider how they have to view their life on Earth, and what sense their existence makes to them."[15] Himself an outsider in the United Nations, Maurice Strong succeeded in engaging individuals with both his passion for the environment and the requisite expertise, without resorting to government- or UN-appointed technocrats. This emphasis on independent intellectual and conceptual contributions was a new model for a UN summit and set an important precedent for subsequent UN gatherings on the environment.

Political tensions between the Global North and the Global South nearly derailed the whole preparatory process. Developing countries threatened to boycott the conference because its initial focus was supposed to be pollution—a problem that they believed was caused by and had to be solved by developed countries, even though developing countries were also experiencing its impacts.[16] In addition, developing countries feared that international action against pollution would likely result in limits on industrialization that would both stymie economic progress and effectively force them to foot the bill for fixing problems they had not created.[17] Strong and the conference secretariat managed to assuage many developing-country concerns and muster support for the conference by convening a panel of twenty-seven economists and scientists from the developing world in Founex, Switzerland, in June 1971. Many of these participants were drawn from the consultant roster assembled by Barbara Ward. The initial nine-day meeting was followed by smaller conferences organized by the UN regional commissions in Asia, Africa, Latin America, and the Middle East.[18]

The *Founex Report* that arose from this gathering elaborated and endorsed the concerns of developing countries, while at the same time countering claims that economic development and environment were diametrically opposed. It established that environmental concerns were both more widespread and more relevant to developing countries' situation than they had appreciated.[19] The report affirmed that the environment should not be viewed as a barrier to development, but as part of it.[20] It also cemented the role of developing countries in the preparatory process, as it assigned specific tasks for delegations to complete prior to the Stockholm Conference such as producing national reports on environmental concerns that they were encountering. Through the Founex meeting, Strong managed to engage world thinkers in a common agenda, reach an agreement, and provide the intellectual foundation for the political negotiations. Strong would later write, "the meeting is inscribed in my memory as one of the best intellectual exchanges I have ever participated in. It had a profound influence both on the Stockholm Conference and on the evolution of the concept of the environment-development relationship."[21] The *Founex Report* articulated the need for an ecological, systemic approach to the management of the issues that affect the future of humanity and was in essence the vision for and definition of sustainable development. Maurice Strong leveraged the *Founex Report* to demonstrate that the environment was connected to every aspect of human existence and thus required a comprehensive, integrated approach.

Despite the consensus emerging among technical experts, politics and ideology remained two of the core challenges for the Stockholm Conference. Notwithstanding calls for inclusion of "mainland China … the Peking regime, the two Germanies, the two Vietnams, and the two Koreas to participate in the Stockholm meeting,"[22] as Professor Richard Gardner articulated in a 1970 *Washington Post* article, the political divisions of the day resulted in exclusion. The West "insisted on excluding East Germany—the German Democratic Republic—from the conference on the grounds that it wasn't a 'real' country but a creature of the USSR," Strong wrote.[23] Consequently, the Soviet Union and most of its allies withdrew from the preparations and did not participate in the conference. It was only through science diplomacy, particularly the work of a Russian scientist named Vladimir Kunin, that political channels stayed open.[24] This makeshift arrangement ultimately worked, and the *New York Times* reported on May 24, 1971, that the scientific director from the Soviet Union's International Organizations Department supported the conference's task "to translate [environmental] concern into action."[25] Nonetheless, Richard Gardner observed, some reluctance towards global cooperation remained as countries maintained that the "new environmental machinery ... should be of an international and not a supranational character."[26] Overcoming nationalism and suspicion of the agenda behind the new institutions would take creativity, compromise, and courage.

At the outset of the conference itself, no one knew how it would actually proceed, including Strong, who recalled that the Swedish security services were worried about security after receiving threats to disrupt the conference from radical groups. Strong, too, had received personal threats.[27] To everyone's relief, the provocations did not materialize. A number of diplomatic challenges nevertheless emerged during the two-week conference, and a serious one was only narrowly averted on the final day—a testament to Strong's deft leadership. The Chinese delegation declared that they could not take a final position on the Stockholm Declaration, a core conference outcome, without authorization from Beijing because of the population issues that the political declaration discussed.[28] This impasse would have led to a sudden walk-out, inevitably dealing a dramatic blow to the esprit de corps. With quick thinking and delicate delivery, Strong devised a way for the Chinese representative, Ku Mu, to leave the official seat during the vote and to take a seat one aisle back and thus effectively be present without voting or abstaining.[29] To everyone's surprise, this technical maneuver worked, both procedurally and politically, and the Stockholm Declaration was adopted.

Thus, against the odds, the Stockholm Conference remarkably succeeded in convening governments and creating a common understanding of the context (the interconnectedness of the one planet we all inhabit) and the goals (the effective resolution of environmental problems). Governments adopted the ambitious Stockholm Declaration with twenty-six principles, an Action Plan with 109 recommendations, and a draft of what would become UN General Assembly Resolution 2997 on *Institutional and Financial Arrangements for International Environmental Cooperation*. Against the initial expectations, the Stockholm Conference generated the political commitment to create a new international environmental institution.

CRAFTING STOCKHOLM'S INSTITUTIONAL LEGACY

As delegates convened in Stockholm in June 1972, multiple international agencies were already active in the field of the environment, and advocates of a new institution realized that any addition would have to be established in full recognition of existing organizations and agreements. The core premise that took hold early on in the negotiations was that "form follows function" and that institutional arrangements would have to be predicated on the specific functions they would be expected to perform. As US Representative to the Preparatory Committee, Christian A. Herter Jr., Deputy Assistant Secretary of State for Environmental and Population Affairs, noted in March 1972, the subject of the institutional implications of the Stockholm Conference had been reserved for last in the deliberations because the wide range of proposed international functions "had to be at least preliminarily surveyed before [deliberations] on the form of organization best suited to carrying them out."[30] The tenet that "form follows function" required negotiators to identify what the existing UN system was already doing and delivering before creating new institutional arrangements with potentially overlapping mandates.[31]

Within the US government, John W. McDonald, then Director of Economic and Social Affairs at the Bureau of International Organization Affairs at the State Department, had been circulating the idea of a new UN agency for the environment and had garnered support from the Nixon Administration. McDonald drafted four resolutions: on the governing body; on the secretariat; on a fund along the lines of the UN Development Programme fund, designed to attract government support for special projects on the environment; and on a coordinating committee that would be chaired by the head of UNEP, with all of the other agencies in the UN system who had a piece of the serious action of the environment sitting together and ensuring that there was no overlap or duplication.[32]

The Committee on International Environmental Programs, which the National Academy of Sciences had created at the request of the US State Department in preparation for the Stockholm Conference, arrived at the same conclusion as McDonald: "We recommend the establishment of a unit in the United Nations system to provide central leadership, to assure a comprehensive and integrated overview of environmental problems, and to develop stronger linkages among environmental institutions and the constituencies they serve."[33] Indeed, by 1972, the US stance on the institutional question was unequivocal. The United States, rivaled only by Sweden in its enthusiasm for effective international action on the environment, strongly advocated for the creation of an intergovernmental body at the highest level in the United Nations that would "enjoy the prestige and public visibility which its subject deserves"[34] and be "placed at the highest possible level in the United Nations administrative structure, i.e., in the Office of the Secretary-General."[35]

The United States also argued for a "strong executive for environmental affairs with broad terms of reference."[36] Regardless of the title of this post—High Commissioner, Under Secretary-General, or Administrator—the US stance was that the "exact position should be determined by that which will provide the office with maximum prestige, strength, and freedom."[37] The US proposal also advocated for an intergovernmental body to advise and support the executive, in contrast to a scenario in which the executive would merely implement the body's guidance and decisions. The United States recognized that only an "active, resourceful, and creative leader"[38] would ensure that environmental concerns received priority. The core functions included catalyzing environmental action, developing policies and guidelines, establishing a global monitoring system, and performing dispute settlement.[39]

The two political documents that governments adopted at the conference contained these decisions: the Declaration on the Human Environment, with twenty-six principles, and an Action Plan, with 109 recommendations. The declaration affirmed that all states were responsible to ensure that activities within their jurisdiction or control do not cause harm to the environment of other states or of areas beyond the limits of national jurisdiction. The Stockholm Action Plan framed three core functions for the new environmental institution: environmental assessment, environmental management, and supporting measures. Environmental assessment included the monitoring of environmental quality, evaluation of the collected data, and forecasting of trends; scientific research; and information exchange with governments and other international organizations. Environmental management was at heart policy development, which included setting goals and standards through a consultative, multilateral process; crafting of international agreements; and devising guidelines and policies for their implementation. Supporting measures referred to what we now term capacity building and development—including technical assistance, education and training, and public information.[40] These functions constitute the core of UNEP's mandate and have stayed constant since UNEP's creation (see figure 3.1 in chapter 3).

WHY UNEP IS NOT A SPECIALIZED AGENCY

When creating international entities within the UN system, states have three main choices: a specialized agency, a subsidiary organ within the UN General Assembly and the Economic and Social Council, or an office within the UN Secretariat.

United Nations *specialized agencies* are autonomous organizations set up independently and linked to the UN through special agreements in accordance with Articles 57 and 63 of the UN Charter. Among the specialized agencies are the International Labour Organization, the World Health Organization, the Food and Agriculture Organization, and the World Meteorological Organization, several of which existed before the creation of the United Nations in 1945. Governments establish these agencies through the adoption and ratification of intergovernmental treaties, and the UN General Assembly has no direct administrative, programmatic, or financial authority over them. Specialized agencies, therefore, need no approval from the UN General Assembly or any other UN authority to make or implement decisions that fall within their mandate. Membership in specialized agencies is universal—that is, any state can join as a member if they ratify the constitutive treaty.[41] States can also withdraw if they wish and can be expelled if they renege on their financial commitments. The budgets for specialized agencies include mandatory financial contributions assessed according to a particular scale based on the relative size of the economy, and they do not receive any funding from the UN's regular budget.

Subsidiary organs are entities created under Article 22 of the UN Charter to address emerging problems and issues in international economic, social, and humanitarian fields. They can have many different formal designations—programmes, funds, boards, committees, commissions, councils, panels and working groups—and governance structures. The UN Development Programme, the World Food Programme, UNICEF, and the UN High Commissioner on Refugees are some examples of subsidiary organs. A UN General Assembly resolution is the instrument through which governments create subsidiary organs. The UN General Assembly exercises oversight over subsidiary organs, which usually have a limited membership designed to be geographically representative.[42] Such organs also rely on a funding mechanism drawing exclusively on voluntary contributions. For some subsidiary organs, a portion of funding may come from the UN regular budget. Subsidiary organs work directly through the United Nations, which gives them access to UN administrative and security services as well as a direct relationship with a number of UN offices and other subsidiary organs.

The third main institutional option is the creation of *an office* within the UN Secretariat with discrete responsibilities in an issue area or overarching coordination functions. For example, the UN Office for Disarmament Affairs (UNODA) provides information on multilateral disarmament issues; engages in norm-setting in the area of disarmament; fosters dialogue, transparency, and confidence-building on military matters; and encourages regional disarmament efforts. It also delivers on the ground through activities such as facilitating the disarmament of former combatants and helping them to reintegrate in society. The Office for Coordination of Humanitarian Affairs (OCHA) is the unit within the UN Secretariat responsible for bringing together humanitarian actors to ensure a coherent response to emergencies. OCHA also creates an overarching response framework, which allows for coordinated contributions from each stakeholder. While relatively small, these offices have gained notable public attention when headed by able leaders.[43]

Negotiators documented clearly how they understood global environmental problems and how they thought the UN system could best address them.[44] They carefully considered various institutional options and decided not to create a specialized agency for three main reasons. First, a new specialized agency would need to assume a wide range of functions already performed by existing agencies, including, among others, the International Labour Organization (ILO), created in 1919; the United Nations Educational, Scientific and Cultural Organization (UNESCO), established in 1946; and the World Health Organization (WHO) and the International Maritime Organization (IMO), both created in 1948. It was determined that none of these organizations could or should relinquish their environmental functions. The scope of work for a new specialized agency therefore would be difficult to define short of an all-inclusive mandate.[45] Moreover, as a US delegate at the conference observed, "Problems of environment are all-pervasive, and to remove environmental responsibility from existing bodies would not only weaken current efforts but deny the basic concept of the complex dependence of man's surroundings on all of his activities."[46]

Second, relegating the entire integrative concept of the "environment" to one specialized agency was deemed disadvantageous because the focus on the environment as another "sector" ran the risk of isolating and miring the new agency in jurisdictional difficulties. As Maurice Strong wrote, the core functions could "only be performed at the international level by a body which is not tied to any individual sectoral or operational responsibilities and is able to take an objective overall view of the technical and policy implications arising from a variety of multidisciplinary factors."[47] Moreover, a new specialized agency for the environment would join the ranks as only one of many existing agencies with activities in the same broad sphere. Were it placed at the same level as organizations with longer traditions and well-established relations with national and international bureaucracies, there were fears that the new agency would have difficulty exercising its catalytic and coordinative functions because it would not have sufficient authority over the other agencies.[48]

Third, conceptualizing and establishing a new specialized agency would take a long time since it could only be chartered after engaging a multiyear treaty process, which would have to be ratified by the national legislatures of the countries involved. The leaders of the Stockholm process and proponents of the creation of a new environmental body recognized that the momentum of the Stockholm Conference and a General Assembly resolution would be the simplest and quickest way of creating the new entity.[49]

Based on these rationales, governments and the conference Secretariat offered proposals for institutional arrangements other than a specialized agency. None of these were adopted in their entirety, but elements of several were present in the final decision about the new institutional form. The UK government, for example, favored "a referral system, a switchboard, putting a person or Government who needs some specialist knowledge in touch with the Government or agency which already has it."[50] The United States proposed three new entities, an Administrator of UN Environmental Programs, a twenty-seven-member Commission for the Environment within the Economic and Social Council, and an Environmental Coordinating Board.[51] The Swedish government suggested a new entity for the environment that would serve as "a central co-ordinating mechanism in the United Nations to provide political and conceptual leadership, methods of avoiding or reducing global environmental risks, methods of working out joint norms, and methods of avoiding or settling conflicts between states on environmental matters."[52] Strong himself envisioned an "institutional 'center' or 'brain' of the environmental network."[53]

Ultimately, the participating governments opted for the new environmental entity to be a subsidiary organ of the UN General Assembly. This followed several recent precedents, including the UN Conference on Trade and Development (UNCTAD) in 1964, the UN Development Programme (UNDP) in 1965, and the UN Industrial Development Organization (UNIDO) in 1966, as well as UNICEF in 1946. Contrary to what has become a commonly-held UNEP creation myth, there is no evidence to suggest that the new institution's status as a subsidiary body rather than a specialized agency was a product of deliberate action to incapacitate the new body. Even declassified confidential materials of the UK government and the Brussels Group show that, while there was interest in restricting the scope of the Stockholm Conference, Britain did not set out to create a weak environmental organization. It accepted that the time had come for new institutional arrangements and that a "new and expensive international organization must be avoided, but a small effective central coordinating mechanism ... would not be welcome but is probably inevitable."[54]

In essence, the institutional form of the new environmental body was designed because it best responded to the core functions of bringing together the different strands of environmental work in the UN system and providing a center of gravity for environmental affairs. Direct association with the General Assembly through the status of a subsidiary body presented major benefits both politically and operationally, as it would enable the institution to work directly through the highest political organ with nearly universal membership.[55] "This," wrote David Wightman, a lecturer in international economic history at the University of Birmingham and a consultant to the Stockholm Conference Secretariat, "should enable it [the new body] to acquire the authority necessary to play a leadership and coordinating role within the UN system as a whole."[56] Creating UNEP as a programme, a subsidiary body of the UN General Assembly, would also benefit the entire UN system, governments agreed, because having the body within the United Nations would "enable the [General] Assembly to effectively tackle problems posed by the interconnexion of development with the need to safeguard the environment and to provide policy guidance thereon."[57] This was the intention and the vision behind the institutional design of the new United Nations Environment Programme.

VOLUNTARY FINANCING AS AN EXPRESSION OF EXPANSION EXPECTATIONS

Creating a new international environmental institution could only happen with the requisite financial support, and such support could only be expected to come from industrialized countries. Commitment by the United States was therefore critical, and the country had significant say about the scope and scale of the financial mechanism. Contrary to popular belief, the United States did not oppose a fund; it envisioned it, created it, and contributed close to 40 percent of it.

In his address to the US Congress on February 8, 1972, President Richard Nixon proposed the creation of an Environment Fund to "stimulate international cooperation on environmental problems by supporting a centralized coordination point for United Nations activities in this field."[58] He explained that, without the financial means, efforts to improve the global environment would accomplish nothing, and that his proposed level of support would provide start-up assistance. The initial suggestion was for a capitalization in the amount of $100 million; the equivalent in 2019, when adjusted for inflation, would be close to $600 million. US participation was expected to be exemplary and a reflection of its status as the world's major polluter.[59]

Despite the commitment from the executive branch and the President himself, however, the US Congress was not in favor of financial contributions to the United Nations. In fact, the United States was already in arrears in its contributions to the United Nations since in 1972, Congress had voted to cut future payments to the United Nations by over 20 percent. This prompted UN Secretary-General Kurt Waldheim to express serious concern over lack of US support to the UN Ambassador at the time, George H. W. Bush.[60] In this context of domestic political tensions, international leadership by the United States was not a given. The team at the State Department, however, had convinced President Richard Nixon, who had just created the US Environmental Protection Agency, of the imperative for international action. The executive branch could create a fund to which the president could commit funds directly, but it could only be voluntary because it would not be subject to congressional oversight.[61] It was also unclear how much funding was necessary to address the growing environmental agenda. Voluntary contributions, therefore, would allow for future growth. As the Advisory Committee on the Stockholm Conference to the US Secretary of State wrote, "We believe that $100 million is a beginning. However, this amount should be viewed as a minimum, a starting figure. It is not yet clear how much money will be required for adequate environmental action. The Voluntary Fund should be of such size as to guarantee that financing will not be a limiting factor to all necessary action."[62] The Environment Fund was therefore designed with voluntary (rather than assessed) contributions not to incapacitate it, but to ensure its establishment and to enable its progression over time.

Developing countries did not welcome the Environment Fund because they feared diversion of development aid into environmental activities and adopted a resolution stating that "resources for environmental programmes, both within and outside the United Nations system, [should] be additional to the present level and projected growth of resources contemplated in the International Development Strategy."[63] They also expressed concern about the existence of numerous and, at times, competing sources of funding within the UN system, which obstructed overall understanding of the UN's financial situation and hindered the elaboration of a coherent development strategy.[64] Voluntary funds, furthermore, were viewed as particularly problematic because developing countries saw them as mostly serving the interests of the donors, not the recipients.[65] Yet, assessed contributions were hardly a politically feasible solution. Set at a certain percentage at the inception of an entity, they commit all member states, including developing countries, to make contributions. This was an unacceptable proposition in 1972, when environmental problems were cast as a consequence of industrial pollution. At the time, the logic was that a voluntary fund would allow for participation by smaller nations in accordance with their capacity. Countries were encouraged to commit symbolic annual contributions of $1,000 (or $5,760 in 2019 dollars) as a means of emphasizing that all have a stake in international environmental protection.[66]

In the end, the decision to proceed with the Environment Fund was determined in large measure by the United States as the primary donor, which committed to "ensure that vital international environmental efforts do not fall by the wayside from fiscal starvation."[67] The Nixon administration adamantly maintained that the new Environment Fund would not be used for development assistance, and that it would indeed be supplementary to funding earmarked for development aid.[68] Keeping with the "form follows function" principle, the United States explained that the Environment Fund would be used for "programs and projects to improve the global environment, rather than for financial assistance to countries to solve specific problems within their own borders."[69] The Fund was therefore envisioned to support UNEP's coordination function by endowing sufficient resources to the UN agencies and thus influencing their activities and priorities. It was to facilitate UNEP's normative role and not be an operational fund for discrete environmental and development projects. The creation of the Environment Fund was "the last step, which [was] in a very real sense the key to launching and coordinating all the rest," Russell Train, Chairman of the US delegation, reported home in a press release in 1972.[70]

The United States had made another important and innovative proposal that was rejected at the time but might be an idea for the future of environmental financing. The suggestion was to create a functional financing scheme based on scaled contributions proportionate to energy consumption. Acknowledging that industrialized countries held a responsibility to improve environmental conditions and should provide the bulk of the new organization's financing, the US Secretary of State's Advisory Committee proposed that the largest consumers of energy, and thus the largest polluters, should contribute to the Fund on an escalating curve. "A formula derived from each nation's consumption of energy," the Committee contended, "could provide the basis for the suggested participation in the United Nations Voluntary Fund for the Environment. Or, it might provide the basis for a long-range system of funding, which could be a matter of assessment rather than voluntary participation."[71] When it was clear that this proposal would not be accepted, the United States affirmed its commitment to ensuring a sufficient level of voluntary financing.[72]

Voluntary contributions were a mechanism for countries to support the functions of the institution, but they also presented a risk of possible decrease or even termination. UNEP's financial situation over the years attests to both of these realities. Despite difficulties posed by oil crises and the subsequent global economic downturn in the 1970s, resources flowed into the Environment Fund, which reached a cumulative total of $100 million in nominal terms in the first four years, 30 percent of which came from the United States. Thirty-two governments contributed in UNEP's first year, 1973, and only six years later, in 1979, the number almost tripled to eighty-eight governments, or 58 percent of UN member states, which contributed $31.5 million, or over $111 million when adjusted for inflation (see figure 2.2).[73]

Contributions in 1979 came in from twenty African states, with Kenya leading at $46,000 (about $160,000 when adjusted for inflation); seventeen states from Asia and the Pacific; ten from Latin America and the

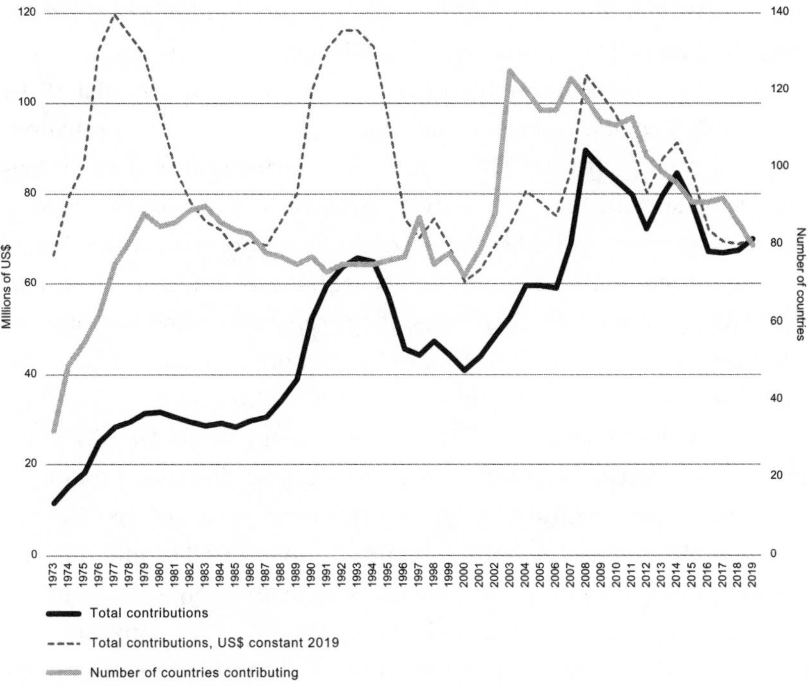

2.2 Environment Fund current vs. constant dollars and number of contributing countries from 1973 to 2019.

Caribbean; seven from West Asia; thirty-two from Europe; and the United States and Canada. Donor interest withered, however, and reliance on a narrow and shrinking donor base constrained UNEP's capacity. In 2019, only 41 percent of UN member states, or eighty countries, contributed to the Environment Fund, including thirty-six countries from Europe, six countries from Africa, twenty-one from Asia-Pacific, eleven from Latin America, four from West Asia, and two from North America, with a total contribution of $70 million. In the span of forty years, between 1979 and 2019, the number of countries supporting the Environment Fund (as percentage of UN member states) decreased by 30 percent, and the amount of financial contributions to the Fund decreased by 38 percent when adjusted for inflation.[74]

While not created as a small and inconsequential body, the Environment Fund has not provided sufficient resources to support UNEP's capacity and growth. When adjusted for inflation, the Environment Fund has not increased since UNEP's first full year in operation in 1974. In 2019, forty-five years after the first year of UNEP's operation, the Environment Fund was at a mere $70 million per year, far below the original 1970s vision of $100 million, or about $600 million when adjusted for inflation. Many scholars analyze UNEP's resources by looking only at the Environment Fund and attribute its paucity to UNEP's design as a subsidiary body and the subsequent voluntary nature of the Fund. Consequently, scholars have suggested that because assessed contributions constitute the financial platform of specialized agencies, they "can avail themselves of more resources and hence influence"[75] and have recommended that UNEP be "upgraded" to the structure and status of a specialized agency.

Yet the Environment Fund has become only one part of UNEP's financial structure, accounting for a mere 12 percent of the total funding of UNEP. Earmarked contributions form a much larger part of UNEP's total resources (84 percent in 2018), amounting to over $340 million. The overall funding for UNEP, a subsidiary body, is thus larger than that of several specialized agencies, including the World Trade Organization, the UN Industrial Development Organization, and the World Meteorological Organization (see figure 1.4). Importantly, the top four UN bodies in terms of finances are all subsidiary organs working on issues of particular interest to governments: the UN Development Programme (UNDP), the UN Children's Fund (UNICEF), the World Food Programme (WFP), and the UN Refugee Agency (UNHCR). Their resources amount to several billion dollars per year and are drawn exclusively from voluntary funds. Their income, however, has fluctuated as interest in their particular issues has shifted.

Careful financial analysis of UNEP's total income over the past fifty years reveals that it is not so much the level of funding as its unpredictability that has been the problem in every decade and under every executive director, as chapter 6 illustrates. The harsh reality of scarce, inconsistent, fragile finances was the result of a political minefield that UNEP had to navigate; under these circumstances, priorities shifted, messages changed, agendas within the United Nations competed, and UNEP was hard-pressed to find its identity and place within the system. "Governments fail to contribute [to UNEP] because there is a lack of trust in the organization," a member state official remarked, and "donors are holding some resources back because of the lack of trust."[76] Heavy reliance on earmarked funding, as noted in a 2019 evaluation report of UNEP by the UN Office of Oversight Services, hinders UNEP's flexibility to respond to requests from member states for core activities, including areas related to science, policy expertise, and capacity-building.[77] This, however, is not an institutional design issue. Rather, it reflects the increased demand for environmental action as well as UNEP's periodic challenges to deliver results for the environment.

FOUNDING UNEP IN NAIROBI

During the short two weeks of the extraordinary first conference on the global environment, governments could not finalize several core aspects, including the exact name of the new institution, its governance structure, and its location. The political representatives of all UN member states would make these decisions during the twenty-seventh session of the UN General Assembly, which took place from September to December in 1972 in New York. Indeed, the name United Nations Environment Programme did not appear until the very end of that session. The core draft resolution on *Institutional and Financial Arrangements for International Environmental Cooperation* mandated governments to set up four organs: a Governing Council for Environmental Programmes, an Environment Secretariat, an Environment Fund, and an Environmental Coordinating Board but did not mention the term United Nations Environment Programme.[78] The name was first specified in the revised version of that document, Resolution 2997, UNEP's founding document.[79]

The debate over the location of the new environmental body was unexpectedly turbulent and contentious.[80] In the fall of 1972, the discussions were no longer the purview of an extraordinary congregation of carefully selected delegates with keen interest in the environment. Instead, the UN General Assembly session comprised career diplomats whose mandate was to represent their countries—and their national interests—at the UN headquarters in New York. International politics thus took center stage during the debates in the Economic and Finance Committee of the UN General Assembly (known as the Second Committee), where the deliberations on the Stockholm Conference outcomes took place. Developing countries sought to become equal partners in multilateral affairs and argued fervently for equity in representation and decision-making in the United Nations, which had been founded on the principle of "one country, one vote." They demanded that a principle of equitable geographic representation and distribution be observed. Industrialized countries, on the other hand, argued that the effectiveness of institutions could be compromised by their location. The decision of where to situate the new environmental institution vividly illustrates these tensions.

In the discussions leading up to and during the Stockholm Conference, it had been assumed that the location would be determined in a way that would provide the new institution with maximum prestige, strength, and freedom, as well as with the ability to link and coordinate the environmental activities of UN agencies, governments, and non-governmental organizations.[81] Maurice Strong had used the same rationale in 1970 when he set up the Secretariat for the Stockholm Conference not in Stockholm but in Geneva, where most of the UN agencies were located. In his opening remarks to a meeting of the UN Preparatory Committee for Stockholm that year, Strong explained:

> I am planning to have most of the substantive work on the programme and agenda of the conference carried out in Geneva. This will permit savings in both salaries and travel for our own Secretariat and most of the other United Nations agencies ... Also, as you know, the Conference Services Division, which is responsible for the conference arrangements, is based in Geneva, and I feel strongly that a successful conference requires the closest possible relationship between the substantive and administrative aspects of its organization. Let me also say that I am fully aware of the importance of maintaining closest possible liaison with member governments through their Missions in New York and with other organizations which can best be serviced from the New York Headquarters. Accordingly, we intend to retain a small office in New York, and I will personally be spending a substantial amount of my time [in New York].[82]

Owing to Geneva's proximity to many of the international agencies, its first-rate communications infrastructure, and the low set-up and operational costs, it was widely believed that Geneva would be the location of the new environmental body. At the conclusion of the Stockholm Conference, however, a number of cities offered to host the new institution. The ten candidates included Cairo, Geneva, London, Malta, Mexico City, Monaco, Nairobi, New Delhi, New York, and Vienna, but the final decision was left for the UN General Assembly discussions in the fall of 1972, when member states were expected to approve all of the Conference outcomes. So strong was the sense that the environmental secretariat would remain in Geneva that the UN Secretary-General had only prepared cost estimates for the new institutional arrangements as they would apply in Switzerland. However, as Peter Stone, senior information advisor to Maurice Strong during the Stockholm Conference, recounted laconically in 1973, "a vast surprise was in store for everybody."[83]

Developing countries had long sought the placement of an international agency in the developing world, and saw in the creation of UNEP a golden opportunity to expand the geographical distribution of the UN system.[84] In 1966, Nairobi had been in the running to host the headquarters of UNIDO, but the Kenyan capital had lost to Vienna in a secret ballot vote that, the Kenyans believed, had been rife with horse-trading between developing and developed countries. Kenyan diplomats had since learned how to run a lobbying campaign for the purpose of headquartering an international organization in Nairobi, and by the time the decision for the location of UNEP came around, they had gathered enough expertise and experience to ensure victory.[85]

Kenya's delegation to the UN General Assembly comprised a team of outstanding diplomats with extensive experience and with the single-minded goal of bringing the new UN agency to Nairobi. To this end, Joseph Odero-Jowi, the Permanent Representative of Kenya to the United Nations, Njoroge Mungai, Kenya's Foreign Affairs Minister, and Donald Kaniaru, officer in the Kenyan Mission to the United Nations, worked tirelessly. On October 24, 1972, Ambassador Odero-Jowi, a forty-three-year-old Calcutta-trained economist considered a rising star in the United Nations, presented a proposal to the Second Committee of the General Assembly that the new environmental body should be located in Nairobi. As Stanley Johnson, author of UNEP's history over its first forty years, writes, "[Odero-Jowi] brought his speech to a climax end with a defiant bid for Nairobi. Not one agency in the UN system, he pointed out, had its headquarters in the 'Third World.' This was unjust and must be rectified, he insisted and called on New York, Geneva, London and Vienna to withdraw."[86] Over the following week, the Kenyan delegation worked to gain the support of African countries, and then additional developing countries, to put forward a resolution on the location of the new UN environmental entity. After Odero-Jowi's proposal on October 24, 1972, several African and Caribbean countries threw their weight behind Nairobi's candidacy.

On November 3, 1972, having convinced the African Group to sponsor a resolution on the location of the new secretariat, Kenya introduced a draft resolution to the Second Committee of the UN General Assembly with two points: first, underscoring the need for more equitable geographical distribution of UN bodies, and second, a proposal to locate the new environment secretariat in Nairobi.[87] Kenya's draft resolution created a conflict between the goals of increasing the equitable geographic distribution of the UN system and maximizing the effectiveness and efficiency of the new environmental body. The "form follows function" tenet governing all previous decisions was cast aside at this juncture, as discussion degenerated from collective strategic planning to divisive, uncompromising politics. The Kenyan delegation was within its rights to demand the placement of a UN body in the Global South; there was nothing inherently sacrosanct about the location of the UN headquarters and of the international agencies in Western Europe and North America. As the UN system grew, furthermore, it was only logical for it to adapt to changing representative distribution by decentralizing its operations and including a broader constituency in its daily operations. Given the functions of UNEP, however, many delegates felt it needed to be located at a center of UN activity, where its role as a coordinator and catalyst would be aided by proximity to the specialized agencies and representatives from all governments. In the words of the UK delegation, "it would be a mistake to locate the environment secretariat far from other units with which it would have to be in close and constant contact."[88] Communication capabilities in the 1970s were extremely limited and expensive—particularly in developing countries. This would have great impact on UNEP's connectivity and ability to be in close and constant communication with its constituents, as the subsequent analysis explains.

Most delegations, even those from developing nations, acknowledged that either Geneva or New York would be the wisest location for UNEP if the organization's effectiveness were the primary concern. In Geneva, all member countries were already represented, and many missions had economic and social experts on staff. By contrast, only twenty-two developing countries had missions in Nairobi, and these were not staffed at a level comparable to those in Geneva. Locating UNEP in Nairobi, therefore, would impose a higher financial cost and might cost developing countries considerable influence over the activities of the organization. As the Colombian delegation pointed out, it was in the collective interest of developing countries to locate the environment secretariat "in a country where United Nations organizations had already been established and where as many developing countries as possible already had accredited representations."[89] The flip side of the argument was that a city in the Global South could become a center comparable to Geneva and New York, and this could only be accomplished by founding a UN agency there. Delegations noted, however, that locating UN bodies out of concern for equitable geographical distribution alone might impair their ability to carry out their mandates.

The Kenyan delegation continued to marshal support from the G-77 nations, an alliance of developing countries that had been established in the 1960s as a part of the United Nations Conference on Trade and Development. Countries recognized the tack Kenya was taking. The representative of Zaire articulated a sentiment shared by several developing countries that "undoubtedly, if only economic criteria were taken into consideration, the location of the environment secretariat would certainly be in New York or Geneva, for the operating costs would be lower in those cities," but acknowledged that Kenya had made the issue political.[90] The Kenyan delegation countered that "a political approach was valid because it could serve to eliminate certain technical considerations and practical difficulties which made a decision impossible. The Second Committee was a political body and its decision had to be political."[91] Economic and technical issues, "difficulties of communications and the problems of remoteness from research centers," the Kenyans submitted, were a small price to pay for this political achievement.[92]

Even those developing countries that admitted Geneva made for a logical choice indicated in the debates that they were lining up in solidarity with the G-77. Leandro Verceles of the Philippines, for example, noted that his government would "prefer the environment secretariat to be located in a city where a United Nations office already existed, for reasons of coordination and efficiency, or where the Philippines maintained a diplomatic presence. However, [the Philippines] delegation was prepared to join in a political decision reflecting the overwhelming sentiment of the developing countries and would therefore vote in favor of the draft resolution."[93] The representative of Tunisia remarked that "if good sense was outweighed by political considerations," his delegation would vote with the Group of 77.[94] Thus, despite the existence of voices within the G-77 pleading that their case of economic costs and diplomatic presence also be considered, the overwhelming duty to vote with the political bloc prevailed.

Developed countries dissented, maintaining that the only criteria that should dictate the choice of location were the future body's effectiveness and efficiency. The Danish delegation felt that "apart from financial considerations, the only other valid criterion to be taken into account was the efficient performance of functions for the benefit of all Members of the United Nations, developing as well as developed countries ... [Denmark's] objections, however, were not based on the fact that Kenya was a developing country; it preferred Geneva because it was of overriding importance for the environment secretariat to be located in a place where it would be most likely to fulfill its task of co-coordinating programmes and advising intergovernmental bodies within the United Nations systems."[95] Spain also maintained that it would be "wrong to rely solely on political or economic arguments, for it was necessary to consider also the purely operational aspects of the matter."[96] The functional mandate of the organization was the key factor that should determine location and the only "valid criterion to be taken into account was the efficient performance of functions for the benefit of all members of the United Nations, developing as well as developed countries."[97]

An open and irreconcilable conflict was emerging in the Second Committee. Three possible courses of action were presented over the course of the session: (1) to put the draft resolution to an open vote; (2) to separate the two issues mentioned in the document—the principle of equitable geographical distribution and the specific location of UNEP—and put each to vote by secret ballot in either the Second Committee or in the General Assembly; or (3) to request that the Secretary-General prepare a report on geographic distribution and a comprehensive survey of all the locations proposed for the environment secretariat, thus postponing a decision on the environment secretariat until the twenty-eighth session of the General Assembly. The developing-country sponsors of the draft resolution rejected any move to postpone a decision on the location of UNEP's secretariat and pushed for an immediate vote, despite objections invoking Rule 155, which stipulated that decisions could not be made before their financial implications were clear.[98]

Shepherded skillfully by the Kenyan leadership,[99] developing countries agreed to support Nairobi's bid for the new secretariat and declare the first course of action as the only acceptable choice. The prospect of a secret-ballot vote made the second option unpalatable to most developing countries and unacceptable to Kenya. The delegates pointed to the precedent set by the secret UNCTAD and UNIDO votes, which had allegedly allowed developed countries to sway the vote and secure the placement of UNCTAD in Geneva and UNIDO in Vienna. While the third possible course of action, calling for a careful consideration of functional issues alongside the political and economic concerns, seemed the most logical and least confrontational, it would have required a new resolution, and by this point in the Second Committee session, procedure precluded the submission of an entirely new resolution.

The decision to locate UNEP in Nairobi was thus the result of an open-ballot vote in the Second Committee in November 1972. Solidarity among developing countries, which far outnumbered developed countries, led to a decisive vote in favor of Nairobi as the site for the first international organization in the developing world.[100] Reflecting upon the results, some countries urged the Second Committee to "propose that the General Assembly take the necessary steps to insert in the rules of procedure to be followed in the future in selecting locations for secretariats of United Nations bodies" the stipulation that in making decisions on the location of a UN unit for which there is more than one candidate, the General Assembly should fully consider each bid, including the financial and operational implications, and that the vote should be taken by secret ballot to ensure free expression.[101] Some delegates noted that they had abstained from the Nairobi vote, rather than cast opposing votes, in order to avoid overt conflict and to promote a spirit of cooperation on environmental action. As the delegate from the United Kingdom declared, "in light of the debate, it would be fiction to pretend that there was a consensus."[102]

Despite the acrimonious debate, there was an overall feeling of collective commitment to helping the new organization function. Testifying in front of the US Congress on behalf of the bill authorizing the appropriation for a US voluntary contribution to the recently established United Nations Environment Fund, H.R. 5696, Christian Herter commented on the location of UNEP in Nairobi, "When this was first suggested as the location, we very much opposed it and we opposed it right down to the wire when, frankly, the United States and other countries were greatly outvoted. The issue having been decided, however ... the United States in the General Assembly said, in essence: 'All right, the matter is decided. We will now do our darndest to make it work.'"[103] The foundation of UNEP in Nairobi was clearly not a premeditated plot to incapacitate it, and all countries were committed to supporting its efforts and enabling it to succeed. But both internal and external dynamics would change over the years and present various obstacles to the functioning of UNEP, as this book explains.

On December 15, 1972, the UN General Assembly adopted, on the recommendation of the Second Committee, Resolution 2997 (XXVII) and thereby established the institutional and financial arrangements for international environmental cooperation. The resolution combined the elements that the US State Department officer, John W. McDonald, had envisioned several years earlier. In recognition of his "outstanding contribution to international environmental activities" and his "vital role in developing the US position on an institutional framework within the United Nations to effectively co-ordinate and carry out future environmental activities," the Department of State awarded John W. McDonald its Superior Honor Award in 1972.[104]

CONCLUSION

The creation of UNEP was the major outcome of the 1972 Stockholm Conference, commonly referred to as the starting point of global environmental governance. Existing literature about UNEP claims that the organization is deficient by design, that governments saddled UNEP with its

2.3 Samuel de Palma, left, Assistant Secretary for International Organization Affairs, presents the Superior Honor Award to John W. McDonald, with his wife, Christel McDonald, by his side, and Christian A. Herter Jr., Deputy Assistant Secretary of State for Environmental and Population Affairs. Credit: From the archives of Christel McDonald.

particular form, function, and financing in order to incapacitate it. The conventional wisdom is that UNEP is weak because it is a subsidiary body rather than a specialized agency, because it has an impossible mandate, and because its financing is from voluntary rather than assessed contributions. Some scholars also contend that UNEP was located in Nairobi as a result of a pact between the Global North and South, and others see it as a scheme by industrialized countries to exile an unwelcome new secretariat to a place distant from the political centers of power.

The archival evidence, financial records, and conversations with the founders, however, tell a very different story. None of these decisions sought to incapacitate UNEP, and any resultant deficiency was *not* "something that was painstakingly designed into the system" as scholars contend.[105] Rather, UNEP was the product of thoughtful and deliberate institutional design.

UNEP was not constituted as a programme to diminish its authority. The institutional status of a subsidiary body was the fastest option for creating a new entity and was intended to prevent the organization from competing with existing agencies. It was also expected to avoid encumbering the new environmental institution's operations with the customary administrative structure of specialized agencies, and to prevent the marginalization of the environment as just one "sector" among many.

UNEP's normative mandate was not supposed to consign the body to irrelevance but to ensure it would serve as a focused catalyst and coordinator in a cluttered institutional landscape. As John Matuszak, international affairs officer at the US State Department, exclaimed in 2018, "UNEP's mandate is pretty strong. You can drive a truck through it. If governments renegotiated the mandate now, it would not be this solid."[106] The voluntary financial structure was not designed to starve the new international institution of resources, but to allow an even greater cash flow than could come from the then-impoverished United Nations and reluctant member states.

The decision on UNEP's location was taken later in the design process and was the most vividly contested issue in UNEP's creation. It was the result of a political calculus that sought to affirm developing countries' stature in global governance. Developing countries commanded majority in the United Nations and voted as a political bloc. Situating UNEP in Nairobi was a successful attempt to affirm the role of developing countries as equal partners in multilateral affairs and overturned the accepted practice of placing UN headquarters in the industrialized world. This political decision molded the identity of the anchor institution for the global environment.

3

DELIVERING ON AN EVOLVING MANDATE: RECONCILING NORMATIVE AND OPERATIONAL EXPECTATIONS

Tasked with protecting the foundations of human society (nature and human health) but provided only minimal resources, UNEP has done extraordinary work identifying environmental problems, conducting relevant research, coordinating international efforts, framing constructive solutions, and catalyzing needed action. The world and humanity would be much poorer without UNEP's continued efforts.

—Daniel Magraw, President and Chief Executive Officer of the Center for International Environmental Law (2002–2010)[1]

Created as the focal point for environmental action and a "permanent institutional arrangement within the United Nations system for the protection and improvement of the environment,"[2] the UN Environment Programme is a normative body that provides policy guidance for the direction and management of environmental programs. The raison d'être for its establishment was the coordination of environmental activities across the UN system. The new institution was to catalyze synergies among existing UN agencies, with a view to ensuring that the system's whole was greater than the sum of its parts, minimizing overlap and maximizing the use of resources.[3]

In addition to this coordination mandate, the three-part functional framework of the 1972 Stockholm Action Plan—"environmental assessment," "environmental management," and "supporting measures"—shaped the other core functions of UNEP. Environmental assessment, UN coordination, and policy development have stayed at the center of UNEP's mandate over time, with supporting measures integrated across all of these issues as UNEP provided assistance to nations in developing the necessary institutional capacity for science, policy and law, and implementation.[4] Figure 3.1 illustrates the ways in which the mandate has evolved through the core documents that have articulated UNEP's functions since 1972, and showcases the continued emphasis on the three core functions envisioned in Stockholm.[5]

UNEP's mandate reflects the aspirational goals at the time of its creation and the vision of becoming an important source of authority and legitimacy.[6] It has defined UNEP's work and place in the international system over the past fifty years. Governments see the mandate as robust, and staff view it as stimulating. The viability of UNEP's mandate has been a disputed subject among scholars, with some considering it impossible to realize and others criticizing it as insufficient.[7] As this book illustrates, however, UNEP's mandate is ambitious and achievable, inspirational and meaningful.[8] The core functions were grounded in the logic that nothing can be done about global environmental problems without accurate scientific data, and that these data should be used for the development of sound environmental policies and management strategies.

At its core, the mandate to set the global environmental agenda and serve as the advocate for the global environment is highly normative. Indeed, as UN Deputy Secretary-General and former environment minister of Nigeria, Amina Mohammed, remarked in our interview in 2018, "The United Nations is normative. Operative work is for the countries and the UN helps with input and advice on how to enhance government capacity to deliver." To this end, she added, it is important "to understand what instruments are available, what the regulatory environment is, and how to integrate processes."[9] UNEP's core functions were to lead the development of environmental policy and coordinate the environmental activities in the UN system. However, most developing countries required assistance in creating their environmental institutions, policies, regulation, and infrastructure, and UNEP was the logical place to turn to for such material assistance. Although created as a normative institution, UNEP often has been called to act in an operational capacity, and

UNEP's ability to deliver on these operational requests has often been insufficient.

Headquartered in Kenya, in a country and a region where natural resource challenges demand urgent action, UNEP staff could not remain indifferent as they bore witness to environmental problems and their interconnectedness with social justice, economic development, and political change. Over the years, the organization has been drawn into an operational role in supporting countries with their concrete needs on the ground. Thus, UNEP has had difficulty projecting a clear identity as it has struggled with the tension between normative and operational expectations. In light of these competing demands, how has UNEP fared in delivering on the core functions in its mandate, and what have the results for the environment been? This chapter assesses UNEP's performance in its functions of coordination of environmental activities in the UN system, scientific assessment, and policy development; chapter 4 evaluates the achievements and challenges in addressing key environmental concerns. Together, these two chapters create a baseline that can assist in articulating and implementing a vision for the future.

It is impossible to state definitively whether UNEP has been effective or not, because, in short, it has been both effective and ineffective across issues and over time. Throughout the 1970s and 1980s, under the leadership of Maurice Strong and Mostafa Tolba, UNEP developed as a new institution in a new field. Its greatest challenges came in the 1990s as the end of the Cold War altered the political and economic reality across the world. The result was not the expected increase in financial resources for environmental activities but a neoliberal economic order that led to a single-minded focus on economic growth, a sharper division among states on issues of inequality, uneven technological development and thus uneven access to information and connectivity, and dramatically diminished financial contributions to UNEP.[10] In fact, while public concern with environmental issues increased, awareness about UNEP as the anchor institution for the global environment decreased. In the aftermath of the 1992 Rio Earth Summit, governments created and invested in new institutions that eclipsed UNEP in capacity and credibility, effectively marginalizing it.

In the final analysis, however, UNEP delivered on its mandate. Expected to protect nature and human health but largely marginalized and possessing

COORDINATION

1972 General Assembly Resolution 2997 (XXVII) "Institutional and Financial Arrangements for International Environmental Cooperation"	• provide general policy guidance for the direction and coordination of environmental programs within the UN system (I.2.b) • coordinate, under the guidance of the Governing Council, environmental programs within the United Nations system, to keep their implementation under review and to assess their effectiveness (II.2.b) • advise, as appropriate and under the guidance of the Governing Council, intergovernmental bodies of the United Nations system on the formulation and implementation of environmental programs (II.2.c)
1997 Nairobi Declaration UNEP Governing Council's 19.1. Nairobi Declaration on the Role and Mandate of the United Nations Environment Programme	• further … the development of coherent interlinkages among existing international environmental conventions (3.b) • strengthen its role in the coordination of environmental activities in the United Nations system in the field of the environment … based on its comparative advantage and scientific and technical expertise (3.d) • promote greater awareness and facilitate effective cooperation among all sectors of society and actors involved in the implementation of the international environmental agenda … (3.e) • provide policy and advisory services in key areas of institution-building to governments and other relevant institutions (3.f)
2012 Rio +20 outcome document "The Future We Want," paragraph 88	• enhance the voice of UNEP and its ability to fulfill its coordination mandate within the United Nations system by strengthening UNEP engagement in key United Nations coordination bodies and empowering UNEP to lead efforts to formulate United Nations system-wide strategies on the environment (88.c)

3.1 Evolution of UNEP's mandate.

ASSESSMENT	POLICY
• keep under review the world environmental situation in order to ensure that emerging environmental problems of wide international significance receive appropriate and adequate consideration by governments (I.2.d) • promote the contribution of the relevant international scientific and other professional communities to the acquisition, assessment, and exchange of environmental knowledge and information and, as appropriate, to the technical aspects of the formulation and implementation of environmental programs within the United Nations system (I.2.e) • secure the effective cooperation of, and contribution from, the relevant scientific and other professional communities in all parts of the world (II.2.d)	• promote international cooperation in the field of the environment and to recommend, as appropriate, policies to this end (I.2.a) • provide, at the request of all parties concerned, advisory services for the promotion of international cooperation in the field of the environment (II.2.e) • maintain under continuing review the impact of national and international environmental policies and measures on developing countries, as well as the problem of additional costs that may be incurred by developing countries in the implementation of environmental programs and projects, and to ensure that such programs and projects shall be compatible with the development plans and priorities of those countries (I.2.f)
• analyze the state of the global environment and assess global and regional environmental trends … (3.a) • provide … early warning information on environmental threats … (3.a) SCIENCE-POLICY INTERFACE serve as an effective link between the scientific community and policy makers at the national and international levels (3.e)	• provide policy advice … (3.a) • catalyze and promote international cooperation and action, based on the best scientific and technical capabilities available (3.a) • further the development of its international environmental law aiming at sustainable development … (3.b) • … stimulate cooperative action to respond to emerging environmental challenges (3.c) • advance the implementation of agreed international norms and policies, to monitor and foster compliance with environmental principles and international agreements … (3.c) • strengthen … its role as an Implementing Agency of the Global Environment Facility … (3.d)
• disseminate and share evidence-based environmental information and raise public awareness on critical as well as emerging environmental issues (88.e) SCIENCE-POLICY INTERFACE promote a strong science-policy interface, building on existing international instruments, assessments, panels and information networks, including the Global Environment Outlook, as one of the processes aimed at bringing together information and assessment to support informed decision-making (88.d)	CAPACITY-BUILDING ELEMENT • provide capacity-building to countries, as well as support and facilitate access to technology (88.f) • progressively consolidate headquarters functions in Nairobi, as well as strengthen its regional presence, in order to assist countries, upon request, in the implementation of their national environmental policies, collaborating closely with other relevant entities of the United Nations system (88.g)

3.1 (continued)

minimal capacity, UNEP has called public and political attention to key environmental problems, developed a robust body of international environmental law, framed constructive policy options, and catalyzed needed action. Even though it stumbled in providing a one-stop shop for state-of-the-environment assessments, in coordinating the UN's numerous environmental activities, in supporting implementation of international environmental agreements, and in providing consistent and reliable assistance to national environmental efforts, UNEP has delivered more than could be expected given the obstacles in its course.

COMPETITION AND COHERENCE CHALLENGES IN THE UN SYSTEM

Coordination is a critical precondition for the resolution of global problems through successful collective action; such collective action is in turn essential for realizing the ideals of the United Nations. The complexity of the global environmental governance system and the lack of any authority structure make coordination of the various actors, institutions, and norms critically important.[11] Coordination requires being both *in* authority and *an* authority—having the mandate and the money to coordinate as well as the knowledge, expertise, and credibility. Since its creation, UNEP has been in authority to coordinate as it has had both the legal mandate and a financial mechanism to do so. UNEP's authority—its expertise and credibility—have, however, been tested over the decades. Struggles in meeting the core coordination function have no doubt contributed to the widely diverging conclusions on the feasibility and appropriateness of UNEP's mandate and on the organization's ability to perform. Why, observers have asked, has UNEP not succeeded in becoming the central forum for debate and deliberation in the environmental field, like WTO has done for trade or WHO for health?

The conventional answer has been that UNEP does not have the status and therefore the authority and resources of a specialized agency.[12] Indeed, the financial resources at UNEP's disposal are grossly inadequate for resolving the set of evolving global environmental problems it faces, but this is not a result of its institutional form. Being a relatively small entity in terms of staff and funding has often led to the perception that an increase in size, through a change of institutional form, would translate into improved coordination. Yet, as the analysis of resource availability to various UN bodies illustrated, subsidiary bodies, programmes, and funds such as UNDP, WFP, UNHCR, and UNICEF command the largest resources in the UN system, and several specialized agencies including UNIDO, WTO, and WMO have smaller budgets than UNEP (see figure 1.4 in chapter 1). Change in institutional design, therefore, or what many proposals term an "upgrade," would not yield the desired effects.

UNEP's institutional design, its form and function, is not the liming factor and root cause of the coordination and coherence challenge. Rather, capacity and credibility are. And they have been shaped by location and leadership. The turbulent political, economic, social, and security situation in Nairobi affected UNEP's capacity and connectivity. The severe security concerns were an obstacle to attracting staff, and the long distances for travel and absence of state-of-the-art communication technologies affected its credibility and ability to raise the requisite resources. Meanwhile, leadership determined the authority of the institution among particular constituencies. While Maurice Strong had the personal power and influence to convene the directors of the World Bank, IMF, and consequently all the specialized agencies, his successor, Mostafa Tolba, did not manage to maintain their interest and convince them to make the long trips to Nairobi. A dedicated and talented scientist, Tolba carried considerable legitimacy in environmental circles but did not possess Strong's convening power necessary for the leadership of the international agencies. UNEP gained reputation as a scientific organization but lost much of the networking power that Maurice Strong envisioned it would possess. Effective coordination requires a strong organizational identity and the authority to convince others to undertake actions toward common goals; this is an area in which UNEP's influence has waxed and waned.

Well before UNEP was created, environmental issues had been part of the portfolios of a number of UN agencies, including ILO, FAO, UNESCO, WHO, WMO, IMCO, IAEA, ICAO, and UNDP.[13] Each UN agency has its own mandate, budget, and governance structures and is accountable to a particular subset of member states. All possessed some environmental responsibilities and feared that they might lose parts of their work program, budget, and staff if duplication were eliminated.[14] Opposition to the creation of UNEP, therefore, came not from national governments but from UN agencies that feared competition, because the design of the UN system is stacked in favor of separate rather than coordinated and collaborative efforts. This competition has been present throughout UNEP's history and in 2019, 80 percent of UNEP's respondents to a survey by the UN Office of Internal Oversight Services noted that there was critical competition for donor resources with other UN entities.[15]

UNEP's architects foresaw these challenges and created an organizational structure for coordination with a healthy funding mechanism at its core in order to incentivize participation by other agencies. As documented in chapter 2, UNEP was purposefully designed as a subsidiary body rather than as an independent specialized agency so that it would be better positioned to coordinate environmental activities across the UN system. Resolution 2997 of 1972 created an Environment Coordination Board (ECB) to ensure cooperation and coordination among all UN bodies concerned in the implementation of environmental programs. It charged the secretariat—under the leadership of the executive director—to serve as a focal point for environmental action and coordination in the UN system. It also established the Environment Fund to provide financial incentives for the direction and coordination of environmental activities.

During its first few years, UNEP engaged in intensive and effective large-scale consultation and interaction with other UN agencies through the Environment Coordination Board. In its first report to the UNEP Governing Council, the Board emphasized that "the subject of the environment demonstrated the process of evolution of new networks of relationships, the formation of new links between institutions, the establishment of new institutions and the search of new roles by exiting institutions."[16] As the UN entity with authority for coordination, UNEP led the formulation of UN policy on environmental matters and provided money, personnel, and content guidance. In 1978, however, the Environment Coordination Board was eliminated and its functions relegated to the UN's Administrative Committee on Coordination (ACC) in New York. This decision to abolish the ECB "was the worst decision taken by the United Nations," Mostafa Tolba argued in 2009.[17]

Multiple other entities would follow over the years, as illustrated in box 3.1.[18] The frequent changes in the institutional vehicle for coordination

Box 3.1

Coordination Mechanisms: Trying to Find the Right Formula

The Environmental Coordination Board (ECB) comprised the Executive Heads of the UN agencies, and its principal mandate was to ensure cooperation and coordination in the UN system on environmental programs. The Board initiated, defined, and developed much of the environmental program of the UN system and instituted joint programming as a valuable method of collaboration among governments and UN agencies. It consulted with a wide range of UN bodies and facilitated the formulation and implementation of a variety of collaborative projects and programs. In 1978, in the context of a broader UN reform effort to increase coherence and coordination within the system, the UN's **Administrative Committee on Co-ordination (ACC)** fully assumed the functions of the ECB.

System-Wide Medium-Term Environment Programme (SWMTEP) was created along with a new group of UN officials, **Designated Officials for Environmental Matters (DOEM).** Through these mechanisms, UNEP encouraged other UN agencies to inject environmental considerations into their own programs and developed shared environmental activities, created common methodologies, harmonized program budgets and plans, and initiated joint programming. This did not produce the system-wide coherence necessary for effective collective action. A 1993 UN report noted that "DOEM falls short in their support and functional roles for the ACC; that [it] needs revitalizing and re-directing in order for it to meet the challenges offered by the new post-UNCED [Rio] phase."

After the Rio Earth Summit in 1992, governments established the **Inter-Agency Committee on Sustainable Development (IACSD)** with the mandate of identifying major policy issues and ensuring effective cooperation and coordination of the UN system in the implementation of Agenda 21. The IACSD was to be "the only body to prepare decisions for ACC in the areas of development and environment." With the focus having shifted away from the environment and UNEP having lost its leadership position, the DOEM, too, lost influence, and in 1995 it itself was replaced by the **Inter-Agency Environment Management Group (IAEG)**. This group only met twice and was then replaced by the **Environment Management Group (EMG)** in 2001. That year, the ACC was transformed into the **UN System Chief Executives Board (CEB) for Coordination**, and the Inter-Agency Committee on Sustainable Development ceased to exist.

The **Environment Management Group (EMG)** was established in 2001, pursuant to Resolution 53/242 of July 1999, with the goal of improving coherence and collaboration among UN agencies and the secretariats of Multilateral

Box 3.1 (continued)

Environmental Agreements (MEAs). It comprises forty-eight members, including specialized agencies, programmes and funds of the UN system, and MEA secretariats. It also includes the Global Environment Facility (GEF), the Bretton Woods institutions, and the WTO. Its goal is to provide an effective, coordinated, and flexible United Nations system response to environmental concerns; to facilitate joint action; and to promote coordination among its members. The EMG consists of senior-level officials of member organizations and is chaired by the executive director of UNEP. UNEP also provides the secretariat for EMG in Geneva.

shifted the centrality of UNEP in the environmental coordination work within the UN system. None of the subsequent coordination mechanisms delivered the value-added kind of coordination envisioned by UNEP's founders because of the pervasive competition dynamic in the UN system as well as the major challenges to UNEP's authority because of the difficulties in connecting, communicating, and collaborating with the rest of the UN system. Geographical distance and technological challenges were important determinant factors until well into the 2000s, as chapter 5 outlines.

Much of the influence of UN agencies derives from the perceived authority of the national ministries with which they are associated—ministries of health, development, agriculture, environment, or other issues. These ministries form the core membership and thus political base of the respective international organizations. The support of member states—political, financial, operational, and normative—is critical to the international organizations' ability to operate and command authority among peers. A novelty in the 1970s, environment ministries never garnered the power and resources of other line ministries such as health, development, industry, or foreign affairs. They have limited clout because they are usually small, underfunded, and marginalized. They tend to focus on cleaning up the impacts of other ministries' actions and mistakes, rather than managing to change these ministries' strategies before mistakes happen. As Jim MacNeill, the Secretary General of the 1987 Brundtland Commission, noted, "They were told to take development as a given and to worry about ways and means to ameliorate the effects of development on health, property and ecosystems. And to do so almost exclusively with add-ons: add-on technologies, add-on policies, and add-on politics."[19] This dynamic led to the core challenge of environmental ministries and agencies—they failed to make the economic, trade, and sectoral institutions in any way responsible for the environmental implications of their policies and actions. Moreover, in many countries, environmental ministers tend to have short terms in office and move on to other careers, making it difficult to build a strong corps of national-level environmental leaders. The absence of strong national environmental institutions has led to gaps in oversight and continuity for UNEP and ultimately to the lack of adequate support from national governments. And since every UN agency is accountable to a different line ministry, incentives for coordination are minimal. "It is extremely difficult to get the agencies to look across the board," Kofi Annan pointed out. "They look to where their money is coming from, and it is not from UNEP or New York."[20] Their funding comes from member states, and they seek to develop demand for their work from recipient states as well as support from donor countries.

During its first two decades, UNEP utilized the Environment Fund to work effectively with other agencies. It leveraged its finances for coordination, leading to successful partnerships among several agencies including WHO and FAO and the creation of common work programs on health and environment and pesticide management. "We had a rule, a standing rule which Mostafa Tolba imposed on us," a UNEP staff member recalled, "and it was very frustrating at times, but one third of the Environment Fund had to be executed through the specialised agencies. That was a massive motivator of environmental action and seed projects and programs in the UN system."[21] In 1984–1985, for example, 16.5 percent of the Environment Fund (which totaled approximately $61.5 million at the time, or $148.8 million when adjusted for inflation) was spent on projects with other UN agencies for a total of over $10 million (slightly over $24 million when adjusted for inflation).

As UNEP established itself and countries sought its assistance, it began using more of the Environment Fund resources to support its own technical assistance activities rather than to invest in the other UN agencies to motivate the rest of the system. By 1992–1993, for example, only 6.9 percent, or about $9 million (over $16.2 million when adjusted for inflation), of the Environment Fund was used for collaborative projects with UN agencies, governments, or NGOs (see figure 3.2). The Environment Fund thus came to be seen as UNEP's budget rather than as the funding mechanism for environmental activities across UN agencies because, as UNEP's evaluation office noted, the Fund "pays for almost half of the UNEP staff and a large portion of its resources go to internal projects."[22] Without resources explicitly earmarked to support cooperation between UNEP and the specialized agencies, such initiatives became increasingly superficial and geared mainly toward administrative and procedural work rather than substantive issues.[23] UNEP, therefore, became more of a competitor than a coordinator. Ultimately, this inadequacy of resources was a major limiting factor.

The 1990s marked a difficult period in UNEP's history and the most significant challenge to coordination. In 1989, the Berlin Wall fell and with it, the entire Soviet Bloc. That same year governments committed to convene the UN Conference on Environment and Development, later known as the Rio Earth Summit, in 1992. The end of the Cold War ushered in a neoliberal economic model, which, combined with the minor economic recession that occurred in the early 1990s, led the international community to focus on economic growth, often at any cost.[24] Political support for the environment and its main international institution plummeted.[25] Furthermore, Kenya was suffering from corruption, insecurity, and uncertainty under the regime of President Moi, as chapter 5 explains. As a result of these factors, contributions to the Environment Fund plunged more than 30 percent in less than five years, from close to $130 million in 1992–1993 to $90 million in 1996–1997.

The United States disengaged and diminished its contributions from the all-time high of $21 million per year in both 1993 and 1994 to $5.5 million in 1997. The Soviet Union had contributed $6 million in 1990 but, after its dissolution in 1991, contributions from the Russian Federation, which assumed its responsibilities, fell to $500,000. Struggling with the dual impacts of the aftermath of the dissolution of the Soviet Union and the Yugoslav Wars, the European states were weak and divided. Without strong support from developed countries, UNEP found itself confined to a narrow interpretation of its mandate, with its actions limited by funding.

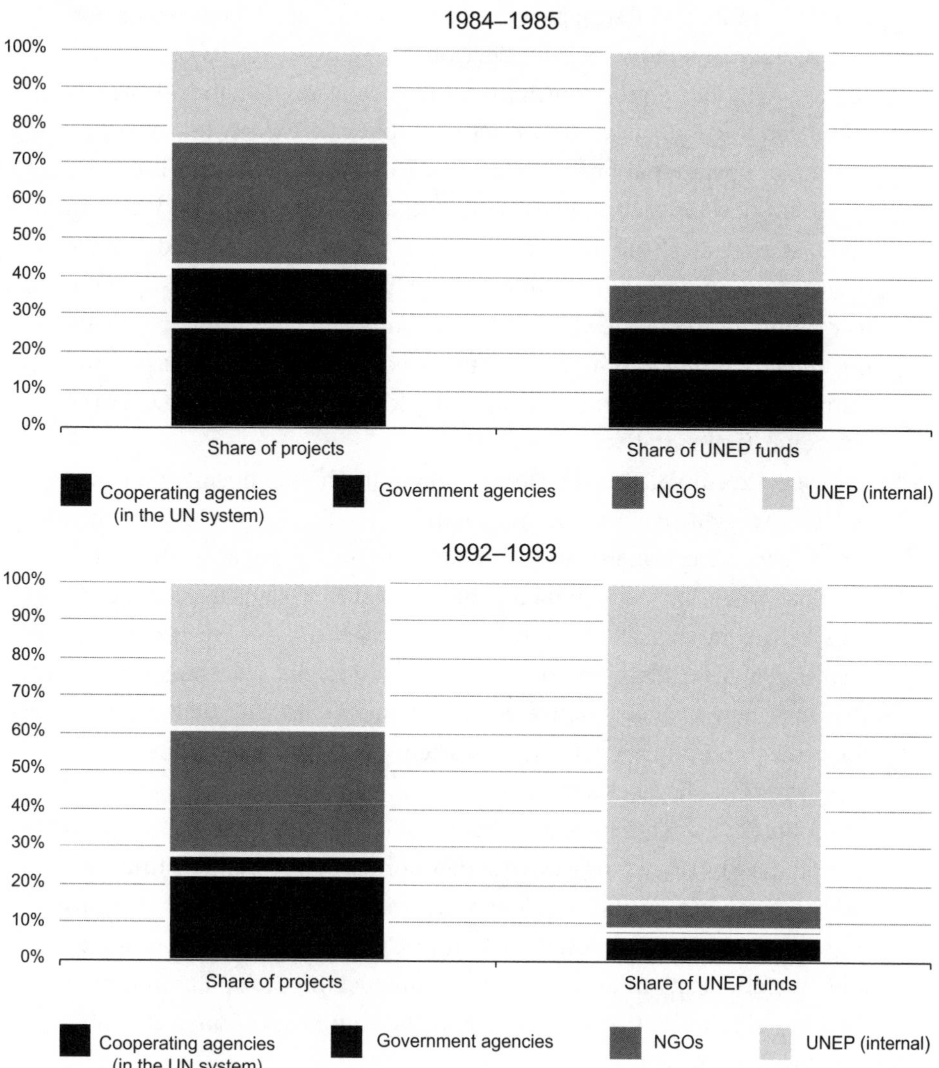

3.2 Shift in share of collaborative projects and funds with UN agencies supported by the Environment Fund.

In the 1990s, UNEP struggled to address the mismatch between its normative mandate, requests from developing countries for its operational engagement, and donor contributions to meet such demands. Formally mandated to conduct normative activities but consistently asked to support more operational ones, UNEP constantly shifted between roles and could not develop a clear, consistent, and compelling identity. When in 1992, as a result of the Rio Earth Summit, governments created a range of new environmental institutions, UNEP had an opportunity to reclaim its coordination role. However, it had all but lost its preeminent convening and coordination power in the field because it had not engaged substantively during the Rio Earth Summit and had little influence over the environmental narrative.

UNEP Executive Director Dr. Mostafa Tolba had deliberately chosen not to engage actively in the preparations for the Earth Summit, thus effectively ceding leadership to the conference secretariat and other international organizations, a dynamic that chapter 6 explains in more detail. This led to the marginalization of UNEP when substantive issues were deliberated, new activities planned, and follow-up arrangements discussed. A new global narrative about sustainable development replaced the earlier environmental focus, and attention moved away from UNEP's core expertise. The Rio Earth Summit became the defining event in global environmental governance, as it transformed the international environmental stage by catalyzing a wave of new norms, policies, and institutions. Governments set up independent secretariats for the new conventions on climate change and desertification in Geneva (later moved to Bonn) and on biodiversity in Montreal. They launched the Global Environment Facility (GEF) in Washington, DC, and the Commission on Sustainable Development in New York.[26]

The GEF became the main financing instrument for environment, including for several of the conventions that UNEP had facilitated. The Commission on Sustainable Development assumed the leadership role in convening the world's environmental constituency for two weeks every year in New York, which effectively eliminated the incentive for environmental ministers and other actors to convene in Nairobi and to engage substantively with UNEP. The center of gravity thus moved to Washington, DC, and New York. UNEP's elaborate coordination mechanisms became redundant and were promptly eliminated.[27] Political attention shifted from the environment to sustainable development, the divide between the Global North and South deepened, and the institutional landscape became very crowded. The result was a "punch to the solar plexus" for UNEP as its authority as coordinator and attractiveness as collaborator diminished, and its credibility suffered as a result.[28] Though a more integrated environment and development agenda emerged, UNEP was not in a position of leadership in this new landscape.

Widely sought after and seldom achieved, coordination remains a modern-day quest for the philosopher's stone, and it has been UNEP's greatest challenge. "No one likes to be coordinated," explained Donald Kaniaru, the officer at the Kenyan mission in New York who had worked with Ambassador Odero-Jowi in getting UNEP to Nairobi and who later joined UNEP as a lawyer.[29] Without a stable center of gravity in environmental governance, institutional specialization took hold, and, with no clear division of labor, fragmentation ensued. UNEP has clearly "fallen short in exercising effectively its original mandate to coordinate all environmental initiatives in the United Nations system," a major evaluation by the UN inspector general concluded in 2008.[30] As a result, it continued, "an overarching authority for global environmental governance is lacking within the United Nations system," and "[r]esponses to environmental challenges have become sector-specific, specialized and fragmented."[31] These critiques came as governments were undertaking another attempt at reforming international environmental governance.

Coordinating the activities of intergovernmental agencies with bigger budgets, larger governing bodies, longer histories, and greater authority among member states was certainly a herculean task. The coordination difficulties challenged UNEP's authority and capacity to serve as an effective anchor institution and, ultimately, one observer noted, "UNEP could no more be expected to 'coordinate' the system-wide activities of the UN than could a medieval monarch 'coordinate' his feudal barons."[32] Over time, the explicit emphasis on coordination softened to collaboration and cooperation. Working through clusters on concrete issues presented an opportunity for UNEP to deliver on its coordination and coherence mandate while sharing the leadership role and diminishing competition. The clusters approach, which brings together various institutions working on similar issues around a common focused agenda, Mohamed El-Ashry, founder and former CEO of the Global Environment Facility, recalled, "would give UNEP the leadership in areas where it really has the strength. So that it's not twenty-two or twenty-four organizations of the UN all doing environment, all doing water resources, all doing energy."[33]

The Environment Management Group, the main body in the UN system for coordinating environmental work since 2001 (See box 3.1), also moved toward collaborative projects and the clusters approach. The EMG used programmatic expertise, knowledge, and capacity to provide the foundation for joint programming and to reduce overlap. It harnessed the multiplicity of institutions to explore opportunities for synergies and more effective implementation, but it has had limited effectiveness in system-wide concerns.[34] The EMG has been a "great way to engage with the UN system on specific issues," explained Janos Pasztor, its first director. "People want to work together by definition. We managed to turn around the UN system attitudes by becoming a UN initiative rather than a UNEP initiative and making clear we were playing a different game. We listened to people and collectively developed a program on how to make the UN climate neutral."[35] This approach worked and other topics followed, including e-waste and marine litter and microplastics. These thematically driven efforts happened through issues-management groups and task forces, which have enhanced the coherent delivery on several issues, including biodiversity, drylands, sound management of chemicals, and green economy, but have not amounted to a coherent system-wide approach. It was not until 2016 that the EMG launched an initiative to create a system-wide framework of strategies on the environment that seeks to integrate environment into the implementation of the 2030 Agenda on sustainable development.

As discussed previously, effective coordination depends on the existence of a legal mandate and financial means, being *in* authority. But it is also determined by the ability to influence, to use its expertise and reputation and be *an* or *the* authority. Integrating these two notions of authority is critical. "Coordination comes when there is a common goal, when resources are pooled together for greater impact," Kofi Annan remarked. Coordination becomes natural when the reputation of an institution attracts others to its sphere of influence. "And good leaders are able to do that," Annan continued.[36] UNEP's leaders have been pushed to advance the goals of the organization and protect it from undue outside influence. Operating in a climate of strong competition, they have more often than not chosen to strengthen the institution as an independent actor that delivers to member states—to be *the* authority—rather than as simply the convener and coordinator. Chapter 6 explains the competitive reality that each executive director faced and the choices they made in response. Following the 2012 Rio+20 conference and the conclusion of the reform process, governments abolished the Commission on Sustainable Development and replaced it with a new political body—the High-Level Political Forum. The division of labor across the UN system on environment, development, and sustainable development, however, still remains unclear and reinforces the often unproductive competition among the agencies.

WHAT IS MEASURED IS MANAGED

Since Rachel Carson called attention to environmental concerns in the 1960s, science has been a prominent foundation for policy and action.[37] Policymakers asked, What is the state of the environment, why, and what is to be done? Existing monitoring and measurement systems could not produce a clear answer. Worldwide monitoring of air, soil, or water quality; of hazardous substances; and of species abundance and distribution was in its infancy. Environmental information was sparse and of varying quality, and no central data facility existed. International agencies across various issue areas—food and agriculture, labor conditions, health—continued to measure indicators and substances they considered relevant, developed guidelines, and carried out environmental programs.[38] However, the guidelines, principles, and policies various organizations had been producing were disparate and incoherent. The multiple efforts at measurement rarely produced comparable results, even when focused on the same problems. And without coherent measurements, environmental management would be futile. UNEP was expected to fill the existing knowledge gap. And, against steep odds, it did. There are, however, further gaps to be filled.

With a mandate to "keep the world environmental situation under review," UNEP engaged in monitoring, tracking, and recording environmental data and sought to bring science to bear on policy with the goal of resolving environmental problems. It harnessed science, and scientific advances, in the service of setting global priorities. It put the spotlight on specific environmental issues—from the pollution of the Mediterranean to ozone depletion—and lay the foundation for the creation of legal, policy, and institutional frameworks to address these issues at both the national and international level. It created a body of scientific knowledge on chemicals and waste, on ecosystems and species, as well as scientific institutions on climate change and biodiversity, such as the IPCC (Intergovernmental Panel on Climate Change) and IPBES (Intergovernmental Science-Policy Platform on Biodiversity and Ecosystem Services).

Without an institutional center of gravity for environmental monitoring, assessment, and analysis, however, systematic data on the state of the environment, on the status of policy responses, and on linkages between policy implementation and the state of the environment remains absent. "In health we track how many people are treated and cured," John Matuszak of the US State Department remarked, "in economic development we track the increase of economic activity, in environment we track laws, studies, meetings, but [we] cannot tell whether the environment is better."[39] Substantive, reliable data on the state of the environment is insufficient, which makes it impossible to establish causal connections between the existence and implementation of multilateral environmental agreements and the condition of the environment. Despite significant successes in bringing scientific data to bear on environmental policy, therefore, UNEP has room for improvement.

Creating a strong scientific foundation for environmental policy was at the core of UNEP's mandate to provide the "best available objective knowledge … for rational decision-making"[40] and to deploy rigorous and robust science in an institutionally innovative and politically powerful way. One of the first decisions governments took during the inaugural UNEP Governing Council in 1973 was to create Earthwatch, a program to coordinate, harmonize, and integrate observation, reporting, and assessment activities across the UN system.[41] This innovative venture was to provide common baselines to assess environmental concerns, determine priorities for action, and spur the development of policy responses.

Earthwatch was a trailblazing initiative: it focused on creating methodologies for monitoring, establishing global databases and quality control, providing technical support, and delivering overviews and trends in the state of the environment. Through Earthwatch, UNEP was able to exercise its catalytic coordinating role in environmental monitoring and assessment, and also collected and processed information from existing sources rather than acquire its own stations, equipment, and highly specialized staff. However, over the years, the constraints of financing, connectivity, and political commitment undermined Earthwatch's ability to deliver on its original tasks. It was therefore reconstituted several times, and did not grow into the data coordination hub originally envisioned.

Nevertheless, UNEP catalyzed environmental data collection, analysis and dissemination, and established a credible scientific baseline for the development of a body of international environmental law. Global environmental monitoring and assessment requires the ability to identify and measure environmental problems, warn of looming crises, research long-term environmental hazards, and facilitate information exchange. Baseline studies set up the measurements for environmental phenomena that need to be addressed. They are "notoriously difficult to carry out," Richard Sandbrook of the International Institute for Environment and Development in the UK warned in 1976, because determining "the quantities of various pollutants ... and their effect on the biological system is almost an impossible task; the state of the initial biological system is usually not known, is probably inherently variable, and the pathways of the pollutant far from clear."[42] UNEP, however, delivered reliable data on a number of environmental issues, including, among others, changes in the mass balance of glaciers as an indicator of climate change, methyl mercury levels in regional fisheries, and pesticide levels in human tissue.[43]

Armed with solid scientific findings, UNEP launched initiatives that coordinated global efforts to address global pollution and resource management. It carried out successful scientific assessments that "shed light on rates of desertification, deforestation, loss of biological diversity and stratospheric ozone depletion," explained Peter Thacher, UNEP's deputy executive director from 1977 to 1983. They provided the foundation for policy, motivated public engagement, and contributed to the successful conclusion of international environmental agreements.[44] UNEP's assessment of ozone-layer depletion, for example, provided the necessary impetus for policymakers to develop international environmental law and to move toward a common solution to the runaway use of chlorofluorocarbons (CFCs), a group of synthetic chemicals used widely as aerosols, solvents, and refrigerants. UNEP successfully convened and engaged many scientists across the world at numerous conferences, placing the issue in the public sphere. Explicit support from scientists and a call for action by policymakers generated agreement on the need for action and, ultimately, a legal treaty articulating goals and means of implementation. UNEP's leadership in marshalling the science to directly influence policy in order to resolve the problem was exemplary. Its executive director at the time, Mostafa Tolba, "simply got hold of the [ozone] issue and wouldn't let it go," remarked David Runnalls, former President of the International Institute for Sustainable Development, "and when finally the science became clear we got the fastest agreement that I think anybody's ever had." The successful work on ozone depletion through the Montreal Protocol increased UNEP's visibility, authority, and impact.

Throughout the years, UNEP produced numerous high-quality reports that articulated the science and urged for a policy response. The reports on chemical pollution, for example, set the standard for high-quality assessments in UNEP's early years. "UNEP collaborated with the WHO [World Health Organisation] to produce what was called environmental health criteria on almost every single chemical," Professor Calestous Juma, the inaugural Executive Secretary of the Convention on Biological Diversity, recalled. In the late 1970s, "UNEP mobilized scientists and the first report was on mercury. These were very high quality. Technically, the series was the best thing coming out of UNEP. It was excellent," Juma remarked.[45] A decade later, UNEP would begin to oversee the drafting of conventions to regulate chemicals, hazardous waste, and, some years later, mercury.

UNEP's focus on monitoring the environment evolved from tracking indicators to synthesizing data into environmental assessments. The expectation was that UNEP would produce a "concise yet comprehensive State of the Environment Report" and publish it every three years, a 1982 evaluation of UNEP noted.[46] The report was to be drafted by a small group of experts and "published under the exclusive authority of the executive director, possibly in consultation with an independent advisory group of scientists, and without any formal intergovernmental review prior to its public release."[47] These assessments sought to examine not only the state of the environment and the pressures on it—what is happening and why—but also the impacts on human and natural systems as well as the range of existing and new responses—the chain of interactions between society and environment. They therefore expanded the excellent technical work into more comprehensive assessments of cause-effect dynamics.[48]

The first integrated environment assessment, the *Global Environment Outlook* (GEO), was published only in 1997. It has since become the flagship publication on the environment and is released every five years, for a total of six reports published through 2020.[49] Building on the IPCC model of multi-stakeholder engagement, the GEO has sought to provide timely scientific input on important policy issues, engage renowned scientists and experts from around the world, and deliver objective analysis with high policy relevance (see box 3.2).[50]

In climate change, UNEP's reports and collaborative work with WMO set the stage for the creation of the IPCC and the UN Framework Convention on Climate Change. Despite the fact that they became independent entities located in Geneva and Bonn respectively, as chapter 4 explains, UNEP continued to produce flagship assessments, including the Integrated Assessment of Black Carbon and Tropospheric Ozone, the Emissions Gap Report, the Production Gap Report, and the Integrated Assessment of Short-lived Climate Pollutants in Latin America and the Caribbean. "One of the very useful inputs from UNEP into the climate change negotiations," noted Michael Zammit Cutajar, the first Executive Secretary of the climate change convention, "was the emissions gap report, which is a really good piece of political journalism. It gives you information that you can absorb and understand and a really strong political message."[51] Where UNEP continues to struggle is linking reports to policymaking and producing the required change in decisions and behavior. As Amina Mohammed noted in 2018, "The GEO is useful, but it is not used enough. Even UNEP does not use the GEO. It should be in the briefcase of every UNEP officer."[52] In 2019, the annual *Emissions Gap Report* received high levels of media and public attention and recognition for driving home the dangers of high emissions and climate change,

Box 3.2
Global Environment Outlook

The *Global Environment Outlook* (GEO) is the flagship assessment through which the UN Environment Programme carries out one of its core functions: reviewing the state the global environment. GEO's goal is to produce scientifically credible and policy-relevant assessment of the state of the global environment and to enhance the capacity of a wide range of actors to perform integrated environmental assessments.

Six GEO reports have been published to date: GEO-1 in 1997, GEO-2000 in 1999, GEO-3 in 2002, GEO-4 in 2007, GEO-5 in 2012, and GEO-6 in 2019. A multi-stakeholder process engages experts from around the world in the drafting of the report. Each iteration has resulted in the creation of related products, such as GEO assessments at regional, national, and city levels, and editions targeted at specific audiences, such as summaries for decision makers, specialized reports, thematic assessments and reports for Youth, Cities, and Business.

Each GEO cycle has employed a different approach to process design, with an overall tendency toward greater consultation and engagement and increasing the capacity of the organizations involved. In its earliest stage, the GEO process involved a network of twenty collaborating centers and gathered data through regional policy consultations. The trend with each subsequent GEO report has been to increase the number of organizations and individuals as authors, contributors to the methodology and process planning, and reviewers of multiple drafts.

The most important contributions of the GEO process have been developing capacity, raising awareness about global and international environmental issues, and fostering engagement and participation. The GEO publications offer overarching trends by issue and geographic area; they do not provide comparative feedback to countries and regional networks on the policies' implementation and efficacy. Funding and management for the production and publication of the report remain a critical challenge.

including floods, heat waves, and ocean acidification, to the general public. But, as UN Secretary-General António Guterres remarked, "For ten years, the Emissions Gap Report has been sounding the alarm—and for ten years, the world has only increased its emissions."[53] Translating science into policy is indeed challenging and has yielded uneven results. On the whole, UNEP executive directors have not prioritized the assessment function of the original mandate and have not accorded it the requisite attention and investment.

Over the years, UNEP designed and launched a number of initiatives that sought to put issues on the policy agenda. It also built capacity in countries through a network of assessment-supporting collaborating centers that provided a mechanism for input from developing countries. It developed integrated assessments in post-crisis countries for reducing risks from disasters and conflicts, and this in turn created demand in member states for UNEP to engage in improvement of environmental emergency prevention, preparedness, assessment, response, and mitigation.[54] Follow-through and long-term investment were insufficient, however, making many of the initiatives short-lived rather than consistent and continuous programs with sustainable outcomes. The State of the Environment assessments published in 1982 and 1992, for example, were "one-off" reports that did not provide a rigorous basis for comparison over time.[55] In 1994, UNEP's office for the Harmonization of Environmental Measurements published a directory of environmental information and assessment programs—seemingly in an effort to shed light on the range of activities undertaken by UNEP, and possibly to encourage transparency and coordination. However, due to lack of funding, the program was abandoned, and a second directory was never published. UNEP also stopped working closely with the collaborating centers and began engaging with individual scientists instead. This change in process was pivotal, as collaborating centers were designed to address issues holistically, whereas individuals tend to have deep expertise but limited scope. New people came on board too often or too infrequently, and oversight and continuity suffered. Consequently, focus on regional capacity in assessments diminished.

Scholars have lauded UNEP for achieving "considerable success in alvanizing international environmental concerns"[56] and making "a great contribution ... on the use of shared natural resources,"[57] but UNEP has been unable to maintain the momentum, the demand, and the justification for continued support.[58] UNEP also made poor internal investment decisions and chose to follow new trends rather than to invest core funding in its core mandated functions. Despite the publication of numerous reports, it has been difficult to track the impact of UNEP's actions on overall environmental quality. As a result, UNEP's legacy is made up of a collection of discrete efforts that each in their own way were promising, but did not as a whole deliver the needed monitoring of the progress on environmental issues.

Importantly, UNEP did not instill coherence into the monitoring system, nor did it catalyze cooperation in assessments. UNEP worked on urban air-pollution monitoring with WHO, on food quality with WHO and FAO, and on water quality with WHO, FAO, and UNESCO. In the face of the structural constraints in the UN system, the response was the creation of siloed sectoral programs rather than integrated ones. UNEP produces the *Global Environment Outlook* and the *Global Chemicals Outlook* as well as various reports through the International Resources Panel; UNESCO publishes the *UN-Water World Water Development Report*, FAO the *Global Food Security Update*, and the IEA the *World Energy Outlook*. At most, only two of these domains have been paired together—water and energy, water and food, energy and agriculture, and the interconnectedness of all dimensions of the water-food-energy nexus has been difficult to map out and analyze systematically.[59] An integrated approach to assessment across all environmental issues would require coordination and coherence among institutions *within* these areas as well as coordination and coherence *across* them.

Producing scientific reports is not coterminous with influencing policymaking, and spurring policy action in response to assessments has been a challenge for UNEP. In addition, as environmental issues have multiplied, becoming more acute and more interconnected, and powerful lobbies have been spurred to advocate for maintaining the status quo. Despite the large number of reports generated, there is no direct link between UNEP's reporting and international negotiations on environmental issues. "UNEP is very poor in linking science to decision-making," remarked Niko Urho, a former official in the ministry of environment of Finland. "They have these massive reports coming from here and there; that looks good. But how much do they actually support the negotiations? They don't. They don't have that type of documentation."[60] Moreover, the environmental policy community has not applied any serious pressure in support of good data collection for tracking the impacts of policy responses. Without measuring the extent of implementation of international environmental agreements, it remains impossible to assess whether these agreements solve the problems they were designed to address.

UNEP has not adequately invested in its data and science expertise and authority. Despite the importance of scientific assessments, or perhaps because of it, UNEP has not consistently directed funds from its core budget into assessment. Following the logic of the "Washington Monument syndrome," UNEP has chosen not to allocate core resources to assessment, knowing that someone will come in with the funding because the issue is too important to ignore. Extrabudgetary resources, however, are unpredictable, volatile, and scarce, and financial uncertainty undermines institutional confidence and commitment. Many of the areas in which UNEP had comparative advantage, such as pollution and chemicals, or areas in which it had an explicit mandate to keep the environment under review, have not received funding from UNEP's core resources. UNEP has instead used the Environment Fund to chase the hot topic of the day. This has reinforced the tendency to react to and prioritize new events—wild fires, tsunamis, river clean ups, or reconstruction after disasters—and to then move resources, staff, and attention to these issues. "At UNEP we chase the first bus we see, hoping it will take us to our destination," exclaimed Gerry Cunningham, former Head of Partnerships at UNEP.[61] As a result, trust has eroded, member states have not delivered contributions, and the Environment Fund has decreased.

Much like the challenge to UNEP's coordination function, new institutional arrangements have emerged and vied for attention and resources to deliver environmental assessments. In 2005, governments created a new global initiative and platform, the Group on Earth Observations, which even carries the same acronym as UNEP's flagship environmental assessment, GEO. This Group includes 105 governments and 127 participating organizations and seeks to provide "comprehensive, coordinated and sustained observations of the Earth system" as well as "timely, quality long-term global information as a basis for sound decision making."[62] Located in Geneva, it provides a platform for coordinating monitoring, assessment, and early-warning information as well as timely, accurate, long-term scientific information as the basis for policymaking; in essence, this Group has in essence been tasked with one of the core mandates envisioned for UNEP in 1972. The question, therefore, is whether UNEP is at risk of losing a part of its mandate that it has done relatively well.

Continuous assessment of the state of the global environment that draws on national and global monitoring will remain a critical function in global environmental governance. As the anchor institution for the global environment, UNEP will always have an important role in assessment, if it is willing and ready to assume it. As per the original vision for UNEP, science was not an end-in-itself; it was, instead, intended to inform policy. Governments and UN agencies have recognized the need to break the silo approach and work across issues and across institutions to ensure that global resources are appropriately and efficiently managed.

The Sustainable Development Goals—regarded as indivisible—offer an opportunity to develop an integrated vision and a range of new collaborative approaches and initiatives to instigate necessary institutional transformation and action. UNEP's engagement in this work could add value.[63] UNEP could potentially help transform the many reports and efforts into a more consistent initiative to influence decision-making and assess the impact of resulting actions in terms of change in behavior of nation states and in the state of the environment. A UNEP-led systematic monitoring effort could also engage civil society in the collection of data and deploy new partnerships with business in using AI and earth observation technologies. In the contemporary reality of hyper-connectivity and close collaborations across institutions, sectors, and geographies, having multiple organizations working on information collection, compilation, and comparison is not detrimental, indeed, it is necessary. Powerful computing platforms—and UNEP is working on making Environment Live such a platform—can present coherent overviews of the state of the environment, from a hyper-local to a global level; the state of policy formulation; and the trends in policy implementation.

Substantial, systematic, comparable data is fundamental to effective environmental policy, and systematic data collection is necessary for identifying problems and tracking the impact of policy responses. UNEP has been successful in building on its scientific assessment function, and its communication has been clear and simple—we have identified a problem, we are determining its root causes and its effects, and we are gathering all parties concerned to design solutions and the necessary legal frameworks. This model produced a notable body of international environmental law, as chapter 4 explains, but an explicit connection to enacted policy could be improved. Will UNEP be able to take this model to the next level and analyze the impact of policy implementation on the resolution of the problem at hand and the collateral effects on other connected issues?

CREATING DOMESTIC AND INTERNATIONAL ENVIRONMENTAL LAW

A core mandate of UNEP is to formulate and evaluate policy options and catalyze action to implement them. In 1972, governments termed this "environmental management," including comprehensive goal setting and planning as well as international consultation and agreement to protect and enhance the environment. The creation of appropriate policy and legal instruments was envisioned in response to the assessments UNEP carried out and in tandem with its coordination mandate. The vision was that UNEP would provide support with institutional, technical, and policy advice and engage in public awareness and education, thus enabling governments, civil society, and business to implement necessary actions.

Using the scientific evidence accumulated through its assessment function, UNEP developed policy frameworks on a range of environmental concerns. It established a range of multilateral environmental agreements on stratospheric ozone, climate change, regional seas, biodiversity, desertification, and chemical and waste regulation, as chapter 4 illustrates. It fostered the establishment of domestic legal, regulatory, and institutional structures for environmental action. "UNEP's work on environmental law," noted Dan Magraw, former director of the Center for International Environmental Law, "has been remarkably effective in designing national legal frameworks, training judges about environmental science and law, and fostering the creation of and administering multilateral environmental agreements."[64] UNEP also carried out research; maintained a register of environmental agreements, conventions, and protocols; prompted governments to adhere to the conventions; and supported them in addressing difficulties related to adherence.[65] While it is possible to track the development of international environmental law, assessing the level of implementation at the national level has not been feasible making accountability and improvement difficult.

Development of international environmental law has been one of UNEP's landmark successes. Strictly speaking, creating international environmental law was not directly part of UNEP's original mandate.[66] Principle 22 of the Stockholm Declaration called for state cooperation to develop international environmental law, and a number of UN documents also assigned the organization a quasi-legislative role.[67] UNEP Executive Director Dr. Mostafa Tolba led this initiative. As Mark Allan Gray, First Secretary at the Australian Permanent Mission to the United Nations, wrote, "UNEP [was] always calling for legislation and treaties, and developed guidelines and model laws to assist legislators and diplomats."[68] A natural scientist, Tolba recognized the need to develop legal instruments for collective action toward the resolution of environmental problems and invested his personal energy toward this end. In 1982, UNEP adopted the Montevideo Programme for the Development and Periodic Review of Environmental Law, which has been renewed every ten years. The Montevideo Programme was designed to support the development of environmental law and legal frameworks, improve implementation at the national level, and support capacity-building for member states and a range of stakeholders.

Three first-tier priorities formed the core of the Montevideo Programme: (1) marine pollution from land-based sources, (2) protection of the stratospheric ozone layer, and (3) transport, handling, and disposal of toxic and hazardous waste. To address these priorities, UNEP developed international environmental agreements and specialized institutional and financial instruments to facilitate this work. In the first two decades, these became some of UNEP's most compelling successes. The global treaties on ozone-layer protection, regulation of chemicals and hazardous waste, climate change, desertification, and biodiversity were all created and concluded with UNEP's engagement.[69] Indeed, during the first decade of UNEP's operations, almost as many international agreements were created as during the previous sixty years.[70] Since 1973, Professor Peter Haas noted, UNEP has catalyzed the development of more than 40 percent of "multilateral environmental treaties adopted outside the

European Community."[71] Although many scholars point to the existence of hundreds of multilateral environmental agreements, there are twelve to fifteen truly global environmental agreements—those concerned with a global rather than regional issue and with close to universal membership (see table 3.1).

However, UNEP's "biggest success has also been the biggest failure," remarked Gus Speth, founder of major international environmental NGOs and former Administrator of UNDP. UNEP developed most of the multilateral environmental agreements currently in existence, and, Speth pointed out, "this is the biggest thing that has happened in terms of creating global environmental governance." But, he continued, "very few of these agreements are actually succeeding in their intended purposes, and that, to me, is the failure. The UNFCCC's failure in particular is very serious, and from 1989 forward this failure is mainly attributable to the United States. We really need to step back and think about how to effectively implement legislation at the international level."[72] Indeed, the quantity of new international agreements is not necessarily reflective of their impact on the environment. States voluntarily create international agreements to govern their relations through legal responsibilities, and there is no overarching judicial or penal system to ensure enforcement of these agreements. Parties face no penalties for not meeting their commitments, and breaches are not punishable by sanctions. Compliance and implementation have to be enticed rather than coerced.

Once launched, the conventions have become quasi-autonomous entities with separate, legally independent structures, decision-making bodies, and procedures, each with its own Conference of the Parties (COP), secretariat, and subsidiary bodies with influence often exceeding that of UNEP. This dynamic, much like that with the other UN agencies, has led to competition rather than cooperation. This perhaps became most evident at the 1992 Rio Earth Summit and the creation of the conventions on climate, biodiversity, and desertification. Over the years, UNEP backed away from the conventions and did not assist in their implementation, and, as a result, lost political influence with governments it could have leveraged strategically.

The successful creation of a such a body of international environmental law has led to some critical challenges. First, creating multiple new

Table 3.1 Global environmental conventions

Adopted/entered into force		Convention	No. of parties	Issue area	Location
1971/1975	Ramsar	Convention on Wetlands of International Importance especially as Waterfowl Habitat (Ramsar Convention)	170	Biodiversity	Gland
1972/1975		World Heritage Convention (WHC)	193	Biodiversity	Paris
1973/1975	CITES	Convention on International Trade in Endangered Species of Wild Fauna and Flora (CITES)	183	Biodiversity	Geneva
1979/1983	CMS	Convention on the Conservation of Migratory Species (CMS)	130	Biodiversity	Bonn
1985/1988 1987/1989	UN environment programme	Vienna Convention for the Protection of the Ozone Layer (Vienna Convention) and Montreal Protocol on Substances that Deplete the Ozone Layer (Montreal Protocol)	198	Atmosphere	Nairobi
1989/1992	BASEL CONVENTION	Convention on the Control of Transboundary Movements of Hazardous Wastes and Their Disposal (Basel Convention)	187	Chemicals and Waste	Geneva
1992/1994		United Nations Framework Convention on Climate Change (UNFCCC)	197	Atmosphere	Bonn
1992/1993	Convention on Biological Diversity	Convention on Biological Diversity (CBD)	196	Biodiversity	Montreal
1994/1996	United Nations Convention to Combat Desertification	United Nations Convention to Combat Desertification (UNCCD)	197	Land	Bonn
1997/2005	IPPC	International Plant Protection Convention (IPPC)	184	Biodiversity	Rome
1998/2004	ROTTERDAM CONVENTION	Rotterdam Convention on the Prior Informed Consent Procedure for Certain Hazardous Chemicals and Pesticides in International Trade (Rotterdam Convention)	161	Chemicals and Waste	Geneva
2001/2004	STOCKHOLM CONVENTION	Convention on Persistent Organic Pollutants (Stockholm Convention)	184	Chemicals and Waste	Geneva
2013/2017	UN environment programme	Minamata Convention on Mercury	117	Chemicals and Waste	Geneva

Source: Maria Ivanova, "Coloring the UN Environmental: The Catalytic Role of the UN Environment Programme," *Global Governance* 26 (2020): 318.

environmental agreements led to institutional multiplicity that increased demands on member states' time, attention, and resources. "I can spend all my time going from one international meeting to another and not do my job of running the ministry," an environment minister of one developing country noted.[73] Second, the proliferation of independent environmental agreements, with their own headquarters, staff, budgets, and COPs, has led to tough competition, much like that among UN agencies in the 1970s discussed in the earlier section on coordination. The result has been a strained relationship between UNEP, the conventions it administers, and the more autonomous conventions. Third, implementation of the complex and growing body of international environmental law has been and remains a significant challenge for countries, and thus for UNEP to fulfill its mandate in supporting their efforts. Without targeted support to countries lacking the capacity to implement treaty provisions, progress has been slow. Little information is available on the extent to which countries implement their obligations and therefore on the extent to which environmental agreements address the problems they were designed to resolve.[74] Finally, without systematic support for implementation, whether through UNEP or other means, international environmental agreements have remained aspirations rather than plans of action incorporated into domestic legal practices.

Furthermore, the governance relationship between UNEP and the conventions has been tense. The COP is the primary governing body of each convention and the parties make all the decisions. "They tell the secretariat what to do and see the executive secretary as their person that is buying services from UNEP," explained Professor Calestous Juma, the first Executive Secretary of the Convention on Biological Diversity. "UNEP, however," Juma emphasized, "sees the relationship exactly reverse. Because the executive director of UNEP appoints the Executive Secretary of the convention, they see him as a UNEP person."[75] UNEP provides the secretariat for fifteen global and regional agreements. As John Scanlon, the then Secretary-General of CITES, told governments gathered at the Global Ministerial Environment Forum in Nairobi in 2012, "UNEP is, in many instances, playing a role that is akin to a 'middle man' between the convention secretariat(s) and the service provider(s), which comes at a cost." Administering the conventions is not UNEP's comparative advantage, he explained; where UNEP is needed most and performs best is on programme, financing, and UN system-wide support.[76] Rethinking the relationship with the conventions will be critical when considering the future of UNEP.

The key question for governments has been how to keep the various conventions working cooperatively toward common objectives. "It's difficult enough within one organization," Michael Zammit Cutajar remarked, "but much more so when you spin off in different directions and only pay lip service to coordination."[77] The conventions have very different administrative set ups: UNESCO hosts the World Heritage Convention, IUCN hosts the Ramsar Convention on wetlands, UNEP hosts CITES, the chemicals conventions, and CBD under different agreements, and the climate and desertification conventions (UNFCCC and UNCCD) are autonomous, stand-alone institutions under the UN umbrella. Moreover, the convention secretariats are geographically distributed across Nairobi, Montreal, Geneva, Bonn, and Paris, which has presented a range of communication and coordination challenges.

Creating international environmental law is one of UNEP's most notable successes, but, lacking capacity and resources itself, UNEP has been challenged to assist member states in the implementation of these laws. Governments adopted the Bali Strategic Plan for Technology Support and Capacity Building in 2005 as "an effort to thread the needle to make UNEP help countries with implementation without taking on high administrative cost of having country offices," John Matuszak of the US State Department explained.[78] "Its purpose," he added "was to strengthen the [UNEP] regional offices to be responsive to member states' needs to implement existing agreements and strengthen national environmental programs and policies." The Bali Strategic Plan aimed to assist countries in the Global South to achieve environmental and development goals through greater focus on capacity building and technology transfer but fell short in articulating adequate guidance to put goals into practice and remains largely unfulfilled.[79] Indeed, "no mechanism exists to support implementation of the conventions and agreements," explained Youba Sokona, special advisor for sustainable development at the South Centre, in 2018.[80] With a limited operational budget, UNEP has not been able to provide the kind and scale of assistance necessary for member states to improve delivery on complex environmental concerns. Without such support, countries remain unable to deliver on their international obligations, and the environment continues to be at risk.

A core problem with the policy function of UNEP has been the focus on development of law and policy rather than on implementation and accountability.[81] As new problems emerge, UNEP cerates new agreements, and governments take on new obligations at every international conference. Governments have become accustomed to endorsing and signing new agreements with no regard for having to do anything to implement them. Neither UNEP nor the convention secretariats nor the NGO community have held governments accountable for delivering on their obligations set out in these legal instruments.[82] Although one might expect civil society to step up to this challenge, UNEP's governance arrangements have disincentivized such a development. Under the rules of the UNEP Governing Council (the governance arrangement in place from 1973 until it was replaced with the universal membership UN Environment Assembly in 2012 as discussed in chapter 7), in order to participate in Governing Council meetings, civil society groups had to receive funding from UNEP for travel expenses and a generous daily subsistence allowance. As a result, civil society has become quite timid in its relationship with governments attending the UNEP Governing Council. Given these lucrative financial aspects, selection was based on relationships. "This is what I think killed robust civil society engagement," explained Annabell Waititu, who had represented civil society at UNEP meetings. "With such financial dependency, you have nothing to say or you have no issues that you really want to drive home."[83] When a push for accountability from strong public actors is absent, ambitious environmental action is also lacking. Relatedly, there have been no systematic, time-series empirical assessments of the degree to which countries have implemented their commitments under global environmental conventions. Therefore, no baseline data exists against which to assess performance, actions, or even expectations. In the absence of implementation measurement, it is impossible to determine whether these conventions solve the problems they were created to address. Moreover, without understanding what enables or prevents countries from implementing their obligations, no serious actions can take place either at the national or international level to promote their success. This is an area where UNEP has the potential to leverage its mandate, but has yet to do so.

CONCLUSION

At its creation, the United Nations Environment Programme was designed to help resolve global environmental problems; to do so, UNEP was given the means to undertake scientific assessment, create environmental law and institutions, enhance the capacity of countries across a range of functions, and coordinate and collaborate with other UN agencies toward a common goal. Designed as a normative body but facing increasing demands for support of concrete initiatives within member states, UNEP was often walking a line between normative programs and operational activities and results (this tension will be addressed further in chapters 4 and 5).[84] There is no doubt that developing countries needed concrete assistance—both normative and operational—on many issues. Responding to multiple demands, UNEP worked on strengthening judicial systems, supporting the development of financial instruments to assist policy development, developing tools and training on eco-labelling, life cycle analysis, certification, and awareness. The gravitation toward project work was driven by powerful drivers: more readily available funding for concrete projects, the clear credit an institution would receive, and the continuous demand for on-the-ground engagement.

Throughout the years, UNEP has come to embrace these two aspects of its mandate and now acknowledges that it is both a normative and an operational entity that exercises leadership on environment within the UN system and beyond.[85] The shift from a normative, catalytic function to one that also encompasses implementation and operational roles has, however, further obscured the line separating UNEP from operational agencies. As a result, UNEP's role in providing technical assistance and improving capacity remains unclear, as does its role vis-à-vis UNDP and the World Bank; these entities now resemble competitors more than partners. And yet, the niche identified in 1972 is no less in need of being filled: none of these other institutions have the potential to systematically conceptualize, launch, implement, and scale up environmental programs on a nation-by-nation basis. In this, UNEP has yet to deliver on its promise. On the other hand, the need for assistance with environmental activities at the national level remains unfulfilled. It may indeed be inevitable that UNEP's support function will be elevated to stand equally with the coordination, assessment, and policy development functions of its mandate.

Ultimately, UNEP has been both an astounding success and a disappointment on core functions that demand collective action at the global level. The biggest obstacles have been the lack of a common vision, consistent priorities, and recognized identity at UNEP.[86] Embracing the need for effective support that has been part of its core mandate since creation, and UNEP could yet be a bridge for collaborating with the various multilateral environmental agreements and member states. As the organization rethinks its identity for the next fifty years, it could draw on lessons from the past and chart a vision for the future that embraces improved monitoring, reporting, and implementation, and connects the fulfillment of international obligations to the attainment of environmental results across issues and across countries.

4

ADDRESSING ENVIRONMENTAL PROBLEMS: SUCCESSES AND CHALLENGES

I was telling governments what they should do. I was taking the stance that I am a civil servant. I am a citizen of the world. I'm not any human being; I'm a scientist, able to see the danger. My responsibility is to help protect the environment, so I'm defending it.
—Mostafa Tolba, UNEP executive director (1976–1992)[1]

At inception, UNEP faced the challenges that come with being a startup institution with a big vision and modest resources. Undeterred, UNEP took risks and spurred governments to adopt agreements, commit funding, embrace ethical imperatives, and deliver on promises. Despite gaps in connectivity and communication, remoteness from the centers of political power, and growing competition with a range of existing and emerging institutions, UNEP persevered. Its work program encompassed natural resource and ecosystem management issues, including the protection of biodiversity and forests, the stemming and reversal of land degradation, reversal of the depletion of the ozone layer, and control of climate change. The standard UNEP procedure for addressing these challenges was to follow the core functions of its mandate and identify the problem based on scientific assessment, convene scientists and policymakers, and facilitate the development of the necessary legal, regulatory, and institutional mechanisms that set the goals and supported countries to achieve them. This model delivered results in marine pollution, ozone depletion, and chemicals and waste management. During the first two decades, one long-term staff member remarked, UNEP's mandate and mission were clear to all staff; they were focused on work in pollution, waste, energy, climate change, ozone, desertification.[2] After the 1992 Rio Earth Summit, however, UNEP's leadership position shifted.

The Rio Earth Summit transformed the international environmental stage by catalyzing a wave of new norms, policies, and institutions for the global environment. The international environmental community, however, did not recognize the full impact of Rio. Assistant Secretary-General and UNEP Deputy Executive Director (1986–1992) Bill Mansfield remarked, "We were looking at Rio as an environmental success, and I don't think that in the end it was."[3] The conference established a new global paradigm—sustainable development—and created consensus around the need to resolve a range of environmental issues UNEP had brought to international attention. But as a result of the Rio summit, UNEP lost the leadership it had held on these issues. Originally created to be a catalyst in the environmental field, UNEP had to redefine its value proposition to better respond to the broader notion of balancing people, planet, and prosperity. As a 1997 report by the UN Office of Internal Oversight Services noted, UNEP was "de facto divorced from most of the operational activities carried out by the United Nations system related to environmental issues" and had difficulties demonstrating concrete results.[4]

The major success in global environmental governance at large—the reversal of the depletion of the ozone layer—is one of UNEP's landmark successes. The institution, and governments and other agencies alike, have, however, struggled with a range of other concerns, including biodiversity, forests, desertification, and resource efficiency. Difficulties arose when demands from member states increased but did not align, when financial support was absent, and when the tension deepened between priorities of member states and between normative and operational requests. The rift between the Global North and South seemingly lies at the core of many of these concerns. It stems from the fact that many of the environmental problems confronting developing countries are not necessarily transboundary or international but are urgent local problems such as clean water, sanitation, and air pollution. Global concerns about biodiversity, forests, and species have very concrete local repercussions that governments would like to have control over. This chapter offers a nuanced story of what has worked and what hasn't—with views from a few, though not all, of the environmental issues UNEP has taken on—and provides insights into why, an issue that subsequent chapters will take on in greater depth.

OZONE DEPLETION

Reversal of the depletion of the ozone layer is perhaps UNEP's greatest achievement. The resolution of the ozone-depletion problem created "a model for effective multilateral action" for tackling major global problems, according to Ambassador Richard Benedick, chief US negotiator and a principal architect of the Montreal Protocol on depletion of the ozone layer.[5] The ozone issue came onto the international political agenda in the mid-1970s when Mario Molina and Sherwood Rowland articulated a hypothesis that CFCs were destroying the stratospheric ozone layer. At the request of the Natural Resources Defense Council (NRDC), a major environmental NGO in the United States, UNEP took the lead on ozone and received approval from its Governing Council to launch an investigation and international discussions. In essence, UNEP's effective use of the science-policy-support trifecta led to action on ozone, in what has been recognized as a clear success.

This success has been explained by a range of factors, including the positive engagement by parties, especially the United States; the relatively narrow scope of the problem; the compelling science undergirding policy decisions; the leadership of industry, DuPont in particular; the existence of epistemic communities (expert networks); and the creation of human, social, and cultural capital (among negotiators).[6] By all accounts, however, the common denominator was the leadership role of Mostafa Tolba, for whom ozone became a defining issue.[7] Professors Penelope Canan and Nancy Reichman, scholars of the ozone regime, explain that Tolba "pushed UNEP to assume responsibility for getting a treaty because he felt so strongly that a formal agreement was essential for planetary survival"[8] and demonstrated "the very model of how a UN agency should operate in a complex international negotiation."[9] The importance of Tolba's leadership is elaborated in box 4.1.[10]

Box 4.1

Mostafa Tolba's Leadership in Reversing Ozone Depletion

Policymakers credit UNEP, and in particular its executive director at the time, Dr. Mostafa Tolba, with the greatest success in global environmental governance, the resolution of the ozone problem in the late 1980s. "Tolba pleaded, provoked, cajoled, shamed, and sometimes bullied reluctant governments ever closer to the treaty provisions that he, as a scientist, knew were necessary for the world," wrote Richard Benedick, the chief US negotiator. "It was an unforgettable virtuoso performance, a role that he undertook with unflagging energy and with absolutely no consideration for his own personal popularity." Investing the entire energy of the institution he led was critical to the resolution of this global problem. So too was the engagement of the governments of all countries as part of one global team. "If the 'ozone story' can be likened to the preparation of a Michelin three-star feast," Benedick wrote, "then Dr. Tolba was the master chef: the rest of us were cook's apprentices—salad chefs, pastry chefs and onion peelers." A certain level of discomfort with the activist executive director, however, led many member states to pull back from UNEP subsequently as they became "gun shy and thought 'we can't leave it to Tolba who will push us,'" one member state representative recalled.

Tolba's leadership translated into UNEP taking a lead in managing the agreement and creating the institutional structures to support it. The Multilateral Fund was created to finance member-state actions, national ozone units were set up within governments to support the implementation of the treaty, and the ozone secretariat was created within UNEP to support international collaboration. These institutional structures facilitated a nearly 100 percent level of compliance with the reporting obligations and an equally high implementation rate over the years the Protocol has been in force. This can be explained by the work of the national ozone units in collecting data on the production, export, and import of groups of substances regulated by the Protocol and submitting the information to the Ozone Secretariat and to the funding mechanism, the Multilateral Fund.[11]

Scientific knowledge was an important foundation for the political process that led to this success. In 1976, UNEP called for an international conference, and in 1977, scientists from thirty-two countries convened in Washington, DC, and established a "world plan of action" for

the ozone layer. That year UNEP created the first official expert panel on the ozone layer. This panel established a common body of data and analysis and diminished the degree of data uncertainty. It also provided a basis for influencing public opinion; clear scientific evidence of a hole in the ozone layer over Antarctica motivated action on the issue. Environmental organizations linked the ozone hole to an increased risk of skin cancer and made the issue personal. In 1978, the United States banned the non-essential use of CFCs as aerosol propellants. In 1980, UNEP's Governing Council requested that it "undertake measures to protect the ozone layer from modifications due to human activities, and in 1981 [it] called for a convention."[12] The Governing Council also noted that "the progressive development of environmental law is necessarily a slow process [and] negotiating a new instrument takes a long time. Nevertheless, considerable progress has been made towards the achievement of this goal," governments emphasized, "in spite of the fact that as originally conceived the goal was over-optimistic considering the delicate nature of some of the subject areas chosen."[13]

Working with scientists and national academies, UNEP was instrumental in creating public awareness about the causes and consequences of ozone depletion. It performed a catalytic role in building a consensus on the science, the policy, and potential implementation strategies. It continued to keep the problem of stratospheric ozone depletion on the international agenda and to work with governments to devise the legal regime for collective action. Science provided a "major turning point in the negotiations," Professor Ernst Haas wrote in 1990, when Mostafa Tolba convened "atmospheric modelers and instructed them to compare their models and assessments of ozone depletion." The report from the meeting, Haas explained, provided support for measures advocated by the United States and UNEP and "given the authority of the scientists involved, this report was sufficient to compel the recalcitrant European nations to accept the need for speedy controls over a wide variety of CFCs—a position which they had previously opposed."[14] In 1985, governments signed the Vienna Convention, the framework convention on ozone-depleting substances. The Vienna Convention promoted international cooperation on the protection of the ozone layer through systematic scientific observations and research, information exchange, and public awareness. It obligated parties

to create legislation to regulate activities with potentially harmful effects on the ozone layer. However, Tolba saw this as insufficient, remarking that "these framework conventions are nothing but governments saying, 'Oh, we love one another, we have to protect the environment, but we need more resources.'" He also pointed out that he asked the government of Canada to continue the negotiations for a protocol. "And to my great surprise," he exclaimed, "the Canadians jumped at this, and they said—it was 1985—'We are ready to host the ministerial conference to adopt a protocol in Montreal in 1987'—that's a two-year period."[15]

Mostafa Tolba—and thus UNEP—led the difficult negotiations during the following two years. Initially, the various negotiation positions differed widely. There were seven mathematical models—from UNEP, from the United States, and from the Soviet Union—and each had different assumptions and different projected results. UNEP convened the modelers in Germany for a week in 1986 to compare their assumptions and adjust their models. Tolba recalled, "six of them ended up with the same result: that stratospheric ozone is depleting and fast and it cannot recover in less than seventy years, even if we stop everything tomorrow. The only exception was the Soviet Union; they did not think that they would suffer from the ozone depletion and that they were receiving more pollution than they were sending. But when they looked back into what was actually happening, it turned out that they were exporting more pollution than they were receiving. So, they started changing their position. That meeting was really crucial."[16] While agreement on the problem was attained, there were certainly wide disagreements on how it could be resolved. Since the political positions of governments were widely divergent, as Lee Thomas, then Administrator of the US Environmental Protection Agency, remarked, the adoption of the Montreal Protocol showed an "unprecedented degree of cooperation among nations of the world in balancing economic development and environmental protection."[17]

With leadership from UNEP, in 1987, twenty-four countries convened in Montreal and "promised to halve the production and use of ozone-destroying chemicals by 1999."[18] The Montreal Protocol committed countries to specific actions to control ozone-depleting substances, including banning the use of and trade in these chemicals. It contained economic

incentives for participation and compliance, provisions for technology transfer, and stipulations for assessment of efficacy and for readjustment.[19] The financing mechanism to support the implementation of the convention was a substantial institutional innovation, which was critical to ensuring collaboration from developing countries and in practice has proven significant to the successful implementation of the treaty. Since its inception, the Multilateral Fund has received more, and more stable, funding than UNEP's Environment Fund. Since 1990, countries have contributed an average of $275 million per biennium, for a total of $3.85 billion in the period 1990–2017 (see figure 4.1).[20]

Scientific evidence is now sufficient to show that "the Montreal Protocol is working."[21] A January 2018 study by scientists at NASA confirms that chlorine from CFCs "is decreasing in the Antarctic stratosphere and the ozone destruction is decreasing along with it." The Antarctic ozone hole is expected to continue to progressively recover, although complete closing of the hole will take decades. "CFCs have lifetimes from 50 to 100 years, so they linger in the atmosphere for a very long time," noted

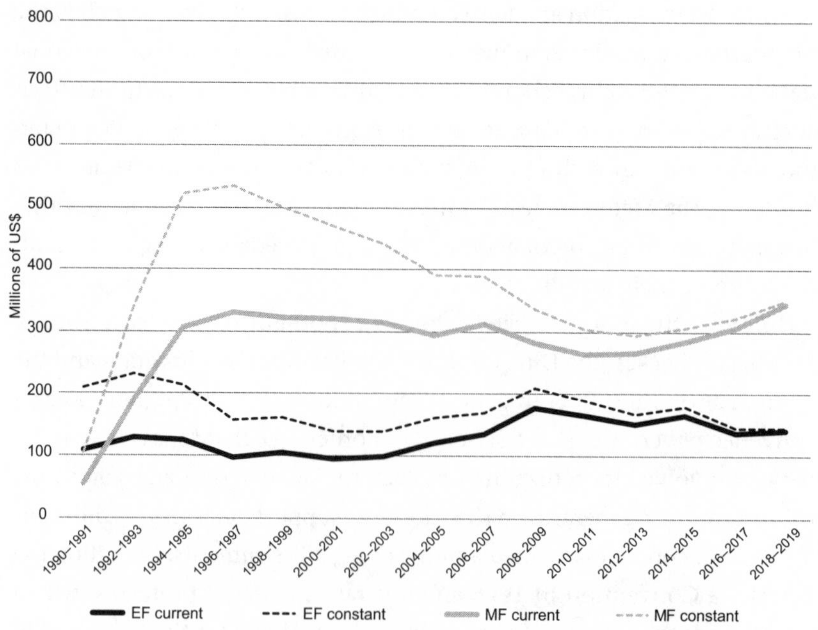

4.1 The Environment Fund and the Multilateral Fund from 1990 to 2019.

Anne Douglass, an atmospheric scientist at NASA and one of the study's two authors. "As far as the ozone hole being gone, we're looking at 2060 or 2080."[22] Scientific assessment, public awareness and outcry, individual and institutional leadership with financial incentives and governance mechanisms all came together to shape this successful environmental regime.

MARINE POLLUTION

The health and productivity of marine ecosystems were among the first of UNEP's topic-specific initiatives and continue to be an emphasis for its work, with the goal of supporting countries in maintaining and restoring their long-term functioning. This work began in 1974 with the Regional Seas Programme, which mobilized the power of science and the authority of the new institution to convene various actors. Eventually, the program included fourteen regions and over 140 states. Responding to concerns about marine pollution in the Mediterranean, UNEP convened governments in Mediterranean coastal states to develop an action plan for the protection of the marine environment and ensured a balance between scientific investigation and legal commitment. As a result, it launched the Mediterranean Sea Programme and facilitated the creation of a regional network of over eighty laboratories and research institutions from fifteen coastal states to share data for baseline studies, pollution source determination, and research. Through these efforts UNEP enabled the states bordering the Mediterranean—often antagonistic to each other in other international fora—to collaborate to an unprecedented degree to limit pollution of their shared sea.[23]

In 1981, the *New York Times* shined a spotlight on the leadership of Dr. Stjepan Kečkeš, the Director of UNEP's Regional Seas Program and the "principal optimist" behind the Mediterranean Action Program. Kečkeš convened governments at a six-day UN conference that "showed that the nations involved recognize the problem and are determined to do something about it," generating $13 million to support activities.[24] Under his leadership, countries adopted a range of legal instruments, including the Barcelona Convention in 1976 and several subsequent protocols, which established standards for discharge levels and criteria for the treatment of industrial wastes, municipal sewage, and runoff of agricultural pesticides

and fertilizers, and committed parties to reporting on implementation.[25] As Kečkeš remarked, "We have had complete agreement on an agenda from a group that includes Israel, Syria, Lebanon, Libya and Tunisia—countries that agree with each other on very little else."[26]

The Regional Seas program catalyzed science and convened, guided, and shaped policy direction for technical programs, which made it highly influential and successful in initiating and shaping treaty negotiations.[27] While some of the Regional Seas conventions have struggled with funding and the challenge of elevating environmental issues on governments' agendas,[28] UNEP generally considers the Regional Seas agreements "extraordinarily effective" in engaging governments in environmental protection.[29] Scholars agree with this assessment, and many have pointed to the Regional Seas Programme as one of UNEP's most successful undertakings, exemplifying the catalytic role that international organizations can play in resolving environmental problems.[30]

DESERTIFICATION

Desertification came onto the international agenda after a series of droughts afflicted the Sahel[31] in the late 1960s, causing famine in several countries between 1968 and 1972 and spurring intense humanitarian, political, and scientific concern.[32] In 1975, UNEP and UNESCO co-sponsored a study of the status of desertification in northwestern Sudan.[33] Hugh Lamprey, an ecologist and bush pilot, carried out the study and noted that the desert in the Sudan had moved southward by ninety to one hundred kilometers over a period of seventeen years.[34] Based on the urgency and importance of the issue, desertification became one of UNEP's core program areas. UNEP invested considerable resources into continued research and scientific assessment of the gravity of the problem, deployed its convening and awareness-raising power to elevate the issue politically, and created the necessary policy and legal framework at the international and national levels.

In its 1979 annual report, UNEP emphasized that "the loss of arable soil is probably the greatest single environmental threat to the future well-being of the planet."[35] Two years earlier, UNEP put the issue on the international political agenda when it hosted the first UN Conference on

Desertification in Nairobi. The scientific basis for the conference included four extensive reviews of existing knowledge about desertification and its relationship to climate, ecological processes, society, and technology, as well as a number of case studies and a set of desertification maps.[36] The conference triggered greater scientific interest and catalyzed the development of national policies. The policy outcome was the United Nations Plan of Action to Combat Desertification (PACD) that was to be implemented at the national level with the goal of preventing and halting desertification. The Plan provided the framework for policy action and remained the main policy instrument from 1977 to 1992, yet little implementation took place. UNEP submitted annual reports to the UN General Assembly on implementation of the Plan and the status of desertification and the challenges in addressing it. Scientific assessments in 1984 and 1991, as Mohammed Kassas, former President of the International Union for the Conservation of Nature (IUCN), wrote in 1994, showed the worldwide advance of desertification and that "efforts undertaken since 1977 were too modest to be effective."[37]

UNEP harnessed scientific knowledge of the complexity of desertification as a "crisis narrative"[38] and made desertification a truly international concern at the 1992 Rio Earth Summit.[39] The first edition of UNEP's *World Atlas of Desertification*, published in 1992, summarized scientific knowledge showing that large areas of the world and large populations were experiencing soil degradation.[40] Desertification, however, has been a disputed topic, as it highlighted the tension between scientific concerns and political priorities (see box 4.2).[41] The calls for global political action and an international legal instrument continued and, in 1994, governments signed the United Nations Convention to Combat Desertification (UNCCD). They located its secretariat in Geneva, Switzerland, and, in 1999, the secretariat moved to Bonn. The Global Environment Facility provides the convention's financing mechanism.

Despite increased political attention, scientific studies, and regulatory approaches, desertification—or land degradation, as it is now known—"still remains a largely unresolved issue," Steve Lonergan, director of the science division at UNEP, wrote in 2005.[42] And, fifteen years later, the problem has only been exacerbated. The journal *Nature* reported that over 70 percent of Africa is impacted by drought, and scientists from

Box 4.2
Desertification Disputes

Desertification was among UNEP's early priorities that presented challenges to its scientific reputation and political clout. Scholars criticized UNEP for unsubstantiated science, an alarmist political stance, and inability to deliver on a solution to the environmental problem at hand. The methodologies for the monitoring and assessment of desertification that FAO and UNEP had employed in the 1980s and early 1990s were disparaged as imprecise, mixing quantitative and qualitative measurements and having a large number of implicit assumptions. UNEP's scientific assessment of the early 1990s estimated that 70 percent of all drylands had been affected by desertification and that "at least one third of the present global deserts are man-made, [and] the result of human misuse of the land."

Ultimately, scholars noted, "although large amounts of resources were invested to inventory desertification during the 1980s and early 1990s, these did not translate into a significant increase in our knowledge of desertification status." The global assessments revealed that basic knowledge about desertification was insufficient and that the methodologies used were "more like an autopsy than a preventive diagnostic: once soil is lost, the chances of preventing further desertification and the economic feasibility of restoration are almost nil."

Without clear scientific grounding, it has been difficult to create, support, and implement the policy framework for action. National development plans did not integrate anti-desertification measures, and legislation to stop human-induced drivers was lacking. Despite the personal interest and investment of Executive Director Mostafa Tolba, who felt compelled to press for action, desertification did not become a priority for African governments or donor countries. The Inter-Agency Working Group on Desertification that governments created generated little interest and attracted a mere $167,000 in the ten-year period of 1978–1988, prompting the UN General Assembly to close the account.

the continent are turning to the UN Convention to Combat Desertification to assist them with research and data.[43] While there is a need for improved data and methodologies in environmental monitoring, more rigorous assessment models, accurate databases, and integrated information systems, desertification is no longer a part of UNEP's program of work.[44] The desertification convention is independent, with its own COP, Secretariat, and institutional and administrative mechanism in Bonn,

Germany, and relies on the GEF for its finances. The Executive Secretary, Ibrahim Thiaw, assumed office in 2018 after serving as deputy executive director of UNEP under Achim Steiner and Erik Solheim.

CHEMICALS AND HAZARDOUS WASTE

Much of the original impetus for the modern environmental movement came from the realization of the harmful effects of chemicals on the environment and human health. These effects came into sharp focus in the early 1960s with the publication of Rachel Carson's book *Silent Spring*, which presented a compelling case about the danger of pesticides, DDT in particular. The book catalyzed an environmental movement and led to a ban on the use of DDT in agriculture in the United States, enabling the recovery of endangered species like the bald eagle. It also triggered the creation of the US Environmental Protection Agency in December 1970 and the establishment of an environmental regulatory system. In light of this timing, the issue of chemicals featured prominently on the agenda of the Stockholm Conference and in the Stockholm Action Plan.

As with other international challenges, UNEP began its work on chemicals through the lens of scientific assessment. In response to Recommendation 74 of the Stockholm Action Plan on addressing the effects of "man-made pollutants," UNEP first took action on chemicals in 1976 when it set up the International Registry of Potentially Toxic Chemicals (IRPTC) to ensure the "most appropriate and least damaging use of chemicals and to provide a global early-warning system concerning undesirable environmental side effects."[45] IRPTC was to use information collected by other UN agencies such as FAO, UNESCO, WHO, IARC, IMCO, and ILO,[46] as well as from governments and NGOs. Other agencies were also engaging in this field, and in 1979 countries signed the Convention on Long Range Transboundary Air Pollution, which had been developed by the UN Economic Commission for Europe. They had also recently modified MARPOL, the International Convention for the Prevention of Pollution from Ships, developed under the aegis of the International Maritime Organization. In 1980, WHO, UNEP, and ILO established an International Programme on Chemical Safety.[47] By 1992, the register of that program contained data profiles for over eight hundred chemicals and special files on about eight thousand others that were subject to national regulation.

New, more stringent environmental regulations in the 1970s increased disposal costs and heightened public resistance to disposal of hazardous wastes, leading to a rise in NIMBY (Not In My Back Yard) actions. The result was a pressure to dispose of waste beyond the borders of the countries where it was produced, and companies sought cheap disposal options in Eastern Europe and the developing world, where environmental awareness was nascent and regulation absent. In only a couple of years, as the *Christian Science Monitor* reported, "Western industrial nations ha[d] shipped more than 3.5 million metric tons of toxic waste" because the cost differential was enormous. "Treatment and disposal costs in many industrial countries can hit $1,250 a ton," the *Monitor* reported in 1988. "In Africa, where debt-ridden countries have tended to be short on expertise and on regulations governing toxic wastes, such materials can be dumped for as little as $3 a ton."[48] The exported waste was disposed of in flimsy or corroded containers and leached into the soil, causing serious health damage (see box 4.3). This "garbage imperialism" prompted the development of a convention on the movement of hazardous wastes, the Basel Convention.

Environmental NGOs launched campaigns around this movement of hazardous waste. They sought to raise awareness, stop waste traders by publicly shaming them, and influence the negotiations of an intergovernmental treaty. The intergovernmental process for regulating the trade of toxic waste had begun in the early 1980s when UNEP drafted the Cairo Guidelines on the Environmentally Sound Management of Hazardous Wastes, which the Governing Council approved in 1987. In the mid-1980s, the European Community and the OECD had also established regulations on the trans-frontier movement of hazardous wastes among their member states and amended them in 1986 to include third parties. UNEP played an important role in leading the negotiations for a formal convention. After an intense and politically charged negotiation period of just over a year, governments adopted the convention in 1989.

The convention was hard-fought because a deep division emerged from the start on how to reconcile the principle of free trade with the

Box 4.3
Hazardous Waste in the Village of Koko, Nigeria

In the 1980s, the discovery of dumped toxic waste in African countries awakened environmental awareness in new ways. The fishing village of Koko, Nigeria, made international headlines in 1988 when a Nigerian newspaper, the *Daily Times*, published reports about "over 2,000 drums, sacks, and containers" that were leaking hazardous waste in a vacant residential lot. Reporters had discovered that two Italian firms had negotiated the storage of 18,000 drums of toxic chemicals disguised as building materials for the price of $100 per month. Sitting in the hot sun, the barrels burst open and released the industrial waste contaminated with polychlorinated biphenyls (PCBs) and asbestos. Several people in the village became seriously ill because some had used the barrels to store drinking water. The incident caused an international scandal, and the Nigerian government compelled Italy to take back the waste, which spent many months at sea as no port would accept the toxic-waste barge.

The village of Koko was not an isolated case—there were hundreds of cases of hazardous-waste exports around the world. Western media followed such stories and prompted increased concern about the plight of countries in Africa and Eastern Europe that had nothing to do with the waste generation, were unaware or unable to deal with the environmental and health consequences, and received little or nothing in exchange. The waste trade was therefore labeled "toxic colonialism" and "garbage imperialism."

movement of hazardous waste across borders. Prompted by the private companies that produced and managed the waste, industrialized countries argued for legalized trade with certain regulations. Developing countries, on the other hand, argued for a global ban on waste exports from rich to poor states because they considered regulation as "merely legalizing of a conspicuously unjust practice" and simply a new means of exploitation.[49] Greenpeace actively supported and lobbied for a ban and worked closely with developing-country negotiators. The sharp divisions threatened the demise of the negotiation process that UNEP was shepherding, and Mostafa Tolba worked hard to ensure that the process concluded with the adoption of a convention.

UNEP had committed to the stance that trade should be regulated, not banned completely, taking into account the interests of developing countries. The argument was that some states could not dispose of their toxic materials safely and had to export them to countries where disposal could be carried out in a safe manner. Such trade would happen from countries with low capacity to countries with higher capacity. UNEP recognized the right of developing countries to refuse the import of waste, and as Professor Jennifer Clapp explains, UNEP "saw the main purpose of the [Basel] convention as protecting the rights of developing countries to refuse waste imports."[50] Just like with the Montreal Protocol, agreement on the text of the convention was only achieved in the very last hours of negotiation, in no small measure because of Tolba's "determination and skill in negotiating delicate political issues interspersed with some judicial browbeating."[51] However, as Gerry Cunningham recalls, the intensive process had strained Tolba, and he was hospitalized. After being discharged, he returned immediately to the conference. He donned his suit over his striped pajamas and pulled down the leg of the pajamas over his shoes so delegates could see it, and he made an emotional plea to them: "I had to get out of my sick bed to come and convince you to come to a close."[52] The Basel Convention was adopted on March 22, 1989, and entered into force in May 1992 after ratification from twenty member states.

The Basel negotiations had been extremely difficult and confrontational, as states held widely divergent positions. The Convention got off to a fragile start, as disappointment with the outcome was prevalent, though for opposite reasons, both among industrialized countries and their industries, and among developing countries and environmental NGOs. Developing countries and Greenpeace continued to lobby for a ban to the transport of hazardous waste and, in 1995, the Ban Amendment to the Basel Convention was adopted.[53] The Ban prohibits the export of hazardous waste for any reason, including recycling, from a list of mostly OECD countries to developing countries. The Basel Ban amendment entered into force in December 2019. The European Union, Norway, and Switzerland had already fully implemented the Basel Ban through their own legislation.

In 2019, parties to the Basel Convention adopted an amendment that adds plastic waste to the scope of regulated wastes subject to prior notification and consent as established under the convention. In establishing a Partnership on Plastic Waste, parties committed to public-private cooperation, exchange of best practices, and technical assistance to minimize and manage plastic waste. The amendment will make it harder for developed countries to export plastic waste for processing in developing countries, which, the *Guardian* stated, mismanage more than 70 percent of their own plastic waste.[54]

UNEP has undertaken scientific assessments of chemicals and produced two editions of a comprehensive *Global Chemicals Outlook* (in 2015 and 2019). It has actively engaged and collaborated with other UN agencies, including FAO and WHO, and worked on a range of chemical regulations, many of which resulted in international treaties, including the 1989 London Guidelines for the Exchange of Information on Chemicals in International Trade, the 1998 Rotterdam Convention on Prior Informed Consent promoting shared responsibility between exporting and importing countries of hazardous chemicals, the 2001 Stockholm Convention on Persistent Organic Pollutants, and the 2013 Minamata Convention on Mercury. It also provides administrative support and hosts the secretariat of the Strategic Approach to International Chemicals Management (SAICM), a policy framework that promotes chemical safety around the world. These treaties and instruments were the result of multi-year science and policy collaborations that both responded to and generated increased international concern about pollution and hazardous waste.[55]

With the proliferation of regulatory instruments and conventions, UNEP has sought to step into its coordination role and created a joint secretariat for the three chemicals conventions it manages—Basel, Rotterdam, and Stockholm. Rolph Payet, the executive secretary of the joint secretariat, noted that the "synergies [processes] brought scientists together and the secretariat became more effective." However, he warns, "negotiations became more challenging" since the issues are now joint, making them more complex and engaging more actors. "Cooperation with other agreements, however, is limited," Payet remarked, and "at UNEA, there is not enough representation."[56] Moreover, the UN Environment Assembly (UNEA), as chapter 7 explains, is a political forum where discussions are broad and not as specific as they are during the conferences of the parties to the various multilateral environmental agreements.

CLIMATE CHANGE

Climate change had been on the international agenda even before the Stockholm Conference. General Assembly Resolution 1721 (xvi) on international cooperation of the peaceful uses of outer space, adopted in 1961, triggered the establishment of the World Weather Watch program at the World Meteorological Organization (WMO) and the joint Global Atmospheric Research Programme of WMO and the International Council for Science.[57] The evolution of the climate change regime illustrates the importance of the sequential arrangement of initiatives—a scientific conference that issues a joint call for action, the creation of an international legal instrument and institutional arrangements, and their subsequent implementation. Member states are not the only actors within this progression but certainly hold the power to create legal arrangements and ensure their operation. It also evidences the dynamics between international institutions and member states, the importance of the geopolitical context at the time, and the influence of individuals.[58]

The sixth special session of the UN General Assembly in 1974 set up the WMO Executive Committee Panel of Experts on Climate Change, which collaborated with UNEP and other UN agencies and scientific organizations to convene "a world conference of experts on climate and mankind"—the first World Climate Conference—in 1979 in Geneva. Over 350 specialists from fifty-three countries and twenty-four international organizations participated, representing a wide range of disciplines.[59] The conference called for the "urgent development of a common strategy for a greater understanding of the climate system and a rational use of climate information, and proposed the establishment of the World Climate Programme."[60] The World Meteorological Congress established the World Climate Programme in 1979 with the aim of developing scientific knowledge and understanding of the climate system for the benefit of societies dealing with climate change.[61] The program was an interagency, interdisciplinary effort among WMO, UNEP, and ICSU, with a mandate to collect and assess climate-related data, conduct research, evaluate impacts and response systems, and operationalize climate action.[62] Under this umbrella, the international and scientific institutions worked together and engaged the research community in understanding and communicating the role of increasing greenhouse gas concentrations in the atmosphere on global warming. In the process, they applied the sequence that had worked so well for ozone: conference, call for action, legal instrument, and/or institutions.

In October 1985, UNEP, WMO, and ICSU convened the Villach Conference for an assessment of the role of greenhouse gases on climate change. The conference produced a highly influential statement noting the risk of global warming in the first half of the twenty-first century, calling on the three institutions to carry out periodic assessments of the state of scientific understanding and its practical implications, and to begin the development of a global convention.[63] As a result, in 1988, UNEP and WMO initiated the creation of the Intergovernmental Panel on Climate Change (IPCC) to provide policymakers with regular assessments of the scientific basis of climate change, its impacts and future risks, and response strategies for mitigation and adaptation. It was at this point that discussions about a global climate convention began. More than 300 scientists and policymakers gathered at the World Conference on the Changing Atmosphere: Implications for Global Security, held in 1988 in Toronto, Canada. The Toronto Conference Statement called upon governments, the United Nations and its specialized agencies, industry, educational institutions, NGOs, and individuals "to take specific actions to reduce the impending crisis caused by the pollution of the atmosphere."[64] It also advocated support for the proposed IPCC and for the development of a comprehensive global framework convention on climate change.[65] UNFCCC would be signed several years later, in 1992 at the Rio Earth Summit.

UNEP—in collaboration with WMO and the scientific community—was instrumental and highly influential in the creation of the international climate regime. It collaborated effectively with agencies in the UN system to raise awareness about the risks of climate change and linked it to health, agriculture, food security, and natural disasters. For example, the findings of a 1996 study on climate and health that UNEP, WHO, and WMO conducted established that climate change would affect the health of a large number of people across the world. The study warned of a multitude of new and reemergent diseases, including a resurgence of infectious diseases such as malaria.[66] With strong scientific evidence and active political pressure, countries came to a strategic judgment that the climate issue was important and that it was much bigger than the classic pollution issues. Governments, however, also began to move climate out of UNEP's orbit.

Michael Zammit Cutajar noted that "governments were not looking for a secretariat that would lead the negotiations, headed by a strong, assertive leader, as had been the case with earlier convention negotiations under UNEP auspices."[67] The driver for moving climate into UN central as opposed to UNEP, he argued, was also the fact that some governments—initially Brazil and Mexico—having analyzed the first assessment of the IPCC, concluded that climate change was a serious economic issue, much more important than the classic pollution issues, and their political judgment was that it was central to economic strategy. Such governments, therefore, had to keep the issue under their own control, and began taking the negotiations out of UNEP.

Even so, currently climate change shapes much of UNEP's substantive work, and one of its seven subprograms is on climate change. The two large divisions—economy and ecosystems—each have full-fledged programs on climate change. About half of the work for the ecosystems division is on climate change, as is about a quarter of the economy division's. UNEP also hosts the secretariat of the Green Climate Fund with over $40 million in project funds. Climate change is thus bigger than all the other subprograms.[68] Some of UNEP's achievements in climate-change mitigation include the launch of the UN Secretary-General's global initiative Sustainable Energy for All, which UNEP helped to shape, and the creation of the UNFCCC Climate Technology Centre and Network, which UNEP hosts collaboratively with UNIDO.

Ultimately, UNEP's key goal is a transition to low carbon, resource-efficient, equitable, sustainable development. This broad goal, an internal evaluation states, "doesn't pin down the changes UNEP hopes to contribute to in the longer term in terms of impact on the environment and human well-being," but it provides a clear vision for the trajectory of the organization's work.[69] UNEP's assessment work is instrumental in moving toward this goal, including the influential black carbon assessment, emissions gap report, and the assessment of short-lived climate pollutants, among others.[70] Climate, however, is an overarching concern and has a strong convention secretariat in Bonn, where powerful executive secretaries have carved out discrete institutional space. "The distance from New York allowed the UNFCCC secretariat to develop its own corporate culture," remarked Christiana Figueres, Executive Secretary from 2010 to 2016.[71] The climate convention engages actively with stakeholders, and its annual conferences of the parties held around the world have become convening platforms for individuals and institutions, not just bully pulpits for governments. Climate change has indeed mobilized an engaged global constituency of activists.

The youth movement Fridays for Future, the international movement Extinction Rebellion, and Fire Drill Fridays, led by Jane Fonda in Washington, DC, starkly illustrate the power of civil society in climate activism. During COP25 in Madrid, Spain, in December 2019, half a million people participated in a climate strike led by Greta Thunberg. Climate activists protested and urged ambitious action from industrialized states, and over three hundred people were banned from the venue.[72] By not allowing activists in the plenary, member states rolled back the slim progress the UN had made over the last years in engaging civil society.

BIODIVERSITY

Biological diversity is being depleted and degraded faster than ever before in human history. Much like with climate change, "humans are the main culprit in biodiversity loss."[73] Conservation of wildlife was one of the central topics of the Stockholm Conference in 1972, and biodiversity was a priority for UNEP from the outset. An international legal regime for biodiversity, however, was already in existence and comprised a range of longstanding legal instruments and institutions. One of the first biodiversity treaties, the Convention for the Regulation of Whaling, was signed in 1946. The Ramsar Convention on International Wetlands and the World Heritage Convention were adopted in 1971 and 1972, respectively, and are administered by the International Union for the Conservation of Nature and by UNESCO. Two other conventions followed—the Convention on the International Trade in Endangered Species of Wild Fauna and Flora (CITES) in 1973 and the Convention on the Conservation of Migratory Species (CMS) in 1979—and UNEP assumed their administration.

UNEP became a key player in international biodiversity research and conservation.[74] It served as a convening agency of the Intergovernmental Science-Policy Platform on Biodiversity and Ecosystem Services (IPBES), the intergovernmental body which, in response to requests from decision makers, assesses the state of biodiversity and of the ecosystem services it provides to society. IPBES seeks to harness expertise across scientific disciplines and knowledge communities, provide relevant and timely knowledge to decision makers, and facilitate implementation of policies. In 2019, its first *Global Assessment Report on Biodiversity and Ecosystem Services*, prepared by 145 leading experts from fifty countries, stated unequivocally that one million species are at risk of extinction. The unraveling of the planetary web of life threatens the survival of humanity. Tom Lovejoy, the conservation biologist known as "the Godfather of Biodiversity," warns that "we now sit at the fail-safe point and must decide what to do."[75] The assessment articulates the challenges and urges action to ensure a viable future for humanity and the rest of the species on earth. But former Director General of IUCN Julia Marton-Lefèvre argues that there is hardly a need for two separate intergovernmental panels on biodiversity and climate change. "Healthy ecosystems have a huge role in both adaptation and mitigation. And so why do we need to address this in two different ways, in two different places on the planet? In 1992 many of us said at least put them in the same city, so they could help each other."[76] The institutional landscape for biodiversity itself is complex, with about a dozen conventions and protocols, many focused on different species and ecosystems. In 1989, governments requested that UNEP lead negotiations for a new legal instrument, a framework convention with the purpose of rationalizing existing activities in the rather crowded institutional landscape for biodiversity.[77]

From the early stages of the negotiation process for the Convention on Biological Diversity (CBD), UNEP faced several challenges. Some came from UN agencies, others from member states. During the initial rounds of negotiations, FAO was "reluctant to shed parts of its turf"[78] and share authority. It was concerned that CBD would interfere with its newly established International Undertaking on Plant Genetic Resources.[79] The other conservation conventions also valued their independence and were not enthusiastic about a framework convention. In addition to feelings of mistrust, the negotiations for the CBD were fraught with vagueness and political strife. Unlike with ozone or climate change, a strong body of scientific evidence was lacking for the protection of species, which was part of the difficulty the biodiversity convention had in capturing the attention of the world community. Climate change was an issue with a long tradition of scientific research which connected to the public. Biodiversity was not. As Professor Calestous Juma remarked, "CBD was really negotiated purely as a consolidation of existing instruments, and so it was more of an administrative convention as opposed to being a substantive convention. Even when I was in CBD," Juma recalled, "and I knew it was driven by lawyers rather than scientists, I never thought of the consequences." An important issue, he noted, was the difficulty of having a discussion on technology in the CBD. While the climate convention endorsed the role of emerging renewable energy technologies as a solution, "CBD became hostile to biotechnology by negotiating the biosafety protocol to regulate GMOs, and anyone who had any idea about how technology could be used in conservation just never went to the CBD."[80]

Biodiversity negotiations were strenuous and divergent because of the persistent conflict between developing and developed countries. The natural resource endowments of the Global South generally outweigh those of the North, and attempts to regulate them echoed the debates about environment and development that had happened in the build-up to the Stockholm Conference. Developed countries saw biodiversity as a common heritage, while developing countries perceived it as an attempt to implement nature conservation outside developed countries' own territory. Developing countries sought to protect their sovereignty over the biological resources within their borders; to provide settlements, food, transport, and raw materials for their people; and to receive a fair share of the benefits from the use of genetic resources. They also wanted developed countries to limit demand for resources and to help finance biodiversity protection in the South.[81] Over time, these divides seemed insurmountable, and "the Convention's detractors dismiss[ed] it as a prisoner of its own politics rather than being based on sound science."[82] The signing and ratification of the CBD, therefore, was another environmental achievement against long odds.

The tensions between the Global North and South were real, however, and extended into the CBD's implementation phase. For example, UNEP had launched the *Global Biodiversity Assessment* in 1993 and completed it in 1995 when results were presented at a meeting of the Subsidiary Body on Scientific, Technical and Technological Advice (SBSTTA) to the biodiversity convention. Some delegates declared the assessment illegitimate, however. As one of the national delegates put it "we didn't ask for it, we don't want it, and if it is produced we won't use it!"[83] The assessment was science-driven, engaging more than 1,550 scientists across the world, and confirmed that "biodiversity is especially important to provide resilience to ecosystems, enabling them to adapt to changing conditions."[84]

Given these enduring political tensions, the biodiversity regime has faced structural challenges and has become highly fragmented.[85] There are tensions within the scientific community, as Ehsan Masood explained in *Nature*. "The world of biodiversity research is like an extended family that has split into feuding factions. Scientists from less-prosperous southern countries have squared off against colleagues from the wealthier north, and researchers from more empirical disciplines are arguing with those from humanities and the social sciences."[86] Even UNEP, a driving force behind IPBES, also runs a somewhat competing study on The Economics of Ecosystems and Biodiversity (TEEB).

UNEP has undertaken efforts aimed at enhancing coherence and coordination and has initiated a process of harmonizing reporting requirements for the five biodiversity-related conventions—the Convention on Biological Diversity, CITES, the Convention on Migratory Species, the Ramsar Convention on Wetlands, and the World Heritage Convention—and the two regional seas conventions with biodiversity-related protocols—the Barcelona and Cartagena Conventions.[87] While a common website and a biodiversity clearinghouse mechanism have been established, there has been little substantive progress toward the practical implementation of a common reporting framework.[88] The various conventions have different institutional homes, making synergies difficult to achieve. UNEP also recently launched initiatives to identify options that enhance synergies among biodiversity conventions toward the implementation of the Sustainable Development Goals, though that effort is too nascent to assess.[89]

FORESTS

Deforestation emerged as an important concern in the mid-1970s, when scientific assessments pointed to a pressing problem. In 1979, the US Department of State held an international conference on tropical forests, and in 1980 UNEP organized an expert meeting on the topic.[90] A decade later, in 1990, the United States proposed the negotiation of a global forest convention, and UNEP received a mandate to lead this process for developing new international environmental law. Despite prolonged negotiations on a legal instrument, however, no international convention for forests could be established because of the deep divide between the Global North and South. Like biological resources more generally, most forests are located in the Global South, and developing countries have been protective of their sovereignty and their development agendas.[91] In addition, deforestation is driven by a growing demand for timber from industrialized countries, making the negotiations politically combustible.

As a result, in 1992, governments negotiated and adopted non-binding Forest Principles rather than a forest convention, yet left a window open for a binding agreement at a later stage.[92] To date, multiple attempts to bring this question back onto the agenda have not succeeded, and the forest-related institutional framework remains divided and contested.[93] With a relatively modest work program on forests, UNEP plays a catalytic role and has to undertake activities in partnership with a number of other organizations, including UNDP, FAO, UNESCO, the World Bank, and other development banks.[94] UNEP is also part of the UN's Inter-Agency Task Force on Forests, where it plays a leading role and, jointly with UNDP and FAO, established the UN Collaborative Program on Reducing Emissions from Deforestation and Forest Degradation in Developing Countries (UN-REDD). In 2000, UNEP produced a scientific assessment to again underscore the importance of deforestation and in 2008 facilitated the creation of the governance structure of the Congo Basin Forest Fund to mobilize resources to support the equitable and sustainable use, conservation, and management of Congo Basin forests and ecosystems. Professor Wangari Maathai of Kenya co-chaired the Fund, along with Canadian Prime Minister Paul Martin. Despite its relevant work in the global forest regime, however, UNEP never became the driver or center of gravity in this space.[95]

UNEP engages in activities across a range of environmental concerns, but it acts as one among many institutions. What is missing in global environmental governance is the space for all institutions to come and piece together the larger puzzle. UNEP's governing body, the universal UN Environment Assembly, could possibly provide such an opportunity, as chapter 7 explains.

CONCLUSION

Ultimately, UNEP is a small organization with a large mandate and an expectation that it will address global environmental problems. Resolving the depletion of the ozone layer is perhaps UNEP's most successful achievement. The institution effectively deployed all of its functions—scientific assessment, policy development, and coordination of actions across the UN system and across governments—and its leadership committed fully to addressing this global problem. It developed the capacity—human, institutional, and financial—connected to the relevant constituencies, and gained authority as it delivered a solution. Over the years, UNEP identified a range of other environmental problems, developed scientific knowledge about them, informed and developed policy, and prompted governments to act upon assessments by creating international environmental law. It set in place scientifically rigorous systems for environmental assessments, raised awareness, created legal regimes, and developed policy instruments. Indeed, because of its work, governments created a range of multilateral environmental agreements and a range of new institutions.

In the first two decades, commanding leadership by Executive Director Mostafa Tolba elevated UNEP's authority. Inevitably, however, the commanding style alienated some governments. Desertification, biodiversity, forests, and climate change were all concerns that UNEP had been working on for years before the 1992 Rio Earth Summit. It had engaged scientists, raised awareness, and appealed to enlightened self-interest and the common public good. It had produced studies and reports, convened conferences, created networks, and harnessed public opinion. However, serious commitment to action remained hamstrung by tensions between the priorities and expectations of industrialized and developing countries.

Developed countries promised financing but did not deliver, and developing countries had difficulty utilizing resources effectively. Fundamental difficulties arose in conceptualizing and operationalizing economic, political, and social models that could maintain essential ecological processes and life support systems in the face of excessive exploitation to satisfy growing consumption needs. As environmental problems grew ever more complex and global, and as the geopolitical reality shifted toward heightened tensions and increased conflict, UNEP found it challenging to exhibit the requisite authority.

Rapid worldwide expansion of economic activity relying on extraction of natural resources, destruction of habitats, and growing consumption was a major cause of environmental decline. "Yet," Gus Speth warned, "the world economy, now increasingly integrated and globalized, is poised for unprecedented growth" that would prove damaging to the natural capital upon which all life on Earth depends.[96] With the dichotomy between economic growth and environmental protection deeply lodged in the outlook of individuals and governments worldwide, UNEP has been close to powerless to change behavior considerably, and its achievements have been hard-won.

The geographic dispersion of the convention secretariats has taxed UNEP's ability to administer, manage, and coordinate. Meanwhile, the emergence of sustainable development as the new paradigm that subsumed environment affected UNEP's standing and authority. "The flourishing of new international institutions," UN Secretary-General Kofi Annan noted in 1998, "pose[d] problems of coordination, eroding responsibilities and resulting in duplication of work as well as increased demand upon ministries and government."[97] Without the ease of communication—in person and virtually—that is necessary to connect with organizations, governments, groups, and individuals, collaboration has been difficult. Connectivity requires functional and affordable infrastructure. Communication also hinges on leadership and the skills to convey a message in a relevant, relatable manner. The next two chapters turn to the impacts of location and leadership.

5

PLACE MATTERS: IMPACTS OF LOCATION ON CAPACITY AND CONNECTIVITY

From our tower in the heart of Africa, we must envisage the whole earth, and foresee the challenges that face each man in the proper use of the earth's resources so that all people may thrive and no one suffer needlessly. Working together—HARAMBEE—should become the theme ... for a world that now has the capability, knowledge, and opportunity to create a better human environment for all people. The ingredient most needed to bring about this kind of world is the spirit of HARAMBEE—let's work together.

—Maurice Strong at the inauguration of UNEP's Headquarters in Nairobi, 1973[1]

Traditionally used by porters in coastal Kenya, the term *harambee*, a Swahili word meaning "let us all pull together," came to symbolize a way of life in Kenya and became Kenya's national motto, inscribed on its coat of arms. As the nation gained independence, President Jomo Kenyatta used the word to rally Kenyans and mobilize citizen contributions to nation building through donations of funds, materials, and labor.[2] This noble initiative, however, became the epitome of corruption and patronage politics in Kenya.[3] When Kenya became the first developing country to host the headquarters of a United Nations organization, the spirit of collaboration for a new and better global order was palpable. However, Nairobi experienced serious security challenges and has continued to struggle with debilitating corruption. In its first three decades, Kenya experienced notable communication and infrastructure difficulties. This, in turn, affected UNEP's capacity and connectivity and, ultimately, its credibility as the authoritative anchor institution for the global environment.

In 1972, Kenya made a compelling argument that developing countries needed a stronger voice in the UN system and that hosting the headquarters of a UN body would ensure equitable distribution of UN institutions around the world. The Nairobi location has been a source of pride, as it became the first and only city outside the Global North to host one of the three UN offices away from headquarters, along with Geneva and Vienna. UNEP's presence in Nairobi did increase Kenya's stature in global governance, presented new opportunities, and spurred innovation. It did not, however, automatically lead to greater input from developing countries, as originally envisioned. Fifty years after UNEP's creation, only 36 percent of developing countries have diplomatic missions in Nairobi. Furthermore, travel to Kenya from most developing countries continues to be expensive and time-consuming. The lack of reliable connectivity in terms of communications and infrastructure has limited UNEP's ability to connect to constituencies and the rest of the UN system. As a result, UNEP's marginalization was particularly acute into the 1990s. These issues have since been addressed as Kenya transformed into a communications-technology hub in Africa in the 2000s. Insecurity and corruption, however, continue and impose high costs not only in financial terms (since the United Nations has to maintain security capacity) but by contributing to uncertainty and anxiety, which ultimately affects Nairobi's attractiveness as a duty station.

As a result of the constraints it faced in its first few decades, UNEP experienced difficulties in recruiting and retaining staff. Its visibility suffered, and its credibility diminished. Without consistent communication with constituencies, UNEP was challenged to raise the resources necessary to sustain and expand its operations. Moreover, as the first UN organization headquartered in a developing country, UNEP had a responsibility to respond to the needs, contribute to the capacity, and elevate the voice of the countries whose interests remained neglected. As a means of meeting this need, UNEP staff moved toward greater operational engagement than the mandate outlined. Ultimately, the bold vision (or, some might say, the political gamble) to locate the headquarters in Nairobi has been

5.1 Opening ceremonies of UNEP Headquarters in Nairobi. Left: President Jomo Kenyatta (center) with Foreign Minister Dr. Njoroge Mungai (left) and UNEP Executive Director Maurice Strong (right). Right: President Kenyatta signing the visitors' book at UNEP. Credit: Nation Media Group Plc Library and Standard Group Plc Library.

beneficial in many respects, both to UNEP and to Kenya as the host country. While many have expressed concern, the fear that the headquarters might be moved to another city, such as Geneva or New York, has made a systematic examination of the location largely taboo.[4]

This chapter addresses the location question head on, but it is not intended to serve as a compendium of Nairobi's challenges nor of its unique features. Rather, it seeks to foster a deeper understanding of how UNEP's location has shaped its performance in its first fifty years and how UNEP has in turn affected its host community. It shows the promise of Nairobi, examines its realities, and analyzes location effects on UNEP and on Kenya. Nairobi, a city of paradoxes, has been challenging in terms of security and connectivity but also inspiring with its profound connection to the environment and its technological dynamism and innovation. Location has influenced UNEP's capacity in terms of staff, resources, and connectivity. Its Nairobi location has demanded greater operational engagement from the anchor institution for the global environment. Torn between a normative and an operational role, UNEP has been both constrained and enabled by its location in Kenya, and this has intensified its search for identity.

KENYA'S POWERFUL PROMISE

Until Kenya's successful bid for the location of the headquarters of the new UN environmental body, UNEP, in 1972, all headquarters of international organizations had been located in the Global North. Kenya's vision was to claim a greater role in the UN system through direct participation in the work of UN agencies. The United Nations was a "global body and it was unfair that its agencies should be confined to North America or Western Europe," Kenya argued in the UN General Assembly in 1972, and, as chapter 2 explained, there was nothing inherent or sacrosanct about that fact.[5] As the UN system grew, it was only logical for it to adapt to the new realities, decentralize its operations, and include a much broader constituency in its daily operations. The expectation was that hosting the UN Environment Programme would bring political capital to the developing world and enable countries to be equal partners in global policymaking. Economic and technical issues, "difficulties of communications and the problems of remoteness from research centers," the Kenyan government argued, were a small price to pay for this political achievement.[6]

Indeed, Kenya offered a powerful promise. It had gained independence from the United Kingdom in 1963 and adopted a political path that rejected both rampant capitalism and doctrinal socialism. Navigating Cold War politics adeptly, Kenya became a strategic regional partner to the West, which sought to stop communist influence from Ethiopia and Tanzania and infused foreign aid, making Kenya one of the most prosperous African countries. Significant foreign investment flowed into Kenya, economic growth increased, employment opportunities emerged, and education and health care expanded. Kenya was a nation on the rise, often described as the Switzerland of Africa and a Garden of Eden.[7] The country boasted a range of landscapes: a coastline on the Indian Ocean, savannahs, and snow-capped mountains as well as a mild climate. Several national parks, including Nairobi National Park and the Maasai Mara National Reserve, among others, had been created long before independence and made Kenya a desirable destination offering a unique quality of life.

The oil crises of the 1970s and a decline in coffee prices led to some uncertainty and economic decline, but Kenya's overall economic performance was stable and strong from 1964 to 1980, recording an average

GDP growth of 5 percent each year. Subsequently, however, the 1980s and 1990s marked a difficult period in Kenya's economic and political history under President Daniel arap Moi (1978–2002). The country bounced back during the terms of President Mwai Kibaki (2002–2013) and Uhuru Kenyatta (2013–present) and restored its position as "the anchor" in the East African Community. Kenya's vibrant and resilient economy is now considered "Africa's powerhouse," as it attracts major flows of investment and trade, is relatively stable, and operates within a "somewhat democratic" political environment.[8] Kenya also boasts an advanced human-capital base, a dynamic private sector, and a cutting-edge information communication and mobile money services sector. This evolution has been connected to the presence of UNEP and the United Nations family in Nairobi, which has been an important driver for improvements in Kenya's infrastructure and institutions as well as in its human-capital capacity. The demand for connectivity by the international organizations located in Nairobi and the international community they attract contributed to the development of technological and financial capabilities and to Kenya becoming the "Silicon Savannah" in East and Central Africa.

Kenya's promise launched the country on a trajectory of influence in the region and beyond. It has, however, been marred by security concerns and by corruption scandals that have earned Kenya the rank of the third most corrupt country in the world.[9] And, as Kenya's Ethics and Anti-Corruption Commission announced in 2018, every year the country loses one third of its state budget, or $6 billion, to corruption. As a result, the public has lost confidence in law enforcement and the state institutions.[10] Although the UN operations in Nairobi have stayed clear of corruption and are relatively insulated from the country's security problems, the continued presence of these acute societal challenges in the host country has impacted Nairobi's attractiveness as a duty station. Kenya has presented a paradox of promise and peril that has shaped the capabilities of the United Nations Environment Programme that it hosts.

THE NAIROBI PARADOX

Kenya's political trajectory and its economic, institutional, and security context have evolved over the decades since independence. Jomo Kenyatta, an ardent fighter for independence, became Kenya's first president and provided powerful symbolic leadership. He helped create a solvent, functional economy, the *New York Times* wrote in 1975, but the *Times* also noted that he abused his power, amassed a fortune, and allowed high-level officials to operate with impunity.[11] As Kenya's population grew rapidly, unemployment, hunger, poverty, and disease persisted, and the country lacked the infrastructure and communication services necessary to ensure the smooth operation of an international agency. Insecurity became a pressing, prevalent problem in Kenya.[12]

A deadly explosion at a Nairobi hotel on New Year's Eve in 1980 illustrated that Nairobi was a soft terrorist target, and a 1982 coup attempt against President Moi resulted in anarchy, widespread looting, and chaos in the streets of the capital. This led to a government crackdown on universities that were suspected to have been infiltrated by rebels, withdrawal of support from African-owned private banks (which led to their collapse), political repression, economic downturn, and increased securitization of the state. The economy plunged and poverty struck Kenya's populace. With an average annual Kenyan income as low as $1 a day, bad governance and rampant corruption took hold, and Kenya became known as "one of the most corrupt countries in the world."[13] The two and a half decades of the Moi presidency (1978–2002) were characterized by increased crime and pervasive uncertainty, insecurity, and lawlessness. Armed robberies and carjackings became commonplace in Nairobi, earning it the nickname "Nairobbery." "Sudden brutal attacks, brazen threats, encounters with young hoodlums desperate for quick cash became normal on the streets of Nairobi," Dr. Edwin Gimode of Kenyatta University wrote in an analysis of crime and insecurity in Kenya.[14] Government corruption led to major crimes going unpunished "even if they attracted considerable attention and censure in the press"[15] because the police force and the justice system were consistently ranked by international agencies as the two most corrupt institutions in in the country. Basic security and justice were thus completely lacking in the country.[16]

Yet civil society fought relentlessly and won some important battles. Wangari Maathai, the founder of the Green Belt Movement, one of the most prominent grassroots women's organizations in the world, and subsequently a Nobel Peace Prize Laureate, led the opposition to the plundering of Karura Forest, the largest urban forest in Africa, in the late 1990s. The Moi government had divided the forest into thousands of parcels and sold or gifted them to its political allies. Construction started deep inside the forest in the hope that it would go unnoticed, but Maathai discovered it and led the civil disobedience against the powerful interests responsible for deforestation. She went to court, held press conferences, and led groups into the forest to stop the trucks destroying it. She was arrested, jailed, and beaten.[17] "If I ever thought I would lose my mother, this was one time," Wanjira Mathai, Maathai's daughter and now regional director for Africa of the World Resources Institute, exclaimed. "My mother led this campaign that grew to include a collective of clergy, politicians, students and the general public—people who showed up at every march to say 'No' to corruption and greed. Very quickly the wave was too big for the authorities to subdue and the forest was finally saved."[18] Wangari Maathai's fight and her important victories inspired a vibrant civil society and strengthened the power of democratic actors in Kenya.

Adding to these challenges, conflicts erupted in Africa, several of them in close proximity to Kenya, including the Somali civil war in 1991, the Rwandan genocide in 1994, and the Congo wars in 1996. A massive explosion ripped through the American embassy in Nairobi in August 1998, killing more than two hundred and injuring thousands; Al Qaeda claimed responsibility. The attacks added to ongoing ethnic violence in Kenya facilitated by the widespread availability of cheap weapons.[19] In 2001, the International Civil Service Commission (ICSC) downgraded Nairobi's security rating from a B to a C to reflect increasing tensions and decreased security.[20] International financial institutions and donor governments reduced their aid as a way to demand political and economic reforms, and Kenya lost its reputation as one of Africa's most stable and prosperous countries.[21]

While in 2002 the transition of power to Mwai Kibaki was peaceful, the 2007 presidential election—a contest between Mwai Kibaki and Raila Odinga—resulted in tribal hostility and violence that brought Kenya to the brink of civil war and rattled the entire East Africa region.[22] Violent attacks ensued, homes were burned, and families were forced to flee. More than 1,100 Kenyans died in the post-election violence, and 350,000 were displaced.[23] The African Union's Panel of Eminent African Personalities,

5.2 The environmental activist Professor Wangari Maathai in police custody, and in Karura Forest in November 1998. Credit: KTN Kenya and Standard Group Plc Library.

chaired by Kofi Annan, mediated an end to the conflict and brokered a power-sharing agreement. The post-election violence highlighted the fragility of democracy and peace in Kenya, ultimately resulting in high levels of crime and violence, reduction in quality of life, constraints on mobility, and erosion of trust in the state.

Kenya has continued to struggle with safety and security. Uhuru Kenyatta (referred to as Uhuru), the son of Kenya's first President, Jomo Kenyatta, became the country's fourth president in April 2013, and in September of that year, an attack at the upscale Westgate shopping mall claimed seventy-one lives, including sixty-two civilians.[24] Attacks in the provinces followed, with bombings in Mpeketoni, Lamu County, and Garissa University in the northeast. In 2015, even though ICSC upgraded Kenya back to level B, the country ranked as the twenty-first most fragile state out of 178 countries as measured by the Fragile States Index.[25] In January 2019, another attack shook the Kenyan capital when explosions and shootings occurred at a cluster of upmarket shops and hotels in the middle of the afternoon, leaving over twenty dead and forcing hundreds to flee. To this day, pervasive insecurity undermines Kenya's stability and poses a threat to the safety and well-being of all.

Much of the insecurity traces back to what the *Sunday Standard* called "runaway corruption" that has become the norm and has resulted in the "plunder of a nation."[26] The scale and scope of corruption are mobilizing an increasing public outcry. "Greed and selfishness have become embedded into Kenya's fabric," Wanjira Mathai noted in her TED talk in 2019. "From greedy politicians lining their pockets at the public's expense to shady business dealings, [corruption] is everywhere."[27] Kenya's Auditor General, Edward Ouko, reported that one trillion Kenyan shillings, roughly the equivalent of $10 billion, is lost every year. This amounts to more than the Kenyan government's annual expenditures on health and education combined and is the equivalent of the GDP of entire countries such as Chad or Madagascar.[28] "Sh368 billion [$3.6 billion] of the Sh1 trillion [$10 billion] is spent without any accountability," the *Sunday Standard* reported. "Not even the chief government gate keeper can keep tabs on the hemorrhage of public funds."[29] Rampant corruption has crippled Kenya under all four regimes. "Neither Jomo Kenyatta nor Daniel arap Moi nor Mwai Kibaki nor Uhuru Kenyatta," states Joe Khamisi in his book, *Kenya: Looters and Grabbers: 54 Years of Corruption and Plunder by the Elite, 1963–2017*, "managed to extinguish the overwhelming fire of graft. Each one of the Kenyan presidents—together with their families and cronies—amassed enormous personal wealth through means which were not entirely lucid or honest." They came from humble beginnings and used their positions of authority to acquire vast amounts of exclusive public land, build luxury residences and buy lavish cars, ransack treasuries, and stash funds in offshore accounts. Each administration, meanwhile, promoted a strong anti-corruption narrative. Kenyatta described corruption as an "enemy" and planned to deal with it. Moi established a range of institutions to fight corruption but all of them failed. Kibaki discussed the need of "slaying the dragon." Uhuru contended that corruption was "the foremost danger facing the country." It has, however, proven too big to handle.[30]

The promise of making UNEP more accessible for developing countries was one of the major reasons why developing countries supported Kenya's proposal to host the new institution in 1972, leading to an overwhelming vote in favor of Nairobi, as chapter 2 illustrated. In reality, the accessibility challenge continues. Developing countries are underrepresented in terms of diplomatic missions, and travel to Nairobi remains expensive and time consuming. Creating diplomatic missions in Nairobi and building a solid diplomatic corps was a tall order, as it entailed financial and human-resource investment. Only 36 percent of developing countries have missions in the Kenyan capital. Even developed countries are represented at only 54 percent, a much lower number compared to New York, Geneva, other European capitals, and even Addis Ababa. As figure 5.3 illustrates, 95 percent of developing countries are represented in New York, 54 percent in Geneva, 73 percent in Bonn, 61 percent in Vienna, 59 percent in Rome, and 46 percent in Addis Ababa.[31] The Latin American and Caribbean Group (GRULAC) has a notably minimal presence in Nairobi. Only seven out of thirty-three GRULAC countries, or 21 percent, are formally present in Nairobi. Given this relatively low concentration of diplomatic representation in Nairobi, channels for interaction and communication with member states have been limited, affecting reputation and opportunities for support, material or otherwise. Furthermore, non-governmental organizations, academics, and other groups have few direct means of

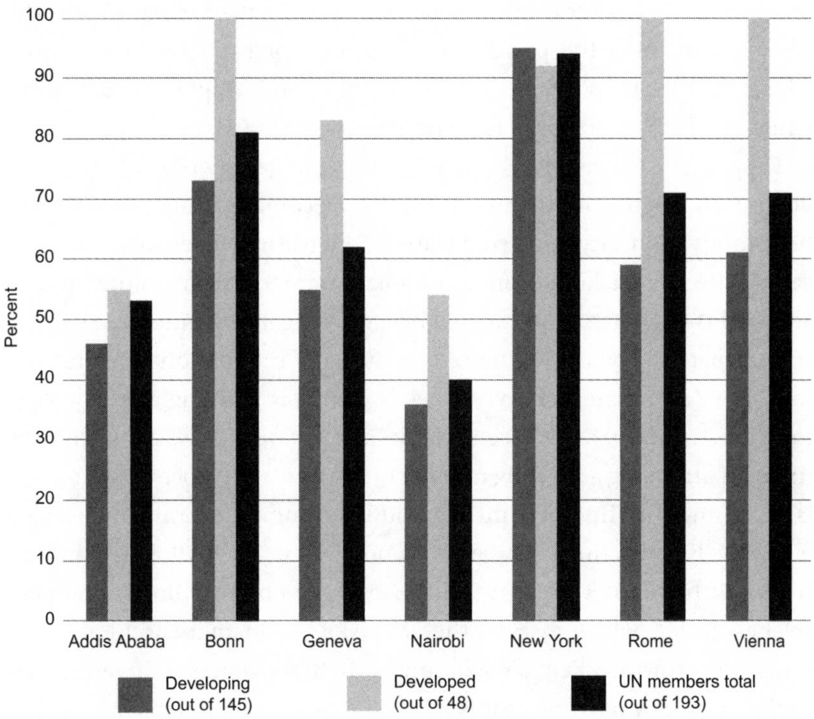

5.3 Member state permanent missions to the United Nations around the world.

interaction, and the temporal, economic, and professional costs to attend events in Nairobi preclude their systematic engagement.

For much of UNEP's existence, the lack of airport connections within Africa meant that delegations from developing countries needed to first fly to a developed-world hub and then connect back to Nairobi. Developing countries have therefore encountered profound difficulties, which, while somewhat ameliorated in recent years, still persist. For example, even in 2019, Ambassador Amal Mudallali, Permanent Representative of Lebanon to the United Nations and co-chair of the ad-hoc working group on a Global Pact for the Environment,[32] remarked that negotiations were hobbled because 60 percent of countries are not represented in Nairobi. None of the small island developing states have missions there, and, lacking the capacity and finances, they simply cannot engage with UNEP.[33] The resulting exclusivity of environmental debates detracts from their legitimacy. Furthermore, the financial cost of convening intergovernmental meetings in Nairobi continues to be much higher than in New York. The cost of convening the preparatory meetings for the negotiations on a Global Pact for the Environment in Nairobi, for example, was $300,000, while in New York it would have been only $80,000.[34]

Despite these challenges, Nairobi has emerged as one of the most vibrant and dynamic African cities. It is becoming a high-technology, high-innovation city that could attract increasing investment, specifically if the political and economic climate were to become more predictable and trustworthy.[35] Stimulated by a growing influx of foreign capital, spurred partially by the existence of a cluster of international institutions in Nairobi and their technology needs, Kenya is building a technology-infrastructure hub, Konza Technology City, just outside Nairobi, with the intent of attracting a growing number of software developers. The country is becoming a technology, media, and telecommunications hub, which is positively impacting its large youth population. In 2019, Kenya ranked ninety-fifth among the 141 countries evaluated by the Global Competitiveness Index, which assesses the drivers of productivity and long-term economic growth.[36] Kenya's standing and attractiveness to investors has increased over time, though it is subject to ebbs and flows in conjunction with the political stability and security situation in the country. Tangible assets such as infrastructure could improve dramatically in a short time frame, and these would in turn strengthen the intangible assets of knowledge and information. Nairobi's rapid technological development will be very positive if coupled with a supportive political climate in Kenya and improvements in institutional reputation, government policies, and public perceptions. Such developments would complement the country's technological base and facilitate the flow of capital, goods, services, and staff. The international organizations located in Nairobi would then attract greater investment, which would make Kenya more visible on the global stage.

LOCATION INFLUENCE ON UNEP

People shape the identity and determine the capacity of an organization. Scholars argue that if an "institution's secretariat does not attract talented staff, it is more likely to die" or become a "zombie organization."[37]

Recruiting and retaining top talent has been UNEP's top priority and one of its biggest challenges. In UNEP's early years, the supply of highly qualified staff was limited, given the novelty of the environmental-policy field. UNEP's ambitious and novel mandate, however, attracted motivated, committed people to leadership positions.[38] "It was difficult to get good people to move there permanently," Maurice Strong remarked, but "it proved relatively easy to recruit them for stints of a few years."[39] Eventually, however, as the organization grew, it was challenged to grow its staff at a pace proportionate to the demands upon it. In 1980, in his address to the Governing Council, Executive Director Mostafa Tolba told governments that it had become "extremely difficult to attract experienced administrative personnel ... and substantive staff" to UNEP.[40] He therefore decided to move functioning units of UNEP to Nairobi. For example, the Regional Seas Programme relocated from Geneva to Nairobi in the 1980s; unfortunately the effect was disastrous, as box 5.1 illustrates.[41]

Recruitment became increasingly difficult as Kenya's economy deteriorated in the 1980s and 1990s and tensions with the Moi government increased. Insecurity was the biggest problem, and UNEP's difficulty in delivering on its core functions affected its reputation and authority. Security is an important lens through which life in Nairobi has frequently been experienced and has long affected the attractiveness of Nairobi as a duty station. Once regarded as one of Africa's safest cities, Nairobi's crime rates soared during this period. "The main problem," a UNEP official remarked, "is that crime in Nairobi is more violent than would be the average in other UN headquarter cities, and this is a major issue when we try to recruit new staff."[42] International staff members were particularly vulnerable as their relative affluence attracted attackers. In our interview, UNEP Executive Director Mostafa Tolba recounted a break-in of his own home while he was sleeping. "They came at night, past the main guarded gate, through the side, cut through the hedge. I woke up in the morning and found something looked wrong. I had a sofa and chairs with red zip covers. Now there was something white in the room and I noticed that the furniture was missing its covers and also that the whole stereo set and television and video were all gone. I saw that the door and window were open. They had used the covers to carry the loot. I told the government that this was much too much. So, they sent me twenty-four-hour

Box 5.1

Regional Seas Programme Relocation

Operated out of Geneva, the Regional Seas Programme was forced to relocate to Nairobi in the early 1980s, when Mostafa Tolba made the decision to dramatically change the entire program. Arthur Dahl, former deputy assistant executive director at UNEP and a long-time staff member, noted that Tolba "felt that Regional Seas was looking too big and too good and was out of his control, so he ordered Regional Seas to move to Nairobi." Stjepan Kečkeš, who was running the programme, refused to move to Nairobi and resigned because he considered the Geneva location critical to the programme's effectiveness as an interagency collaborative initiative that relied on direct communication and personal relations with the other UN agencies. Most of the staff resigned in solidarity, and only one secretary relocated to Nairobi, along with the programme's files. After a year and a half, Kečkeš agreed to rejoin the programme and rebuild it. However, he submitted his resignation every year in protest of the decision to relocate the office. Years later, Peter Sand, chief of the Environmental Law Unit at UNEP from 1983 to 1986, noted, "Stjepan never forgave me for having supported Mostafa Tolba's idea of moving OCA/PAC [Oceans and Coastal Areas Programme Activity Centre] from Geneva to Nairobi. In retrospect, of course, Stjepan was right, and I was wrong." Ultimately, the relocation of the programme from Geneva to Nairobi significantly affected its staffing, visibility, and ability to deliver, which are the core elements of UNEP's authority.

guards."[43] As crime levels increased and UNEP took responsibility for ensuring security for all its staff members at their residences, security costs mounted.[44]

Working and living in seclusion—behind high walls, guarded gates, and barbed wire—diminishes uncertainty about safety but also increases exclusivity. Exclusion is built into Nairobi's architecture, with its private malls and gated communities.[45] Security, and securitized living, therefore, is not only about the absence of crime but also about exclusivity and prestige, a question of both risk and status. This, however, undermines the very principles of engagement, enhancement, and inclusion that UNEP had been created to promote. Importantly, UNEP and the United Nations Office in Nairobi cannot ensure a work environment that is inclusive and safe for all. Kenya continues to criminalize Lesbian, Gay, Bisexual, Transgender, and Queer (LGBTQ) relationships, and has made violence, discrimination, and abuse of LGBTQ people impossible to prosecute and punish. UN staff, therefore, can be exposed to blackmail, with no recourse from the judicial system or the United Nations, a clear abrogation of the UN Human Rights Council resolution that condemns discrimination and violence against LGBTQ people.[46]

Life for an expatriate in Nairobi has also presented logistical challenges. "Just getting through the day here [in Nairobi] can be a triumph," the *Christian Science Monitor* wrote in 2001. "Water stops running in the middle of your shower; the car gets stuck in a crater-size pothole; and the electricity is forever flickering. Phone lines can take a month to fix, e-mail can take two hours to connect. And if you haven't paid off the street kids, they may just puncture your tires while you're visiting some government office to complain about it all."[47] Many of these challenges were addressed in the 2000s after President Moi left office and economic development stabilized, institutions engaged in governance, and technological progress took hold. Nairobi, however, did not offer the conditions necessary for recruiting, retaining, and rewarding scientists. "They got stuck in Nairobi," Arthur Dahl, former deputy assistant executive director noted, "away from the scientific mainstream, unable to go to scientific meetings, and became frustrated former scientists, people with expertise that wasn't appreciated by UN bureaucrats."[48] UNEP Deputy Executive Director (2013–2018) Ibrahim Thiaw also noted that Nairobi is simply not as attractive to the intellectual community and does not carry the same prestige as New York.[49] Nairobi, however, brought issue experts into closer contact with the problems they were trying to fix and attracted people drawn to direct intervention and implementation. Nairobi, therefore, was a place where operational experts gained valuable time in the field. For those with more political- and management-oriented career aspirations, however, Nairobi represented the risk of personal safety and well-being, as well as a hindrance to maintaining professional connections in their field. This reinforced the move toward more operational activities, as UNEP attracted funding for particular projects and initiatives, as explained in chapter 3.

As a catalyst and coordinator, UNEP was mandated to convene and connect. "For us to be relevant, people have to see us," Dechen Tsering, director of the UNEP's Asia Office, remarked. For its first two decades,

UNEP experienced operational challenges that other UN bodies did not. Located far from the UN centers of power and from the capitals of major financial donors, UNEP was isolated. The high cost and low reliability of phone calls, not to mention the non-existence of the internet and the limited number of flights linking Kenya to the world, made connectivity one of the greatest challenges. At the beginning, "Nairobi was a black hole," staff recalled.[50] In 1972, a three-minute telephone call from Nairobi to New York cost 75 Kenyan shillings and to Geneva, 72 Kenyan Shillings, or $10.50 and $10.08, respectively[51]—roughly the equivalent of $60 today. Moreover, communication was unreliable. As one staff member remarked, "the telephone and fax have been a major problem for many years. Calling from abroad, one usually would get a recording, 'all lines to Nairobi are busy, please try later.'"[52] The connectivity limitations made it critical for UNEP staff to travel in order to facilitate in-person interaction, a reality which would last for decades.

Counterintuitively, Nairobi was not at that much of a disadvantage over other UN centers in the 1970s and 1980s, since all faced constraints of expensive communication, though face-to-face interaction was easier in cities with a high concentration of agencies. In the 1990s, however, Nairobi truly fell behind by not taking advantage of telecom advances. To address these constraints, in 1993, six member states of the European Space Agency donated a $14 million satellite system, the Mercure system, to UNEP to facilitate communications; however, the equipment could not be used for several years. According to Arthur Dahl, this was because "the Kenyan government refused to authorize its connection to the satellite, probably for fear that its telephone revenues would drop." Dahl also explained that by the time the Mercure system was implemented, it was already dated and expensive to maintain.[53] In 1995, an ECOSOC evaluation pointed out that "the location of UNEP in Nairobi was a serious handicap,"[54] citing the substandard communication facilities to and from Nairobi, and the demand for frequent travel to meetings which mostly took place at the headquarters of the World Bank (in Washington, DC) or UNDP (in New York). The evaluation further noted that the poor state of communication facilities considerably undercut the ability of international organizations to interact effectively with UNEP programme managers as well as the ability of governments to communicate efficiently with their respective missions and capitals.[55]

Eventually, communications with a range of constituencies improved, and internal communications were enhanced. But the decades of isolation had already left a considerable impact on the organization's reputation and the professional connectivity of its staff.[56] Isolated from the political centers of power, with low political presence of member states and ongoing communication challenges, UNEP's leadership has had no choice but to travel extensively, as chapter 6 details. When UNEP staff do travel to participate in various fora, this comes at a large cost of time and resources as well as considerable carbon emissions.[57] Nairobi is at least eight hours away by air from most major cities in any direction. UN staff are entitled to business class tickets for flights longer than nine hours, and on average, business class costs roughly four times as much as economy. When the fairly generous per-diem allowances for UN employees are added in, the travel costs associated with doing business become substantial. Accordingly, most staff have not been able to travel. Without continuous and systematic interaction with the rest of the UN system, they have been less likely to be recognized by other agencies and less likely to hear of opportunities for advancement. Their mobility within the UN system has therefore been limited. Geographical distance, however, has also insulated UNEP and enabled it to withstand political pressure and develop its own identity.

UNEP's location has also shaped its governance structure. The Committee of Permanent Representatives (CPR) is an important governance body established in 1985. A subsidiary body of the UNEP Governing Council (and now of the UN Environment Assembly), the CPR is expected to monitor the implementation of decisions by the governing body and provide government oversight of administrative, budgetary, and programmatic issues at UNEP. It has traditionally comprised members from the permanent missions in Nairobi, and because only 40 percent of member states have missions in Nairobi, deliberations have not been representative. Furthermore, most of the representatives in Nairobi are in political posts with duties in several countries in the region, including Somalia, Eritrea, and Ethiopia, which limits their ability to engage systematically and fully. Only a few countries, such as the United States and several EU countries have specially appointed Permanent Representatives, often with solid environmental backgrounds, whose primary responsibility is to work with UNEP and UN Habitat.

For many countries, representatives in the committee are often officers from the ministries of foreign affairs and have somewhat limited environmental knowledge and expertise when they take their posts in Nairobi. Given the intense engagement with UNEP, meeting formally at least six times a year to discuss the work program and budget, review the status of resolutions, and deliberate on a range of relevant issues, government officials gain knowledge and skills. There is a dichotomy, however, between the universal UN Environment Assembly engaging environmental ministries that meets every two years and the non-universal Committee of Permanent Representatives that relies on representatives of foreign-affairs ministries and meets in Nairobi almost daily. Both bodies have the responsibility to prepare for the meetings of the UN Environment Assembly, which leads to confusion among member states and frequent frustration in the UNEP secretariat.

Location is a highly political decision, as earlier chapters discussed, but the implications are intensely practical. The secretariat of the UN Framework Convention on Climate Change has also experienced the benefits and the challenges of a location outside the main centers of political power. "Headquartering the UNFCCC in Bonn has both a logistical and a strategic advantage," Christiana Figueres noted. "Logistically it has excellent internet and telephony quality, allowing staff to minimize travel. When travel is indispensable, it is located in the center of Europe, with ample train and flight connections from nearby Cologne airport." Strategically, remoteness from the UN Headquarters in New York has enabled the secretariat to develop its own corporate culture, specifically focused on the particular needs of the climate negotiations and the Parties to the Convention. One of the challenges, however, Figueres noted, is "the fact that Bonn is a small town with few employment opportunities for spouses, which complicates the capacity to hire the best and the brightest."[58]

Ultimately, UNEP's location in Nairobi has not been all good or all bad. It has affected UNEP's capacity to be a purely normative organization, to participate consistently in global environmental discussions across the UN system, and to convene actors at short notice. This has led it to undertake more operational activities, which has resulted in an identity crisis that UNEP is still in the process of resolving.

UNEP'S IMPACT ON KENYA

Hosting an international organization is a source of great prestige in the international community and, in a sense, a dream for any city. Indeed, from 1944 to 1946, enticed by the opportunity to transform themselves into the "Capital of the World," more than two hundred cities and towns across the United States mobilized to attract the headquarters of the newly created United Nations. The question of location of the UN headquarters was a difficult, high-stakes decision. At the heart of it were key individuals who had lived through great change and believed that they could create positive change in the world.[59] The United Nations headquarters was established in New York City in 1946 and was followed by the UN Offices in Geneva, Vienna, and Nairobi. Socially and economically intertwined with their local communities, UN organizations play integral roles in the local economies and have had significant positive impacts on their host cities, as box 5.2 illustrates.[60] Embedded in their host countries and communities, the UN institutions exert influence through tangible and intangible means, including economic power, human and intellectual resources, and technological advances.[61] For example, UNEP's new eco-friendly headquarters, which opened in 2011, was designed to generate as much energy as its 1,200 occupants consume, setting an example for sustainability in Africa.

Kenya has become a center of gravity in the East Africa region. "If a country has to make a decision where to locate their diplomatic focus in Africa," Donald Kaniaru explained, "Nairobi ranks high up because of the significant UN presence and its proximity to the African Union in Addis Ababa."[62] Seventy-five foreign missions and twenty-three international organizations are now based in the Kenyan capital and influence the nation's politics, policies, and economy. Nairobi has attracted a cluster of international institutions, diplomatic missions, NGOs, and consultancy companies whose presence has brought "prestige, projects,

Box 5.2

What Is the Economic Benefit of a UN Headquarters?

New York City became the site of the UN Headquarters in 1946. The UN office in New York employs over five thousand staff members and hosts the seats of the General Assembly, Security Council, Economic and Social Council, Trusteeship Council, and the Secretariat. New York also hosts the headquarters of nine UN agencies, funds, and programmes, including UNICEF, UNDP, UNFPA, and UN Women. The New York City Mayor's Office for International Affairs conducts an extensive assessment of the economic and fiscal impact of the United Nations on the economy of the city. In 2014, the UN community directly and indirectly supported about 25,040 full- and part-time jobs in New York City, and total earnings paid to New York City employees in relation to the UN amounted to close to $2 billion. The UN community accounted for $3.7 billion in output and $3 billion in value added. The estimated net fiscal benefits to New York City were $56 million.

Geneva hosts the UN Office in Geneva (UNOG), which was established in 1966. Dubbed "International Geneva," this global hub hosts thirty-eight international organizations with more than 10,400 staff members of 171 nationalities. The headquarters of the Economic Commission for Europe (ECE), the Office for the Coordination of Humanitarian Affairs (OCHA), the Office of the High Commissioner for Human Rights (OHCHR), and the United Nations Conference on Trade and Development (UNCTAD) are located in Geneva. In 2018, the various UN entities in Geneva hosted over 120,000 meetings, which bring visitors to the city and boost the local economy.

Vienna is the home of the UN Office in Vienna (UNOV), created in 1980. Around five thousand UN employees from more than 125 countries work at the more than forty international organizations based in Vienna. The sector spends about €725 million per year, which results in a macroeconomic demand effect of about €1.4 billion. In 2012, the city estimated an overall positive economic effect of €503.9 million. International organizations create approximately ten thousand jobs in and around Vienna. The number of conference days of international organizations in Austria has increased, and convention tourism contributes about €230 million to Austria's GDP.

Nairobi hosts the UN Office in Nairobi (UNON) since 1996. More than eighteen UN agencies operate in Kenya employing some five thousand local and international staff. The United Nations' contribution to the Kenyan economy was estimated to be in excess of $350 million annually in 2004, bringing in four times more foreign exchange than coffee, Kenya's primary export. In the late 1990s, a time of bad governance in Kenya and falling commodity prices worldwide, the United Nations provided the only steady source of foreign exchange, bringing in more money than horticulture or tourism. The UN contribution was equivalent to 3 percent of Kenya's GDP, or 19 percent of exports, and was second only to tea. International meetings at the UN office in Nairobi provide an important contribution to the Kenyan economy.

5.4 The eco-friendly headquarters of UNEP and UN-Habitat in Nairobi. Credit: Maria Ivanova and UNEP.

scientific research, employment and ... ideas," Donald Kaniaru pointed out.[63] Being host country for the United Nations has also empowered Kenya politically, helping it to become a "beacon and an anchor in diplomacy and politics" in the region, according to Moses Wetang'ula, former minister of foreign affairs.[64] The country has also ratified most multilateral environmental agreements, partially as a result of the international environmental institution's presence in the country, and these global conventions have contributed to a global sense of Kenya's leadership in championing key causes. As Ambassador Kipyego Cheluget wrote in 2017, Kenya is "the only country that regularly disposes of illegally acquired but widely traded wildlife products such as ivory, rhino horn and leopard skin by public burning."[65] This leadership on environmental issues is in stark contrast with Kenya's policies and behavior in the 1970s and 1980s, for example, when the illegal ivory trade was a serious problem in the country and the region.

The impact of the UN in Kenya has been very positive economically, politically, socially, and technologically. Kenya has hosted, co-chaired, and participated in negotiations on many global issues, including climate change, the Sustainable Development Goals, and global trade. It has anchored the peace processes in the Horn of Africa and East and Central

Africa, and has grown into the largest humanitarian hub in the region.[66] As a result of the UN's presence, new political, economic, social, and technological opportunities have opened up for Kenya, and convening international conferences and leading negotiations have advanced Kenya's political experience and standing. Kenya assumed a leadership role in creating the African regional governance architecture, and Kenyan diplomats imagined and created the Intergovernmental Authority on Development (IGAD) as a diplomatic forum where the heads of state in the Horn of Africa could meet to tackle escalating conflicts.

CONCLUSION

Deciding where to situate a new international body (including headquarters and secretariats) usually results from political deal making; as detailed in chapter 2, competing bids are often put forward, and coalitions and alliances are required to broker outcomes. Often, such wrangling may have little to do with the substance of the issue at hand, but the dynamics that bring about such decisions may present political puzzles that prove institutionally impactful in the long run. Establishing UNEP in Nairobi was a successful political move that aimed to increase the presence of UN institutions in developing countries.

Place matters, however, and even the "distance-destroying" capacity of modern technology has not made geography irrelevant. Locating the secretariat of the climate change convention in Bonn, for example, was driven by a domestic political calculus in Germany in the 1990s. Following reunification, the national capital was moving from Bonn to Berlin, and Germany needed to ensure that Bonn would continue to function as an administrative center. In the years since, and with significant investment from the host government, Bonn has become an important UN hub and home to a cluster of international organizations working on sustainability (including the headquarters of the climate and desertification conventions). Removed from the major UN agencies, the Bonn location has allowed for the development of the UN climate change secretariat as an independent actor in global affairs. Similarly, Nairobi has established itself as a main UN hub, the third UN office away from headquarters in New York. Retaining UN institutions in Nairobi has been a political priority for Kenya, but the government has not invested anything near the amount committed by Germany, Geneva, or Vienna, the other hosts of official UN offices.

As a place-based anchor institution, UNEP has shaped, and has in turn been shaped by, its host community. Notably, the Nairobi location influenced UNEP's identity. It demanded that the anchor institution transcend a purely normative mandate of coordination of the UN system's environmental activities, a feat which was simply impossible to achieve without adequate connectivity, communication, and capacity. The Nairobi location required UNEP to become more operational and responsive to concrete environmental challenges. As a result, UNEP has been moving into a more operational role, but in the absence of a clear mandate, requisite capacity, and necessary resources to fulfill such a role. Its identity and place within the UN system, therefore, remain in flux.

As UNEP nears its fiftieth year in operation, this intertwining of UNEP and Nairobi has at last laid to rest suspicions of UNEP's relocation; as the *Daily Nation* remarked in 2014, "the UN family, a trusted and committed partner of Kenya, is here to stay."[67] Location, and the evolution of the context within which the day-to-day reality of UNEP has unfolded, is certainly one part of the story that helps to make sense of UNEP's track record over five decades. And yet, independent from geography and its resulting issues with connectivity and insularity, UNEP's leadership and management have also shaped what the organization has and hasn't achieved. Indeed, it is common among staff and observers to refer to the respective era of each executive director much as one describes the specific time periods in Kenya by each president. Chapter 6 provides a detailed analysis of the tenure of each of the first six executive directors in UNEP's trajectory.

6

EXECUTIVE LEADERSHIP: THE INDIVIDUAL AND THE INSTITUTION

Leadership in times of change is about deeply understanding the contextual reality, clearly setting out the destination that needs to be reached, and then fertilizing the ground of possibilities that help steer toward the desired destination.
—Christiana Figueres, UNFCCC Executive Secretary (2010–2016)[1]

Leadership is the ability to create a compelling vision, translate it into action, and sustain it.[2] Leadership shapes the vision, management, and culture of an organization, its sense of identity and purpose.[3] Although leaders of international organizations possess much weaker formal powers than the heads of multinational corporations or even public administrations at the national level, they hold meaningful agenda-setting power, shape debates around particular issues, frame visions, and instigate, sustain, and manage change. They have access to important "bully pulpits" and can reach a large number of people with their message. They possess administrative powers over budgetary procedures and priorities, financial controls, personnel, and procurement policies and face legal-political, resource, and bureaucratic constraints.[4] They shape the organizations they lead and, as Professor Robert Cox explained in 1969, "[t]he quality of executive leadership may prove to be the most critical single determinant of the growth in the scope and authority of international organization."[5]

Undeniably, the executive director of UNEP has a critical and important role. The explicitly normative mandate, the voluntary financing mechanism, and the organization's remoteness from the rest of the UN system have created a strong reliance on the executive director. The director is expected to continuously promote UNEP, elevate its profile, and garner political and financial support from donors whose attention might be captured by operative priorities in organizations with which they interact more frequently. Internally, the executive director is largely responsible for providing direction and vision. Externally, the executive director is critical for securing steady funding and is integral to keeping UNEP and environmental concerns more broadly on the international agenda. Thus, in effect, UNEP demands that its leader seamlessly integrate the roles of outstanding technical expert, manager, politician, and visionary. The executive directors, however, are enabled or constrained by the environment and the historical moment within which they operate. Power in international affairs is critical, but its exercise changes with shifting ideologies, economic realities, and geopolitical forces.

To make sense of UNEP's first five decades, it is essential to bring individuals back into the study of the institution and explain their influence. Effective leaders are associated with institutional growth and evolution. They attract resources to inspire and sustain creativity and innovation, and they cultivate a distinctive institutional image and identity. Indeed, perceptions of an institution are influenced by perceptions of each leadership era. In other words, people remember developments in the organization by identifying and associating them with the particular leader who oversaw a given change. "Key leaders personify an institution's image—both internally and externally," David Whetten explains. "They try to exemplify an image consistent with core institutional values."[6] There is, however, no universally effective leadership type or style. Leadership qualities are intrinsic to the individual leader but are also shaped by the historical context in which they act. The executive's own leadership type and style determine what processes they are able to initiate and implement within the institution. Externally, the evolutionary state of the institution and the specific social-environmental context shape the field within which a director is able to operate.

At the time of UNEP's creation, the United States, as the government leading the process, offered a vision for a "United Nations Executive for Environmental Affairs." The most important function of the executive officer was to catalyze environmental concern among nation states.[7] To this end, the Advisory Committee to the US Secretary of State wrote, the environmental executive was to be an "active, resourceful, creative leader" who would be "empowered, by the broadest possible terms of reference short of enforcement, to initiate consultations with governments [and] to go directly to the people of the nations."[8] UNEP's first leader, Maurice Strong (1973–1975), was the architect the institution needed. Strong had envisioned and to a large extent designed the institution, as explained in chapter 2. In its early years, UNEP was a catalyst and collaborator, reflecting Strong's personality. When his deputy, Mostafa Tolba (1976–1992), assumed the post of executive director, he led the organization on an evolutionary path from the initial startup moment to an established entity. UNEP developed scientific expertise and international environmental law authority, and became a competitor to other organizations. Strong and Tolba had to craft the new institution, fight for it to have a place at the table, and implement the vision articulated at its creation.

Subsequent executive directors took on the roles of consolidator, reformer, or steward of the organization. Elizabeth Dowdeswell (1993–1998) had to carve out a role for UNEP in the age of sustainable development following the 1992 Rio Earth Summit, to remake its organizational culture, and to consolidate its disparate parts. The search for UNEP's identity continued in the late 1990s and early 2000s during the age of UN reform championed by UN Secretary-General Kofi Annan. Klaus Töpfer (1998–2006) brought political energy to institutional reform and increased UNEP's visibility and resources. The reform process concluded formally only in 2012, during the second mandate of Achim Steiner (2006–2016). Having become the steward of the reform process, he received an extension of his term for another two years to begin implementation. Steiner was at the helm of UNEP during the age of the technological revolution of the 2000s and improved communications and recognition and, as a result, UNEP's authority and financial feasibility. Indeed, UNEP's overall financial resources have increased with every executive director, as figure 6.2

6.1 The five UNEP executive directors since 1972 (left to right): Achim Steiner, Maurice Strong, Mostafa Tolba, Elizabeth Dowdeswell, and Klaus Töpfer at the Global Environmental Governance Forum in June 2009 in Glion, Switzerland. Credit: Satishkumar Belliethathan.

illustrates, but the sources have changed as earmarked contributions have come to constitute the majority of revenues.

In 2016, Erik Solheim joined an organization on the rise. Only two years later, in 2018, amid turmoil, the new executive director suddenly had to step down and leave the organization after a highly critical UN audit report. The report identified persistent gaps in accountability, transparency, and management of travel funds, as well as deliberate defiance of rules.[9] Inger Andersen assumed the post in June 2019 and will guide UNEP as the organization assesses its performance in its first five decades and envisions the next five.

This chapter traces the historical arc of UNEP's leadership in order to trace institutional development and evaluate performance. It presents a profile of each executive director that outlines their background, leadership type and style, vision for the organization, and the methods they used to translate their vision into action. The profiles also explain the financial situation during the tenure of each executive director and situate

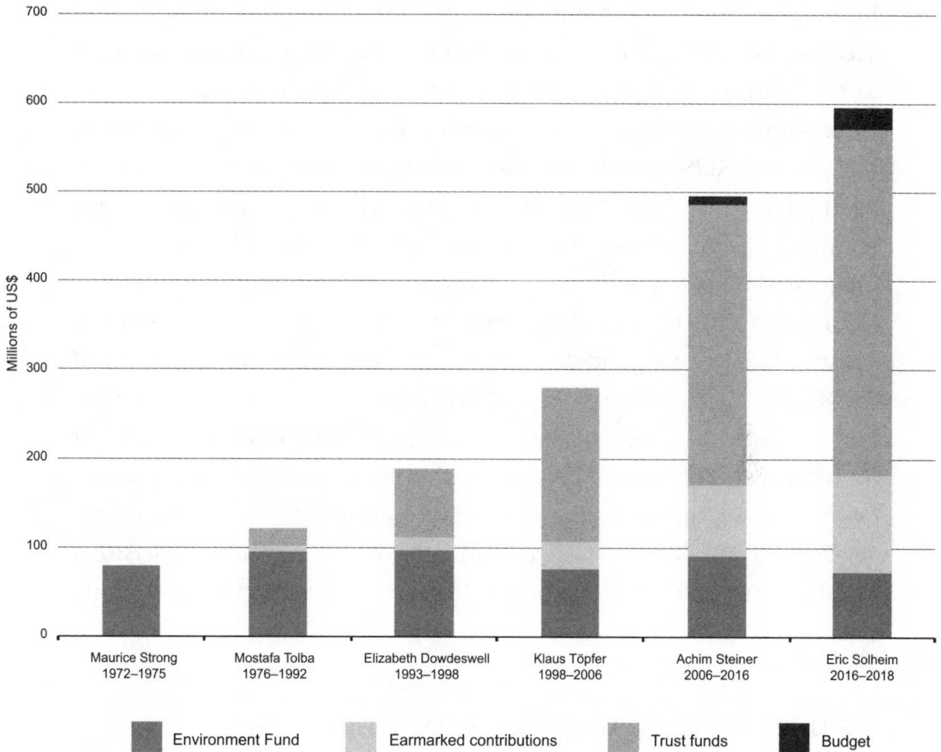

6.2 UNEP average annual income, adjusted for inflation, by category and executive director.

them within the geopolitical reality of the time, the moment in history in which each leader found themselves that enabled and constrained them.

MAURICE STRONG (1973–1975)

Effectively, the Maurice Strong era began in 1970 when the UN General Assembly appointed him Secretary-General of the planned United Nations Conference on the Human Environment. Chapter 2 described his leadership during the preparatory process and the two weeks of the Stockholm Conference. On December 13, 1972, the UN General Assembly unanimously elected Maurice Strong to the post of executive director of the new United Nations Environment Programme, but Strong took on the job reluctantly. "This was not at all what I had planned," he wrote in his memoir, *Where on Earth Are We Going?* He had accepted the position of Secretary-General of the Stockholm Conference with a clear commitment to return to his post in the government of Canada. His entrepreneurial leadership was critical to the success of the Conference, and governments had recognized how indispensable it would be for the successful launch of the new institution. After the decision was made in the fall of 1972 to site UNEP in Nairobi, the Swedish and other industrialized governments pushed particularly hard for Strong to become executive director. "Distance [from the other UN organizations] was seen as a real impediment," Strong noted, and "they wanted to minimize the difficulties of the Nairobi location by at least avoiding a potentially divisive and uncertain search for an acceptable head, and they knew I'd have broad support from all regions."[10] After consultations with Canadian Prime Minister Pierre Trudeau, Strong accepted the offer to become UNEP's first leader. "I agreed to a full term," he recalled, "but it was privately understood that I'd return to Canada as soon as I felt the new body had been firmly established."[11]

VISIONARY AND PRAGMATIC LEADERSHIP

Both a visionary and a pragmatist, Strong was the original architect of UNEP. In 1973, UNEP "consisted of nothing more than a General Assembly Resolution and me," Strong wrote, "and I needed to start from the ground up in translating it into a reality." Strong's vision was to create a source of power and authority for the environment that could coordinate and rationalize environmental activities within the United Nations family. He was convinced that the new environmental institution should not have operational functions so it would not have to compete with the organizations it was expected to influence and that it should be a collaborator, a catalyst, and a coordinator.[12]

His first tasks were pragmatic: he needed to recruit people to Nairobi and establish the organization's physical presence. Mostafa Tolba, the energetic Egyptian minister who had been such an asset during the Stockholm negotiations, had impressed Strong as a highly qualified scientist. Strong requested that UN Secretary-General Kurt Waldheim appoint Tolba as Deputy Director of UNEP, and a small and dedicated team of international experts followed. As a UNEP staff member noted, Strong "hand-picked his staff and had confidence in people to do the job."[13] He was able to attract individuals with both a passion for the environment and the requisite expertise. In this endeavor, Strong built on the network he had created in the run-up to the Stockholm Conference, where he had managed to assemble a team of over 150 scientific and intellectual leaders from fifty-eight countries to serve as consultants for the conference. As Mostafa Tolba observed, "Strong had a talent for spotting people to work with him and created top notch combinations."[14] His extensive personal contacts and the respect he commanded in the business and government sectors contributed to his ability to put forth a progressive environmental agenda and galvanize support at a macro and micro level.

Strong's second priority was to identify a physical location for the fledgling entity. For this purpose, he opted to move from the original offices in the Kenyatta Conference Center in downtown Nairobi, which were not "symbolic of our environmental purposes," as Strong noted, and not suitable for future expansion. He secured a large coffee farm in the outskirts of Nairobi to build a new complex that would suit the needs of the organization. UNEP remains in the Gigiri district of Nairobi, next to the Karura forest, and Gigiri has become the home of the UN complex, which hosts over twenty UN bodies.

The framers of UNEP at Stockholm had set out a powerful new vision for a catalytic institution, and Strong laid the groundwork to deliver on UNEP's core mandate to monitor the environment and catalyze environmental action across the UN system. In its early years, UNEP also helped create new national environmental institutions in countries around the world. Strong, building on relationships forged in the lead-up to the Stockholm Conference, engaged with governments around the world in setting up environmental ministries and agencies. In just one example among many, Strong recalled the creation of such an agency in China: "Stockholm created a binding relationship for me and China, because as I went on to head UNEP, they at the same time created their environmental agency—first an environmental protection unit, which would grow into an environmental protection agency and an environmental ministry."[15] Within only a few years, national environmental institutions would spring up within most of the world's governments.

Although he had little formal education, Maurice Strong exercised impressive intellectual leadership. He had a talent for coining new catch phrases that would become powerful intellectual concepts. "Outer limits" and "eco-development" became key concepts in his advocacy for an ecological, systemic approach to the management of global risks that would impact humanity's future. As a result, UNEP established an "outer limits" program to identify major global risks, including climate change and, as early as 1973, convened scientists to review the state of affairs on climate change. Charismatic and inspirational, Strong motivated followers and nurtured a culture of excitement. His vigorous pursuit of a clear and compelling vision stimulated performance. His management experience and acumen, ability to establish trustful personal relations, and outstanding diplomatic skills made his short tenure at UNEP quite successful. "He had the skills to help people who didn't agree to work together, and people who were pessimistic or overly utilitarian to see that they could change things," wrote reporter John Ralston Saul.[16]

CATALYTIC MANAGEMENT

In his own words, Maurice Strong's management approach was "never to confront but to co-opt, never to bully but to equivocate, and never to yield."[17] He had built a successful though controversial career as an oil tycoon in Canada and had been an outstanding manager. He invested in enabling UNEP to fulfill its core mandate to review and assess the state of the environment. "Right from the beginning," Strong recalled in our interview, "it was envisaged that UNEP would be engaged in monitoring what was happening through Earthwatch. But that didn't mean it did it all. It meant it had to put it all together."[18] He saw UNEP as bringing all the component elements of the environment together in one framework within the UN system. Often, however, UNEP found itself in competition with other UN bodies. "We had only the reluctant cooperation of the agencies," Strong remarked, "that saw us as a competitor especially when we did anything that was operational." UNEP therefore worked on providing guidance to the agencies in their operational work. From the beginning, Strong envisioned close collaboration between UNEP and UNDP, the two bodies working on the twin issues of environment and development, but he was not able to deliver on that vision. "I proposed that UNDP develop a policy on environment [and] that UNEP have a unit to work with UNDP and UNDP have a unit to work with UNEP," Strong noted. "That UNDP do the operational part of our program. And even that UNDP run our fund, the Environment Fund. That never happened."[19] Indeed, the inertia in the system was too strong to overcome, and without regular interactions, political incentives, and adequate financial means, such transformation was impossible.

PUSH FOR PARADIGM CHANGE

In the geopolitical context of oil crises and an economic downturn in the 1970s, the environment began slipping down on governments' agendas. With UNEP rather removed from the centers of power and the mainstream UN discussions, sustaining substantive interest and financial support became a challenge.

The environment–development linkage was one of Strong's priorities, and he worked on integrating the ideas from the Founex workshop that had ensured the success of the Stockholm Conference into the work of UNEP (see chapter 2). In 1974 Gamani Corea of Sri Lanka, one of the Founex participants, became Secretary-General of UNCTAD, the main UN body working on trade and development. Strong worked with Corea and several of the other leading intellectuals of the Stockholm Conference to convene a joint UNEP/UNCTAD symposium on "Patterns of Resource Use, Environment and Development Strategies" in 1974 in Cocoyoc, Mexico. Barbara Ward of the United Kingdom chaired the symposium, and Johan Galtung of Norway and Ignacy Sachs of France wrote the first draft of the proceedings, which would become the flagship Cocoyoc Declaration. Seen by some as radical and provocative, the declaration was "the first international document that articulated the need for change in the lifestyles and patterns of production and consumption," Branislav Gosovic, a UN official who joined UNEP in 1974, wrote. It pointed out that poverty and the environmental crisis stemmed from the same root cause of "maldevelopment" and called for "structural, systemic and paradigm changes in the existing world economic, political, as well as technological order."[20] As Gosovic recounts, soon thereafter, "Strong received, in Nairobi, a long telex from the State Department, signed [by Secretary of State] Kissinger ... The telex stated that most of these problems had no place either in the document or on the agenda of an environment organization, and should be left to other competent fora to deal with, while UNEP should limit itself strictly to 'environmental problems.'"[21] UNEP was beginning to attract opposition from countries that perceived the organization as a threat to their interests.

At the same time, developing countries united behind a proposal for a New International Economic Order (NIEO) that sought to directly address the enduring inequalities in the international system, which sharpened tensions between developed and developing countries. This threatened the established economic and political status quo, and when, in 1974, developing countries passed the declaration on the New International Economic Order, the Charter of Economic Rights and Duties of States, and the Cocoyoc Declaration within the United Nations, this reinforced the perception that the United Nations supported radical, systemic changes that might result in a move away from capitalism.[22] UNEP came down clearly on one side of the political argument as it argued explicitly that economic inequalities had led to grave environmental problems, especially in developing countries, and were a "barrier to the harmonious development of mankind."[23] Thus, while UNEP had been at the core of political debates at its inception, as governments changed, especially in industrialized countries, and priorities shifted, it was pushed out of the political debate and forced to be more of a technical organization.

The financial implications were notable. Although major donors did not decrease their financial contributions, they did not augment them and, in the context of the inflation crisis in the early 1980s, UNEP's income plummeted (see figure 2.2 in chapter 2). Governments had urged integration and linkage among the range of issues that demanded international attention, but these remained hollow statements at international fora, and a silo approach continued. Separate institutions focused on separate problems but vied for attention and resources from the same governments, which fostered competition rather than cooperation and reinforced the existing economic and political structures, as chapters 3 and 4 illustrated. In this context, as early as December 1974, a former staff member remarked, Strong "was already saying he was just there to start something and then he was going to leave. He wasn't an administrator; he liked to create and catalyze things, get them going and then go on to something else."[24] Aware of Strong's intention to leave UNEP early and return to Canada, UN Secretary-General Kurt Waldheim asked Strong to meet and engage with Javier Pérez de Cuéllar, the Permanent Representative of Peru at the United Nations and President of the Security Council in 1974. The meeting in New York, Strong recalled in our 2008 interview, would eventually lead to Strong's appointment as head the Rio Earth Summit many years later.

In 1971, to ensure the backing of developing countries and the Soviet Bloc in the contested selection of a UN Secretary-General, Waldheim sought support from Peru, which was emerging as a leader among developing nations. Pérez de Cuéllar, Peru's Ambassador to the UN at that time, had just been called from his post in Moscow, where he had opened the first Peruvian embassy. As Strong explained, "Waldheim had promised the Peruvians to make Pérez de Cuéllar an Under-Secretary-General, and the only post he could see possible was the executive director post in UNEP." Since Strong was preparing to leave, Waldheim saw an opportunity to deliver on his promise. During the meeting with Pérez de Cuéllar, however, Strong understood that "he didn't know anything about the field, had not the least bit of interest in going to Nairobi, and would have been a terrible choice." So, rather than convincing Pérez de Cuéllar to take the job, Strong decided to tell Waldheim that he would remain executive director for another year, so that Pérez de Cuéllar would not have the option to accept or decline. A few years later, in 1980, Pérez de Cuéllar would become UN Secretary-General. "And we laughed," Strong recalled, "and said 'if you had gone to Nairobi, you would have never become Secretary-General.'" This, Strong acknowledged, "affected my appointment for Rio because Pérez de Cuéllar was Secretary-General at that time and appointed me to the post."

Strong left UNEP at the end of 1975, after only a couple of years at the helm, at a point when the organization was still weak and fragile. As Mark Halle, one of his close associates, remarked, Strong "left too early. People really liked the idea [of UNEP], but it really needed to be worked out and all the kinks ironed out so that it could develop into something a lot more solid before stepping back and letting it develop on its own.

It's not so much a critique of Maurice because that's the kind of person he was but it soon slipped back into a more traditional vision of how a UN organization should work."[25] This transition took place during the tenure of Mostafa Tolba, Maurice Strong's deputy who would lead the institution for the next seventeen years and put a lasting stamp on it.

MOSTAFA TOLBA (1976–1992)

At the end of 1975, Mostafa Tolba succeeded Maurice Strong as executive director. The clean transfer of power lent legitimacy to Tolba and to the organization. Tolba was unanimously elected by the UN General Assembly to complete the final year of Strong's term and ensure continuity in the organization. He was then subsequently elected for four consecutive four-year terms and would become the longest-serving executive director with a total of seventeen years at UNEP's helm.

CONVINCING AND COERCIVE SCIENCE DIPLOMACY

Tolba possessed core competencies in both science and diplomacy and was particularly adept at combining them.[26] He brought to bear intellectual, structural, and entrepreneurial leadership. As Oran Young explains, intellectual leaders produce intellectual capital and create systems of thought that determine outcomes; structural leaders translate acess to material resources into bargaining leverage; and entrepreneurial leaders exhibit negotiating skills that foster creative deals.[27] Tolba deployed intellectual innovation, bargaining leverage, and negotiating skills. "I went into my position as executive director of UNEP with varied experiences," Tolba recalled in our conversations, "academic, science, planning, diplomatic, political, and executive. I think that that helped me a lot in moving ahead with UNEP."[28] He had unquenchable thirst for knowledge and impressive interdisciplinary technical capacity and was known for continuously retraining himself. "I'm a microbiologist," Tolba noted, "but I taught myself law because of the international treaties; I taught myself economics because of the cost-benefits of Montreal and climate change from economists or international lawyers. I sat with them in their meetings, as a student, learning from them."[29] During Tolba's tenure, UNEP's intellectual prowess increased as it focused on keeping the environment under review. For example, UNEP installed GIS stations around Africa and strengthened its climate impact studies program, and developed a series of major multilateral environmental conventions. In the process, UNEP evolved into an authoritative environmental institution.

Tolba's intellectual drive shaped global environmental governance. He coined the term "development without destruction," which was effectively the foundation for what would come to be known as sustainable development. Tolba wrote in 1982 that "One of the most fundamental problems confronting mankind at present is how to meet the basic needs and requirements of all people on earth without simultaneously destroying the resource base, that is the environment, from which ultimately these needs have to be met."[30] This was five years before the Brundtland Commission officially defined sustainable development as "development that meets the needs of the present generation without compromising the ability of future generations to meet their own needs."[31] Throughout his tenure with UNEP, Tolba adhered to "development without destruction" as his guiding philosophy—both personally and for the organization.[32] This ideology effectively emphasized the environment as a core precondition for human life and development. As UNEP's slogan for World Environment Day 1988 proclaimed: "when people put environment first, development will last."[33]

Tolba's leadership style derived from his powerful personality and high visibility. Able to broker deals that were perceived as impossible, he was convincing and, where necessary, coercive. A hardnosed negotiator, he described himself as a "head basher." He forged conventions and agreements by the force of his character, leveraging both his charisma and extensive scientific knowledge. He recognized that there were two sides for every convention—the demands of developing countries and those of developed countries—and, in between the two, there was the issue of the money.[34] Tolba knew that he could not deal with these issues as mathematical equations but instead had to approach them as political equations. He was an innovator who blended the structural power he derived from his connections to developing countries with his extensive technical knowledge. Tolba played a critical role in translating rapidly evolving scientific knowledge into political, policy, and legal terms relevant to the intensive institutional bargaining that took place at the time.[35]

Both an African and an Arab, Tolba could connect directly with a number of countries on their own terms. Perceived as an overt supporter of developing countries, he also had the backing of the Eastern Bloc countries and was therefore often seen as opposing what the United States considered to be its interests.[36] As a former high-level US official noted, "Mostafa had made himself the darling of the Group of 77 and was seen to be pretty much in their camp."[37] Tolba, however, considered himself an honest broker among the various countries and interests. Adept at political maneuvering, he was able to move UNEP's agenda forward, but in the process, he often alienated the United States and its Western allies. His behavior with member states grew confrontational when he saw any one government as a possible obstacle to his agenda.

Tolba became infamous for his "bullying, cajoling, wheedling and threatening tactics," noted Fiona McConnell, who led the UK delegation in the biodiversity negotiations leading up to the 1992 Convention on Biological Diversity. "He was unwaveringly courteous to the US because as he told us all, he did not want to give them an excuse to walk out. But to everyone else he distributed his contempt even-handedly. Japan was accused of taking up space and saying nothing. India was attacked for talking too much. The UK was blinkered, mean and would not listen to Darwin if he were still alive."[38] In essence, while Tolba's intellectual leadership helped carve out substantive authority for UNEP, the organization's appeal as a collaborator began to diminish in the face of the harsh diplomatic approach employed by the executive director both internally and externally.

VISION FOR NORMATIVE AND OPERATIONAL REACH

Tolba's vision for UNEP was that it would develop the environmental agenda along with a framework of law, practice, and incentives and that it would provide the necessary support for implementation, especially in developing countries. He chose to put his unflagging energy into getting large pieces of the environmental policy infrastructure in place and launched nearly all of the major environmental conventions, thus making UNEP a clear normative leader. Indeed, Tolba was widely regarded as "solely responsible for the ozone and biodiversity conventions."[39] As explained in chapter 4, the achievements of the Montreal Protocol and the success story of the ozone regime can be traced to Tolba's and UNEP's leadership.

Tolba was impatient with the Maurice Strong vision of a highly normative agency and preferred to work on an agenda of tangible activities that he was confident he could accomplish.[40] For Tolba there could be no normative impact without an operational footprint: he firmly believed that any organization that could not give practical help to countries was never going to get support, be it political or financial. Tolba's measure of success, then, became what the organization could deliver on its own, rather than its effectiveness as a catalyst within the UN system. This focus, however, meant that UNEP was seen as more of a competitor than a collaborator by other UN agencies. Facing increasing demands from developing countries, UNEP became a support agency with greater on-the-ground delivery. This was a move that would be difficult to reverse and would lead to tensions that still affect the organization today.

AUTHORITARIAN MANAGEMENT

The commanding leadership and controlling management style of Tolba led to a clear direction in the organization, but it also created a cult of personality. Imposing and commanding, Tolba could not be challenged, and the institution evolved in a highly hierarchical manner. Tolba "brought to UNEP the management style of his culture from Egypt, loyalty to the top man," a former staff member noted.[41] Another called his management style "pharaonic" and commented that the management culture was "that of a pyramid. God speaks and everybody responds."[42] Mark Halle remarked that Tolba "was an authoritative figure but very quick to support you and congratulate you when he thought you were doing good work, and to acknowledge that work, and pretty quick to come down on you hard if you messed up."[43] This authoritarian leadership and management style drove productivity, but the need to claim credit led to turf battles among divisions and a political environment in which staff had to fight for the leader's favor.[44]

This organizational culture became one marked by territoriality. Indeed, there were "cultures within culture,"[45] as staff noted, and these persisted for years after Tolba's departure. This atmosphere, coupled with prolonged absences due to his heavy travel schedule, presented challenges to establishing, exercising, and delegating authority. Tolba trusted very few individuals to make decisions in his absence, which caused backlogs. As a result, UNEP "gained the reputation of being an incredibly sluggish bureaucracy, impossible to get anything done," Mark Halle noted, "particularly because Tolba insisted that he, personally, should approve things that should have been decisions taken three or four levels down."[46]

Tolba recognized that his leadership style was seen as coercive and that it had engendered opposition among governments, and he acknowledged that this resulted in environmental issues being steered away from UNEP and into alternative institutional arrangements. This was perhaps most obvious when governments established a negotiating committee, and later a secretariat, for climate change under the UN Secretary-General rather than within UNEP or the World Meteorological Organization, the two institutions that had been most assertive on the need to address climate change at the global scale and had jointly created the Intergovernmental Panel on Climate Change. "Obviously," Tolba lamented, "the West did not want to give climate change negotiations to UNEP, to Mostafa Tolba. They clearly did not want another Montreal Protocol."[47] Indeed, as new environmental institutions emerged, they became independent of UNEP and ultimately more competitors than collaborators, which presented a challenge to UNEP's core functions, as the analysis in chapter 3 illustrated.

LAISSEZ-FAIRE CAPITALISM AND FALLING FINANCES

The original high financial ambitions for UNEP did not materialize. "The United Nations Environment Programme has been having an uncomfortable time of late," wrote Richard Sandbrook of the International Institute for Environment and Development in the UK in a 1976 issue of *Nature*. "Not only are funding problems now hampering the agency; there also appears to be increasing dissent about the work programme, both within and without the Secretariat."[48] As laissez-faire capitalism gained ground, some governments—the United States and the United Kingdom in particular—lowered taxes and decreased regulation, and attention shifted to domestic economic priorities. Environmental issues took a backseat to pressing economic concerns, and contributions did not reach the levels envisioned at the time of creation.[49] "Some Western leaders," Barbara Ward wrote in 1982, "are starting to abandon the concept of our joint voyage on Spaceship Earth, and to dismiss any concern for the environment or for underdeveloped nations as 'do-goodism.'"[50] This political context had considerable economic and therefore performance repercussions.

Hyperinflation in the 1970s reduced the value of the financial contributions of all governments, even as they maintained the same level of contributions. In 1980, Tolba admonished the Governing Council that "the resources currently available to the Environment Fund affected as they are both by inflation and stagnation are not of such importance as to offer any but the most minimal inducement to our partners."[51] He reiterated this message two years later at UNEP's ten-year anniversary. "In 1982 we find ourselves in very different circumstances," he told governments. "The problems we faced in 1972 have been compounded, and instead of stepping up efforts aimed at solving them we find that the Stockholm commitment has begun to flag. In the face of the global economic recession the temptation has been for the international community to relegate the environment to a position of secondary importance."[52] In real terms, the Environment Fund decreased from close to $247 million in 1978–1979 to $149 million in 1984–1985, a 40 percent plunge, which rendered UNEP powerless (see figure 2.2 in chapter 2).

Political developments in the United States, originally the strongest advocate of UNEP, led to a dramatic decrease in diplomatic and financial support to multilateralism and the environment and thus to the United Nations and UNEP. With the Reagan administration taking office in 1981, UNEP lost its most important champion, which resulted in a gradual decrease in global contributions. The Reagan administration was "defensive and even hostile towards multilateral cooperation for resolving global environmental problems," a 1981 UN General Assembly report about UNEP noted.[53] Anne Gorsuch, the Administrator of the Environmental Protection Agency, had little knowledge about UNEP, the UN system, and the environment-development nexus. Analysts observed that the US delegation in Nairobi was "widely perceived as abdicating its advocacy role."[54] US financial contributions declined from $10 million in

1980 to $7.8 million in 1982 and stayed below $10 million for the duration of Reagan's term in office, which, coupled with inflation, reduced resources considerably. In the mid-1980s, European countries began increasing their contributions and would ultimately become the biggest donors to UNEP (see figure 6.3).

These financial difficulties translated into operational challenges and diminished authority. When governments created the Global Environment Facility, as chapter 3 explained, UNEP both suffered some loss in authority and gained a source of financing as it became one of the three implementing agencies for the GEF, along with UNDP and the World Bank. Mostafa Tolba had a chip on his shoulder about the GEF. "Tolba and I were just completely at loggerheads," recalled Mohamed El-Ashry, the inaugural CEO and Chairman of the GEF, because of the issue of national environment versus global environment. "In all global forums,

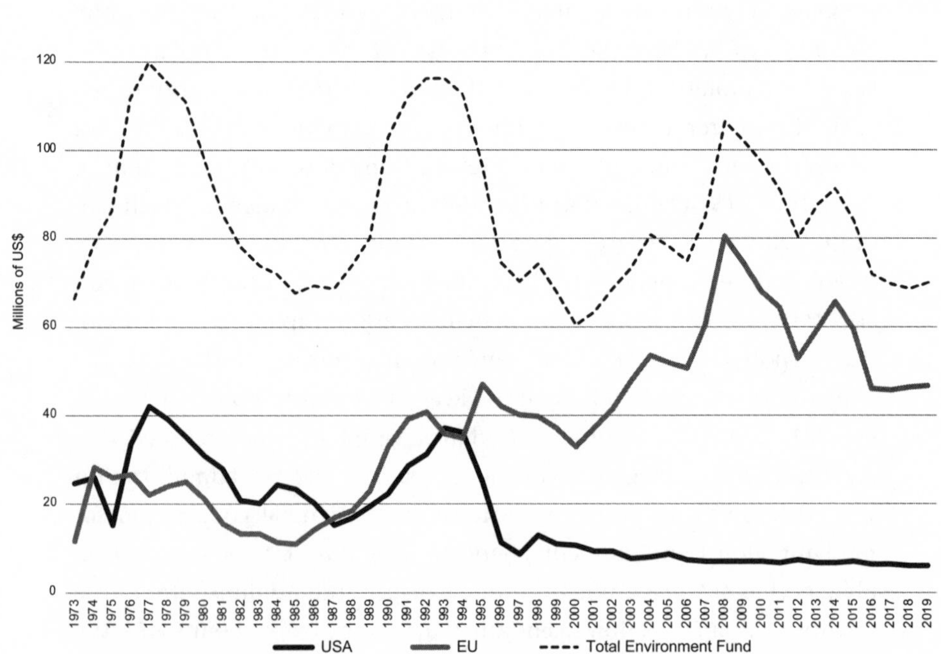

6.3 US and EU contributions to the Environment Fund, adjusted for inflation, from 1973 to 2019.

UN or otherwise," El-Ashry explained, "Tolba would say in his remarks the 'Global Facility for the Environment.' And I would come back and say it's the 'Global Environment Facility' because it deals with the global environment and not all environment. So, he would just nod his head and the next time he makes a remark he would say the 'Global Facility for the Environment' again. That was ongoing."[55] While Tolba's commanding leadership had made UNEP successful initially, in time countries and partner organizations began to see Tolba's influence as an increasing threat. He continued to vehemently defend environmental pursuits but was faced with an increasingly unreceptive milieu.

UNEP ON THE SIDELINES

In 1983, UN Secretary-General Javier Pérez de Cuéllar (who served from 1982 to 1991) created the World Commission on Environment and Development to review issues at the nexus of environment and development, assess the achievements in the fifteen years since Stockholm, and imagine how to take a quantum leap forward.[56] Even though UNEP had been the primary institution leading this agenda, the twenty-member commission was independent, and Pérez de Cuéllar appointed then–Prime Minister of Norway Gro Harlem Brundtland as Chair. Maurice Strong was a member of the Commission but not Mostafa Tolba, which alienated the executive director and, as a result, the entire institution. Tolba had really wanted to run the commission and felt that producing the report was "UNEP's job" and that all the "attempts to innovate and create something new were ... a threat to what he was trying to do," Mark Halle explained.[57] In 1987, the Brundtland Commission produced a report, *Our Common Future*, which defined sustainable development, put it firmly on the map of international affairs, and strongly influenced the agenda of the 1992 Rio Earth Summit.

Tolba expected that the preparations for the 1992 Rio Earth Summit would largely be entrusted to UNEP, or that at the very least he would have a major, controlling role in it. In February 1990, before the first preparatory committee for the conference, Pérez de Cuéllar appointed Maurice Strong as the Secretary-General for the conference. Tolba was unhappy with this choice and opted to withdraw individually and institutionally.

As a result, and to its detriment, UNEP did not play an active role in the two-year preparatory process for the Rio Earth Summit.

Maurice Strong had insisted that all UN agencies contribute and engage in the drafting of the voluminous documentation for the conference and that they focus more on substance than on their own institutional interests. However, according to Ambassador Lars-Göran Engfeldt, UNEP was the one agency that did not cooperate. He noted that throughout the process, UNEP "acted largely on its own and made only minimal contributions to the collective effort."[58] Moreover, a member of the Rio secretariat recalled that senior UNEP staff had clear instructions from the executive director not to provide any data or information for the conference.[59]

Tolba was driven by a desire to protect UNEP from the negative effects of organizational changes in the UN system and acted in a manner that was remarkably similar to that of the UN specialized agencies in advance of the Stockholm Conference. He protected his organizational turf as best he could, and the geographical remoteness of UNEP allowed him to disengage from the Rio Earth Summit preparations. It also insulated UNEP from interaction with others. As Mark Halle remarked, Tolba "felt that if UNEP could simply ignore [the conference] and show that they were peeved, people would come running to UNEP, but they never did."[60] The sidelining of UNEP in the lead-up to Rio left a lasting impression on Tolba. In 2008 he bemoaned:

> I was the one who suggested to the Governing Council of UNEP that we should have an international conference to commemorate the twenty years after Stockholm, and they made that recommendation to the General Assembly. And they wanted it as a session of a special character, like the one in '82. And we prepared—[the report] *The World Environment 1972 to 1992: Two Decades of Challenge*. So, it was UNEP all through. Maurice Strong came and found all that ready and put all that we—UNEP, FAO, UNESCO, and WHO—did on the environment into one book and came up with Agenda 21. One of the things I was telling Maurice all throughout—he and his deputy came to Nairobi several times—and I said, "For God's sake, this is a *huge* agenda and people will put it on their shelves and nobody will implement anything. Pick one or two examples—water, air, whatever—that *can* be corrected, and say how much it will cost the world and where are the responsibilities of the developed and developing countries and give them a cost estimate." So that, when they look into the rest of their agenda, they have a clear vision of the cost and their priorities. They didn't do that, they wanted to come with the Rio Declaration and Agenda 21.[61]

Dr. Mostafa Tolba implemented the vision for UNEP and led the institution when it was a pioneer in the field. He shaped UNEP as an authority in its own right, asserted its scientific eminence, and created a body of international environmental law. He pushed through a series of global environmental agreements on a range of important issues, but he stayed too long and outlasted his legacy.[62] Importantly, as the world was preparing for the 1992 Rio Earth Summit, Tolba misread the fact that governments were ready for another wave of thinking on the environment and another phase of experimentation with environmental institutions. He saw a threat and removed himself and UNEP from the Rio process. Somewhat ironically, some of Tolba's core achievements—the conventions on climate, biodiversity, and desertification—were finalized at the Rio Earth Summit, but two of the three conventions were set up as completely independent entities.

Consequently, UNEP became one of many institutions rather than the center of gravity it was envisioned to be, and it has come to be perceived as weak and ineffective. That perception has persisted for decades. In 2018, at the height of the controversy around the resignation of Executive Director Erik Solheim, the Norwegian newspaper *Aftenposten* reported that "There are many who don't think UNEP is functioning as it shall, and that there are other means of promoting environmental issues that can be more effective."[63] In the final analysis, however, the Mostafa Tolba era at UNEP was characterized by the creation of a robust body of international environmental law and the resolution of key environmental problems, the most important being ozone depletion. "If you start listing what Tolba achieved," Mark Halle noted, "it's an amazing record. But I guess it depended far too much on his personally. That was the downside of it."[64]

ELIZABETH DOWDESWELL (1993–1998)

Canadian Elizabeth (Liz) Dowdeswell assumed the post of UNEP executive director in 1993, a particularly challenging time in its history. This was the end of an era, as the two previous holders of this post had been directly involved in its conceptualization and had, over the subsequent twenty years, both put their stamp on the organization and helped shape global environmental governance. Just a year after the Rio Earth Summit, she had to keep UNEP afloat while making it relevant to the new international priorities. Dowdeswell also had to deal with governments that were distrustful of UNEP and unwilling to lend it full support. The geopolitical context was qualitatively different from UNEPs first twenty years, as "economic recessions, fratricidal conflicts, natural and man-made disasters" required that governments act, but the steps they were taking to address the relationship between population, consumption, and natural resources were too few and too slow.[65] Moreover, every UN agency now defined their programs in terms of sustainable development, and the competition among them for political attention and financial resources was intense.

BIG PICTURE VISION, DISRUPTIVE CONSENSUS SEEKER

Although neither a scientist nor an environment minister, Dowdeswell was keenly aware of the interconnections among environmental and social issues. She had served as Canada's Assistant Deputy Minister of Environment with responsibility for the Atmospheric Environment Service and for negotiating the UN Framework Convention on Climate Change. Within the Canadian government, Dowdeswell had worked on a variety of issues, and what distinguishes her from most of UNEP's executive directors is the breadth of her engagement in social causes. "I've worked in culture and the arts, in education, science and technology, innovation," she noted in an interview in 2014. She sought to create consensus about the identity and place of the institution she was heading, but she would have to disrupt the existing state of affairs in the process.

Entrepreneurial and committed, Dowdeswell joined UNEP with a clear recognition of the requirements of a leader of an international institution and the need to transform UNEP. She sought to build on its strengths, tackle its weaknesses, and work with others in expanding UNEP's agenda. Seeking consensus within and outside the organization, she set out to rethink UNEP's unique role in the post-Rio reality but was beset by extraordinary difficulties, many beyond her control. UNEP had to reinvent itself and redefine its value proposition to better respond to the notion of balancing of people, planet, and prosperity.

Dowdeswell envisioned UNEP as an organization that looks at the world as a whole and communicates the big picture. She saw an organization that brings governments together to try and find pathways that actually work for everybody, and one that helps countries that need help in terms of finances and capacity. She was committed to attaining that vision by pursuing a drastically different style of management, one based on consensus rather than commanding top-down directives.

She had come into UNEP with the conviction that an effective leader needed to perform both a leadership function and a management function. The leadership function was to provide insight and inspiration and move the institution to where it needed to be both externally and internally. But she recognized that a leader was also responsible for the sound management of both financial and human resources. So, Dowdeswell remarked, "I needed to step back and look at the original vision and mission and say: 'Is that still valid?' And if it is so, given this new context, how is that actually interpreted, how is that vision operationalized, and what may change? And I needed to consider whether we had the right set of skills and abilities within the organization, the right structure, and the conducive political reality so I could move ahead."[66] That required rethinking and reorganization.

In her first meeting with UNEP staff, Dowdeswell started by saying, "I am going to cause constructive damage to the status quo,"[67] a comment that many staff members considered threatening. When asked in a 2014 interview what she meant by this statement, she responded that her comment was grounded in the realization of the extent of environmental change. "Evidence was piling up about the unprecedented pace and breadth of environmental degradation occurring around the world," she explained, and "it was becoming apparent that there really wasn't any room for complacency." Dowdeswell was convinced that the attitudes and behavior of institutions and individuals would be difficult to change but that it was imperative to do so. "I think that's what I meant by causing constructive damage," she noted.[68] But change had to happen within the organization as well and many staff were wary of the threat to the status quo.

PARTICIPATORY MANAGEMENT AND SEXISM CHALLENGES

Mostafa Tolba's departure had left a massive vacuum. The whole institution had evolved around a personality and had melded with him to have an almost synonymous identity. Everything at UNEP had been done vertically. Dowdeswell set out to change that, which made many staff members wary, suspicious, and fearful. Her attempts to create a new vision for UNEP were met with resistance even from program proponents.[69] One observer noted that the permanent representatives in Nairobi opposed Dowdeswell "with blood and body; she just could not convince them of her attempts at reform."[70] Many staff members remained loyal to Tolba and blocked any attempt at reform. "I was told that these were simply concepts of Western management that were not appropriate and wouldn't work in the UN system," Dowdeswell observed.[71] Or, as a former staff member pointed out, they knew how to deal with Tolba but didn't know how to deal with Dowdeswell, who broke down the familiar verticality. UNEP went from one extreme—a top-down management style—to another, a horizontal management style.

Committed to working in partnership, Dowdeswell sought to build consensus through participation or what many called a "Canadian approach." Managing through consultation and participation was a painstaking, drawn-out process that clashed with the conventional tactics of what staff called the Tolba feudal empire.[72] The "participatory management style angered many, dismayed others, and alienated the rest," a staff member remarked. Many of the professionals at UNEP had no experience with such a management style, either prior to joining the organization or during their time at UNEP. Dowdeswell's push for democratic leadership created paralysis, increased resentment, and resulted in inefficiency, which generated a perception that the executive director could not make decisions. Difficulties in attaining goals precipitated a vicious cycle of declining internal productivity, coupled with rapidly evaporating international relevance.

Committed to introducing accountability and results-based management, Dowdeswell challenged staff to be clear about what their mandate was, what they were going to be held accountable for delivering, and how they interacted with other parts of the system.[73] She recognized that improving environmental governance required systems thinking and integrated approaches. She pushed for change in UNEP's existing work, which was based on projects and organized in twelve sectors. She structured task teams to re-plan the organization from the bottom up. "What was amazing to me from some of those meetings," one staff member noted, "[was that] you would see staff members from the same division talking about what they were doing and discovering for the first time what their next-door neighbor was doing."[74] Dowdeswell broke silos within the organization, a process that inevitably caused some consternation and dissatisfaction.

Dowdeswell also adjusted the relationship between UNEP's headquarters and its regional offices so that their directors became her direct deputies around the world. Along with this, she set out to disrupt the political nature of staff appointments and institute an apolitical recruitment process, a performance appraisal system, and accountability mechanisms. "In my view," she noted, "politics is not the basis on which a sound organization should be built. But certainly, the organization I inherited had positions earmarked. I was told that this was essentially a Japanese position and this was a European position and so on. This reality, however, was not only what UNEP experienced, it was throughout the whole UN system. And ... the system's that way for whatever reason so you can't change everything overnight, but I tried to." Over time, UNEP "began to develop a culture of accountability and a results orientation," Dowdeswell reflected. She created a trust fund for managerial innovation and excellence. "It was a time where we were trying to up our game in terms of attracting financial resources and also in the management and development of our human resources—learning to work as multidisciplinary teams, having real performance appraisals, holding people to account."[75] The political challenges, however, were serious, because she was a bureaucrat rather than a politician and thus did not excel at handling the ministers from a range of different countries and backgrounds with the special treatment they expected.

The new executive director was also hampered by overt sexism. Ambassador Engfeldt noted that there were "embarrassing elements of a gender bias in attitudes of some diplomatic representatives in Nairobi and within the Secretariat."[76] In the 1990s, there were very few women in high positions at the United Nations, and Dowdeswell had an inherently more difficult time building legitimacy as a woman from the Global North holding a position of power in a paternalistic environment recently vacated by a traditional masculine leader. As one UNEP staff member recalled, "I can remember one of the senior African managers in the organization said one day, 'In my country there's an expression: when you have a woman general, be prepared to die bravely.'"[77] Sexism was prevalent in the high levels of Kenya's government at the time, which inevitably curbed Dowdeswell's authority and effectiveness. As Joe Khamisi recounts, when US Ambassador Smith Hempstone left Kenya in February 1993, two women took on the post consecutively, Aurelia E. Brazeal (1993–1996) and Prudence Bushnell (1996–1999). Kenyan President Moi considered that a signal of America's disregard for his country. "Moi was convinced that the US government was intentionally sending him women as a message that he was just not good enough to merit a white male," Bushnell wrote.[78]

The explicit sexism and the fierce opposition Dowdeswell encountered from some of the permanent representatives in Nairobi and some of the staff at headquarters detracted from her ability to assert positive, authoritative leadership in a context in which excessive reliance on and deference to top management had prevailed. Some member states, however, recognized the challenges she had to overcome. "I was impressed by Liz Dowdeswell," said Idunn Eidheim, former deputy director general of the Norwegian Ministry of Environment. "Tolba had run UNEP like his own organization, and she sought to be an effective administrator."[79] The environment within which she had to operate, however, was not conducive to her management style and hampered many of her efforts.

NEOLIBERAL ECONOMICS AND PRECARIOUS FINANCING

Significant economic and political shifts affected the attention to and investment in UNEP during Dowdeswell's tenure. The new neoliberal economic model, combined with the minor economic recession that occurred in the early 1990s, led the international community to focus on economic growth, often at any cost.[80] It was an "awfully ungrateful time to be running an environment agency," Mark Halle remarked.[81] Environmental issues had fallen precipitously down the political agenda in many countries and were increasingly couched in terms of economic costs rather than human rights. Driven by global competition for market share, governments put short-term economic gains at the top of their priorities. Under this framing, even if developing countries were to willingly adopt measures to halt environmental deterioration, they would risk their place in the global economy in the immediate term. Saddled with huge debts, developing countries were forced by the existing economic and political realities to adapt their national strategies to the neoliberal dynamic of unrestricted economic growth.

Political support for the environment, and for its main international institution, plummeted.[82] In the United States, the 1994 "Gingrich revolution" during President Bill Clinton's first term in office resulted in the takeover of both houses of Congress by Republicans.[83] The new legislators were skeptical and even hostile to multilateral institutions and the environment, and as a result the United States stopped contributing to the United Nations and all of its agencies and programmes.[84] Contributions to UNEP diminished from an all-time high of $21 million in both 1993 and 1994 (or $37 million when adjusted for inflation) to $5.5 million in 1997 (equivalent to $8.7 million), a more than 76 percent drop (in real terms). "The requests from the Clinton administration remained at or near 1993–94 levels through the remainder of their term in office," explained John Matuszak, international affairs officer at the US State Department, "but they were never approved by Congress."[85]

The vacuum left by the United States could not be filled by other states.[86] Europe was struggling with the dual impacts of the aftermath of the dissolution of the Soviet Union and the Yugoslav Wars. Countries in the former Soviet Bloc stopped contributing because of the economic and political crises they were experiencing. Larger Western European countries also diminished their support. France, for example, slashed its contribution by 75 percent, from the $2 million it had contributed annually from 1990 to 1994 to less than $500,000 in 1995, and it failed to contribute at all in 1996. Smaller European countries, on the other hand, stepped in and increased their support. Denmark's contribution increased in the 1990s—from $575,000 in 1990 to $2.4 million in 1998—as did that of the Netherlands, from $790,000 to $2 million in that period. The 1990s, therefore, were very challenging for UNEP financially and politically.

Without strong support from developed countries, UNEP found itself confined to a narrow interpretation of its mandate and limited in action by its funding.[87]

Overall, contributions to the Environment Fund plunged more than 30 percent in less than five years—from close to $130 million in 1992–1993 to $90 million in 1996–1997. The precarious financial situation exerted significant pressure on UNEP's leadership and management. At the same time, a survey of environmental financing available in UN entities showed the enormous disparities in the system. In the mid-1990s, expenditures for environmental projects within the International Labour Organization were $50 million per year, at the Food and Agriculture Organization $51.3 million, and at UNDP $170 million.[88] Ultimately, the expansion of the number of institutions with environmental portfolios and the reduction of UNEP's resources substantially eroded the organization's central role in global environmental governance.

The difficult financial situation led to program adjustments and staff reductions, propelling UNEP into what some analysts call a "doom loop." The result was stagnation, irrelevance, and a consensus that "UNEP was adrift."[89] These problems made the task of the new executive director very demanding. The need to reinvent the organization in the new geopolitical and institutional landscape led to an inward-looking period that lasted until mid-1998.

ROOTS OF REFORM

In the 1990s, there was a real mismatch between the kind of institution that UNEP was and the kind of institution it wanted to be. Mostafa Tolba had pursued a broad normative agenda of environmental law and institutions but had also developed many ways to engage directly on the ground. Having agreed to sustainable development as the overarching goal, developing countries increasingly demanded that UNEP actively support concrete projects within their jurisdictions. Developed countries resisted these demands and argued that UNEP's normative mandate precluded such involvement.

Dowdeswell wanted UNEP to evolve toward broad scientific policy and away from local projects, and she went on record supporting UNEP's withdrawal from implementing fieldwork projects at the local and national levels—a principal legacy of Mostafa Tolba that included work in developing countries on drinking water purification, soil conservation, and pest control.[90] This institutional metamorphosis was a direct challenge to the interests of the G-77, and dissatisfaction with UNEP grew, setting the stage for the beginning of reform efforts.[91]

During the nineteenth session of the Governing Council, which met in January and February 1997, the G-77 formally objected to the programmatic and budgetary shift away from local projects. In response, Dowdeswell urged the Governing Council to support "deep and far-reaching organizational reform" that would entail "examination of the role and focus of UNEP, and also of its governance, and the provision of a sound and adequate financial base."[92] Governments, however, could not agree on the creation of a high-level committee for policy guidance to UNEP and suspended the session on its last day. After subsequent meetings in Geneva, delegates reconvened in Nairobi in March. One of the most notable outcomes of the session was the 1997 Nairobi Declaration on the Role and Mandate of UNEP, which confirmed UNEP's role as the leading environmental authority and its ambitious mandate in science, policy, and support. The mandate to be the leading authority, however, did not provide UNEP with any explicit authority over the environmental conventions and their secretariats nor with any capacity to hold secretariats or UN entities accountable. This paper-tiger mandate has been a challenge. In 1997, the UN Office for Internal Oversight Services carried out an evaluation and identified UNEP's core problem: "The basic issue facing UNEP is the clarification of its role," the report concluded, "It is not clear to staff or to stakeholders what that role should be. The lack of clarity has had consequences for … staff morale and esprit de corps." The recommendation was to focus on fewer priorities and increase UNEP's effectiveness and impact.[93] This identity challenge has persisted and continues to be a major obstacle to effectiveness and impact.

Ultimately, despite all the difficulties within and outside the organization, Elizabeth Dowdeswell was deeply committed to making a difference. During her tenure at UNEP, she sought to bring about positive operational, cultural, and environmental change. She created new programs in areas where the organization had not been active, including a vibrant trade and environment program, and in spite of opposition and sexism became a prominent player in this field.[94] Yet, despite the process of rethinking that Dowdeswell initiated, the role of UNEP remained contested, its value added misunderstood.[95] Notwithstanding the challenges and open resistance she faced, progress was made during the final phase of Dowdeswell's tenure that enabled UNEP to emerge with a new sense of purpose.[96]

KLAUS TÖPFER (1998–2006)

In 1998, Dr. Klaus Töpfer, former German environment minister and one of the key negotiators at the Rio Earth Summit, was appointed executive director of UNEP. Kofi Annan had assumed the office of UN Secretary-General the previous year and had launched an effort aimed at comprehensive UN reform. Environment emerged as a critical concern. "Of all the challenges facing the world community in the next century," Annan stated in the 1998 Secretary-General's report on *Environment and Human Settlements*, "none will be more formidable or pervasive as the attainment of a sustainable equilibrium between economic growth, poverty reduction, social equity and the protection of the Earth's resources, common and life-support systems."[97] Annan appointed Klaus Töpfer as the leader of a new Task Force on Environment and Human Settlements. This meant that Töpfer had a leadership position in the UN system from the start of his term. With experience as an academic, a government official, and a minister, Töpfer commanded respect from UNEP's core constituency, the world's environment ministers,[98] who saw him as "both a committed 'green' and a pragmatic manager."[99] During his two terms, Töpfer stabilized UNEP and expanded its operations.

CONSUMMATE POLITICIAN

Having served as a politician, a minister of both planning and environment in a prominent country, and a university professor, Töpfer had deep knowledge of the issues and the system. He also knew what was going on in UNEP as he had led the German delegation to the UNEP Governing Council, participated in the annual informal ministerial consultations, and served as a contributor and leader in the Rio Earth Summit. As Mostafa Tolba remarked, "He knew what was there before he came, and that is why we were all putting our eggs in his basket."[100]

Töpfer's entrepreneurial leadership was externally focused and politically driven. He had high personal political ambitions and saw UNEP as a stepping stone to becoming EU Commissioner of Environment or President of Germany. This ambition was evident from the start, and throughout his two terms as executive director he retained his links to the European political scene. Staff members noted that Töpfer was very attentive to EU priorities and to German concerns and "always kept a foot in his old pond while fishing in UNEP's."[101] A consummate politician, Töpfer saw the environment as political. "Whether or not solutions are effectively applied will continue to rely upon politics and policy," he wrote in 1998, "upon the aptitude of leaders, parties and their constituents and upon a complex cross-referencing and cooperative system involving international agencies, national environmental agencies, nongovernmental organizations, and international conventions and agreements."[102] In this political context, member states were UNEP's primary constituency that demanded close attention, and civil society was an important ally.

As minister of planning in Germany, Töpfer had presided over the move of the German capital from Bonn to Berlin in the mid-1990s. When he was appointed as UNEP's executive director in 1998, many thought that he would be "a Trojan Horse" for the relocation of UNEP to Bonn under the guise of transforming UNEP into a specialized agency, a UN (or World) Environment Organization.[103] Instead, Töpfer became an ardent supporter of UNEP's location in Kenya and reaffirmed it in nearly every speech to the international community. His intellectual leadership instigated a change in narrative at UNEP, moving the organization toward a more central role in sustainable development. He advocated for integrating social and economic concerns with the ecological and cultural dimensions of the natural and built environment. "When I went to Kenya eight years ago as German minister for the environment," he told the German Council for Sustainable Development in 2005, "it was not only my English that was miserable. My understanding of the problem was also miserable. My understanding of the problem was much more focused on environmental policy. Today,

I am firmly convinced that the environment is vital to development."[104] Indeed, Töpfer focused on this new narrative, articulated the positive relationship between environment and development, and promoted a UNEP motto "Environment for Development."

Töpfer's vision for UNEP was to engage in any effort that had political momentum and value. He sought to create institutional mechanisms to engage constituencies and secure their support. As chair of the Task Force on Environment and Human Settlements in 1998, he led an analytical and political process that set out a vision for reforming UNEP that, when completed years later, led to reform of UNEP's governance structure, as chapter 7 explains.

FUNDAMENTAL RESTRUCTURING

From the outset of his term in office, Töpfer acknowledged UNEP's achievements in science, law, and policy but noted that the work had taken a sectoral or issue-based approach. Recognizing that the Rio Earth Summit demanded a more integrative approach, he created a fundamentally different organizational structure. UNEP had been organized around particular issues with Program Activity Centers. Töpfer moved to a focus on functions—environmental assessment and early warning, development of policy instruments, enhanced coordination with environmental conventions, technology transfer and industry, and support to Africa—and created divisions within each of these topics.[105] The expectation was that the new organizational structure would result in greater coordination and clarification of the lines of authority and responsibility within the organization. Töpfer envisioned that specific sectoral issues such as water, air, and ecosystems would be dealt with in every division. He also addressed new areas such as conflict and environment, for example, and created the post-conflict assessment branch, which governments have relied on for a number of assessments and advice in conflict situations.

Achieving a coordinated, concerted approach within the organization underscored the need for communication, information exchange, and an overarching strategy, areas in which UNEP had been struggling. Divisions, however, operated as silos and lacked organizational unity. This alienation was even more pronounced at the outpost offices at the regional and country level, where employees identified as professionals working on a concrete issue rather than as UNEP staff.[106] Under the new structure, it was not uncommon for various divisions to focus on different life-cycle periods of the same issue—for example, assessment of water pollution, policy development, policy implementation, and communication on water pollution actions—which meant that groups that were fundamentally working on the same issue were competing for scarce resources and attention. This resulted in ad hoc financial requests from divisions and a perception of competition within the organization. A major shift in organizational culture was necessary to improve communication and collaboration, but management challenges and the prolonged absences of the executive director from Nairobi led to continuous struggles to articulate UNEP's role and identity.

FINANCIAL VIABILITY AND INSTABILITY

Klaus Töpfer had to dramatically elevate UNEP's diminished visibility and increase its financial resources at a time when the organization was financially weakened, institutionally diffuse, and politically marginalized. In the late 1990s, the world was in the grips of a financial crisis that had spread from Thailand through the rest of the world and challenged the "Asian Miracle" narrative. Financial and political commitments undertaken at Rio remained unfulfilled. The North had not even come close to its 0.7 percent of GDP target for financial assistance it had committed to in 1970.[107] Little progress had been made on resolving global environmental concerns and both the Global North and South had failed to implement their environmental agreements to safeguard biodiversity, reverse desertification, reduce pollution, deal with persistent organic pollutants and hazardous waste, or address climate change. Governments' attention had moved away from the environment into sustainable development, a neoliberal ideology had taken root, and the institutional landscape had become even more crowded. This required the new executive director to invest a great deal of time and effort into mobilizing political support from governments.

As a former minister in the European Union, Töpfer knew how to engage with donors. He was supportive of the notion of "upgrading" UNEP into a specialized agency.[108] Driven to gain political stature, increase UNEP's exposure, and affirm its leadership role on the global environmental stage, Töpfer was quick to start new initiatives, mobilize attention, and raise funding. "So, when there was a tsunami in the world," Mark Halle remarked, "Töpfer was worried about how you deal with victims and UNEP dropped everything they were doing and shifted over to running and setting up a tsunami program." In the immediate aftermath of the tsunami in 2003, for example, Töpfer created the Asian Tsunami Disaster Task Force to assist governments in assessing and responding to the environmental impacts of the tsunami. UNEP deployed experts to Indonesia, Sri Lanka, Thailand, the Maldives, the Seychelles, and Yemen to engage in operational work.[109] Töpfer created new partnerships and new UNEP centers around the world, which increased UNEPs presence in the field but also scattered focus and attention and detracted from its normative mandate.[110]

Töpfer also sought out opportunities to speak about the work of the institution. He received an increasing number of requests to address member states, and as a result, UNEP became more visible. Projecting a positive picture of UNEP was to lead to increased donor confidence and resources, and in its communications and programming, UNEP focused almost entirely on successes and avoided ineffective initiatives or lessons learned. This strategy resulted in the expected positive perception, but it also contributed to an organizational culture with strong aversion to criticism. The negative consequence, a staff member noted, was that UNEP was "permeated by fear of being criticized and is not adult enough to deal with criticism."[111]

Overall, the executive director succeeded in achieving his financial goals. UNEP's finances increased from close to $260 million in the 1998–1999 biennium ($401 million when adjusted for inflation) when Töpfer took office to about $580 million in 2006–2007 ($723 million when adjusted for inflation) when he left, representing an increase of 80 percent when adjusted for inflation (see figure 6.4). This growth was due exclusively to an increase in extrabudgetary resources. During Töpfer's term, income from those sources more than doubled, from $153.7 million in 1998–1999 ($247.5 million when adjusted for inflation) to $394.3 million in 2004–2005 ($524.4 million when adjusted for inflation). During his eight years in office, Töpfer created fifty-nine new trust funds, more than any other executive director in UNEP's history.[112] The "earmark craziness,"[113] former Assistant Executive Director Anthony Brough remarked, has reshaped UNEP's financing over time, and such funds now constitute over 80 percent of UNEP's income.[114] The Environment Fund stayed relatively constant but at a very low level. During Töpfer's two terms, UNEP's average annual income from the Environment Fund adjusted for inflation was at $76 million, lower than all except for Erik Solheim's term ($72 million; see figures 6.2 and 6.4).

The move away from core funding to earmarked contributions led to an increase in revenues, a large number of funds, and consequently, to a proliferation of projects. While the additional resources are necessary and welcome, the growing number of new funds also drained staff members' time and effort and diminished UNEP's independence and flexibility. The incessant need to secure new resources led to a vicious circle reinforcing the importance of extrabudgetary resources.

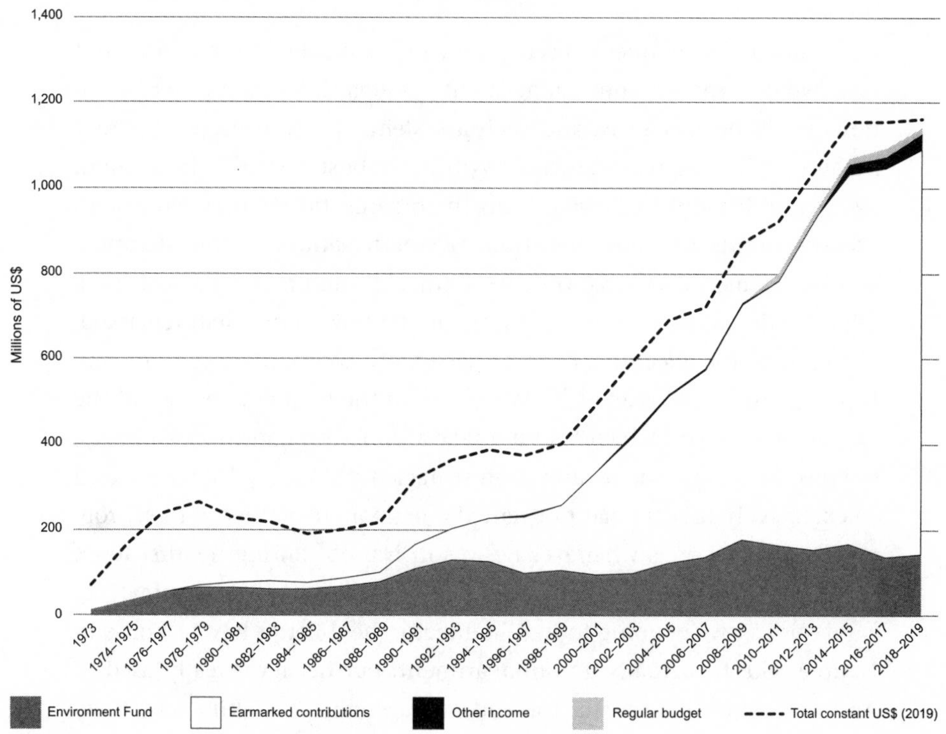

6.4 UNEP income from 1973 to 2019 by category.

THE TRAVEL TRAP

Töpfer's top priority was to regain the support of important contributors and improve UNEP's financial health. To increase visibility and bolster funding, he engaged with many countries, in many issues, at many sites. "If that meant frequent absences from Nairobi and hard political graft in national capitals," Stanley Johnson wrote in 2012 after interviewing Klaus Töpfer on the occasion of UNEP's fortieth anniversary, "then that—in Töpfer's view—was a price that had to be paid."[115] Indeed, Töpfer came to be known as "one of the top ten people who travel most around the world," a distinction he acknowledged with some pride.[116] "When I first came to Nairobi," he recalled, "they told me this joke about Dr. Tolba. 'What is the difference between Dr. Tolba and God the Father?' And the answer? 'God the Father is everywhere. Dr. Tolba is everywhere except Nairobi!' Well, now you can cross out Tolba and put Töpfer there instead."[117] The prolonged absences of the executive director from the Nairobi headquarters, however, affected UNEP's management and operations, and the morale of the staff.

Because of his frequent absences, the executive director had not built effective governance and management systems that could cover operations while he was away, and such a system was even more necessary because of his extensive absence. Without robust systems, the vacuum of internal leadership slowed down the organization and angered staff. "No one minds the store when Töpfer is not in Nairobi"[118] and "no one is allowed to make decisions while he is away,"[119] staff members explained. Töpfer had to approve any activity, no matter how minor, staff remarked, stating that the executive director personally approved or rejected any trip over twenty kilometers.[120] As a result, in the frequent absence of the executive director, UNEP could not take a stance on controversial issues; hobbled by delays, the organization struggled.[121] Indeed, Töpfer traveled so extensively that he had not rented a permanent residence in Nairobi and stayed in hotels whenever he was in Nairobi during his first term. "So, the staff actually rose up in arms," one government official remarked, "and said: 'If we're going to have a director, he'd better have a house in Nairobi.' So, he actually got an apartment, but he never really used it. And that was a big part of the bad management."[122] Ultimately, however, the executive director could not have increased UNEP's authority and financing without being able to connect directly with governments around the world, which did require extensive travel.

REGAINED VISIBILITY

Töpfer's political savvy and competence were critical to making UNEP more recognizable, more visible, and a more sought-after partner. In emphasizing the environment as the foundation for development, Töpfer advanced the eco-development ideas that Maurice Strong and Mostafa Tolba had articulated. He did not focus on engaging in international environmental lawmaking in the way that UNEP had done in the early years but extended the work that Liz Dowdeswell had begun after the Rio Earth Summit by bringing the environmental dimension into the mainstream of the development debate. Töpfer took advantage of the broader operating space that the 1997 Nairobi Declaration had provided and engaged governments more intensively than any previous executive director. The Töpfer Task Force also produced an ambitious and widely accepted report on environment and human settlements with twenty-four recommendations for reforming and creating structures, rules, institutions, political processes, relations, and systems. The report recommended, for example, the creation of a Global Ministerial Environment Forum, a platform for the world's environment ministers to convene both in Nairobi and in countries around the world in a special session in alternate years; the establishment of the Environment Management Group, a problem-solving, results-oriented interagency mechanism to achieve effective coordination and joint action on key environmental and human-settlement issues throughout the UN system; and the reform of the membership of the UNEP Governing Council from limited to universal, i.e., in line with the UN General Assembly. These recommendations would appear in the reports of multiple intergovernmental groups working on international environmental governance and would be enacted over the following years as part of UNEP's reform process.

In May 2000, UNEP convened the first Global Ministerial Environmental Forum in Malmö, Sweden. Over one hundred ministers gathered along with more than five hundred delegates from over 130 countries and adopted the Malmö Ministerial Declaration. The Declaration recognized the challenge of the increasing number of international environmental agreements and their implementation, called for reinvigorated international cooperation and solidarity, and urged a closer partnership with civil society and the private sector, issues that would resurface regularly as priorities over the years.[123] The Declaration sounded the same alarm bells that had rung in the UN Millennium Survey, in which 57,000 adults from sixty countries had responded that they thought their governments had not done enough to protect their environment.[124] Töpfer was positioning UNEP to play a leadership role in the planning for the 2002 World Summit on Sustainable Development in South Africa.[125]

Töpfer led UNEP through the 2002 Cartagena process on reforming international environmental governance, which moved the reform agenda forward. He established central functions in Nairobi while also strengthening UNEP's presence in Geneva and New York.[126] The reform process would ultimately result in important changes to UNEP's governance structures (many of which were articulated in the 1998 Töpfer Task Force report) years after Dr. Klaus Töpfer had left office and under the leadership of UNEP's subsequent Executive Director, Achim Steiner.

ACHIM STEINER (2006–2016)

In September 2005, at the High-level Plenary Meeting of the sixtieth session of the UN General Assembly, Achim Steiner, representing civil society as Director General of IUCN, addressed member states. "In order to make poverty history," he stated, "we need to make environment the future."[127] Less than a year later, in June 2006, Steiner was appointed to the position of executive director of UNEP with the explicit mandate to catalyze and promote international cooperation and action to safeguard the environment. On his first day as UNEP's executive director, Steiner reiterated his commitment to connecting poverty and ecosystem vitality, saying, "For too long economics and environment have seemed like players on rival teams. There have been a lot of nasty challenges and far too many own goals. We need to make these two sides of the development coin team players, players on the same side."[128] He thus picked up the theme that all UNEP executive directors had been working on since the organization's inception: bringing environment and development into a coherent framework. Steiner served two four-year terms with one two-year extension to see through the governance reforms.

CHARISMATIC LEADERSHIP

Steiner had the competency and tact to operate in the international community in a politically savvy fashion similar to that of Klaus Töpfer, but he was bolder, more articulate, and more ambitious in undertaking substantive work. Born and raised in Brazil to a German farmer, Steiner enjoyed extraordinary legitimacy among developing countries because of his stance on addressing environment and development as connected challenges, his experience and knowledge of different cultures and development contexts across four continents, and because of the understanding and empathy he exhibited. "I wanted to assist in realizing a far more focused and responsive institution," he noted, "so that when governments request action, the system is already aligned to deliver."[129] He approached issues with a positive attitude and engaged with potential partners with new ideas, solutions, and initiatives.

He projected a sense that his was a fresh approach and was able to convince others that this genuinely was a new start for UNEP. His political and diplomatic skills made him, and thus UNEP, relevant, and often critical, to the positive outcomes of many high-level, high-stakes discussions. He succeeded in making governments feel comfortable with him and in engaging productively with the governing bodies. As Ambassador Julia Pataki, Chair of the Committee of Permanent Representatives from 2014 to 2016, remarked, Steiner "had it all. He could discuss everything in a holistic manner, had good political sense, related well to people, and was accessible."[130] As an intellectual leader, Steiner brought to UNEP a clear appreciation for the need to embed environmental policy into the political economy of society, to treat nature as capital, and to integrate the value of ecosystem services into national policy.[131] Upon taking office, he committed to work on ensuring that markets and international treaties could support environmental and social goals. In addition, Steiner successfully engaged governments and the private sector.

INTEGRATIVE VISION

For Steiner, the environment was more than just one of the three pillars of sustainable development (along with the economy and social issues), as the 1992 Rio Earth Summit had emphasized; instead, the environment was the foundation for all life on Earth. "The natural services provided by the land, the air, the biodiversity, and the world's waters have been frequently treated as free and limitless," Steiner declared. "While money may make the world go round," he said, "what makes money go round is ultimately the trillions of dollars generated by the planet's goods and services from the air cleaning and climate change countering processes of forests to the fisheries and the coastline protection power of coral reefs."[132] Steiner's priority, therefore, was to decouple economic growth from resource use and demonstrate that environmental protection is fundamental to a stable society and economy. His conviction shifted the prevailing narrative away from the "three-pillars" approach of Rio.[133] The green economy and green finance became landmark initiatives of Steiner's tenure.

Articulating a compelling vision was one of Steiner's core strengths. As UN Secretary-General Ban Ki-moon noted in our interview, Steiner is "very passionate and very eloquent and has deep knowledge."[134] He could work successfully with a range of actors and convince them to support his vision and his efforts. Steiner saw UNEP as "an ever-brighter beacon of intellectual leadership, scientific assessment, and an energetic catalyst for the deep and meaningful policy reforms and revolutions so urgently needed worldwide."[135] To this end, he set out to make the organization efficient and effective by introducing results-based management and focusing on a few key priority initiatives, including the Design of a Sustainable Financial System, The Economics of Ecosystems and Biodiversity (TEEB), and the Portfolio Decarbonization Coalition, among others. He also introduced a Medium-Term Strategy to help measure the organization's performance. The strategy provides the vision and direction for all UNEP activities for three-year periods through cross-cutting thematic priorities. The goal was to enable UNEP to deliver on its mandate by creating a framework for focused, effective, and efficient delivery of results; and for transparent monitoring and evaluation of performance.[136]

MANAGEMENT CONTESTATION

At the outset, Steiner improved staff morale. People felt a new sense of hope because he believed in UNEP and was able to communicate his passion. Initially, there was also hope that Steiner would help heal rifts within the organization and foster discipline and self-motivation among staff. Similar to other bureaucracies, however, the internal workings of UNEP have remained rather inscrutable. And while reform of UNEP's internal structure was necessary, this required a range of difficult actions that Steiner was not able to push through.

As had every executive director before him, Steiner reorganized UNEP's internal structure. He sought to return to the issue-focused approach of Tolba's period, but without changing the functional approach and divisional structure that Töpfer had created. The result was a complex organization—a matrix structure that staff consistently characterized as burdensome and ineffectual. As one staff member noted, "During Steiner's time all divisions were doing everything, each was a mini UNEP."[137] Another challenge was the increased emphasis on projects as the delivery mechanism for achievement of the program of work. In this system, the cycle for projects is two years, and at the end of every project staff may be dismissed. This put considerable pressure on staff to constantly justify their employment, which was compounded by the pressure to attract funding and to ensure that new projects were in the pipeline. The need to manage and deliver on projects while having to raise funds to maintain staff levels creates a stressful work environment: "One-year contracts keep staff in suspense and create fear and a culture of not speaking up," a staff member reflected.[138] In essence, this meant that UNEP was managed on a personal level. "Jobs are promised, recruitment is pro forma, and there is retaliation through contract extension," they lamented.[139] Some of these issues are part of the larger UN system and not unique to UNEP, and they certainly present challenges to every executive director. How that leader handles these problems can be telling.

"There was no better communicator than Steiner," Idunn Eidheim of the Norwegian Environment Ministry remarked, "but he traveled a lot and was not able to delegate enough responsibility. The executive director should be able to speak for the organization, and communication skills are critical, but a skilled administrator is also crucial."[140] Steiner's management philosophy was that a good manager could manage anything, and he focused on hiring people with management expertise rather than trying to find potential managers with issue expertise among UNEP staff. Steiner would not recognize mistakes he had made in appointments, however, and would "stick with them far beyond the time it became clear they were not working at all," Mark Halle remarked.[141] Staff commented that Steiner's management style was very hierarchical, that he managed the organization through a shadow cabinet, and that he relied on a small network of close friends and associates, which alienated many competent staff who felt excluded and ignored. Steiner had assembled a senior leadership team of a few top-echelon staffers—the directors of the divisions, the deputy director, the head of the New York office, and the chief of the executive office—and convened over 250 meetings of that team. He took time to discuss and deliberate, but avoided making tough decisions, and UNEP remained top-down.[142]

The challenges with management at UNEP have been essential for every executive director. Steiner sought to introduce results-based management, but "an intergovernmental institution such as the UN does not lend itself to quick fixes and easy change," he told the Governing Council in 2010.[143] Communications, data and analysis for strategic management, human resources, and capacity and skills development remained critical concerns and an obstacle to timely and effective delivery. Significant reform, however, requires bold decisions and upsetting the status quo, a difficult proposition to deliver on. The two directors who openly challenged the status quo—Elizabeth Dowdeswell and Erik Solheim—only served one term and half a term, respectively.

TECHNOLOGY REVOLUTION AND FINANCIAL EXPANSION

Steiner's term at UNEP was defined by technological advances the likes of which had not been seen in generations, including remarkable progress in communication capacity, which led to an increase in transparency. At the same time, member states were demanding management reform and a move to a more results-based organization. "When I arrived," Steiner remarked, "a lot of the governments were saying 'okay, we know why we have UNEP, but can it be re-tuned so that it delivers far more in very practical terms?'"[144] Recognizing the importance of working with other UN organizations, Steiner put a lot of energy into building stronger ties with them. "The challenges are so immense that, only by working together in mutual self-interest, can we realize internationally agreed goals and deliver a stable, just and healthy planet for this and future generations," he noted.[145] Accordingly, Steiner improved UNEP's relations with other UN bodies, especially with UNDP and the World Bank. Though challenges in delivering the desired results persisted, his strategy was to refocus and revive UNEP, and create an understanding of UNEP as the environment programme of the UN. As a result, UNEP gained attention and prominence in the UN system.[146]

Steiner also managed to elevate the standing of UNEP's New York office in the UN system by raising the status of its director from a D1 (director) post to an Assistant Secretary-General, one of two UNEP staff (the other being the Deputy Director) at that level . This effectively signaled that it was a leadership position, not just a high-level management job.[147] In the political system of the United Nations, such status is critical, as former Secretary-General Ban Ki-moon noted in our interview.[148] Every UN member state is represented in New York by a permanent representative with the status of an Ambassador. Ambassadors are reluctant to meet with counterparts if they don't hold equally high positions and would often avoid or refuse to interact directly with the director of UNEP's New York office while that position was at the D1 level. An Assistant Secretary-General commands respect and attracts attention.

Steiner continued on the trajectory set by Klaus Töpfer in improving UNEP's financial health. Contributions increased from the very start of his term in office and continued to rise. During his term (2006–2016), the total income of the organization per biennium almost doubled from $580 million in 2006–2007 to over $1 billion in 2015–2016. The Environment Fund stayed constant during that period at $91 million per year, while earmarked contributions and trust funds increased by over 90 percent. The increase in overall finances came from extrabudgetary funds that imposed restrictions on how the money could be spent and inserted an additional level of oversight; however, this stream also allowed for entrepreneurship by the executive director in reaching out for support of various initiatives that would be of interest to partners. Steiner thus continued the trend that had taken off under Töpfer's leadership and brought in substantively higher annual amounts of financial contributions over his ten years in office when compared to other UNEP executive directors (see figure 6.2).

REGAINED AUTHORITY

Steiner's proactive attitude improved UNEP's reputation and helped increase its authority among governments and within the UN system. The integrated approach to environment, society, and development encouraged developing countries to step up and assist with solutions, even though they were not responsible for causing many of the problems that were being addressed. Developing countries argued that they did not cause climate change but nevertheless agreed to be part of the solution. They also came to take responsibility for helping to solve the problems of endangered species and deforestation, and restated the importance of land and culture, advocating for the rights of indigenous peoples and the rights of mother earth.[149]

Steiner walked the talk on sustainability and led a far-reaching physical transformation. When he took office, he declared that he was "fully committed to ensuring that UNEP's headquarters becomes ever more a world-class facility, on par with cities like New York or Geneva," because, he explained, "Africa and the developing world deserve nothing less."[150] He delivered on that promise a few years later, in 2011, when the new Nairobi headquarters for UNEP and UN-Habitat opened its doors. Featuring energy-efficient lighting, natural ventilation systems, rain harvesting, and gardens with hardy indigenous plants, this eco-building set a new standard for sustainability in buildings. It has six thousand square meters of solar panels—the largest installation on a roof in East Africa at the time—that generate all the electricity necessary for the 1,200 building occupants. In its first year of operation, the solar-powered building saved at least 650,000 kilowatt-hours of electricity and up to 1.4 million shillings (about $14,000) in electricity bills compared to a standard building of the same size. It also supports employee well-being with a pleasant work environment that highlights greenery and natural light. "It's a brilliant building to work in; the light around our office space is wonderful and it's nice not to hear the sound of generators and to have everything running efficiently," one staff member noted, adding that it was a building of the future (see figure 5.4).[151]

Steiner's ambitions for UNEP were driven by his aspiration to bring countries together and advance a shared agenda. During his ten-year tenure, he obtained political support, increased financial resources signicantficantly, and sought to align UNEP and the UN system to advance environmental priorities. He worked to make environment ministers more effective in their own national debates and in their own countries by building connections beyond their offices. He also moved the dialogue beyond governments and engaged civil society and the private sector, which increased UNEP's recognition and influence on the international stage to a level comparable to that of the Tolba era. In 2016, after leaving UNEP, Steiner joined the Martin School at Oxford University, but only a few months later, in 2017, he became the Administrator of UNDP, a major competitor and collaborator for UNEP.

ERIK SOLHEIM (2016–2018)

Erik Solheim became executive director of UNEP "at a critical point in UN efforts to tackle global warming, green finance flows and protect diminishing stocks of endangered flora and fauna," environmental news outlets noted at the time of his appointment in 2016.[152] He came into an organization on the rise, actively seeking to assert its place as the global authority on the environment. Having served as environment and development minister in Norway, Solheim had a plan for the organization. A risk-taker by nature, he came in with a new management style. He focused on the outside world and set out to create a new narrative; engaged with new constituencies, China and India in particular; and sought to restructure the administrative systems.[153] Solheim found the UN bureaucratic and stifling and was defiant in his disregard for rules that he found antiquated and wanted to change. Dissatisfaction with his management style spurred an audit report by the United Nations Office of Internal Oversight Services of official travel at UNEP. The investigation resulted in negative press, the critical findings led to the freezing of funds by some member states, and Solheim's reform plans were halted.[154] "I trusted the strong marching orders for reform of the UN we were given by the UN Secretary-General and was absolutely confident he would support reformers," Solheim remarked in our 2020 interview. "I didn't realize it was all reform talk, not reforms."[155] Less than two years into the job, in November 2018, Solheim resigned from UNEP at the request of UN Secretary-General António Guterres.

CHANGING THE CONVERSATION

Solheim came into UNEP with a clear plan to connect with people so that they can act and encourage their governments to act, but he lost his leadership position amid the controversy that ensued. His foremost priority was to change the conversation in order to inspire and empower people to protect their environment. His conviction was that environmental progress would only happen if people demand change, politicians regulate markets and stay consistent, and the private sector engages fully. "Our challenge is that we need to bring people on board, and to do this we need to stop talking in acronyms and speak a language that people understand," he said in our interview in 2017.[156] He laid out a vision for UNEP as people-centered, politically engaged, simple, and decentralized. He saw UNEP's role as "a moral voice" and a forum for interaction and action.

Perhaps Solheim's most visible reform effort was the sudden renaming of UNEP to UN Environment. Acronyms had beleaguered the organization's public narrative for decades; they fostered the perception that the UN was an anonymous, opaque institution. Solheim set out to rectify that by changing the name and making language simpler and more understandable to the broader public. The executive director cannot unilaterally change the official name of the intergovernmental institution, but they can initiate an informal change that, over time, can become normal practice. In UNEP's case, however, the change resulted in further confusion about purpose and identity.

Three months after assuming office, Solheim announced to his staff that they should refer to the organization as UN Environment. "UN Environment requires us to breathe a nanosecond longer and to spend longer time at the computer. The reward is that everyone on the planet understands what it is about," he wrote in a memo to all staff. The change was envisioned to be internal, but it soon led to change of the logo; the website URL was changed to https://unenvironment.org, and staff began referring to UNEP as UN Environment. Becoming UN Environment did not entail any change of the legal structure but resulted in needless expense of political capital because UNEP had been at a similar point before. In the 1990s and 2000s, the international environmental governance reform process instigated heated analytical and political debates on whether

UNEP should become a World Environment Organization or a UN Environment Organization. A change in name, therefore, was automatically associated with the potential for other, more substantial changes—in function, form, financing, and perhaps location. As Mohamed El-Ashry, the founder and first CEO of the Global Environment Facility, exclaimed, "Calling it UN Environment brings us back again to focusing on names and not focusing on functions and outcomes."[157] Accordingly, governments reacted strongly against the change because they had not been consulted. "Any changes to the nomenclature, mandate or nature of the Programme should follow the same process as in the General Assembly of the United Nations and be conducted in an open, transparent and inclusive manner," the African Ministerial Conference on the Environment stated in 2017.[158] Solheim's failure to observe legal rules and procedures inflamed controversy and confusion about the name change. In essence, the institution was challenging its own identity again.

A name is the baseline of an organization's identity, and Solheim felt that changing it was a necessary first step to forging a new image of the organization, despite his legal team's advice to the contrary. Solheim's vision was essentially the original vision of the governments that created UNEP in 1972: an entity to serve as the anchor institution for the environment in the UN system. But the organization had operated within the UN system for over four decades, and transformation could not happen overnight. "Erik Solheim was fresh and different but did not understand the nature of the team he was playing in," Mark Halle remarked. "You cannot play rugby at Wimbledon. UNEP is part of the system."[159] The result was increased confusion about identity, and despite the change in branding and websites, there was no consistent use of names. United Nations Environment Programme, UN Environment Programme, UNEP, and UN Environment were all used, and observers even began to say UNE as an acronym for UN Environment, which defeated the very purpose of the name change. Executive Director Inger Andersen, who took office in 2019, reverted back to the original UN Environment Programme and UNEP, but UN Environment remains sprinkled throughout the website. An important legacy of Solheim's initiative to change the language is the new nomenclature for UNEP's core building blocks, the divisions: DELC (Division of Environmental Law and Conventions), DTIE (Division of

Trade, Industry and Environment), and DCPI (Division of Communication and Public Information) became the Law Division, the Economics Division, and the Communication Division, respectively.[160] And these titles are here to stay.

ERRATIC MANAGEMENT

When UN Secretary-General António Guterres took office in 2017, he demanded that all UN agencies transform into more modern, transparent, and open institutions and engage actively in frank debates and discussions. "Nothing will make me deviate from that mission," Solheim wrote to UNEP staff in March 2018. "We need to be much more political and concrete. We shall focus on people, impact and changing behaviours. We will turn ourselves outwardly, adjust past practices, simplify and decentralize our internal processes, communicate better."[161] Solheim urged staff to embrace reform and not be afraid that change within the institution might eliminate jobs. "It is exactly the opposite," he told staff during a town hall meeting in March 2018. "Without reforms, our budget will shrink, and there is no way to keep the staff. The way to increase our budget is to do reforms."[162] Restructuring of the organization was thus in order.

Internally, Solheim restructured the executive director's office with the goal of improving management but noted that he considered organizational culture more important than structure.[163] "The culture of innovation, the culture of debate, the culture of coming up with new ideas and new solutions, is much more important than the exact way it's structured," he remarked. UNEP, however, has struggled with its organizational culture, as it has been very hierarchical and often managed through fear rather than motivation.[164] Debate and innovation are contingent upon effective management, which has been a weakness of many of the executive directors. Solheim also acknowledged that he had used all of his energy on projects out of the office, and spent too little time on administration.[165] Indeed, his erratic management style created dysfunction. He "brought in or elevated his own people," former UNEP staff member Oli Brown wrote, "who wielded tremendous power over budgets, jobs and opportunities in what soon turned into a 'game of thrones' saga of individual power games, patronage and fiefdoms."[166] As media coverage explained, some senior staff members were allowed to break the rules and received better benefits. His chief of staff, for example, continued to be based in Paris, her hometown, rather than moving to Nairobi. Staff perceived Solheim's management style as one of preferential treatment, which generated resentment. Norwegian newspaper *Aftenposten* reported that those who criticized Solheim were often told they were too bureaucratic and difficult, while those close to him "felt they could do as they liked."[167]

Externally, Solheim recognized the imperative for partnership. "UN Environment is a small organisation when you think that we are working for the entire planet," he noted. "So, everything we want to achieve will require partnerships—with governments, business or citizens."[168] His priority was to engage UNEP with China and India and to work much more closely with business, a strategy which required extensive travel. Solheim firmly believed that working with the private sector was common sense and that UNEP needed to be present in that space—though some observers cautioned that engaging business should not come at the expense of engagement with governments. Others warned that financial support from China might have led to Solheim's unconditional praise for China's Belt and Road Initiative, a global infrastructure project, which "set alarm bells ringing in capitals around the world."[169] Solheim disagreed with the US criticism that China was using UNEP to greenwash its vast and environmentally impactful infrastructure undertaking, and he noted that countries other than those in North America and Europe could also lead the way in global infrastructure development. He thus challenged the status quo in the UN system.

Solheim was also severely criticized for engaging UNEP as a sponsor of a regatta, the Volvo Ocean Race, at a cost of $500,000. He argued that this was an investment in raising UNEP's profile and a way to increase awareness about marine plastic litter, but the cost was criticized as exorbitant and the benefit elusive. In 2019, the Office of Internal Oversight Services evaluation of UNEP noted that the organization could not provide a consolidated list of partners and had entered into "questionable partnerships" in recent years.[170] Partnerships are essential, but there is a possibility of choosing the wrong partners—those who might simply seek benefits from association with the main UN environmental institution, or even engage in greenwashing. "If partnerships run bad and if UNEP's brand is used for publicity reasons, the whole institution suffers and loses credibility," said Ambassador Franz Perrez of Switzerland.[171] UNEP's eagerness to do work on the ground and engage in more partnerships, therefore, requires a full-fledged, systematic risk assessment and risk-management strategy.

PARTNERSHIPS, CAMPAIGNS, AND CONTRIBUTIONS

Integrating environmental goals into development objectives had become a baseline after 2015, when governments unanimously adopted the seventeen Sustainable Development Goals. Solheim's aim, therefore, was to work with various businesses on environmental issues relevant to their own interests—working with shipping and fishing, for example, to "clean up the oceans, get rid of the enormous volumes of marine litter that are destroying life, and make fisheries sustainable," or working with the tourism industry to protect wildlife.[172] UNEP launched and engaged in a series of campaigns, including Wild for Life, Breathe Life, and Clean Seas, and partnerships such as the Global Partnership on Marine Litter. It also launched an international law-enforcement operation against marine pollution with INTERPOL and EUROPOL called 30 Days at Sea and an awareness campaign called #PollutionCrime. The operation was "to make sure that there is no impunity for the perpetrators of marine pollution crime," Solheim noted.[173] Indeed, plastics regulation became a landmark initiative for UNEP and is an issue that Norway continues to invest in.

Solheim increased engagement with business and launched the Science-Policy-Business Forum, an incubator of joint initiatives with the private sector such as a digital platform on marine litter developed by IBM and cooperation with the international nitrogen initiative. As Isis Alvarez, who represented the women's major group at the UN Environment Assembly in 2017, noted, however, some saw this as a "corporate takeover of the UN."[174] Concurrently, UNEP's engagement with civil society shifted. Civil society has been a core constituency of UNEP providing expertise, support, outreach, and legitimacy. Whenever issues became controversial, however, UNEP leadership has kept civil society out. "When civil society said something that might not be pleasant for governments or for UNEP, anything perceived as criticism, they were excluded and shunned," a staff member said. "This dynamic still holds."[175] As a normative agency, UNEP is not able to deliver on the ground without relying on civil society's capacity to produce results; civil society, therefore, is indispensable in project work. The relationship with civil society, however, is mostly one of tokenism. "UNEP never valued civil society," Annabell Waititu remarked. "They wanted to look politically correct but always kept civil society on the periphery. They did not use the agenda setting powers and implementation capacity of civil society."[176] The effect has been a downward spiral, and many civil society groups have lost interest in working with UNEP. Solheim inherited a UNEP that had neither a good relationship with civil society nor a strategy for engaging it and his inexperience in this area further contributed to his marginalization.[177]

Heavy reliance on extrabudgetary funds rather than core funding for operations necessitates that UNEP reach out to governments regularly and raise funds for people and projects that align with the agendas of these governments' leaders. Solheim reacted against the limitations this reality entailed: "The European Union wants to give money to what they consider their agenda, not what we want to get money for," he remarked. As previously noted, Solheim supported many of China and India's initiatives, campaigns, and projects, because these governments' priorities dovetailed with his priorities for UNEP. He supported a beach-cleaning campaign in India, but, as a European government official noted, "beach-cleaning campaigns are not sufficient; government action and a level playing field are critical."[178] Solheim praised China's efforts in sustainable development but also cautioned against the country's export of coal power plants to Africa.[179] Solheim's efforts to engage China were successful and China's contributions to the Environment Fund tripled, from the $500,000 that China had contributed from 2010 to 2017 to $1.5 million in 2018. China became one of UNEP's top fifteen Environment Fund contributors that year and has maintained the level of contributions and the top 15 rank (see figure 6.5). In addition, China became a significant donor of extrabudgetary resources. Its contributions jumped from $350,000 in 2015 to $2.5 million in 2016 and to $5.7 million in 2017. In 2019, however, the contribution was down to $1.36 million.

As a result of the controversy that embroiled UNEP and Solheim, some donors pulled away, and Denmark and Sweden froze their financial

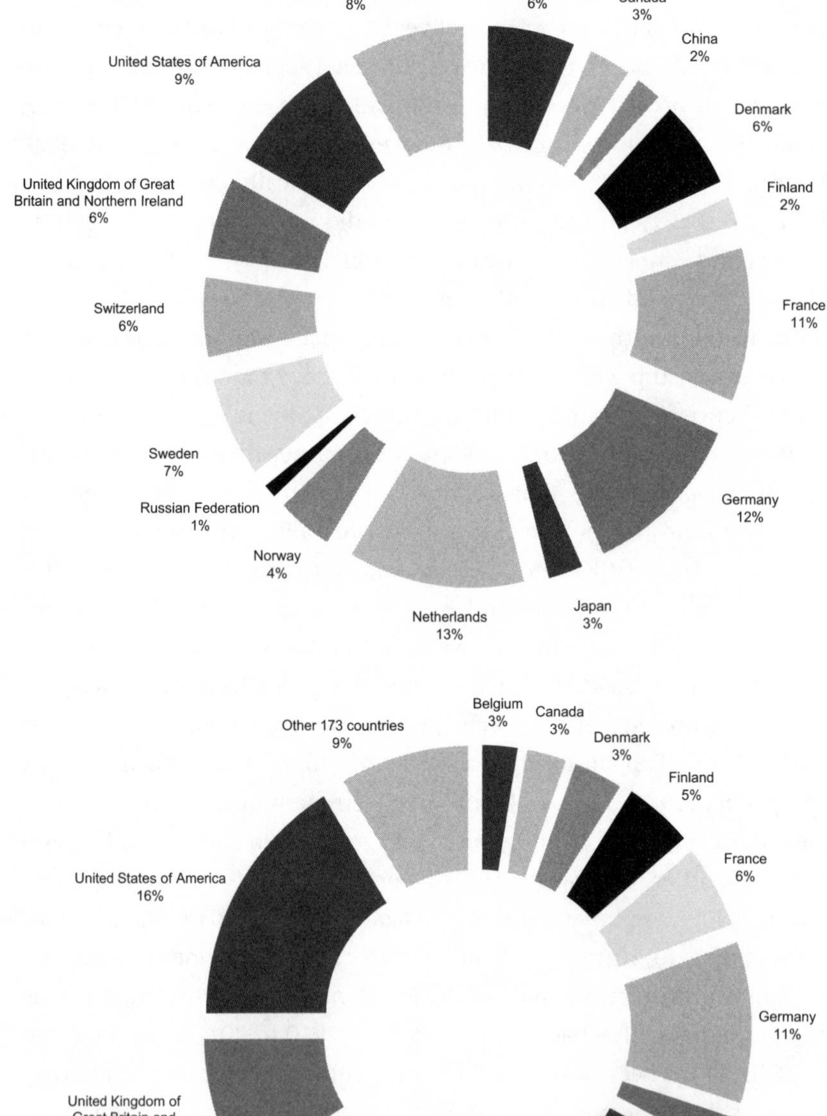

6.5 Top fifteen contributors in 2019 (top) and aggregately since 1973 (bottom).

contributions.[180] In 2018, only eighty-six countries contributed to the Environment Fund, compared to ninety-six in 2014. In 2018, the Fund had diminished by almost 25 percent from the $84 million level in 2014, and was almost at the same level as in 2007, $67.4 million. In 2019, the number of contributors dropped even further; as of January 1, 2020, only eighty countries had contributed a total of $70 million for 2019.

CONTROVERSIAL LEADERSHIP

Erik Solheim's term as UNEP's executive director began on a high note and collapsed with the loss of confidence in his leadership. As Minister of Environment and International Development in Norway, Solheim had been "morally driven, full of energy, and able to take a political situation to advance the issues he cared about, and never his personal agenda," colleagues at the ministry noted. UN Secretary-General Ban Ki-moon also remarked that Solheim had struck him as "a very devoted and committed person and the right leader for UNEP" as he carried out the selection process for an executive director in 2016. Solheim's Norwegian colleagues commented, however, that he was also hyperactive and easily frustrated when rules prevented him from doing what he thought was right. He would break the rules and capitalize on the opportunities that created. Ultimately, Solheim's leadership was highly controversial because of what some considered excessive travel, inept management, and open disregard for UN rules.

The United Nations Office of Internal Oversight Services conducted an audit of official travel at UNEP in 2018 with the objective of assessing the adequacy and effectiveness of existing internal controls. The inquiry into Solheim's travel was a pretext for an inquiry into management misconduct. The report criticized UNEP and its leadership for lack of accountability and transparency, possible mismanagement of travel funds, and deliberate defiance of regulations and rules that senior management deemed "bureaucratic" and "political."[181] Erik Solheim challenged the report and vigorously defended all his travel as a critical part of his job. "I can't ask the leader of Coca-Cola to come see me in Nairobi, I have to go visit him," he remarked, referring to the work he championed on getting rid of plastic bottles and reducing marine litter.[182] Indeed, as the analysis in this chapter shows, every UNEP executive director has had to undertake extensive travel. In the early days, that meant being away from headquarters for months on end. The sheer distance, limited availability of travel options, and the need to directly connect with constituencies, given that 60 percent of countries are not represented in Nairobi and only a few are represented by special environmental envoys, demand that the executive director travel to capitals and conferences.

Extensive travel is hardly unique to UNEP. As the UN Joint Inspection Unit noted in a 2017 Review of Air Travel Policies in the United Nations System, "travel expenses are one of the largest budget components of the United Nations system organizations after staff costs."[183] UNEP's travel costs are average when compared to other UN agencies but increased transparency and accountability exposed irregularities. Controls over the travel authorization process were weak, many trips were not appropriately authorized prior to travel, evidence of the necessity to travel was incomplete or missing, and there was no oversight or accountability mechanism in place to oversee the travels undertaken.[184]

Dissatisfaction with Solheim's management style was perhaps the root cause of the complaints and the audit. In his view, he was trying to change the rigid, complicated bureaucratic system of the United Nations. He saw the need for serious reform to ensure that the United Nations could effectively deliver for people and the planet. As he reflected upon the developments in 2018, Solheim noted, "If we don't stand up for those who try to drive reform, everyone will learn to be risk averse."[185] His insistence on reforming the heavy UN bureaucracy is not misplaced. As Oli Brown wrote, however, Solheim made three main mistakes: he assumed the role of a general and ignored the functions of a secretary, he snubbed the member states, and he made repeated political errors.[186]

CONCLUSION

Leadership is "multi-level, processual, contextual and interactive," and leaders operate in complex social-relational systems.[187] International institutions depend upon a fragile coalition that requires continuous attention and nurturing, which demands that leaders foster respect among the various groups that make up the coalition, that they work continuously to

6.6 UNEP Execurive Director Erik Solheim (left) participates in the largest beach cleanup in history at Versova Beach in Mumbai, India, in May 2018. Credit: UNEP.

create and maintain support for the organization and its mission, and that they respond responsibly to pressures in the organization and its milieu.[188]

Leadership of UNEP takes place within the United Nations as an organization and a system and is influenced by the vision and style of the UN Secretary-General serving at the time. Like each UN Secretary-General, each UNEP executive director articulated a vision for the organization that responded to the dynamics of the time.[189] A compelling vision serves as the bridge from the organization's present to its future. Sustaining a vision and translating it into practice rests on the culture of an organization; the persistent, patterned way of thinking about central tasks; and human relationships within an organization. "Culture is to an organization what personality is to an individual," James Wilson wrote when describing bureaucracies, and "like human culture generally, it is passed from one generation to the next. It changes slowly, if at all."[190] Thus, even as executive directors have changed, UNEP's organizational culture has persisted. It is only through the deliberate efforts of executive directors that the organization culture changes.

Ultimately, the men and women who have led UNEP over time shaped the organization and thus influenced the collective ability of the international community to define and address the environmental issues of the time. Each executive director, except Maurice Strong, UNEP's inaugural director, started off from the baseline their predecessor had established. They all had to operate within a particular socioeconomic, political, and environmental reality that shaped the organization. Mostafa Tolba focused on concrete global environmental problems and, as US Ambassador Richard Benedick remarked, "broke all the stereotypes of the docile United Nations servant to governments."[191] Through Tolba, UNEP took a position in favor of strong international regulation and put in place the building blocks of science and diplomacy for international cooperation. Subsequent directors have focused on enabling UNEP to work across issues and across sectors as the institutional landscape became increasingly crowded and competitive. Their individual leadership types and styles have left an imprint on UNEP, and UNEP has left an imprint on their lives.

In June 2019, Danish economist and environmentalist Inger Andersen became UNEP's seventh executive director. Having served as Director General of the International Union for the Conservation of Nature (IUCN), "the world's largest and most diverse environmental network," and at the World Bank and UNDP, she comes to UNEP with experience across issues, scales, and geographies. "My career has intersected with UNEP's journey many times over the past decades," Andersen noted in our interview in 2019, "and I see the UNEP brand as incredibly strong, with a mandate which is second to none." Yet, she continued, "while the duck may be serene, it is paddling very hard, accomplishing an amazing amount with very little." Andersen comes in at a time when ecosystems are collapsing, political systems are unresponsive, and social systems are buckling under increasing inequality. "Our kids are in the streets," she notes. "Never before have we had such an engaged youth movement that is focused on the sins of our generation and is mercilessly hammering at reform and changing the system. Never have we had the kind of coverage we have now in the media. Never before have we had the kind of interconnectivity that we have today. And we at UNEP need to harness all these forces of impact." As Andersen assumed UNEP's leadership, she acknowledged that change and uncertainty often go hand in hand and that transparency and communication will be important. As global environmental governance evolves, transparency, communication, and public scrutiny become all the more important in these "unusual times." Understanding why and how the United Nations Environment Programme was envisioned and created and what happened to the original plan for a system of global environmental governance is essential. Learning from past experiences will be critical to planning for the future.

7

THE UNEP WE NEED: POTENTIAL FOR TRANSFORMATION

Can [we] reach in time the vision of joint survival? Can inescapable physical interdependence—the chief new insight of our century—induce that vision? We do not know. We have the duty to hope.
—Barbara Ward, *Progress for a Small Planet*, 1979[1]

Created in 1972 at the first United Nations conference on the human environment despite governmental agreement that "no new institutional arrangements would result from the conference,"[2] the United Nations Environment Programme was the product of a powerful common vision. Environmental concerns were just emerging as political issues in industrialized countries, many developing countries had only gained nationhood in the previous twenty-five years, and there were high tensions between the Global North and South, as well as the East and West. Yet, the dynamic preparatory process engaging all countries and many intellectuals from around the world launched an intense and passionate discussion about the planet as a single, shared system, and about the human responsibility to ensure that we could continue to support life in a just and equitable manner. "[W]e are the generation to see through the eyes of the astronauts the astonishing 'earthrise' of our small and beautiful planet above the barren horizons of the moon," Barbara Ward exclaimed in her speech during the opening of the conference. Ward, the British economist and journalist, who had worked with Maurice Strong to assemble a team of over 150 intellectual leaders to produce the background documents for the conference, laid out three elements upon which there was a clear scientific consensus that demanded political action: "We can damage the entire biosphere. Resources are not unlimited. States acting separately can produce planetary disaster."[3] She also emphasized that by acting collectively, states, scholars, and citizens could avert calamity.

Fifty years later, we find ourselves at a more urgent, grimmer juncture. Global environmental change has accelerated, putting pressure on natural resources, decimating species, and altering ecosystem processes. It has pushed the planet to what Maurice Strong termed the "outer" limits for human survival and what contemporary scholars call "planetary boundaries."[4] Meanwhile, the systems of political organization, exacerbated by economic stress, social unrest, and health impacts, are also pushing the "inner" limits of basic human rights such as safety, food and shelter, health, belonging, and self-actualization. Scientific evidence confirms that we are indeed exceeding all conceivable limits. No less than the stability of nations and global peace are at stake, and we need all hands on deck. We need a global vision for collective action, as well as support from activists around the globe.

UNEP'S SUCCESSES AND CHALLENGES

Created as the leading global environmental authority, UNEP sees its core functions as setting the global environmental agenda, promoting implementation of environmental goals and agreements, and serving as an authoritative advocate for the global environment. Its mission is to provide leadership and encourage partnership in environmental stewardship.

UNEP's work has been a success and a challenge. It has made significant strides and delivered progress on several fronts, yet it has also stumbled. It is the setbacks that tend to be remembered, while accomplishments are often taken for granted. Reversing the depletion of the ozone layer is UNEP's major achievement and, indeed, the only global environmental problem that has been successfully resolved. UNEP launched processes for addressing regional seas pollution, chemicals and waste, and plastics. It encountered serious hurdles in tackling land degradation and the loss of species and forests. And not all achievements have been complete successes. UNEP has provided scientific rigor, evidence, and engagement on a number of issues, but has failed to become the main scientific authority for environmental concerns writ large. It spurred the creation of a significant body of international environmental law but has not managed to ensure its coherence and consistent implementation. It motivated national and international action and supported the advancement of scientific knowledge and new technologies but has not had the resources and capacity to provide the support necessary at the national level. UNEP has become one of many organizations active in the environmental field rather than the center of gravity—the anchor institution—because it lacked sufficient capacity, connectivity, and credibility.

UNEP's capacity has been curtailed because of its relatively small staff (barely over 1,200 people spread in forty offices in thirty-eight countries on all continents) and limited resources (less than $600 million per year). UNEP's connectivity was minimal in its first three decades because the infrastructure was limited for air and train travel and rudimentary at best for telecommunications. In addition, the diplomatic representation of nation states in Nairobi remains at a mere 40 percent of UN member states, almost fifty years after the creation of the organization. Without fully functional and engaged missions, countries are less connected and less able to engage in the activities of the organization, which in turn diminishes its authority, legitimacy, and resources. As the environmental field has expanded and many organizations have taken on environmental responsibilities, UNEP has become a competitor rather than the coordinator it was originally designed to be. As it has struggled to find its identity, UNEP's credibility has been challenged, affecting its past and present performance.

Capacity, connectivity, and credibility have been problematic because of institutional design, specifically in terms of mandate and finances, as well as leadership and location. Improving performance will require addressing these critical variables, which have been largely missing from debates about performance and effectiveness. Designed with an explicitly normative mandate, UNEP has attracted staff to policy positions, and governments have committed resources that correspond to a normative mission of setting policy goals. When the organization is charged with providing leadership and vision for global policy but is not present and visible, authority and legitimacy suffer. Effective leadership has the power and potential to boost authority, improve legitimacy, and mobilize people and resources. Finances shape performance, but finances are also dependent on performance. Money flows in to support ideas that donors and recipients support, but the ability to deliver on these ideas also affects donations. Location is a core factor for attracting staff and the critical variable that shapes infrastructure and representation. Infrastructure and representation, in turn, are fundamental to connectivity, the presence of an organization among its constituencies and peers, and they also affect engagement in decision making and priority determination.

With leadership constantly away from headquarters, and without effective management processes and priorities,[5] UNEP lost its voice and some of its original identity and "developed an inferiority complex."[6] UNEP's location in Nairobi, however, has highlighted the urgent support needs of developing countries and pushed it toward more operational work. Yet, when donors expect norm-setting and recipient countries expect support delivery, an identity crisis is inevitable. And with limited presence and visibility, resources dwindle, authority erodes, legitimacy wanes, and all three functionalities—capacity, connectivity, and credibility—suffer, making performance a real challenge.

In addition to these constraints, the performance of the organization was further shaped by limitations inherent to the environmental sphere. The environment is not a priority for many member states and, accordingly, resources have been grossly inadequate to deliver on UNEP's broad and ambitious mandate. Environmental ministries remain weak in national cabinets around the world, and, as a result, UNEP has been marginalized at the international level. The outcome is self-reinforcing: Without a strong domestic constituency, the anchor institution for the global environment is weak. And without a strong international institution, national ministries have less outside support—institutional, normative, financial—and therefore less authority.

Over the past fifty years, governments have engaged in a continuous process of improvement of the anchor institution, a reform that has taken many turns. Most academics engaging with UNEP have done so with an eye toward changing its institutional form. Yet, as this book has demonstrated, the conventional proposal of reforming institutional form and creating a World Environment Organization would not address the problems at hand. Institutional design, in terms of mandate and finances; leadership; and location are critical variables that impact UNEP's functionality and performance. UNEP now faces a daunting task. The world needs to instigate economic and societal transformation at a rate and scale that has "no documented historic precedent," the Intergovernmental Panel on Climate Change underscored in 2018, or we risk driving the Earth system into a new state that may be unable to support human civilization. Prior to considering prospects for future actions, however, it is imperative to understand the existing track record of reform efforts.

PERMANENCE AND TRANSIENCE OF REFORM

"Reform is not a onetime action, it is a permanent attitude,"[7] UN Secretary-General António Guterres emphasized upon taking office in 2016. Reform is indeed a perpetual state for the United Nations because the problems it seeks to address evolve over time and demand new approaches and actions. Addressing global environmental problems required the creation of a new environmental institution and, as chapter 2 explained in detail, governments debated its form, function, and financing extensively before deciding on its structure. These questions have been revisited regularly, with markedly different results as national governments changed and negotiator positions shifted. Although the process of reforming international environmental governance formally concluded in 2012 at the UN Conference on Sustainable Development, Rio+20, the work continues. As UN Secretary-General Kofi Annan often remarked during his time in office, "Reform is a process, not an event,"[8] and, indeed, reform will remain an issue for every UN Secretary-General and every UNEP executive director.

Throughout its history, UNEP has repeatedly been the target of reform efforts, with reformers seeking to change its internal organizational configuration and overall governance structure. Indeed, as detailed in chapter 6, every executive director initiated a reorganization of UNEP's administrative design, which entailed rethinking substantive priorities and reforming the processes through which the organization delivered on its mandate. In contrast to those reorganizations, this section focuses on two specific rounds of UNEP reform, which, not coincidentally, echoed UN-wide reform initiatives.

In the 1990s, twenty years after UNEP's creation, debates about its effectiveness triggered a round of proposals for instituting a new mechanism for environmental governance. The 1992 Rio Earth Summit provided the impetus for these conversations. Sir Geoffrey Palmer, former Prime Minister of New Zealand, advanced a proposal for a new specialized UN agency for the environment, an International Environment Organization similar to the International Labor Organization (ILO), the first UN specialized agency.[9] Two main forces spurred these reform initiatives. First, the sharp increase in world trade liberalization after the end of the Cold War had increased the prominence and power of the international institutions for trade, which were perceived as a threat to progressive national environmental policies.[10] Second, UNEP's authority, visibility, and credibility had declined post-Rio, fueling doubts about UNEP's effectiveness and demands for more deliberate action by governments.

In 1997, Kofi Annan took office as UN Secretary-General, and only six months into his first term, he announced a plan for UN reform that would improve management and coordination across the UN system. "Having been with the UN for many years before becoming SG [Secretary-General]," Kofi Annan recalled in our interview, "I had ideas of what worked and what did not work. I had a keen sense that the world was changing and the UN had to adapt. We had to make the bureaucracy more effective and efficient, and we also needed to pose the question of what should the UN be doing?"[11] Environmental issues had fallen precipitously down the political agenda in many countries and were increasingly couched in terms of economic costs rather than human or environmental rights. In this global context, even if developing countries were to willingly adopt measures to halt environmental deterioration, they would risk their place in the global economy. Saddled with towering debts, developing countries were forced by the existing economic and political realities (and by international financial institutions) to adapt their national strategies to the neoliberal dynamic of economic growth at any cost. In 1997, committed to instilling a greater unity of purpose, coherence of efforts, and agility in action, the UN Secretary-General proposed the creation of a UN Task Force on Environment and Human Settlements.[12] The Task Force was to advance proposals for reforming and strengthening the environmental activities of the United Nations in line with the UN Secretary-General's reform priorities.

At the Rio+5 conference in June 1997, German Chancellor Helmut Kohl called for the creation of a World Environment Organization, a global umbrella body for environmental issues. Brazil's President Fernando Henrique Cardoso, South Africa's Deputy President Thabo M. Mbeki, and Singapore's Prime Minister Goh Chok Tong supported the idea in a Declaration for a Global Initiative on Sustainable Development.[13] The initiative mobilized advocates of reform and encouraged policymakers to acknowledge the need to think more systemically about the shortcomings of global environmental governance. French President Jacques Chirac also became a proponent of a World Environmental Organization.[14] Subsequently, the European Union adopted it as its official negotiating position[15] and repeatedly proposed that UNEP become a specialized agency, a UN Environment Organization, so that it "be recognized as the leader on matters relevant to the environment and perform a coordination function with regard to other UN bodies."[16] These proposals would shape the terms of the process for reforming international environmental governance for more than two decades and generate intense debates.

In February 1998, Kofi Annan appointed UNEP's Executive Director Klaus Töpfer as chair of the Task Force on Environment and Human Settlements to rethink the role of multilateral institutions and to elevate UNEP's diminished visibility. Töpfer seized the opportunity to articulate a far-reaching governance vision. In July 1998, only five months after its creation, the twenty-member Task Force delivered a report with twenty-four recommendations for reforming and creating structures, rules, institutions, as well as political processes, relations, and systems.[17] These recommendations included:

- creating the Global Ministerial Environment Forum, a platform for the world's environment ministers to gather in Nairobi during the regular UNEP Governing Council sessions, and in countries around the world in a special session in alternate years;
- creating the Environment Management Group, a problem-solving, results-oriented interagency mechanism to achieve effective coordination and joint action on key environmental and human-settlements issues throughout the UN system;

- working more closely with the various environmental conventions and protocols;
- enhancing engagement with civil society; and,
- making the membership of the UNEP Governing Council universal, i.e., in line with that of the UN General Assembly.

The report and recommendations were political, pragmatic, and visionary. They addressed directly UNEP's connectivity and sought to improve its capacity and credibility. Following these recommendations, in 1999, the UN General Assembly adopted a resolution that established the Environment Management Group and created the annual Global Ministerial Environment Forum. The resolution also called for strengthening the United Nations Office in Nairobi and emphasized the need to enhance linkages and coordination among the environmental conventions and provide stable, adequate, and predictable financial resources, including from the regular UN budget. Finally, the resolution included language to promote the involvement, participation, and constructive engagement of civil society.[18] The General Assembly opted not to include the recommendation for universal membership for the Governing Council in the resolution, since there was no government support for such a measure at that time.

Opening up UNEP's Governing Council to all the environmental ministers through the Global Ministerial Environment Forum (GMEF) ensured that participation would be de facto universal, even if the Governing Council still formally comprised only fifty-eight member states. This reform increased representation significantly because it formally welcomed ministers from around the world to engage in the Governing Council sessions in Nairobi and because it brought the Governing Council and UNEP to countries around the world. On even years, the GMEF sessions took place as a special session of the Governing Council in a city in any country willing to host the ministerial session, including:

- Malmö, Sweden, in 2000
- Cartagena, Colombia, in 2002
- Jeju, Republic of Korea, in 2004
- Dubai, UAE, in 2006
- Monaco, in 2008
- Bali, Indonesia, in 2010

The result was an improvement in UNEP's visibility, authority, legitimacy, and resources (see chapter 6). Financial contributions to UNEP increased because of the greater political attention and engagement by its leadership. Governments contributed mainly through extrabudgetary funds, however, which limited UNEP's autonomy and initiative.

Klaus Töpfer saw the 2002 World Summit on Sustainable Development in Johannesburg as an opportunity to further augment UNEP's capacity and credibility. Seeking ideas for enhancing UNEP's leadership, he reached out to governments, practitioners, and academics.[19] Governments crafted a reform package at the UNEP Governing Council session in Cartagena, Colombia, in 2002, but made no decisions at the World Summit on Sustainable Development a few months later. The heightened political attention to environmental governance reform had little in terms of an analytical foundation and failed to deliver a substantial, actionable proposal that responded to the political possibilities at the time. The emphasis was on the establishment of a World Environment Organization, and many scholars argued for a central authority that would take charge of the environmental agenda and resolve tenacious global problems. But no analyses dealt systematically with the question of why a World Environment Organization had not been established and why UNEP was not fulfilling the role that so many had hoped it would. The work that scholars advanced was sharply divided among proponents and opponents of the creation of a World or Global or United Nations Environment Organization; as a result, scholars provided little systematic input into the policy process.[20]

Daniel Esty and I were among the scholars who argued that the international environmental architecture was inadequate because of institutional fragmentation, deficient authority, and insufficient legitimacy. We attributed these problems to UNEP's narrow mandate, small budget, programme status, and limited political support. "UNEP's structural handicaps have led to its output being judged as modest and not very useful," we wrote in 2001. "This weak performance results in reduced political support, greater difficulty in attracting highly competent staff, and continuous budget problems as donors look elsewhere for ways to deploy their limited environmental resources. Results further deteriorate, and the downward spiral accelerates."[21] Since we saw the core problem as structural, we deemed a new institutional design to be advisable and indeed imperative. A Global Environmental Organization (GEO), we contended, should craft a coherent and effective international response to global-scale pollution and problems with natural resource management. It should integrate the principles of good governance, including subsidiarity, participation, transparency, and accountability; its main features should be flexibility and responsiveness to change, credibility, commitment to scientific rigor, first-rate staff, and modern management. While we recognized that the organizational design would entail a dramatic reorganization of the existing system and require extraordinary political leadership, we considered the potential benefits to be great and thus saw action as imperative. What we failed to consider, however, was why such an organization did not exist, why the existing institutions (UNEP in particular) had not delivered, and what the various action options might be to attain the results we envisioned.[22]

The political push for reforming global environmental governance continued beyond the 2002 Johannesburg Summit. The French and German governments moved forward with the proposal for an international environmental agency with greater political power and authority, a World or United Nations Environment Organization. In the context of the broader UN reform and because of the political push from important European states, all intergovernmental meetings in the 2000s officially acknowledged the need for more effective and efficient environmental activities in the UN system, with enhanced coordination and improved normative and operational capacity; at these meetings governments were urged to explore the possibility of a more coherent institutional framework.[23] The challenges were consistent: institutional complexity and fragmentation; scientific assessment; gaps in implementation; insufficient, unstable, unpredictable funding; and inadequate use of partnerships.[24] Governments thus acknowledged that UNEP had not fulfilled the core functions of its mandate and sought possible solutions.

A series of consultative reform processes convened from 2006 to 2012, which signaled that debate was progressing. The 2006–2008 informal consultation process on the institutional framework for the UN's environmental activities, co-chaired by Ambassadors Peter Maurer of Switzerland and Claude Heller (and later Enrique Berruga) of Mexico, involved all the UN missions in New York but could not reach agreement.[25] The analyses and the recommendations the consultations produced illustrated the persistence of the need for collective action and effective governance. As Marthinus Van Schalkwyk, Minister of Environmental Affairs and Tourism of South Africa in 2009, remarked with some frustration, "it is not only the system that is fragmented, but also the debate on fixing the system. This debate has been afloat without a compass on a sea of uncertainty marked by competing agendas for far too long."[26]

Governments kept coming back to the same core issues: the need for coordination, for coherent and compelling environmental assessment that links science and policy into actionable priorities, and feasible yet ambitious policy guidance. Progress on any of these fronts, however, developing countries argued, required support. Industrialized states, on the other hand, urged developing states to leapfrog, skipping environmentally destructive practices and adopting a more environmentally friendly trajectory. Without real support, such dramatic advancement would not be possible; but without curbing corruption and increasing accountability, support would not be forthcoming. The challenge, therefore, is consistently at both the international and the national level. Support needs to come from abroad, but results have to come from within a country. Good governance is imperative at both levels, and without it, the trust gap has persisted. Thus, the need for a shared vision was obvious, and from 2009 to 2010 a Consultative Group on International Environmental Governance began convening environment ministers and high-level representatives in several intense working groups. The final agreement, the Nairobi-Helsinki Outcome, articulated a set of core functions and possible reform options that would frame the ensuing negotiations. The options included enhancing UNEP, establishing an umbrella organization for sustainable development, establishing a specialized agency as a World Environment Organization, and reforming the Commission on Sustainable Development.[27]

The international environmental governance reform process concluded formally with the adoption of *The Future We Want* outcome document at Rio+20. The reform outcomes were noteworthy in terms of UNEP's governance, functions, and financing. A new universal assembly, the UN Environment Assembly, replaced the fifty-eight-member Governing

Council and became UNEP's governance body with real political clout. Governments also committed to improving UNEP's funding, voice and coordination, science-policy interface, and public footprint. The document urged that UNEP enhance its regional presence, capacity building, and stakeholder participation as well as consolidate its headquarters functions in Nairobi. In 2016, Achim Steiner characterized this as "the most fundamental governance reform in the environment and of UNEP in its forty-year history."[28]

A major reason for the successful conclusion of the negotiations was that the proponents of a specialized agency accepted the change to universal membership. "I think we were able to get an outcome at Rio+20 on the universal membership because there was a tremendous pressure for a World Environmental Organization," Swiss Ambassador Franz Perrez remarked. "If we had not had that pressure, we probably would not have been able to agree on universal membership. That was seen as a compromise. For us that was more than a compromise; for us that was the best outcome."[29] Governments thus decided that UNEP's original mandate and design, and its form and function, were robust, and they committed to increasing UNEP's finances and authority.

Member states acknowledged the need for more operational engagement from UNEP and stressed the importance of developing a greater regional presence as well as stronger presence in Nairobi. They also committed, and subsequently delivered, resources from the regular UN budget. These reforms laid the foundation for UNEP's legal and formal authority, confirming that the anchor institution was *in* authority in the environmental field. Governments did not, however, directly tackle the issues that have hobbled UNEP from being *an* authority, i.e., its credibility. Although every new political forum and decision reaffirmed UNEP's position as the "leading global environmental authority," such authority is not granted but earned through delivery on mandate and expectations. As chapter 3 demonstrated, UNEP has not been able to fulfill its original mandate of coordinating the environmental activities in the UN system, which has undermined its authority and legitimacy. It also has not been able to meet operational expectations as these exceeded the original mandate and required greater resources. Recognizing the importance of consistent leadership to ensure credibility, UN Secretary-General Ban Ki-moon extended

Achim Steiner's term by two years to allow him to oversee the governance transition within UNEP. His successor, Erik Solheim, however, did not prioritize the governance agenda, and the reform momentum fizzled. With the decrease of the authority and legitimacy of the executive director due to the external audit, as chapter 6 explained, UNEP's credibility plummeted, and contributions to the Environment Fund did not increase.

Yet, with a new universal environmental assembly that could convene all 193 UN member states on the most pressing environmental issues and initiate challenging political debates, UNEP officially positioned itself *in* authority to provide the political center of gravity for global environmental governance. UNEP became "the only forum in the UN where environmental issues are discussed by a ministerial universal body," said Ibrahim Thiaw, former UNEP deputy executive director and current executive secretary of the desertification convention.[30] UNEP's openness to stakeholders and the high-level segment of its governing body allow for governance innovation. When it regains credibility and enhances its connectivity to its constituencies and the global public, the UN Environment Programme will have a chance to fulfill its original potential.

DELIVERING ON UNEP'S POTENTIAL

Ultimately, global environmental governance is in need not just of reform but of transformation that conceptualizes and enacts a range of previously unimagined opportunities. Transformation can comprise change in governance structures and processes, behavioral change that disrupts the status quo, and cognitive change in beliefs, values, and norms.[31] It will be critical for UNEP to strengthen its standing as the global environmental authority starting with an inspirational internal vision, capable management, and a clear, confident voice. UNEP's fiftieth anniversary in 2022 provides a symbolic opportunity for fundamental transformation into *the* authority on the global environment. This commemoration moment has the potential to spur the necessary momentum and political will to launch a transformation through integrated solutions. UNEP could and should become the go-to institution for information on the state of the planet, for a normative vision of global environmental governance, and for support for domestic environmental agendas and non-state actors. It is also time, however, to embrace the two arcs of UNEP's mission—the normative and the operational. UNEP must reevaluate the demands for operational work and integrate them into UNEP's identity, even if it is not formally within its mandate.

OWNING THE NORMATIVE AND OPERATIONAL MANDATE

In the dire environmental reality that we find ourselves, we need to move toward an understanding of our shared existence on this one planet. UNEP could become the primary convener, catalyst, and collaborator in this endeavor. "UNEP is the only UN agency with collective intelligence on key environmental issues with a unique convening and catalytic role," Yunae Yi, UNEP Safeguards Advisor, remarked in 2017.[32] UNEP can jump-start and accelerate actions in the UN system, business, and civil society as well as other international institutions. Entrusted with the mandate to look at the entire global environmental landscape, map connections among issues and organizations, assess the current state of affairs, and identify potential gaps and options for action, UNEP has catalyzed concerted achievement on many issues. But it has to think bigger and present the entire picture, with a full accounting of the interconnections and interwoven responsibilities. UNEP, however, lacks the capacity to do so.

Continuing the core function of environmental assessment and knowledge management will be critical. Releasing a high-quality comprehensive State of the Planet report every three to five years would provide the analytical basis for the development of policy ideas and recommendations. Importantly, overarching trends by issue and geographic area could be supplemented by comparative, time-series data on policy implementation and effectiveness. Such comprehensive information can be harnessed quickly to provide the scientific foundation and societal rationale for a political dialogue. UNEP alone possesses the authority to deliver the scientific foundation and the political dialogue around such State of the Planet reviews. In addition, a close working relationship with the international scientific community will enhance UNEP's capacity and credibility. Establishing a standing interdisciplinary panel of scientific advisors—following the example of the US National Academies of Sciences and the Scientific Advisory Board to the UN Secretary-General—could leverage the knowledge, skills, and authority of the world scientific community and encourage scholars and youth to engage with the United Nations.[33] This will complement the role of the chief scientist of UNEP by bringing in a wide range of expertise and experience on a rotating basis. Such engagement will increase UNEP's connectivity to its scientific constituency and its capacity to produce first-rate systematic analysis. Working with top scientific talent from around the world will also improve UNEP's authority and legitimacy and help it gain credibility. Linking rigorous scientific knowledge to policy action and behavioral change will demand political engagement as well as cultural and emotional intelligence. Engaging with the humanities and the arts will allow UNEP to shape the stories that will compel action.

International environmental governance is defined by commitments countries make and those they fail to fulfill. Closing the implementation gap requires clear lines of responsibility and accountability for reaching internationally agreed-upon goals.[34] UNEP has the potential to leverage partnerships and become the cornerstone of an implementation-monitoring mechanism. Currently, there is no global standard for measuring whether countries are fulfilling their international environmental obligations, what efforts they are taking to implement them, or what gaps in national capacity need to be addressed. Furthermore, there are no systematic review mechanisms to compare the progress of national policies—across countries and conventions—and to understand the strengths and weaknesses of existing instruments. As a result, there is no baseline against which to assess performance, actions, or even expectations; and without empirical evidence, we risk erroneous conclusions and inappropriate regulatory interventions based on assumptions rather than evidence. Furthermore, in the absence of measurement of implementation, it is impossible to determine whether the conventions help solve the problems they intend to address.

A review mechanism would provide a repository for information on the extent to which agreements are implemented, on constraints and challenges, and on best practices. A continuous and transparent reporting effort is critical for comparison within UNEP and with organizational peers. Reporting is also necessary for creating a common understanding of success and failure, of enabling conditions and constraints. Naming and acclaiming countries that report, implement, and improve would generate confidence within their governments, good faith and pride in their citizens, and respect among peers. UNEP can assist countries in their self-assessment and support their domestic environmental agenda. Through such a dynamic process, in collaboration with partners in civil society and academia, UNEP could enable learning and inspire improvement. This would also constructively address both its normative and operative agendas.

The universal UN Environment Assembly is a political forum whose potential is yet to be realized. UNEA accords UNEP the authority to initiate political dialogue and holds the promise of becoming a new forum for constructive environmental politics. It also allows for reaching out beyond environment ministries to heads of state and government. Ultimately, only the UN Environment Programme can convene all member states and all the conventions and present a global snapshot of the state of the environment, the state of environmental policy, and the need for action by drawing upon the work of every member state. Transitioning to a universal-membership UNEA was a big and important step. The assumption was that it would accord UNEP greater authority, but authority is gained through delivering results. The future of UNEP depends on leveraging UNEA as a political forum that assists governments to attain positive outcomes. UNEA could provide the space where governments share experiences and conventions highlight achievements and challenges. The UNEP secretariat can then assist in bringing targeted support and achieving outcomes in a more integrated manner. Created as the hub of the wheel, UNEA offers promise, but the spokes are still to be connected. Harnessing new technological capabilities in Nairobi, UNEP could champion a modern-day fusion of face-to-face gathering with virtual convening. UNEP could mobilize new technologies for presenting and disseminating data through dynamic new tools. Such a platform would alleviate the economic and environmental costs of repeated global gathering and would also improve reach and engagement.

ENHANCING IMPLEMENTATION AND CONVENING THE CONVENTIONS

When asked in 2018 what would be the one thing she would do to improve global governance if she could wave a magic wand, Christine

Lagarde, Director of the International Monetary Fund at the time, replied that she would make sure that governments do what they promised to do.[35] Indeed, the promises and commitments made at each of the global summits and conferences are overwhelming. UNEP could play a valuable role in ensuring governments keep their promises.

To start with, UNEP could make relevant and reliable information available and better equip policymakers to articulate goals, strategies, and actions and mobilize necessary financial, human and institutional resources to improve performance. Moreover, if UNEP were to commit to systematically and continuously assessing implementation, it would be able to determine whether international agreements help solve the problems they were created to address. Facilitating an honest discussion about the advantages and challenges that environmental ministries encounter, and about the contribution governments can make in the age of sustainable development, climate crisis, and worldwide youth mobilization, is an important function for UNEP. It could shift the nature of the debate from identifying problems to initiating and implementing solutions. As Elizabeth Mrema, director of UNEP's Law Division noted, the convention secretariats are not, strictly speaking, engaged in day-to-day implementation on the ground; this is where UNEP and partners come in. UNEP, for example, manages the African Elephant Fund established under CITES and determines the distribution of funds for specific projects in countries implementing the plan. It also supports the ten countries in the Congo basin on adoption and implementation of the Nagoya Protocol on access to genetic resources and benefit sharing. Bridging the policy vision and the concrete actions necessary to implement them through well-crafted strategies, UNEP could facilitate targeted interventions for integrated problem resolution.

Shared risk perception is a key determinant of collective action for risk reduction.[36] The reversal of the depletion of the ozone layer, for example, was possible only because there was a shared sense of urgency among scientists, governments, and citizens, which allowed for coordinated, supported collective action. UNEP's leadership was critical. Inputs across sectors will be important to co-create knowledge and design and implement sound action plans, but UNEP's support will be indispensable. One way to improve the standing and capacities of both environmental ministries and of developing countries is to bring attention to the performance of developing countries that have been implementing their international environmental obligations.

It is commonly argued that developing countries underperform on their international obligations under multilateral environmental agreements.[37] Developing countries' lack of financial, institutional, and human capacity; their low interest in environmental concerns; and their lack of trust in the system fuel this underperformance. As one government official from the Global South remarked, the region has been largely absent from discussions on environmental-governance reform; the reason was "three decades of broken promises and no expectation of any progress except more conditionality on what we are supposed to be doing on development. That's not acceptable for us as an environmental conversation."[38]

However, the conventional wisdom may be wrong. Empirical results on implementation revealed through the Environmental Conventions Index developed by the Center for Governance and Sustainability at the University of Massachusetts Boston show many developing countries outperforming developed states across different conventions.[39] Indonesia, for example, outperforms or performs at the same level as Norway in four out of five global environmental conventions—the Basel Convention on Trade in Hazardous Waste, the Convention on International Trade in Endangered Species, the World Heritage Convention, and the Ramsar Convention on Wetlands. Indonesia, however, encounters significant challenges in complying with the Stockholm Convention on Persistent Organic Pollutants, as do many developing countries, because it is a highly technical convention requiring greater industrial capacity. Armed with knowledge about their performance, countries can gain confidence and bargaining power. They can also summon concrete indicators on which to report and track progress, which can ultimately be used to demand the necessary support. Rwanda has recognized the importance of assessing performance on the achievement of international environmental goals and the opportunity to learn from peers. The ministry of environment requested an analysis of Rwanda's implementation of multilateral environmental agreements and seeks to convene all African countries to exchange experiences and knowledge in an effort to improve performance.[40]

When states perceive important value added from collaboration, they will implement international agreements. Creating a common space for all environmental institutions and actors to convene, consult, and collaborate will be essential to transformative action. This has to be a space where there is an explicit recognition of commonalities and differences, and where a joint narrative can be articulated. The United Nations Environment Assembly offers the opportunity for UNEP to deliver on this potential. It could convene all the conventions in the environmental space (whether administered by UNEP, by another organization, or independently) for a substantive discussion about their work, their needs, and their vision moving forward. Each convention can cover one or a few pieces of the larger puzzle, but UNEP could bring them together and provide a comprehensive overview of the state of the planet and facilitate the political dialogue and the action necessary for the parties to implement their commitments.

Each convention deals with specific environmental problems within its purview, whether it be trade in endangered species, migratory birds, wetlands, climate change, chemicals, or others. None of these conventions, however, are sufficient to resolve an issue by themselves. To protect all wildlife, for example, one needs to tackle issues that are part of the larger context, such as habitat loss, social issues, infrastructure, population growth, and conversion of land for agriculture. "I can't talk about these other issues as the CITES secretariat," John Scanlon remarked, "because that's not my mandate. I can only talk about my little slice of the pie."[41] UNEP is the institutional entity best positioned to ask the big questions and assess the state of the planet in its entirety.

UNEP can finally step up to the role of an orchestra conductor of all the existing conventions and call for their support. "Being a conductor of a major symphony is very difficult," noted Julia Marton-Lefèvre, "but achieving harmony is imperative. Bringing a collective of actors into collective action mode on the global environment is a formidable but essential undertaking. We need a creative coalition of countries, companies and cities, and leadership from UNEP."[42] Currently, much of UNEP's energy goes to administering conventions, which is a burden rather than a privilege and often results in tension with the convention secretariats.

In order to truly take on the role of an effective chief environmental conductor, UNEP should allow the conventions to develop the institutional and economic capacity their parties deem necessary, and then play the role of conductor by ensuring that they talk to each other and that the results are harmonious and positive for the planet.[43]

Contrary to prevailing proposals for integrating all conventions into one global body, UNEP should release the conventions it administers and allow them to develop institutional and economic capacity if they so choose. Currently, providing administrative services does not add value for UNEP, though it may be useful to some of the conventions. Releasing administrative authority to the conventions might work to unify them around substantive issues. UNEP could instead focus on the core elements that would draw the secretariats to UNEA as a common forum. Re-engaging with the conventions on common concerns would revitalize collaboration toward a shared goal—rebuilding abundance in the natural world—and allow for multiple ways for each convention and its parties to contribute. UNEA could offer a space for the convention secretariats and their parties to come together to articulate a coherent vision, identify convergence and potential conflict, and craft strategies for maximizing value and avoiding risk.[44]

FRAGILITY OF FINANCES

Financial revenues are an illustration of power, and many analysts have pointed to UNEP's Environment Fund as an indicator of organizational decline. Created as the core financial mechanism for environmental affairs, the Environment Fund was expected to receive $100 million annually (in 1972) and grow as the global environmental agenda expanded. In the 1970s, as countries contributed resources, the Fund grew, but in the 1980s it plummeted in real terms, i.e., when adjusted for inflation, as a global hyperinflation crisis hit and governments did not augment their contributions. The Environment Fund increased sharply in the early 1990s in the run-up to the 1992 Rio Earth Summit as environmental issues commanded political attention, but the subsequent decline has been difficult to reverse. Importantly, when adjusted for inflation, the Fund has decreased since the late 1970s.

As figure 2.2 in chapter 2 illustrates, contributions to the Environment Fund decreased by 38 percent, from $33 million in 1979, the equivalent of $111 million when adjusted for inflation, to $70 million in 2019. The number of countries supporting the Fund also decreased by close to 30 percent, from 57 percent to 41 percent of UN member states. UNEP's total income, however, increased to $570 million in 2018. This growth came from extrabudgetary resources—trust funds and earmarked contributions—which eclipsed the Environment Fund in 1996 and have since become UNEP's major financial source, accounting for 84 percent of its budget (see figure 6.4 in chapter 6).

These financial circumstances illustrate three important realities. First, the decline in the amount of contributions and in the number of contributors to the Environment Fund—the portion of the budget over which UNEP has discretion—shows that confidence in UNEP's ability to set its own priorities has diminished. As a result, the secretariat increasingly has been deprived of the power to initiate and carry out programs it deems necessary and urgent. Earmarked contributions come with stipulations about the way the resources can be allocated, leaving little, if any, discretion to UNEP staff. The extrabudgetary nature of these funds also entails year-to-year unpredictability. Importantly, this is not an institutional design issue. Rather, it reflects the changes in global attention to environmental concerns and in UNEP's ability to serve as the advocate for the global environment, to promote international cooperation through regional and global conventions, and to deliver results.

The second key trend—a fivefold increase in total funding since the 1980s—shows recognition on the part of governments of the need for international mechanisms, and UNEP in particular, to address environmental concerns. It is not that UNEP is going unfunded so much as countries are turning to UNEP to fund specific projects that come with "strings attached." This has been a trend across the entire UN system. "Governments earmark funding because it gives them a notion of greater ownership and a greater sense of visibility," John Matuszak of the US State Department explained, "which is needed when competing for scarce public funds. With earmarks there are much more tangible results that [officials] can take back to their taxpayers or their congress or whomever appropriates the budget and say, 'Look we achieved this with this expenditure of funding.' Whereas if you just give to UNEP as a whole and to the Environment Fund as a whole it is sometimes difficult."[45] Earmarked contributions are attractive because they allow for easier access to money, and, as one government official noted, "governments are attached to having the national flag fly over a particular office or be associated with an idea."[46] Some of this dynamic, however, is self-induced. UNEP, assuming that governments would provide extrabudgetary funds has, over the last three decades, underfunded its flagship programs where they have a comparative advantage, such as the work on chemicals and environmental assessment. This has undercut its credibility, risked the viability of many programs, and created much anxiety among staff and collaborators. The *Global Environment Outlook* assessments are consistently part of this underfunding pattern.[47]

Third, this proliferation and expansion of extrabudgetary resources has enabled UNEP to support the shift of its original broad normative mandate of coordinating the environmental activities in the UN system, the main purpose of the Environment Fund, to specific programmatic activities within particular geographic regions. With an increasing number of separate funds, administrative costs have increased, management and reporting efforts have become more cumbersome, and focus has dissipated.[48] The extrabudgetary funds have, however, also widened the source of financial support for UNEP, with many member states contributing far more to such funds than to the Environment Fund. They have also complemented the Environment Fund in times of stagnation and added to UNEP's overall capabilities.

Ultimately, the pool of resources for the environment at large has greatly increased. Since its creation in 1991, the Global Environment Facility, which supports developing countries and countries with economies in transition to meet the objectives of the international environmental conventions and agreements, has invested and committed a total of $24.75 billion through 2022. The Clean Development Mechanism has invested $303.8 billion in climate and sustainable development projects between 2001 and 2018, and the Green Climate Fund has provided $10.3 billion in climate financing. In 2019, 80 percent of countries contributing to the Green Climate Fund increased their pledges, augmenting the annual resources by 70 percent to a total of $9.8 billion. In the biodiversity field, the United Nations Collaborative Initiative on Reducing Emissions from Deforestation and Forest Degradation (REDD+) in developing countries, has committed a total of $131.7 million between 2015 and 2019. The World Bank has also been a major contributor of environmental investment and managed the largest source of multilateral development funds for protecting biodiversity, supporting sustainable forest management, and fighting wildlife crime. The Bank's Environment, Natural Resources and Blue Economy Global Practice (ENB) oversees over 150 projects worth $8.06 billion. In 2018, the World Bank Group committed $17.8 billion to climate-related investments, an area in which investments will increase.[49] In 2019, commitments of nearly $1.5 billion supported climate change goals, with much overlap between adaptation, mitigation, and poverty-reduction benefits. Financing for environment, therefore, is gaining momentum in multiple institutions. Though it remains insufficient for the scale and scope of the problem.

Successful resolution of global environmental problems does require significant and stable funding, but such funding does not necessarily have to flow directly through UNEP. Mobilizing and channeling resources into other sectors and organizations is important for solving environmental challenges, but it is not a measure of success that is reflected on UNEP's balance sheet. A different metric of effectiveness is therefore critical, because such initiatives are perhaps among the most effective. In the 1990s, for example, UNEP launched the Finance Initiative, a partnership with thirteen financial-sector organizations to "change finance and finance change."[50] The Initiative has grown to include more than two hundred institutions, including banks, insurers, and investors from over forty countries, and it engages in creating commercially viable and environmentally sustainable solutions. It has created principles for responsible banking, metrics to measure banks' climate progress, and guidance for integrating environmental and social risks into insurance, and it has also launched a coalition committed to portfolio decarbonization, among other initiatives.

If UNEP were to be a primarily normative entity, a think tank at heart, it would not necessarily need to raise funds for its operations; instead it would leverage funds for other organizations to tackle the issues, much like CITES has done with the international consortium on combating wildlife crime. The consortium is a collaboration of five intergovernmental organizations to support national wildlife law enforcement agencies and ensure a formidable, coordinated response. The partnership includes the CITES Secretariat, the World Customs Organization (WCO), INTERPOL, the United Nations Office on Drugs and Crime (UNODC), and the World Bank. The CITES secretariat, a leader of the initiative, mobilized funding on the order of $20 million to address this issue and distributed most of the resources among the partners who worked on implementing the agenda.[51] In this manner, CITES influenced the agenda of the larger agencies and the multilateral system. As the anchor institution for the global environment, UNEP could and should shape the global agenda and mobilize funding for action on the issues; this funding would then be shared among actors, much like the original vision for the Environment Fund.

Relying on fifteen states for over 90 percent of its Environment Fund contributions, and on an even smaller set of donors for the extrabudgetary resources that provide 87 percent of UNEP's total funding, makes UNEP particularly vulnerable to fluctuations in government priorities and attention. Over one-third (35 percent) of UNEP's donor countries have contributed less than what in 1972 was considered a symbolic amount—$1,000 per year, or a bit less than $6,000 per year in 2019 terms. Thus, even an expansion of UNEP's donor base, while necessary, will not be sufficient to generate the required resources. It will be critical to both widen and deepen UNEP's resource base.

Two ideas proposed at the time of UNEP's creation merit reconsideration today: a system of minimum contributions of $5,000 and a system of scaled assessed contributions based on countries' energy consumption (see chapter 2). These mechanisms could bring greater stability and predictability to UNEP's financial resources. Improvement in communicating UNEP's mission and priorities could also improve funding. A financial tracking system to monitor and evaluate environmental financial flows is imperative. Such information could create predictability and reliability of resources, which is important to effective performance. Improvement of reporting on the use and impact of funding in connection to the programme of work will also be essential. Transparency, communication, and recognition of contributions from governments will be the principal elements in building the necessary trust, and "with trust, funding will follow," as a government official remarked.[52]

LEADERSHIP, VOICE, AND IDENTITY

In September 2019, UNEP presented an activist youth organization, Fridays for Future, which had been organizing climate strikes in over two thousand locations around the world, with its highest honor, the Champions of the Earth award. Speaking on behalf of the organization at the award ceremony in New York, fifteen-year-old Kallan Benson declined the prize, stating that young people could not accept it. "Instead," she stressed, "we offer to hold it for you to earn. You at the United Nations hold the power to save humanity from itself. You must act in time to become the real champions of the Earth." The challenge was clear: the United Nations, and UNEP in particular, had to earn the honor to lead.

Leadership is the process of influencing others to achieve common goals toward a greater good. It shapes the vision, sense of identity, and purpose of an organization and gives it its voice. Throughout its history, UNEP's own voice has faltered at times as the organization has struggled to find its identity and its place in the world. The quality of leadership, as chapter 6 explained, shapes UNEP's identity, authority, and credibility. The executive director of UNEP performs an essential role of articulating a vision and carving out authority for the organization as well as mobilizing resources to support its day-to-day work and to explore new opportunities. UNEP's normative mandate and operational demands, its inadequate (and voluntary) financial contributions, and the long distance from the rest of the UN system have made the executive director's role paramount.

The executive director is responsible for the overall vision and direction that give the organization its identity. Externally, they have to secure the necessary financial resources and political attention. When the attention of the executive director shifts or confidence in them decreases, the Environment Fund suffers. It is the litmus test of credibility and confidence in the institution among donors. When Achim Steiner's term was extended for two years, from 2014 to 2016, and he prepared to leave UNEP, for example, the Environment Fund decreased over 20 percent, from $86 million in 2014 to $66 million in 2016. Contributions did not bounce back with a new executive director, however, as governments waited for Erik Solheim to set the agenda and show promise and leadership. The Environment Fund remained relatively stable at about $70 million in 2017 and 2018. However, because the audit by the Office of Internal Oversight Services uncovered possible issues of mismanagement and abrogation of UN rules, confidence fell. As a result, UNEP's total income oscillated between 2014 and 2018, as table 7.1 illustrates.

Tension between the environment and development has created a major challenge for executive directors, which in turn has affected UNEP's ability to deliver on its mandate and mission. They have had to manage conflicting and often mutually exclusive positions of governments. For example, there is no consensus on the value of UNEP's core constituency, the environment ministry. "If I were a prime minister in Africa," stated Youba Sokona, special adviser on sustainable development at the South Centre, "I would never set up a ministry of environment. It should be embedded in the development agenda. We are at the early stages of development and need to merge the two."[53] Others, however, underscore the challenges that officials and institutions for sustainable development have encountered. For example, Manuel Pulgar-Vidal, the former Peruvian Environment Minister, noted that the sustainable development ministries created in Latin America failed. "They failed because they had too much power in relation with traditional government structures,"

Table 7.1 Annual UNEP income (2014–2018) by category, in millions of nominal USD (not adjusted for inflation)

Category	2014	2015	2016	2017	2018
Environment Fund	$86.4	$79.5	$68.2	$69.2	$71
Earmarked Contributions	$81.4	$87.2	$101.2	$93.1	$115.9
Trust Funds	$391.1	$329.9	$426.9	$313.8	$377.6
Regular Budget	$16.2	$20.2	$24	$25.4	$24.3
Other	($12.8)	($9.1)	($13.4)	($14.4)	($18.6)
TOTAL	$562.3	$507.7	$606.9	$487.1	$570.2

Source: UNEP Audited Financial Statements.

he remarked, "and Panama and Bolivia dismantled these ministries."[54] UNEP has understandably struggled to carve out a clear role in the complex contemporary institutional landscape. It continues to struggle with an identity crisis, as it has difficulties taking a position and using its voice. Building up UNEP's identity is thus an important priority for the new executive director, Inger Andersen, to invest in.

Lack of vision has been a serious problem for UNEP. Indeed, the core recommendation of an external evaluation by the Dalberg Group in 2006 was to *develop* (rather than improve) an internal strategic planning and budgeting process.[55] Achim Steiner addressed this concern upon taking office and, with a team of senior staff, developed the Medium-Term Strategy that set out the vision, objectives, priorities, and impact measures for a four-year period. UNEP is currently in its third Medium-Term Strategy (2018–2021). In her first address to the Committee of Permanent Representatives in Nairobi in June 2019, Executive Director Inger Andersen said that "Strengthening organizational performance through our Medium-Term strategy and Programme of Work is critical. It forms the foundation of our organization at this time." Acknowledging the pivotal moment in history in which UNEP finds itself, she reflected on her responsibility as a leader to rebuild the confidence of member states and systematically address accountability, transparency, and financial and program clarity. "As I step into this leadership position," she noted, "I will ensure a well-functioning top leadership team and set the appropriate tone at the top."[56]

The tone from the executive director will be critical to the evolution of UNEP's organizational culture, which, much like its institutional identity, remains conflicted. Staff praise the aspirational mandate, commitment, professionalism, and diversity of the organization. But they deplore its bureaucratic, hierarchical, compartmentalized, and self-centered culture.[57] The disempowering bureaucracy drains power and potential, and staff continue to lament the myopic thinking that hobbles the organization's ability to drive the global environmental agenda.[58] If it is able to generate and gather behind a clear institutional identity, UNEP can regain its focus on the big picture, capitalize on interlinkages among environmental issues, and reinvigorate excellence in management, monitoring, and follow-up. Ultimately, the vision for UNEP has to be a vision of and by UNEP, meaning that it should reflect the views and vision of its staff.

7.1 UNEP Executive Director Inger Andersen at UNEP's Champions of the Earth Award ceremony in New York City on September 26, 2019. Credit: UNEP.

LOCATION, LOCATION, LOCATION

Developing countries argued a powerful case in 1972 when the new international environmental institution was being created. Equity in representation and decision-making at the United Nations was critical in order for the newly independent nation states to join the international organization as equitable members. The principle of "one country, one vote," a core characteristic of the United Nations, presupposed a principle of equitable geographical representation and distribution. Yet, as chapter 2 explained, all international agencies were headquartered in the Global North. Ambassador Odero-Jowi of Kenya ran a powerful and ultimately successful campaign for Kenya to become the first developing country to host the headquarters of a UN agency. The rationale was clear: the United Nations had become a truly global organization and it was time for its agencies to be based in the countries and cities where many of the problems the organization was seeking to resolve were most acute and obvious. This political logic earned Kenya the space as a host country and facilitated the growth of its reputation over the years, as chapter 5 explained. Fifty years later, Kenya remains the only country in the Global South to host the headquarters of a UN agency with a global mandate.

Figure 7.2 illustrates the distribution of UN agency headquarters in twenty-two cities in nineteen countries around the world. The cities with the highest concentrations are Geneva with twelve agencies (24 percent of the total) and New York with ten (19 percent).[59] Europe and North America are the regions with the highest concentration of headquarters within the UN system with thirty (56 percent) and fifteen (28 percent) respectively. Several developing countries host the headquarters of the UN regional commissions, and the United Nations Relief Works Agency for Palestine Refugees has two locations in the region, in Jordan and Palestine. Nairobi remains the sole city in the Global South hosting a global UN institution; and not one but two, UNEP and UN Habitat. If the international community is serious about resolving global problems, it has to engage countries and communities around the world. As Ambassador McDonald noted repeatedly, "the only way to solve a conflict at any level of society is to sit down face to face and talk about it." Indeed, the analysis of global environmental governance achievements and challenges shows that the only way to resolve global problems is to come together face to face to agree on what is to be done, deliver on that agreement in locations around the world, and consistently reconvene to design next steps. To this end, the United Nations will need more people engaging in more locations. The Global South could offer to be both a host and a dynamic actor by engaging top-notch talent.

The ambitious vision for the original location fell short in involving the rest of the developing world and in creating the capacity necessary for the anchor institution to function most effectively. Learning from Bonn and its support for the UN Framework Convention on Climate Change, countries could offer the support necessary to develop powerful platforms for international institutions that would advance the global agenda and revitalize both local economies and a larger vision for sustainability. UNEP's original location decision was highly political. It is time to be political again, but governments must also provide international institutions with the connectivity and capacity necessary for them to deliver on their core mandates and gain credibility.

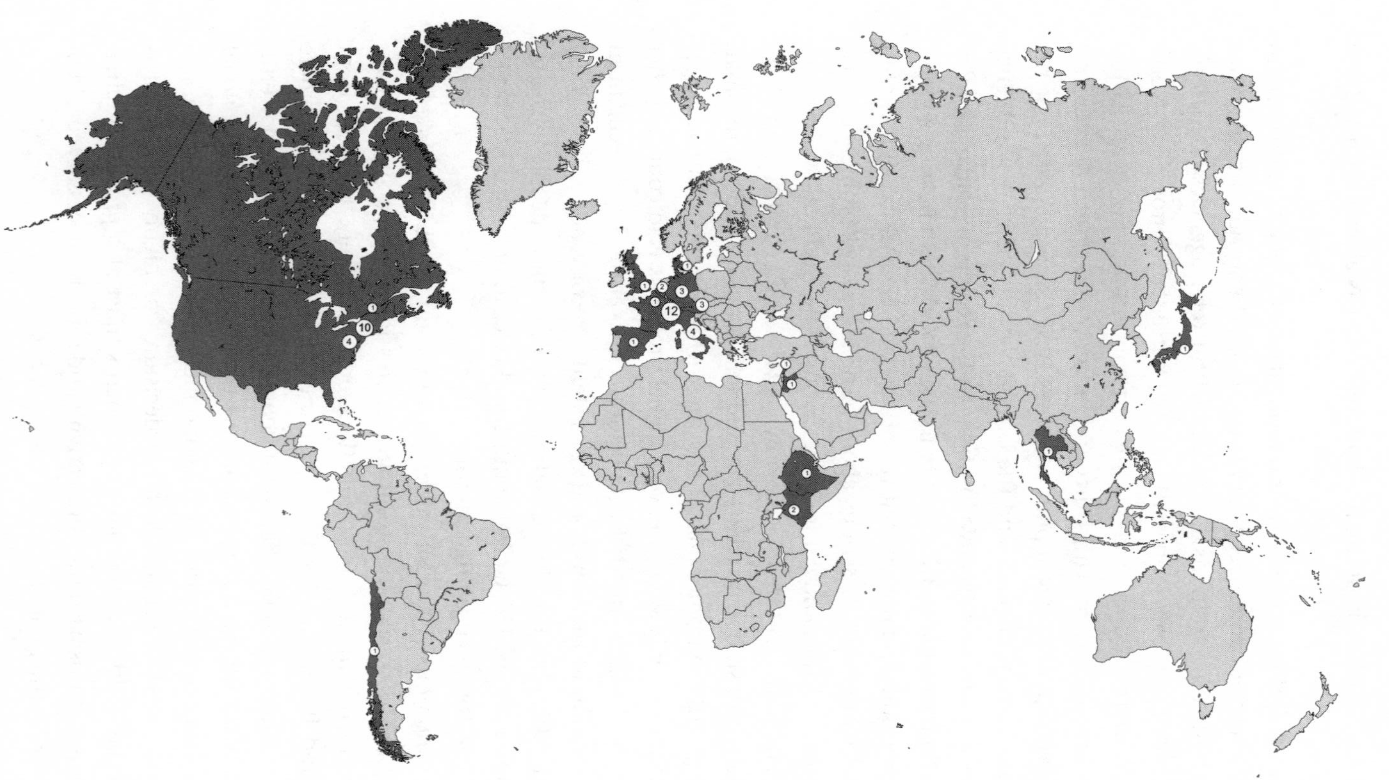

7.2 Number of UN agency headquarters around the world. An interactive version of this map is available at https://www.environmentalgovernance.org/untold-story.

The ability to create new hot spots of international activity does not depend solely on the location of headquarters. Clustering various offices of international organizations will create opportunities for collaboration and training and enhance the potential for staff to learn, grow, and advance in their professional development. There are thirty-two UN agencies with offices in Nairobi, which presents an opportunity for collaboration in the hiring, training, and promotion of staff within the UN ecosystem. Creating nexus units as formal partnerships among UN agencies with different mandates to work in the resource nexus of interconnected issues involving water, energy, land, food, and materials will deliver new opportunities for collaboration and problem resolution.

As previously noted, UNEP's capacity, connectivity, and credibility have been problematic because of institutional design in terms of mandate and finances, and because of challenges related to leadership and location. Actions taken in any single area impact the other interrelated variables. For example, clustering various offices of international organizations in Nairobi (location) will create opportunities for collaboration (connectivity), enhancing staff potential and resources (capacity), and by doing so, would allow UNEP to deliver on its core mandate and gain credibility. Figures 7.3 and 7.4 provide an overview of pragmatic measures to address these critical variables as well as the core design elements.

Capacity and connectivity can be increased even further by expanding this cluster of nexus units to other regions in the Global South, including Asia and the Pacific and Latin America and the Caribbean. And just as UNEP was the product of a powerful common vision, it is time for UNEP's leadership to create a new, compelling common vision and establish itself as the global authority on environmental matters. Part of this may include, for example, creating a common vision for nexus units to work across organizational lines to collectively solve the critical environmental issues we face. Addressing the interconnected aspects of mandate, finances, leadership, and location will allow UNEP to develop a compelling institutional identity and capitalize on its unique location. Ultimately, the host location of the anchor institution will be a critical aspect of its effective operation, which in turn affects UNEP's ability to respond to the needs of the community on which it depends.

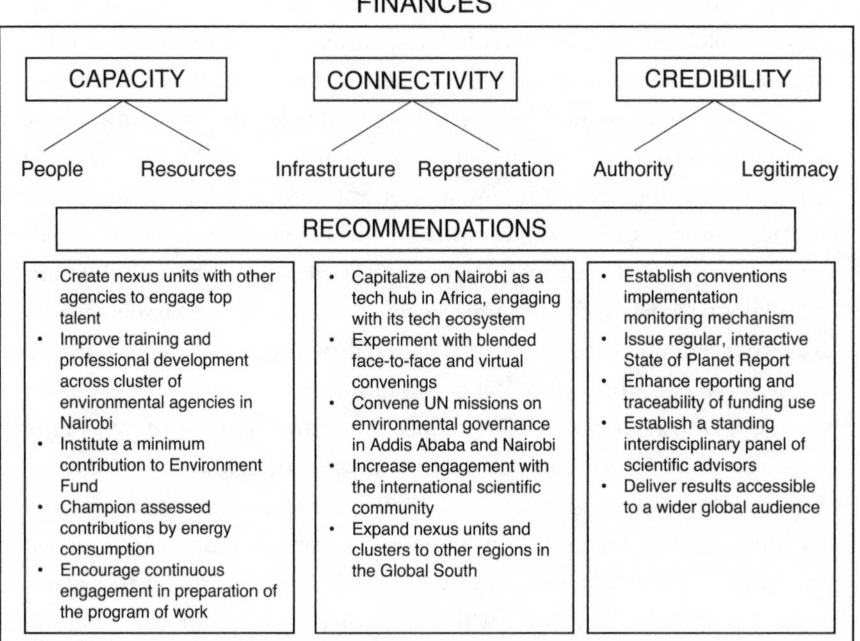

7.3 Key recommendations for enhancing capacity, connectivity, and credibility.

CHAMPION OF THE EARTH

Over the past five decades, the United Nations Environment Programme has delivered on several of its core functions, resolved some global environmental problems, and created the conditions for collective action on others. It has, however, been hampered by external political forces, economic pressures, and geopolitical conflict, as well as by the lack of a common internal vision and coordinated strategy, uneven management practices, and a limiting financial model. As governments and UNEP work through the greatest changes in the environmental governance architecture since UNEP's creation, it is critical to examine the lessons from the past to help build the architecture for the future. UNEP's founders documented clearly how they understood global environmental problems and how they thought the UN system could best address them. While the scale and scope of environmental problems have grown, and with them

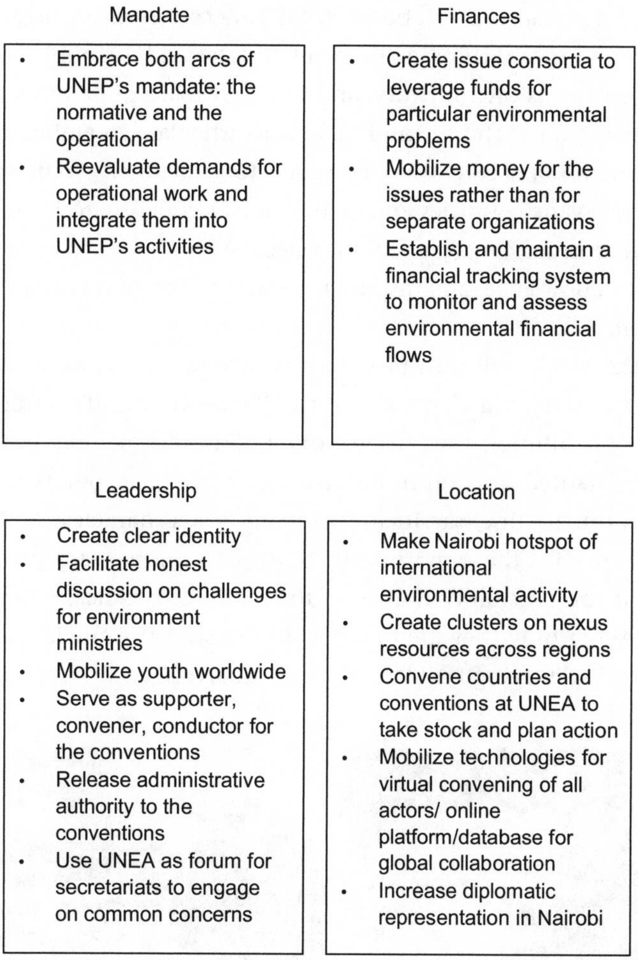

7.4 Key recommendations on design (mandate and finances), leadership, and location.

the urgency of action, the basic functions required of the international environmental governance system remain the same. UNEP was specifically designed to fulfill these functions as a small, highly visible body integrated closely with the rest of the UN system. The reasons for these design choices were valid in 1972; and since the current stated objectives of the governance system correspond to those of the original system, those reasons remain largely valid today.

Resolving persistent environmental problems will require a different approach: one that transcends the identification of issues and delves into the implementation of solutions. What is necessary is an organization that delivers forward thinking to member states and the public, one that is confident in its own identity, and one that takes pride in its mission and its work—an anchor institution able to articulate an ambitious, positive vision and take consequential action to achieve it.[60] To be effective, it would convene countries and conventions frequently to inform them of emerging issues, engage them in collective problem solving, empower them with knowledge, and inspire them with a common vision and concrete examples.

In 2022, UNEP will turn fifty. This anniversary presents an opportunity to envision a transformation for UNEP as the world's leading environmental institution. "It is time," one UNEP staff member put it, "for the disenchanted and burnt-out workers who have put their hearts and lives on the line, sacrificing so many years, nameless and unrecognized, to seize the opportunity the fiftieth anniversary presents to believe in the possibility that the future can look radically better and to realize that only they are in a position to start the crucial search for solutions."[61] Engaging UNEP staff, UNEP analysts, and civil society in a

7.5 Youth gather in Karura forest in Nairobi in solidarity with the global climate youth marches on March 15, 2019. Credit: UNEP.

series of concrete dialogues about UNEP's achievements and ambitions could create momentum similar to the energy generated by the climate change COPs.

We find ourselves in a dynamic context of ever-evolving global problems that demand evolving solutions. There is an extraordinary array of powerful modern tools that connect, inform, and empower to quickly link causes and consequences and devise appropriate actions. Informed decision-making to address current challenges relies on robust scientific input and effective interaction. The only way to generate solutions to the global challenges we face is to co-create knowledge that takes advantage of widely distributed insights to develop a joint vision. Scholars have the duty to shatter taboos and stereotypes; governments have the duty to take responsibility and create a climate of cooperation; and international institutions have the duty to summon bold, unflinching leadership. UNEP has the duty and, indeed, the privilege to serve as a champion of the earth.

NOTES

FOREWORD

1. Ambassador McDonald, Chairman Emeritus, Institute for Multi-Track Diplomacy, wrote this foreword in January 2019 as the manuscript was being prepared for print. He passed away in May 2019.

PREFACE

1. Gordon Harrison, "Is There a United Nations Environment Programme? Special Investigation at the Request of the Ford Foundation" (in the author's possession, 1977), 2.

2. Daniel C. Esty and Maria H. Ivanova, *Global Environmental Governance: Options and Opportunities* (New Haven, CT: Yale School of Forestry & Environmental Studies, 2002).

3. Maria Ivanova, *Can the Anchor Hold? Rethinking the UN Environment Programme for the 21st Century* (New Haven, CT: Yale School of Forestry & Environmental Studies, 2005).

4. "The Quest for Symphony" and "The Quest for Leadership," dir. Maria Ivanova and Joe Ageyo, Global Media & PR Ltd., the College of William and Mary (USA), and Yale Center for Environmental Law and Policy, 2009.

CHAPTER 1

1. In 1989, a wave of revolutions swept through Eastern Europe and toppled the communist regimes. They began in Poland and continued in Hungary, East Germany, Bulgaria, Czechoslovakia, and Romania. In 1991, the Soviet Union dissolved,

resulting in fifteen new countries. Albania and Yugoslavia abandoned communism between 1990 and 1992.

2. Greta Thunberg, "Our House Is on Fire," *Guardian*, January 25, 2019, https://www.theguardian.com/environment/2019/jan/25/our-house-is-on-fire-greta-thunberg16-urges-leaders-to-act-on-climate.

3. Richard Flanagan, "Australia is Committing Climate Suicide," *New York Times*, January 3, 2020, https://www.nytimes.com/2020/01/03/opinion/australia-fires-climate-change.html.

4. William Ruckelshaus, interview by the author, 2009.

5. Richard N. Gardner, "UN As Policeman," *Saturday Review*, August 7, 1971: 47; House of Commons, "Official Report: Parliamentary Debates (Hansard)" (London: Her Majesty's Stationery Office, 1971), 1604; US Congress, House Committee on Foreign Affairs, Subcommittee on International Organizations and Movements, "Participation by the United States in the United Nations Environment Program: Hearings Before the Subcommittee on International Organizations and Movements of the Committee on Foreign Affairs, House of Representatives, Ninety-third Congress, first session, on H.R. 5696," April 5 and 10, 1973 (Washington, DC: U.S. Govt. Print. Off., 1973); UN Information Service, "Preparatory Committee for Conference on Human Environment Completes General Debate" (Geneva, 1971).

6. Jacques Chirac, "Speech to the Plenary session of the World Summit on Sustainable Development," Johannesburg, September 2, 2002, http://www.jacqueschirac-asso.fr/archives-elysee.fr/elysee/elysee.fr/anglais/speeches_and_documents/2002-2001/fi005004.html.

7. Inger Andersen, interview by the author, 2019.

8. Eugénie L. Birch, David C. Perry, and Henry Louis Jr. Taylor, "Universities as Anchor Institutions," *Journal of Higher Education Outreach and Engagement* 17, no. 3 (2013): 9; Camden Higher Education and Health Care Task Force, "A 5 Year Winning Investment: Camden's Anchor Institutions Provide Jobs, Services, and a Bright Future" (Camden, NJ, 2008), 3; Steve Dubb, Sarah McKinley, and Ted Howard, "The Anchor Dashboard: Aligning Institutional Practice to Meet Low-Income Community Needs" (Tahoma Park, MD: Democracy Collaborative, 2013), 27.

9. Michael N. Barnett and Martha Finnemore, *Rules for the World: International Organizations in Global Politics* (Ithaca: Cornell University Press, 2004), 150.

10. UN General Assembly, "Resolution 2997 (XXVII): Institutional and Financial Arrangements for International Environmental Cooperation" (New York, 1972).

11. Robert W. Cox, Gerard Jacobson Curzon, and Harold Karan, *The Anatomy of Influence: Decision Making in International Organizations* (New Haven, CT: Yale University Press, 1973), 6.

12. Harrison, "Is There a United Nations Environment Programme? Special Investigation at the Request of the Ford Foundation," 10.

13. Harrison, "Is There a United Nations Environment Programme," 38.

26. UN General Assembly, "Report of the Preparatory Committee for the United Nations Conference on the Human Environment on the 3rd Session," A/CONF.48/PC.131971.

27. Elizabeth DeSombre, *Global Environmental Institutions* (London: Routledge, 2006), 8.

28. John W. McDonald and Noa Zanolli, *The Shifting Grounds of Conflict and Peace-building: Stories and Lessons* (Lanham, MD: Rowman and Littlefield, 2009), 74.

29. Adil Najam, "Why We Don't Need a New International Environmental Organization" (Working Paper Series no. 64, *Sustainable Development Policy Institute*, 2001), 11.

30. Najam, "The Case against GEO, WEO, or Whatever-Else-EO," 9; Ken Conca, "Greening the UN: Environmental Organizations and the UN System" in *NGOs, the UN, and Global Governance*, ed. Thomas Weiss and Leon Gordenker (Lynne Riener, 1996), 103–19; Konrad von Moltke, "Why UNEP Matters," in *Green Globe Yearbook* (Oxford: Oxford University Press, 1996), 57; von Moltke, "The Organization of the Impossible," 25; Najam, "The Case Against a New International Environmental Organization," 371.

31. In 1975, the UN General Assembly, in resolution 3362 (S-VII), endorsed the recommendation that UNIDO be transformed into a specialized agency. In 1979, the UN conference on the "establishment of UNIDO as a specialized agency" in Vienna, Austria, adopted the new constitution. On June 21, 1985, the new UNIDO constitution entered into force, and the first session of the General Conference of UNIDO as a specialized agency met in August 1979.

32. In figure 1.4, assessed contributions are obligatory payments that member states pay to finance the regular budgets of UN specialized agencies and are based on their level of economic development and per capita income. Voluntary contributions are non-mandatory payments which member states contribute at their discretion to UN programs and humanitarian and development agencies, such as, for example, UNICEF, UNDP, and WFP. The assessed contributions for UNEP include the financing for some of the conventions that UNEP administers.

33. Najam, "The Case against GEO, WEO, or Whatever-Else-EO," 42; DeSombre, *Global Environmental Institutions*, 13.

34. The argument developing countries articulated during the negotiations about UNEP's location at the United Nations in November 1972 was that the United Nations was a "global body and it is unfair that its agencies should be confined to North America or Western Europe." UN General Assembly, Second Committee, "Summary Record of the 1466th Meeting" (New York, 1972), 326.

35. John Scanlon, interview by the author, 2018.

36. Ronald Mitchell, "Evaluating the Performance of Environmental Institutions: What to Evaluate and How to Evaluate It?" in *Institutions and Environmental Change: Principal Findings, Applications, and Research Frontiers*, ed. Oran Young, Leslie King and Heike Schroeder (Cambridge, MA: MIT Press, 2008), 96.

37. Mohamed El-Ashry, "Recommendations from the High-Level Panel on System-Wide Coherence on Strengthening International Environmental Governance: Introduction," in *Global Environmental Governance: Perspectives on the Current Debate*, ed. Lydia Swart and Estelle Perry (New York: Center for UN Reform Education, 2007), 9–10.

38. Najam, "Why We Don't Need a New International Environmental Organization," 11.

39. von Moltke, "Why UNEP Matters," 57.

40. Interviewee 729, interview by the author, 2008.

41. Interviewee 256, interview by the author, 2018.

42. Steve Charnovitz, "A World Environment Organization," *Columbia Journal of Environmental Law* 27, no. 2 (2002): 323.

43. UNEP, "Internal Communication Survey Report" (in author's possession), 11. When asked about the effectiveness of UNEP as the leading UN environmental institution, 64 percent of respondents in 2012 perceived the organization as somewhat effective or very effective, 23 percent considered it ineffective or somewhat ineffective, and 13 were neutral. Four years later, in 2016, only 45 percent of respondents indicated effectiveness, and 33 percent responded as neutral.

44. UNEP, "Internal Communication Survey Report," 27.

45. UNEP, "Internal Communication Survey Report," 23.

46. OIOS, "Evaluation of the United Nations Environment Programme," E/AC.51/2019/7 (2019), 2.

47. Kofi Annan, interview by the author, 2017.

48. Barnett and Finnemore, *Rules for the World: International Organizations in Global Politics*, 24–27.

49. I use "limiting factor" in the way used in natural science—as the conditions that limit growth, abundance, and distribution of an organism.

50. Bill Mansfield, interview by the author, 2008.

51. For a thoughtful analysis of the role of executive heads in international organizations, see Nina Hall and Ngaire Woods, "Theorizing the Role of Executive Heads in International Organizations," *European Journal of International Relations* 24, no. 4 (2018): 865–886.

52. Inger Andersen, "As Voices for the Planet Grow Louder, We Must Get the Job Done" (June 15 2019, Nairobi, Kenya), https://www.unenvironment.org/news-and-stories/story/voices-planet-grow-louder-we-must-get-job-done.

53. Jon Pevehouse and Inken von Borzyskowski, "International Organizations in World Politics," in *The Oxford Handbook of International Organizations*, ed. Jacob Katz Cogan, Ian Hurd, and Ian Johnstone (Oxford University Press, 2016), 15.

54. Scott Krisner, "The suburbs are cheaper, but they don't have what Kendall Square has for biotechs: serendipity," *Boston Globe*, January 26, 2020, https://www

.bostonglobe.com/business/2020/01/26/kirsner/ZgCZqD4TlSJGMvNxZe3EbI/story.html.

55. Figueres and Carnac, *The Future We Choose*, 17.

56. Manuel Pulgar-Vidal, interview by the author, 2018

CHAPTER 2

1. Fitzhugh Green, "Remarks by US Delegate Fitzhugh Green to the Stockholm Human Environment Preparatory Committee," in *World's People Must be Informed, Persuaded to Back Environment Correction Measures*, ed. US Information Service (Geneva, 1972).

2. Maurice Strong, "Closing Statement" (speech, United Nations Conference on the Human Environment, Stockholm, Sweden, 1972).

3. William Clark, "Dedication to Maurice Strong," *The Environmentalist* 4, no. 2 (1984): 89.

4. Åström, *Ögonblick*.

5. Interviewee 532, interview by the author, 2007.

6. Bill Reilly, interview by the author, 2007.

7. Maurice Strong, *Where on Earth Are We Going?* (Toronto: Alfred A. Knopf Canada, 2000), 126. See also Ehsan Masood, "The Globe's Green Avenger," Nature 460 (2009): 454-455.

8. Wade Rowland, *The Plot to Save the World: The Life and Times of the Stockholm Conference on the Human Environment* (Toronto: Clarke, Irwin & Co. 1972), 47.

9. Strong, *Where on Earth Are We Going?*, 129–130.

10. Johnson, *UNEP: The First 40 Years*, 33.

11. Bernardo de Azevedo Brito, "Statement by the Brazilian Representative, Item 11 of the Agenda" (paper presented at the United Nations Conference on the Human Environment, Stockholm, Sweden, 1972).

12. Strong, *Where on Earth Are We Going?*, 124.

13. Engfeldt, *From Stockholm to Johannesburg and Beyond*, 77–79.

14. Mick Hamer, "The Filthy Rich," *New Scientist* 173, no. 2324 (January 5, 2002): 77.

15. Barbara Ward, "Only one Earth, Stockholm 1972," reprinted in *Evidence for Hope: The Search for Sustainable Development: The Story of the International Institute for Environment and Development, 1972–2002*, ed. by Nigel Cross (Earthscan, 2003).

16. UN Information Service, "Preparatory Committee for Conference on Human Environment Completes General Debate."

17. Mostafa K. Tolba, interview by the author, 2008.

18. Rowland, *The Plot to Save the World*, 47.

19. Conference on the Human Environment, *Development and Environment: Report and Working Papers of Experts Convened by the Secretary-General of the United Nations*

Conference on the Human Environment (Founex, Switzerland, June 4–12, 1971), Environment and Social Sciences, 1 (Paris: Mouton, 1972): 5–6.

20. Martin W. Holdgate, Mohammed Kassas, and Gilbert F. White, *The World Environment 1972–1982* (Nairobi: United Nations Environment Programme, 1982), 405.

21. Strong, *Where on Earth Are We Going?*, 128.

22. Gardner, "UN as Policeman." 47.

23. Strong, *Where on Earth Are We Going?*, 121.

24. Strong, 122.

25. Walter Sullivan, "A UN Role is Envisioned in Global Pollution Drive," *New York Times*, May 24, 1971.

26. Gardner, "UN As Policeman," 48.

27. Strong, *Where on Earth Are We Going?*, 130.

28. Strong, 133.

29. Strong, 134.

30. US Mission to the UN, "Statement by Christian A. Herter, Jr., United States Representative, in the Preparatory Committee for the United Nations Conference on the Human Environment, on Item 4, International Organizational Implications" (New York, NY, 1972), 1.

31. Michael Hardy, "The United Nations Environment Problem," *Natural Resources Journal* 13, no. 2 (April 1973): 235–255.

32. McDonald and Zanolli, *The Shifting Grounds of Conflict and Peacebuilding: Stories and Lessons*, 27.

33. Environmental Studies Board, *Institutional Arrangements for International Environmental Cooperation: A Report to the Department of State by the Committee for International Environmental Programs* (Washington, DC: National Academies of Sciences, 1972), 31.

34. United States Secretary of State's Advisory Committee on the 1972 United Nations Conference on the Human Environment (UNCHE), "Stockholm and Beyond: Report" (Washington, DC, 1972), 134.

35. US Secretary of State's Advisory Committee on the 1972 United Nations Conference on the Human Environment (UNCHE), "Stockholm and Beyond: Report," 8. The US Department of State reported, "There is general agreement among countries that a new specialized agency should not be created. One arrangement which is being widely discussed at the UN and among member governments is the creation of a small, high-level staff unit and an inter-governmental committee to give the unit policy direction." US Information Service, "President Proposes Voluntary UN Environment Fund" (Geneva, 1972), 2.

36. United States Secretary of State's Advisory Committee on the 1972 UNCHE, "Stockholm and Beyond: Report," 131.

37. United States Secretary of State's Advisory Committee on the 1972 UNCHE, 131.

38. United States Secretary of State's Advisory Committee on the 1972 UNCHE, 132.

39. Notably, dispute settlement is still missing in the global environmental governance system. By contrast, in the trade system, dispute settlement is at the core of the respective international institutions.

40. United Nations, "Report of the United Nations Conference on the Human Environment, Stockholm, 5–16 June 1972" (New York, 1973), 3–27.

41. In 2015, for example, the World Health Assembly of the World Health Organization comprised 193 states; the World Meteorological Organization had 191 members; the International Labour Organization, 187 members; and UNESCO, 195 members. In 2011, UNESCO members voted to admit Palestine as a full member of the organization, a move that subsequently led to the official withdrawal of the United States and then Israel from the organization in 2019.

42. The UN Forum on Forests is a notable exception. UNFF is a subsidiary organ established in 2000 by the UN Economic and Social Council with universal membership.

43. Sanjay Gupta, "Jan Egeland," *Time Magazine,* 8 May 2006.

44. Maria Ivanova, "Designing the United Nations Environment Programme: A Story of Compromise and Confrontation," *International Environmental Agreements: Politics, Law and Economics* 7, no. 3 (2007).

45. David Wightman, "United Nations Conference on the Human Environment: The International Organisational Implications of Action Proposals: Second Draft" (In the author's possession, n.d); Maria Ivanova, "A New Global Architecture for Sustainability Governance," in *State of the World 2012: Moving toward Sustainable Prosperity* (Washington, DC: Worldwatch Institute, 2012).

46. Gordon J. MacDonald, "International Institutions for Environmental Management," *International Organization* 26, no. 2 (Spring 1972), 373.

47. United Nations, "International Organizational Implications of Action Proposals," in *United Nations Conference on the Human Environment* (Stockholm, 1972). At the third session of the Preparatory Committee, several delegations stated that the conference should not lead to the establishment of any new specialized agency or operational body, and that any coordinating mechanisms which might be necessary should not have operational functions. They also noted the need to avoid rigid institutional structures, which would be rendered obsolete by rapid scientific and technological advances.

48. Wightman, "United Nations Conference on the Human Environment: The International Organisational Implications of Action Proposals: Second Draft"; Environmental Studies Board, "Institutional Arrangements for International Environmental Cooperation: A Report to the Department of State by the Committee for International Environmental Programs," 25.

49. McDonald and Zanolli, *The Shifting Grounds of Conflict and Peacebuilding: Stories and Lessons,* 32.

50. UK House of Commons, "Official Report: Parliamentary Debates (Hansard)."

51. US Mission to the UN, "Statement by Christian A. Herter, Jr.," 4–5.

52. Olof Rydbeck, "Statement by Ambassador Olof Rydbeck in the Preparatory Committee for the United Nations Conference on the Human Environment at Its Fourth Session in New York on Monday, 6 March 1972" (Fourth session of the Preparatory Committee for the United Nations Conference on the Human Environment, New York, March 6 1972), 3.

53. Strong, *Where on Earth Are We Going?*, 12–13.

54. Hamer, "The Filthy Rich," 77.

55. Some participants at a three-day "Mini-Stockholm" convened by the Aspen Institute in Rensselaerville, New York, in May 1971, "urged that environment be kept in the ECOSOC framework so that one institution could face the interrelated issues of development and environment; these people warned that separate bodies on environment and development could result in two sets of conflicting resolutions each reflecting a limited and inadequate perspective. Others urged that environment needed greater visibility and status than could be achieved in ECOSOC, which in their view has an unsatisfactory record." Gardner, "UN as Policeman," 49.

56. Wightman, "United Nations Conference on the Human Environment: The International Organisational Implications of Action Proposals: Second Draft," 6.

57. United Nations, "Report of the United Nations Conference on the Human Environment," 71.

58. US Information Service, "President Proposes Voluntary UN Environment Fund," 1.

59. McDonald and Zanolli, *The Shifting Grounds of Conflict and Peacebuilding*, 117–119.

60. George H.W. Bush, "Telegram from the Mission to the United Nations to the Department of State, New York, May 31, 1972" (New York, May 31 1972), in *Foreign Relations of the United States, 1969–1976*, Volume V: *United Nations, 1969–1972*, ed. Evan M. Duncan (Washington, DC: Government Printing Office, 1972): 334–335. A year later, the United States did decrease its contributions to 25 percent of the general budget for the United Nations rather than the usual 28 percent, prompting the UN to offset its budget by 6.52 percent. See United States Congress, House Committee on Foreign Affairs, Subcommittee on International Organizations and Movements, "Participation by the United States in the United Nations Environment Program," 67.

61. This conflict and impasse between the US executive and legislature would shape much of the US's subsequent behavior in international concerns and result in the inability of the US to ratify key environmental and social global agreements. It has also led to the tendency of US presidents to govern through executive orders, which set policies without congressional approval but can be easily annulled by a subsequent administration.

62. United States Secretary of State's Advisory Committee on the 1972 UNCHE, "Stockholm and Beyond: Report," 131.

63. Egypt, Brazil, Iran, Lebanon, Netherlands, Pakistan, Peru, Philipines, Sudan, Syrian Arab Republic, "Draft Resolution Concerning Development and Environment, A/C.2/L.1236, " (paper presented at the United Nations Conference on the

Human Environment, Stockholm, Sweden, 1972), 7. See also, UN General Assembly, "Official Records: 1466th–1488th Meeting of the Second Committee," ed. Second Committee of the United Nations General Assembly (New York, 1972).

64. UN General Assembly, "Summary Record of the 1478th Meeting," ed. Second Committee of the United Nations General Assembly (New York, 1972), 228.

65. Developing countries had voiced such concerns about the UN Fund for Population and the UN Capital Development Fund, which had diminished along with donor interest. UN General Assembly, "Summary Record of the 1478th Meeting," 228.

66. United States Secretary of State's Advisory Committee on the 1972 UNCHE, "Stockholm and Beyond: Report," 132.

67. United States Secretary of State's Advisory Committee on the 1972 UNCHE, 132.

68. United States Secretary of State's Advisory Committee on the 1972 UNCHE, 132. In a 1972 letter to Maurice Strong, Deputy Assistant Secretary of State Christian Herter explained, "The United States believes that it would be misleading to advance in the context of the Conference on the Human Environment proposals for an increase in the gross total of resources available for development assistance to cover environmental costs. The United States has nevertheless accepted and has urged others to accept the principle that the added cost of development projects necessitated by environmental protection measures are a legitimate part of the projected cost structure and the amount of assistance provided to projects requiring such added factors should take these costs into account." Christian A. Herter Jr., "Letter to Maurice Strong, Secretary-General of UNCHE Commenting on 'A Framework for Environmental Action,'" (in the author's possession, 1972), 2.

69. US Information Service, "President Proposes Voluntary UN Environment Fund," 1.

70. US Information Service, "Success of the Stockholm Conference: Statement by Russell E. Train, Chairman United States Delegation to the United Nations Conference on the Human Environment" (Stockholm, 1972), 2.

71. United States Secretary of State's Advisory Committee on the 1972 UNCHE, "Stockholm and Beyond: Report," 131–132.

72. Ambassador Bush communicated concern over the UN financial crisis to the US State Department. George H.W. Bush, "Telegram from the Mission to the United Nations to the Department of State," 334.

73. These and all following financial figures are as of August 1, 2019, based on data from UNEP-audited financial statements and the "Your contribution" page on UNEP's website, https://www.unenvironment.org/about-un-environment/funding-and-partnerships/why-invest-us/your-contributions. The financial analysis in this book and all relevant figures are derived from UNEP-audited financial statements from 1973 to 2018 (the latest documents available as of the time of writing) as well as from the UNEP Funding Facts portal, https://www.unenvironment.org/about-un-environment-programme/funding-and-partnerships/funding-facts.

74. The total contributions to the Environment Fund in 1979 were $31,493,929, which in constant 2019 dollars amounts to $110,904,179.

75. Frank Biermann, "Reforming Global Environmental Governance: The Case for a United Nations Environment Organization (UNEO)," in *Stakeholder Forum* (London, 2011).

76. Interviewee 364, interview by the author, 2018.

77. OIOS, "Evaluation of the United Nations Environment Programme," 24.

78. Brazil, Argentina, Canada, Iran, Kenya, Jamaica, Malta, Mexico, New Zealand, Swaziland, Sweden, United Republic of Tanzania, United States, "Draft Resolution on Institutional and Financial Arangements for International Environemntal Co-Operation, A/C.2/L.1228 & Corr.1 (Russian Only)" (1972). See also UN General Assembly, "United Nations Conference on the Human Environment: Report of the Second Committee" (1972).

79. In correspondence with Maurice Strong during the preparatory process for the Stockholm Conference, colleagues from governments and other institutions referred to the new body as the Environment Secretariat.

80. For a discussion of the location decision, see Maria Ivanova, "UNEP in Global Environmental Governance: Design, Leadership, Location," *Global Environmental Politics* 10, no. 1 (2010); Maria Ivanova, "Designing the United Nations Environment Programme: A Story of Compromise and Confrontation," *International Environmental Agreements: Politics, Law and Economics* 7, no. 4 (2007).

81. United States Secretary of State's Advisory Committee on the 1972 UNCHE, "Stockholm and Beyond: Report," 131.

82. Maurice F. Strong, "Opening Remarks by Maurice F. Strong, Secretary-General Designate" (paper presented at the Informal Meeting of Preparatory Committee for the United Nations Conference on Human Environment, November 9, 1970), 8.

83. Peter Stone, *Did We Save the Earth at Stockholm?* (London: Earth Island, 1973), 140.

84. Stone, *Did We Save the Earth at Stockholm?*, 142.

85. Donald Kaniaru, interview by the author, 2004.

86. Johnson, *UNEP: The First 40 Years*, 29.

87. The Kenyan delegation maintained that "In order to employ international machinery for the promotion of the economic and social advancement of all peoples, in accordance with the provisions of the United Nations Charter, the activities and headquarters or secretariats of United Nations bodies and agencies should be located having regard to equitable geographical distribution." UN General Assembly, "Summary Record of the 1466th Meeting," 326. Botswana, Algeria, Burundi, Cameroon, Central African Republic, Congo, Dabomey, et al, "Draft Resolution Concerning Location of an Environment Secretariat, a/C.2/ L.1246 & Rev. 1" (1972). Donald Kaniaru, "Kenya: A Special Honor to Have the UNEP Here," *The Nation* (December 19, 2004).

88. UN General Assembly, "Summary Record of the 1487th Meeting," ed. Second Committee (New York, 1972), 301.

89. UN General Assembly "Summary Record of the 1474th Meeting," ed. Second Committee (New York, 1972), 190.

90. UN General Assembly, "Summary Record of the 1483rd Meeting," ed. Second Committee (New York, 1972), 261–262.

91. UN General Assembly, "Summary Record of the 1483rd Meeting," 266.

92. UN General Assembly, "Summary Record of the 1474th Meeting," 191. See also Mauritania's statement affirming that "the candidacy of Kenya was a test of the solidarity of the Group of 77 and of the future of the United Nations itself, because in the past the selection of the location of United Nations units had been based exclusively on financial considerations. [His] delegation was aware that it would be initially more expensive to locate the environment secretariat in Nairobi but felt that the decision to be taken was essentially a political decision." "Summary Record of the 1487th Meeting," 302.

93. UN General Assembly, "Summary Record of the 1487th Meeting," 303.

94. UN General Assembly, "Summary Record of the 1482nd Meeting," ed. Second Committee (New York, 1972), 256.

95. UN General Assembly, "Summary Record of the 1487th Meeting," 302.

96. UN General Assembly, "Summary Record of the 1483rd Meeting," 263.

97. UN General Assembly, "Summary Record of the 1487th Meeting," 302.

98. UN General Assembly, "Summary Record of the 1483rd Meeting." As noted earlier, the office of the secretary-general had not prepared analyses of the financial implications of all location bids, under the assumption that the secretariat would remain in Geneva. The Second Committee requested that such a review be undertaken, and it was quickly compiled based on questionnaires to the candidate countries. It revealed a cost of $2.3 million for Nairobi and $1.3 million for Geneva.

99. Joseph Odero-Jowi, Permanent Representative of Kenya to the United Nations; Donald Kaniaru, Second Secretary at Kenya's Permanent Mission, and Odero-Jowi's "right-hand man;" Dawson Mramba, Permanent Secretary; and Njoroge Mungai, Foreign Minister.

100. Kenya framed the decision as a question of affirming the role of developing countries as equal partners in multilateral affairs. The vote proceeded in two stages. First, governments voted on the operative part of the draft resolution, which included two paragraphs: "1. Decides to locate the environment secretariat in a developing country and 2. Further decides to locate the environment secretariat in Nairobi, Kenya." Second, governments voted on the resolution as a whole. The votes split along the deep rift between the Global North and South. Of the 124 UN member states at the time, ninety-three countries voted in favor of the operative paragraphs, and one country, the United States, voted against. Thirty member states abstained. Among the abstentions were all developed states except Greece, all socialist states except Romania and Yugoslavia, and the developing countries of Fiji, Malawi, Malaysia, Mongolia, and South Africa. The votes were influenced by the fact that Kenya was scheduled to take over the presidency of the Security Council only a

month after the vote. Since the issue of the status of Cyprus came up perennially before the Security Council, Greece supported Kenya and voted in favor of the resolution. Joseph Odero-Jowi, Permanent Representative of Kenya to the United Nations, became the President of the Security Council in February 1973. When countries voted on the resolution as a whole, however, the United States replaced its opposition with an abstention, and the resolution passed with ninety-three votes to none, with thirty-one abstentions. UN General Assembly, "Summary Record of the 1487th Meeting," 302.

101. UN General Assembly, "Summary Record of the 1488th Meeting," ed. Second Committee (New York, 1972), 307.

102. UN General Assembly "Summary Record of the 1487th Meeting," 303.

103. United States Congress, House Committee on Foreign Affairs, Subcommittee on International Organizations and Movements, "Participation by the United States in the United Nations Environment Program," 8.

104. Copy of Department of State Superior Honor Award to John W. McDonald (in the author's possession).

105. Najam, "The Case against GEO, WEO, or Whatever-Else-EO," 36.

106. John Matuszak, interview by the author, 2018.

CHAPTER 3

1. Daniel Magraw, interview by the author, 2018.

2. UN General Assembly, "Resolution 2997(XXVII) Institutional and Financial Arrangements for International Environmental Cooperation."

3. "Governments will want to attach highest priority to the need for co-ordination and rationalization of the activities and programmes of the various international organizations active in the environmental field," the preparatory committee of the 1972 Stockholm Conference agreed. UN General Assembly, "Report of the Secretary General on United Nations Committee of the Human Environment," A/CONF.48/pC 11 (New York, 1971). Resolution 2997 of 1972 establishing UNEP noted that a core function of the executive director was to coordinate environmental programs within the UN system, keep their implementation under review, and assess their effectiveness.

4. These elements include the following, according to the *Mid-Term Evaluation of UNEP's Medium-term Strategy 2010–2013:*

   1. Keeping the world environmental situation under review;
   2. Catalyzing and promoting international cooperation and action;
   3. Providing policy advice and early warning information, based upon sound science and assessments;
   4. Facilitating the development, implementation and evolution of norms and standards and developing coherent inter-linkages among international environmental conventions;
   5. Strengthening technology support and capacity in line with country needs and priorities.

5. Figure 3.1 was created from key documents that established, reiterated and specified UNEP's mandate. Other documents that provided clarifications for UNEP's mandate include, among others, 2000 Malmö Ministerial Declaration, 2002 UNEP Governing Council Resolution SS.VII/I on International Environmental Governance, and 2005 Bali Strategic Plan for Technology Supportand Capacity Building.

6. Other international organizations also have expansive mandates. The IMF mandate, for example, is to "promote stability and growth in the world economy [and] UNHCR's is to protect refugees." See Barnett and Finnemore, *Rules for the World: International Organizations in Global Politics*, 159–160.

7. See von Moltke, "The Organization of the Impossible"; Toru Iwama, "Multilateral Environmental Institutions and Coordinating Mechanisms," in *Emerging Forces in Environmental Governance*, ed. by N. Kanie and P. M. Haas (Tokyo, New York, Paris: United Nations University Press, 2004); Biermann and Bauer, *A World Environment Organization: Solution or Threat for Effective International Environmental Governance?*

8. See Ivanova, "Designing the United Nations Environment Programme: A Story of Compromise and Confrontation"; Ivanova, "UNEP in Global Environmental Governance: Design, Leadership, Location."

9. Amina Mohammed, interview by the author, 2018.

10. Rowan Scarborough, "'Peace Dividend' Apparently Paying Off," *Washington Times*, March 9, 1998; US Congress, "After the Cold War: Living with Lower Defense Spending," OTA-ITE-524 (Washington, DC: US Governmnet Printing Office, 1992). The end of the Cold War led to a dramatic cut in defense spending in the United States. For example, by 1998, the Pentagon reduced its active-duty troops by 700,000 and closed many weapons assembly lines, leading to a defense spending authority of $270 billion in 1999, down from $429.8 billion in 1985 (in 1999 inflation-adjusted dollars) and from $385 billion in 1989. These cuts, however, were not used to invest in global issues but to balance the budget in the United States.

11. Thomas McInerney, "UNEP, International Environmental Governance, and the 2030 Sustainable Development Agenda" (Working Paper, UNEP, 2017), https://wedocs.unep.org/bitstream/handle/20.500.11822/21247/UNEP_IEG_2030SDA.pdf.

12. van der Hel and Biermann, "The Authority of Science in Sustainability Governance: A Structured Comparison of Six Science Institutions Engaged with the Sustainable Development Goals," *Environmental Science and Policy* 77 (2017): 215.

13. International Labour Organization (ILO); Food and Agriculture Organization (FAO); United Nations Educational, Scientific and Cultural Organization (UNESCO); World Health Organization (WHO); World Meteorological Organization (WMO); International Agency for Research on Cancer (IARC); Intergovernmental Maritime Consultative Organization (IMCO, after 1982 known as IMO, International Maritime Organization); International Atomic Energy Agency (IAEA); International Civil Aviation Organization (ICAO); United Nations Development Programme (UNDP).

14. Laurence D. Mee, "The Role of United Nations Environment Programme and United Nations Development Programme in Multilateral Environmental Agreements," *International Environmental Agreements: Politics, Law and Economics* 5, no. 3 (2005): 231.

15. OIOS, "Evaluation of the United Nations Environment Programme," 24.

16. Office of Policy Development and Inter-Agency Affairs, "Review and Analysis of the Environment Coordination Board and Acc Reports and of the Process and Modalities of the Preparation of SWMTEP" (in the author's possession, 1993), 6.

17. Global Environmental Governance Forum: Reflecting on the Past, Moving into the Future (Glion, Switzerland, June 28–July 2, 2009).

18. Source notes for box 3.1: UNEP Governing decision 6/1 of 1978 on program policy and implementation created SWMTEP and UNGA Resolution 33/86 of 1978 affirmed it. UN General Assembly, "Restructuring of the Economic and Social Sectors of the United Nations System," A/Res/32/197 (New York, 1977); Office of Policy Development and Inter-Agency Affairs, "Review and Analysis of the Environment Coordination Board and Acc Reports and of the Process and Modalities of the Preparation of SWMTEP," 13; Office of Policy Development and Inter-Agency Affairs, "Review and Analysis of the Environment Coordination Board and Acc Reports and of the Process and Modalities of the Preparation of SWMTEP," 16; ECOSOC, "In-Depth Evaluation of the Programme on Environment, E/aC.51/1995/3," 8.

19. Jim MacNeill, interview by the author, 2009.

20. Kofi Annan, interview by the author, 2017.

21. Global Environmental Governance Forum: Reflecting on the Past, Moving into the Future.

22. UNEP Evaluation and Oversight Unit, "Management Study on Trust Funds and Counterpart Contributions" (Nairobi, 1999), 27.

23. ECOSOC, "In-Depth Evaluation of the Programme on Environment, E/Ac.51 /1995/3," in *Thirty-Fifth Session of the Committee for Programme and Coordination* (New York: United Nations, 1995), 7.

24. Interviewee 370, interview by the author, 2008.

25. Engfeldt, *From Stockholm to Johannesburg and Beyond*, 217.

26. Designed to tackle global environmental problems and help implement environmental conventions, the GEF began with US$1 billion over three years. Twenty-five years later, the GEF has invested US$14.5 billion, and leveraged US$75.4 billion in additional resources, for nearly four thousand projects in 167 countries. Global Environment Facility, "25 Years of GEF," 2016, https://www.thegef.org/sites/default /files/publications/31357FinalWeb.pdf.

27. UN General Assembly, "Strengthening of the United Nations Environment Programme," A/Res/48/174 (New York, 1993), 2.

28. Gerrard Cunningham, interview by the author, 2017.

29. Donald Kaniaru, interview by the author, 2004.

30. Tadanori Inomata, "Management Review of Environmental Governance within the United Nations System," JIU/REP/2008/3 (Geneva: Joint Inspection Unit, 2008), 10. See also Steiner Andresen, "The Effectiveness of UN Environmental Institutions," *International Environmental Agreements: Politics, Law and Economics* 7, no. 4 (2007), 317–336.

31. Inomata, "Management Review of Environmental Governance within the United Nations System," 30.

32. Mark F. Imber, *Environment, Security, and UN Reform* (New York: Springer, 1994), 83.

33. Regarding the clusters approach, El-Ashry explained his proposal to UNEP Executive Director Dr. Klaus Töpfer and noted that "Töpfer didn't buy it because he wanted the whole thing." The executive director of UNEP was formally the chair of the EMG, but UNEP no longer performs an active coordinating role in the UN system. Mohamed El-Ashry, interviwed by the author, 2008.

34. At the outset, EMG was perceived as an instrument that UNEP used to establish control over the agencies, and it was met with resistance. See Adil Najam, Mihaela Papa, and Nadaa Taiyab, *Global Environmental Governance: A Reform Agenda* (Winnipeg, Canada: International Institute for Sustainable Development [IISD], 2006), https://www.iisd.org/sites/default/files/publications/geg.pdf. Several initiatives to enhance the effectiveness of the EMG have been undertaken. See UNEP/GC/27/2, para. 16; UNEA/1/11, para. 4; and UNEA/2/5. However, fulfilling its mandate is still considered problematic. See UN Secretary-General, "Gaps in International Environmental Law and Environment-Related Instruments: Towards a Global Pact for the Environment," A/73/419, New York, 2018.

35. Janos Pasztor, interview by the author, 2017.

36. Kofi Annan, interview by the author, 2017.

37. For an analytical framework of the science-policy interface, see David W. Cash, William C. Clark, Frank Alcock, Nancy M. Dickson, Noelle Eckley, David H. Guston, Jill Jäger, and Ronald B. Mitchell, "Knowledge Systems for Sustainable Development," *Proceedings of the National Academy of Sciences* 100, no. 14 (2003): 8086–8091. For an empirical study of the science-policy interface in global environmental governance, see Pia Kohler, *Science Advice and Global Environmental Governance: Expert Institutions and the Implementation of International Environmental Treaties* (London, New York: Anthem Press, 2019).

38. Ågesta Group AB Sweden, "Twenty Years after Stockholm, 1972–1992: A Report on the Implementation of the Stockholm Action Plan for the Environment and on Priorities and Institutional Arrangements for the 1980s" (Farsta: Ågesta Group AB, 1982). 13; Norman N. Miller, *The United Nations Environment Programme* (Hanover: American Universities Field Staff, 1979), 21.

39. John Matuszak, interview by the author, 2018.

40. UN General Assembly, "Consolidated Document on the UN System and the Human Environment," *United Nations Conference on the Human Environment* (Stockholm, 1972), para. 111.

41. ECOSOC, "In-Depth Evaluation of the Programme on Environment, E/aC.51/1995/3," 10–12. Earthwatch comprised the International Referral System (IRS), the Global Environmental Monitoring Systems (GEMS), the International Register for Potentially Toxic Chemicals (IRPTC), and the Study of Outer Limits, which included work on climate change, ozone layer depletion, bioproductivity, and weather modification.

42. Richard Sandbrook, "The 'Crisis' in Political Development Theory," *The Journal of Development Studies* 12, no. 2 (1976): 180.

43. Peter S. Thacher, "Multilateral Cooperation and Global Change," *Journal of International Affairs* 44, no. 2 (1991): 442.

44. Thacher, "Multilateral Cooperation and Global Change," 442.

45. Calestous Juma, interview by the author, 2017.

46. Ågesta Group AB Sweden, "Twenty Years after Stockholm," 29.

47. Ågesta Group AB Sweden, 29.

48. This work started with the production of scientific assessments on particular topics. In 1995, UNEP published the *Global Biodiversity Assessment*—the first independent, peer-reviewed, global scientific assessment of biological diversity. The report offered a review of scientific knowledge to date and acknowledged areas of consensus and disagreement. UNEP also continued to produce the International Register of Potentially Toxic Chemicals and use it as the foundation for training experts and providing technical support to developing countries.

49. In 1995, UNEP published the first "independent, peer-reviewed, global scientific assessment of the earth's biological diversity, [a]n authoritative, 1100-page book, *The Global Biodiversity Assessment.*" UNEP, United Nations Environment Programme: Highlights of the Biennium, *1994–1995, UNEP/GC/19/INF.16 (*Nairobi, 1995), 6.

50. Maria Ivanova and Melissa Goodall, "Global Environmental Outlook (GEO): an Integrated Environmental Assessment," *The Encyclopedia of Sustainability: Measurements, Indicators, and Research Methods for Sustainability* (Berkshire Publishing Group, 2012): 207–234.

51. Michael Zammit Cutajar, interview by the author, 2017.

52. Amina Mohammed, interview by the author, 2018.

53. Somini Sengupta, "'Bleak' U.N. Report on a Planet in Peril Looms Over New Climate Talks," *New York Times*, November 26, 2019, https://www.nytimes.com/2019/11/26/climate/greenhouse-gas-emissions-carbon.html.

54. Murat Arsel, "Fuelling misconceptions: UNEP, natural resources, the environment and conflict." *Development and Change* 42, no. 1 (2011): 448.

55. Julia Marton-Lefèvre, "The Role of the Scientific Community in the Preparation of and Follow-up to UNCED," in *Negotiating International Regimes: Lessons Learned from the United Nations Conference on Environment and Development*, ed. Bertram I. Spector, Gunnar Sjöstedt, and I. William Zartman (London: Graham & Trotman/M. Nijhoff, 1994), 173.

56. Desai, "UNEP: A Global Environmental Authority," 139.

57. Michail Nikolaevich Kopylov, "ЮНЕП-35. Сколько еще? (UNEP-35. How Many Ahead?)," *Moskovsky zhurnal mezhduranodnogo prava* 66, no. 2 (2007): 159.

58. ECOSOC, "In-Depth Evaluation of the Programme on Environment—Note by the Secretary-General," 10–12.

59. Maria Ivanova and Natalia Escobar-Pemberthy, "The UN, Global Governance and the SDGs," in *Handbook on the Resource Nexus*, ed. Raimund Bleischwitz et al. (New York, Routledge/Earthscan: 2017): 486–502.

60. Niko Urho, interview by the author, 2019.

61. Gerard Cunningham, interview by the author, 2017.

62. GEO, "GEO, Group on Earth Observations," https://www.earthobservations.org/index.php.

63. Ivanova and Escobar-Pemberthy, "The UN, Global Governance and the SDGs," 491.

64. Dan Magraw, interview by the author, 2018.

65. Norman N. Miller, *The United Nations Environment Programme*, 10; ECOSOC, "In-Depth Evaluation of the Programme on Environment—Note by the Secretary-General," 18.

66. T. C. Bacon, "Role of the United Nations Environment Program in the Development of International Environmental Law," *The Canadian Yearbook of International Law* 12 (1974): 257.

67. UN General Assembly "Resolution 3129 (XXVIII) On the establishment of international standards on shared resources" (New York, 1973). Several Governing Council resolutions also requested the executive director to initiate legal consultations and participate in developing legal principles. See John W. Head, "The Challenge of International Environmental Management: A Critique of the United Nations Environment Programme," *Virginia Journal of International Law* 18, no. 2 (1977–1978): 285.

68. Mark Allan Gray, "The United Nations Environment Programme: An Assessment," *Environmental Law* 20 (1990): 295.

69. Achim Steiner, Lee A. Kimball, and John Scanlon, "Global Governance for the Environment and the Role of Multilateral Environmental Agreements in Conservation," *Oryx* 37, no. 2 (2003): 236.

70. John McCormick, *Reclaiming Paradise: The Global Environmental Movement* (Bloomington: Indiana University Press, 1989), 174.

71. Peter M. Haas, "Institutions: United Nations Environment Programme," *Environment* 36, no. 7 (1993): 44.

72. Gus Speth, interview by the author, 2019.

73. Interviewee 978, interview by the author, 2008.

74. The core policy functions of UNEP as per the 1997 Nairobi Declaration, which rearticulated UNEP's mandate include: Further the development of its international environmental law, including development of coherent interlinkages among existing international environmental conventions; Advance the implementation of agreed international norms and policies, to monitor and foster compliance with environmental principles and international agreements and stimulate cooperative action to respond to emerging environmental challenges.

75. Calestous Juma, interview by the author, 2017.

76. John Scanlon, Secretary General of CITES, "Presentation at the 12th special session of GMEF, Plenary Panel on the Institutional Framework for Sustainable Development" (Nairobi, Kenya, February 12, 2012), https://www.cites.org/eng/news/sg/2012/20120221_UNEP-GMEF.php.

77. Michael Zammit Cutajar, interview by the author, 2017.

78. John Matuszak, interview by the author, 2018. See also UN General Assembly, "UN Reform. Implications for the Environment Pillar," UNEP/DED/040506 (Nairobi, 2006).

79. UNEP, "Mid-Term Evaluation of UNEP's Medium-Term Strategy 2010–2013," 15.

80. Youba Sokona, interview by the author, 2018.

81. Teresa Kramarz and Susan Park. "Accountability in Global Environmental Governance: A Meaningful Tool For Action?," *Global Environmental Politics*, 16, no. 2 (2016): 4.

82. See *Global Leadership Dialogues*, Volume 3, Issue 3: "Environmental Envoy: Achim Steiner." 2016. Center for Governance and Sustainability, University of Massachusetts Boston.

83. Annabell Waititu, interview by the author, 2017.

84. UNEP, "Mid-Term Evaluation of UNEP's Medium-Term Strategy 2010–2013," 7.

85. UNEP, "Medium Term Strategy 2014–2017" (Nairobi, 2015), 40.

86. In 2019, 70 percent of respondents to an Office of Internal Oversight Services survey evaluating UNEP's performance noted that there was no common vision at UNEP on how best to achieve goals, and 60 percent said that quality of work at UNEP suffered due to constantly changing priorities. OIOS, "Evaluation of the United Nations Environment Programme," 20.

CHAPTER 4

1. Tolba, 1998 interview cited in Penelope Canan and Nancy Reichman, *Ozone Connections: Expert Networks in Global Environmental Governance* (Sheffield, UK: Greenleaf Publishing, 2002), 48.

2. Interviewee 710, interview by the author, 2017.

3. Bill Mansfield, interview by the author, 2008.

4. OIOS, "Review of the United Nations Environment Programme (UNEP) and the Administrative Practices of Its Secretariat, Including the United Nations Office in Nairobi (UNON)," A/51/810 (New York, 1997).

5. Richard E. Benedick, *Ozone Diplomacy: New Directions in Safeguarding the Planet* (Cambridge: Harvard University Press, 1991), 6.

6. Benedick, *Ozone Diplomacy*, 6; Philippe G. Le Prestre, John D. Reid, and E. Thomas Morehouse, eds. *Protecting the Ozone Layer: Lessons, Models, and Prospects* (Boston: Kluwer, 1998), 57–58; Edward A. Parson *Protecting the Ozone Layer: Science and Strategy* (Oxford: Oxford University Press, 2003), 142; Karen Litfin, *Ozone Discourses: Science*

and Politics in Global Environmental Cooperation (New York: Columbia University Press, 1994), 201–3; Peter M. Haas "Banning chlorofluorocarbons: epistemic community efforts to protect stratospheric ozone," *International organization* 46, no. 1 (1992): 223; Detlef Sprinz and Tapani Vaahtoranta, "The interest-based explanation of international environmental policy," *International Organization* 48, no. 1 (1994): 78.

7. Thacher, "Multilateral Cooperation and Global Change," 442; Carol Annette Petsonk, "The Role of the United Nations Environment Programme (UNEP) in the Development of International Environmental Law," *American University Journal of International Law & Policy* 5, no. 2 (1990): 367; Benedick, *Ozone Diplomacy*, 54.

8. Canan and Reichman, *Ozone Connections*, 48.

9. Richard E. Benedick, "US Environmental Policy: Relevance to Europe," *International Environmental Affairs* 1, no. 2 (1989): 47.

10. Source notes for box 4.1: Tribute to Mostafa Tolba in Benedick, *Ozone Diplomacy*. Cited in Stephen O. Andersen and K. Madhava Sarma, *Protecting the Ozone Layer: The United Nations History* (London: Earthscan, 2012), 139; Interviewee 676, interview by the author, 2018.

11. In addition, under Article 9, parties report every two years on activities regarding research, public awareness, and exchange of information. There are also reporting requirements established by Meetings of the Parties that require relevant countries to annually submit information on: reclamation facilities and their capacities (Decision VI/19), approved essential or critical uses (Decision VIII/9), and usage for exempted laboratory and critical uses (Decision VI/9).

12. Carol Petsonk, "The Role of the United Nations Environment Programme (UNEP) in the Development of International Environmental Law," 368.

13. UNEP Governing Council, "Review of Major Achievements in the Implementation of the Stockholm Action Plan," UNEP/GC.10/6/Add.1 (Nairobi, 1982), para. 83.

14. Ernst Haas, *When Knowledge Is Power: Three Models of Change in International Organizations* (Berkeley: University of California Press, 1990): 356.

15. Mostafa Tolba, interview by the author, 2008.

16. Tolba, interview by the author, 2008.

17. Tolba, interview by the author, 2008.

18. Glen Garelick, "Environment a Breath of Fresh Air: Delegates of 24 Nations Sign a Historic Pact on Ozone," *Time Magazine*, September 28, 1987.

19. Carol Petsonk, "The Role of the United Nations Environment Programme (UNEP) in the Development of International Environmental Law," 369–370.

20. In figure 4.1 and further in the text, the numbers for the 2018–2019 biennium are based only on the 2018 UNEP audited financial statement, and 2019 numbers are projected based on the 2018 data.

21. Susan E. Strahan and Anne R. Douglass, "Decline in Antarctic Ozone Depletion and Lower Stratospheric Chlorine Determined from Aura Microwave Limb Sounder Observations," *Geophysical Research Letters* 45, no. 1 (2018): 382.

22. Samson Reiny, "NASA Study: First Direct Proof of Ozone Hole Recovery Due to Chemical Ban," https://www.nasa.gov/feature/goddard/2018/nasa-study-first-direct-proof-of-ozone-hole-recovery-due-to-chemicals-ban.

23. Paul Akiwumi and Terttu Melvasalo, "UNEP's Regional Seas Programme: Approach, Experience and Future Plans," *Marine Policy* 22, no. 3 (1998); Stacy D. VanDeveer, "Protecting Europe's Seas: Lessons from the Last 25 Years," *Environment: Science and Policy for Sustainable Development* 42, no. 6 (2000): 10–26.

24. Frank Prial, "Program to Clean up Mediterranian Sea Is Approved," *New York Times*, March 11, 1981, https://www.nytimes.com/1981/03/11/world/program-to-clean-up-mediterranean-sea-is-approved.html.

25. The Barcelona Convention is also known as the Convention for the Protection of the Mediterranean Against Pollution. It was adopted on 16 February 1976 in conjunction with two Protocols addressing the prevention of pollution by dumping from ships and aircraft, and cooperation in combating pollution in cases of emergency. In 1995, the Contracting Parties adopted amendments to the Barcelona Convention of 1976 and renamed it the Convention for the Protection of the Marine Environment and the Coastal Region of the Mediterranean. It entered into force in 2004. Countries adopted the Protocol on pollution from land-based sources in 1980, the Protocol concerning Specifically Protected Areas in 1982, and the Offshore Protocol in 1994.

26. Prial, "Program to Clean up Mediterranian Sea Is Approved."

27. Desai, "UNEP: A Global Environmental Authority," 139.

28. Laurence D. Mee, "The Role of United Nations Environment Programme and United Nations Development Programme in Multilateral Environmental Agreements," 246.

29. UNEP, "UNEP Annual Report 1998" (Nairobi, 1999), 33.

30. Peter M. Haas, "Institutions: United Nations Environment Programme," 45; Peter Hulm, "The Regional Seas Program; What Fate for United Nations Environment Programme's Crown Jewels?" *Ambio* 12, no. 1 (1983): 7; Frank Biermann and Steffen Bauer, "Managers of Global Governance Assessing and Explaining the Effectiveness of Intergovernmental Organizations," paper presented at the 44th Annual Convention of the International Studies Association (Portland, 2003), 11. Other scholars, however, criticize it as insufficient. Mingst, et al. note, for example, that "the plans for various seas have faced a number of difficult problems, including contentious political relationships among participating states." Karen A. Mingst, Margaret P. Karns, and Alynna J. Lyon, *The United Nations in the 21st Century (Dilemmas in World Politics)*, 5th ed. (Boulder: Westview Press, 2016), 213.

31. The Sahel is the semi-arid region in Africa extending from Senegal eastward to Sudan. It forms a transitional zone between the Sahara Desert to the north and the belt of humid savannas to the south. It spans from the Atlantic eastward through Senegal, Mauritania, Mali, Burkina Faso, Niger, Nigeria, Chad, and Sudan.

32. Mohammed Kassas, "Desertification: A General Review," *Journal of Arid Environments* 30, no. 2 (1995): 126.

33. Kassas, "Desertification: A General Review," 127. UNESCO had been working on desertification since 1950, when it launched a worldwide arid zone research program. As a result, two hundred arid-zone research institutions had been activated, thirty volumes of scientific and technical studies published, and dryland ecology emerged as a scientific field.

34. David Waugh, *Geography: An Integrated Approach* (Oxford: Oxford University Press, 2014), 192.

35. UNEP, "1979 Annual Review" (Nairobi, 1979), 34.

36. Steve Lonergan, "The Role of UNEP in Desertification Research and Mitigation," *Journal of Arid Environments* 63, no. 3 (2005): 533.

37. Mohammed Kassas, "Desertification," 123.

38. David S.G. Thomas and Nicholas J. Middleton, *Desertification: Exploding the Myth* (John Wiley and Sons, 1994), 17.

39. Adil Najam, Loli Christopoulou, and William R. Moomaw, "The Emergent 'System' of Global Environmental Governance," *Global Environmental Politics* 4, no. 4 (2004); Najam, Papa, and Taiyab, *Global Environmental Governance: A Reform Agenda.*

40. UNEP, *World Atlas of Desertification* (Baltimore: Edward Arnold, 1992), 23–24.

41. Source notes for box 4.2: Thomas and Middleton, *Desertification: Exploding the Myth*, 17–18; S.R. Verón, J.M. Paruelo, and M. Oesterheld, "Assessing Desertification," *Journal of Arid Environments* 66, no. 4 (2006): 755; Stefanie M. Herrmann and Charles F. Hutchinson, "The Changing Contexts of the Desertification Debate," *Journal of Arid Environments* 63, no. 3 (2005): 538; UNEP, *World Atlas of Desertification 11*; Verón, Paruelo, and Oesterheld, "Assessing Desertification," 756–57; Lindsay C. Stringer, "Reviewing the International Year of Deserts and Desertification 2006: What Contribution Towards Combating Global Desertification and Implementing the United Nations Convention to Combat Desertification?" *Journal of Arid Environments* 72, no. 11 (2008): 2066.

42. Steve Lonergan, "The Role of UNEP in Desertification Research and Mitigation," 534.

43. T. V. Padma, "African nations push UN to improve drought research," *Nature News*, September 13, 2019, https://www.nature.com/articles/d41586-019-02760-9.

44. Steve Lonergan, "The Role of UNEP in Desertification Research and Mitigation," 535.

45. ECOSOC, "In-Depth Evaluation of the Programme on the Environment, E/Ac.51/1995/3", 10–12.

46. Food and Agriculture Organization (FAO), United Nations Educational, Scientific and Cultural Organization (UNESCO), World Health Organization (WHO), International Agency for Research on Cancer (IARC), Intergovernmental Maritime Consultative Organization (IMCO, after 1982 known as IMO, International Maritime Organization), and International Labour Organization (ILO).

47. Johnson, *UNEP: The First 40 Years*, 150.

48. RS, "Halt 'Garbage Imperialism,'" *Christian Science Monitor*, November 15, 1988.

49. RS, "Halt 'Garbage Imperialism.'"

50. Jennifer Clapp, *Toxic Exports: The Transfer of Hazardous Wastes from Rich to Poor Countries* (New York: Cornell University Press, 2001), 40; see also Kate O'Neill, *Waste Trading Among Rich Nations: Building a New Theory of Environmental Regulation* (Cambridge, MA: MIT Press, 2000).

51. Dermot O'Sullivan, "UN Environment Program Targets Issue of Hazardous Waste Exports," *Chemical & Engineering News* 66, no. 39 (1988), 27.

52. Gerard Cunningham, interview by the author, 2017.

53. There have been extensive debates about whether the requirement of three-fourths of the parties to the Convention applies to the current membership, or the membership at the time of the amendment's adoption. In 2011, parties agreed to interpret the clause so that the amendment will have entered into force upon ratification by three-fourths of those that were parties at the time of the amendment's adoption (as detailed in decision BC10/3).

54. Erin McCormick et al., "Where does your plastic go? Global investigation reveals America's dirty secret," *Guardian*, June 17, 2019, https://www.theguardian.com/us-news/2019/jun/17/recycled-plastic-america-global-crisis.

55. Governments adopted the 2020 goal, which commits them to achieving environmentally sound management of chemicals and all wastes throughout their life-cycle by the year 2020. The goal originated in Agenda 21, was confirmed by the Johannesburg Plan of Implementation, and in the 2030 Agenda, which states, "By 2020, achieve the environmentally sound management of chemicals and all wastes throughout their life cycle, in accordance with agreed international frameworks, and significantly reduce their release to air, water and soil in order to minimize their adverse impacts on human health and the environment." Clearly, the goal was not met by 2020, and in 2017 governments launched the "Beyond 2020 process" within SAICM. See http://www.saicm.org.

56. Rolph Payet, interview by the author, 2018.

57. In 2017, at their joint General Assembly in Taipei, the International Council for Science (ICSU) and the International Social Science Council (ISSC) merged into one organization, the International Science Council (ISC).

58. For an overview of the climate change negotiations, see Joyeeta Gupta, "A History of International Climate Change Policy," *Wiley Interdisciplinary Reviews: Climate Change* 1, no. 5 (2010): 636–653.

59. Robert M. White, "The World Climate Conference: Report by the Conference Chairman," *WMO Bulletin* 28, no. 3 (1979): 177–178.

60. WMO, "World Climate Programme (WEP)," http://www.wmo.int/.

61. UNEP, "1979 Annual Review," 28.

62. WMO, "World Climate Programme (WEP)."

63. WMO, "Report of the International Conference on the Assessment of the Role of Carbon Dioxide and of Other Greenhouse Gases in Climate Variations and Associated Impacts, No. 661" (Geneva, 1986).

64. John Zillman, "A History of Climate Activities," *WMO Bulletin* 58, no. 3 (2009): 145.

65. WMO, "The Changing Atmosphere. Implications for Global Security No. 710" (Geneva, 1989).

66. UNEP, "UNEP Biennial Report 1996–1997: UNEP's 25 for Life on Earth" (Nairobi, Kenya, 1997), 45.

67. Michael Zammit Cutajar, interview by the author, 2017.

68. Interviewee 576, interview by the author, 2018.

69. UNEP, "Formative Evaluation of the UNEP Medium-Term Strategy 2014–2017: A Review of UNEP Programming Processes and Documents" (Nairobi, 2015), 14.

70. UNEP and WMO, "Integrated Assessment of Black Carbon and Tropospheric Ozone" (Nairobi, 2011); UNEP, "Emissions Gap Report" (Nairobi, 2018); UNEP-CCAC, "Time to act to reduce short-lived climate pollutants" (2014).

71. Christiana Figueres, interview by the author, 2019.

72. FridaysforFuture. Main page: https://www.fridaysforfuture.org/.

73. Ehsan Masood, "The Battle for the Soul of Biodiversity," *Nature* 50 (2018): 424.

74. Margaret Goud Collins, "International Organizations and Biodiversity," in *Encyclopedia of Biodiversity*, ed. Simon A. Levin (Amsterdam: Academic Press, 2013): 325.

75. Thomas Lovejoy, "Eden no more," *Science Advances* 5, no. 5 (2019).

76. Stephanie Fischer, "Holding on to hope: Q&A with Julia Marton-Lefèvre, former Director General of the International Union for Conservation of Nature," Stanford Woods Institute for the Environment, May 20, 2019, https://woods.stanford.edu/news/holding-hope-qa-julia-marton-lef-vre-former-director-general-international-union-conservation.

77. Fiona McConnell, *The Biodiversity Convention: A Negotiating History* (Kluwer Law International, 1996), 76.

78. Kristin G. Rosendal, "Impacts of Overlapping International Regimes: The Case of Biodiversity," *Global Governance* 7, no. 1 (2001): 102.

79. Rosendal, "Impacts of Overlapping International Regimes," 102.

80. Calestous Juma, interview by the author, 2017.

81. Falk Schmidt and Nick Nuttal, "Contributions Towards a Sustainable World in Dialogue with Klaus Töpfer" (München: Oekom Verlag, 2014), 99. See also Shawkat Alam, Sumudu Atapattu, Carmen G. Gonzalez, and Jona Razzaque, eds., *International Environmental Law and the Global South* (Cambridge: Cambridge University Press, 2015).

82. Désirée McGraw, "The CBD—Key Characteristics and Implications for Implementation," *Review of European, Comparative & International Environmental Law* 11, no. 1 (2002): 19.

83. Anne Larigauderie and Harold A. Mooney, "The Intergovernmental Science-Policy Platform on Biodiversity and Ecosystem Services: Moving a Step Closer to an IPCC-Like Mechanism for Biodiversity," *Current Opinion in Environmental Sustainability* 2 (2010): 1.

84. Timothy Swanson, *Global Action for Biodiversity: An International Framework for Implementing the Convention on Biological Diversity* (Routledge, 1997), 9.

85. Steinar Andresen, "Global Environmental Governance: UN Fragmentation and Co-Ordination," in *Yearbook of International Co-Operation on Environment and Development*, ed. Olav Schram Stokke and Oystein B. Thommessen (London: Earthscan Publications, 2001), 22–23.

86. Masood, "The battle for the soul of biodiversity," 423.

87. UNEP, "Understanding Synergies and Mainstreaming among the Biodiversity Related Conventions: A Special Contributory Volume by Key Biodiversity Convention Secretariats and Scientific Bodies" (Nairobi, Kenya, 2016).

88. For a discussion of the Biodiversity Liaison Group, see K. N. Scott, "International Environmental Governance: Managing Fragmentation through Institutional Connection," *Melbourne Journal of International Law* 12 (2011): 201–203.

89. Examples include the identification of the specific SDG indicators that are related to each of the conventions, the development of action programs that incorporate SDG-related indicators into national biodiversity strategies and action plans, and the establishment of links between Goals 14 and 15 indicators and the Aichi Targets established by the Convention on Biological Diversity.

90. Marie-Claude Smouts, *Tropical Forests, International Jungle: The Underside of Global Ecopolitics* (New York: Palgrave Macmillan, 2003), 29.

91. Deborah S. Davenport, "An Alternative Explanation for the Failure of the UNCED Forest Negotiations," *Global environmental politics* 5, no. 1 (2005): 107; B. Chaytor, *The Development of Global Forest Policy: Overview of Legal and Institutional Frameworks* (London: International Institute for Environment and Development [IIED] and the World Business Council for Sustainable Development [WCBSD], 2001), 5–7.

92. The Forest Principles is the informal name for the Non-Legally Binding Authoritative Statement of Principles for a Global Consensus on the Management, Conservation and Sustainable Development of All Types of Forests.

93. Constance L. McDermott, Aran O'Carroll, and Peter Wood, "International Forest Policy—the Instruments, Agreements and Processes That Shape It" (Department of Economic and Social Affairs United Nations Forum on Forests Secretariat, 2007).

94. Richard G. Tarasofsky, "Assessing the International Forest Regime" (Gland, Switzerland: IUCN Environmental Law Centre, 1999), 21–22.

95. Richard G. Tarasofsky, "UN Intergovernmental Forum on Forests Ends—UN Forum on Forests to Begin," *Environmental Policy and Law* 30, no. 1–2 (2000): 32–33.

96. James Gustave Speth, *The Bridge at the Edge of the World: Capitalism, the Environment, and Crossing from Crisis to Sustainability* (New Haven, CT: Yale University Press, 2009), 178. See also James Gustave Speth, *Red Sky at Morning: America and the Crisis of the Global Environment* (New Haven, CT: Yale University Press, 2004).

97. UN General Assembly, "Environment and Human Settlements. Report of the Secretary-General," A/53/463 (New York, 1998).

CHAPTER 5

1. Johnson, *UNEP: The First 40 Years*, 51–52.

2. Harambee is used to denote community, self-help, and fundraising events but has come under criticism for corruption and the misappropriation of public funds. There have been several attempts to abolish harambee and remove the word from the coat of arms as part of anti-corruption efforts, with the latest in February 2018. See Joseph Karimi, "Efforts to end corruption in harambees," *Standard Digital*, August 28, 2013, https://www.standardmedia.co.ke/article/2000092053/efforts-to-end-corruption-in-harambees; Daniel Psirmoi, "Petition Over Word 'Harambee' Splits Senators," *Standard Digital*, February 15, 2018, https://www.standardmedia.co.ke/article/2001269763/petition-over-word-harambee-splits-senators.

3. David Ndii and Anne Waiguru, "Harambee: Pooling Together or Pulling Apart?" (Transparency International Kenya, 2001). See also Anne Waiguru, "Corruption and Patronage Politics: The Case of 'Harambee' in Kenya," in *Measuring Corruption*, eds. C. Sampford, A. Shacklock, C. Connors, and F. Galtung (Transparency International, 2006), 251.

4. Hierlmeier, "UNEP: Retrospect and Prospect—Options for Reforming the Global Environmental Governance Regime," 770.

5. UN General Assembly, Second Committee, "Summary Record of the 1466th Meeting," 326.

6. UN General Assembly, Second Committee, "Summary Record of the 1466th Meeting," 191. See also Mauritania's statement affirming that "the candidacy of Kenya was a test of the solidarity of the Group of 77 and of the future of the United Nations itself, because in the past the selection of the location of United Nations units had been based exclusively on financial considerations. His delegation was aware that it would be initially more expensive to locate the environment secretariat in Nairobi but felt that the decision to be taken was essentially a political decision" (UN General Assembly, Second Committee, 302).

7. Interviewee 663, interview by the author, 2004.

8. Mwangi S. Kimenyi and Josephine Kibe, "Africa's Powerhouse," Brookings Institution, 2014, https://www.brookings.edu/opinions/africas-powerhouse/

9. Dominic Omondi, "Survey: Kenya Ranked Third Most Corrupt Country in the World," *Standard Digital*, February 26, 2016. https://www.standardmedia.co.ke/article/2000193065/survey-kenya-ranked-third-most-corrupt-country-in-the-world.

10. Ethics and Anti-Corruption Commission, "National Ethics and Corruption Survey, 2016" (Kenya: Report no. 3 of January 2017), http://www.eacc.go.ke/wp-content/uploads/2018/09/Final_EACC_National_Survey_on_Corruption-2016.pdf.

11. Charles Mohr, "Corruption and Repression Mar the Success of Kenya," *New York Times*, October 17, 1975, https://www.nytimes.com/1975/10/17/archives/corruption-and-repression-mar-the-success-of-kenya-kenyas-success.html. Margaret Wambui, President Jomo Kenyatta's daughter, was the mayor of Nairobi from 1970 to 1976 and for ten years thereafter Kenya's representative to UNEP. "Through the United Africa Corporation (UAC) in which she was the major shareholder," Kenyan author, journalist, and diplomat Joe Khamisi writes, "Margaret Wambui exported 50 tons of ivory to Peking (now Beijing) China in 1972." Joe Khamisi, *Kenya: Looters and Grabbers: 54 Years of Corruption and Plunder by the Elite, 1963–2017* (Zionsville, IN: Jodey Book Publishers, 2018), 100.

12. Kipyego Cheluget, *Kenya's Fifty Years of Diplomatic Engagement: From Kenyatta to Kenyatta* (Nairobi: Moran Publishers and Worldreader, 2018), 24.

13. Khamisi, *Kenya: Looters and Grabbers*, 56; World Bank Data Kenya, https://data.worldbank.org/country/kenya; Grey Phombeah, "Moi's Legacy to Kenya," *BBC News*, August 5, 2002, http://news.bbc.co.uk/2/hi/africa/2161868.stm; Xan Rice, "The Looting of Kenya," *Guardian*, 2007.

14. Edwin Gimode, "An Anatomy of Violent Crime and Insecurity in Kenya: The Case of Nairobi, 1985–1999," *Africa Development Journal* 26, no. 1/2 (2001): 298.

15. Gimode, "An Anatomy of Violent Crime and Insecurity in Kenya," 315.

16. World Bank, "Violence in the City: Understanding and Supporting Community Responses to Urban Violence" (Washington, DC: World Bank, 2011), 218.

17. See Wangari Maathai, *Unbowed: A Memoir* (New York: Alfred A. Knopf, 2006).

18. Wanjira Mathai, "3 Ways to Uproot a Culture of Corruption," TED talk, 2019, https://www.ted.com/talks/wanjira_mathai_3_ways_to_uproot_a_culture_of_corruption.

19. The flow of guns across Kenya's borders for as low as $65 each fueled insecurity. See Daniel Branch, *Kenya: Between Hope and Despair, 1963–2011* (New Haven, CT: Yale University Press, 2011), 254.

20. The UN classifies the various duty stations using a hardship rating system that ranks 422 cities in 156 countries where UN personnel operate. The ratings range from A through E, with E being the most dangerous. The ratings only apply to areas the United Nations has identified as potentially hazardous, and therefore no cities in the United States, Canada or Western Europe are included in the rankings. The UN uses the ratings as guidelines for salary adjustments and contract lengths. Staff are entitled to a hardship allowance of up to 25 percent of base pay.

21. "From the top to the bottom of society," Daniel Branch, a scholar of East African politics, explained, "those that thrived under Moi's final decade in power were the agents of disorder, who built their political powerbases, economic wealth and social status on their ability to manage and exploit the conditions of violence and criminality." Branch, *Kenya: Between Hope and Despair, 1963–2011*, 267.

22. Stephanie McCrummen, "Incumbent Declared Winner in Kenya's Disputed Election," *Washington Post*, December 31, 2007, https://www.washingtonpost.com/wp-dyn/content/article/2007/12/30/AR2007123002506_pf.html.

23. See Gabrielle Lynch, *Performances of Injustice: The Politics of Truth, Justice and Reconciliation in Kenya* (Cambridge: Cambridge University Press, 2018), 1; BBC News, "Kenya election violence: ICC names suspects," December 15, 2010, https://www.bbc.com/news/world-africa-11996652.

24. See Constance Smith, *Nairobi in the Making: Landscapes of Time and Urban Belonging* (Oxford: James Currey, 2019), 103.

25. The Fragile States Index assesses nation states' vulnerability to conflict or collapse and serves as early warning for the potential of states to fail. See https://fundforpeace.org/2019/04/10/fragile-states-index-2019/.

26. Vincent Achuka, "Sh1 Trillion—Shocking Numbers in the Plunder of a Nation," *Standard Digital*, December 9 2018.

27. A survey by the East African Institute in 2016 showed that 58 percent of young people in Kenya would do anything to make money, 35 percent would take or give a bribe, 45 percent believe corruption is profitable, and 73 percent are afraid to stand up for what they believe in, for fear of retribution. Quoted in Wanjira Mathai TED talk.

28. $10 billion equals 12.6 percent of Kenya's 2017 GDP, which was $79,263,000,000. In 2015, Kenya's annual expenditure on education accounted for 5.3 percent of the total GDP, and the country's health expenditure accounted for 5.22 percent of the total GDP.

29. Achuka, "Sh1 Trillion—Shocking Numbers in the Plunder of a Nation." The Ministry of Devolution and Arid and Semi-Arid Lands was established in January 2018 and is responsible for land management. The exposé continues, "In the 2015/2016 financial year, Sh40,286,583,945 [~$391 million] was stolen while Sh3.7 billion [~$36 million] collected from the public by various agencies never made it to the Treasury. Out of this amount, Sh27 billion [~$265 million] was lost in just two ministries, Agriculture (Sh16 billion—$156 million) and Devolution (Sh10.4 billion—$102 million)."

30. Khamisi wrote that "The *Africa Investor*, a South African investment magazine, estimated the Kenyatta family wealth to be US$10 billion (KES1 trillion)."

31. The percentage of permanent missions has been calculated based on data from the UN official website. For cities that are not capitals—Bonn, Geneva, and New York—the number includes embassies in the respective capital cities considering the geographic proximity and easy of travel to those locations.

32. See UN General Assembly, "Resolution 72/277 Towards a Global Pact for the Environment," A/72/L.51 & Add.1(as amended by A/72/L.53) (New York, 2018).

33. Remarks by Ambassador Amal Mudallali at a September 24, 2019 conference at Columbia University, "The Global Pact for the Environment and the Sustainable Development Agenda."

34. This is because there are no permanent interpreters in Nairobi, and they have to be flown in. In New York, interpretation costs are covered. Interviewee 173, interview by the author, 2018.

35. Harriet Constable, "Why Millenials Are Heading for a Wilder Tech City," *BBC Capital*, January 15, 2018, https://www.bbc.com/worklife/article/20180115-why.

36. The Global Competitiveness Report by the World Economic Forum assesses the factors and attributes that drive productivity, growth, and human development. Indicators are organized into twelve "pillars": Institutions, Infrastructure, ICT adoption, Macroeconomic stability, Health, Skills, Product market, Labour market, Financial system, Market size, Business dynamism, and Innovation capability. See Klaus Schwab, ed., *Global Competitiveness Report 2019*, World Economic Forum (2019) https://www.weforum.org/reports/global-competitiveness-report-2019.

37. Pevehouse and von Borzyskowski, "International Organizations in World Politics," 16; Julia Gray, "Life, death, or zombie? The vitality of international organizations," *International Studies Quarterly* 62, no. 1 (2018): 11. See also Richard T. Cupitt, Rodney L. Whitlock, and Lynn Williams Whitlock, "The (Im)Morality of international governmental organizations." *International Interactions* 21, no. 4 (1996): 401.

38. Strong recruited a leadership team that included as Deputy Executive Director Mostafa Tolba, the Egyptian Minister who had greatly impressed Strong in the preparations for Stockholm, and as Assistant Executive Director Robert Frosch, a theoretical physicist who had been Assistant Secretary for Research and Development in the US Navy. Paul Berthoud of Switzerland served as the Director of the Environment Fund, Richard Foran as Director of Administration, and Peter Thacher, who had directed the secretariat for the Stockholm Conference, became director of UNEP's European Office in Geneva.

39. Johnson, *UNEP: The First 40 Years*, 52.

40. Cited in Mostafa Tolba, *Development without Destruction: Evolving Environmental Perceptions* (Dublin: Tycooly International, 1982), 140–141.

41. Source notes for box 5.1: Interviewee 369, interview by the author, 2007. Peter Sand's statement appears on a website that colleagues and friends of Stjepan Kečkeš created to share notes and impressions of him and celebrate his excellence, leadership, accomplishment, and good humor in the field of international marine protection and conservation.

42. Interviewee 558, interview by the author, 2004.

43. Mostafa Tolba, interview by the author, 2008.

44. In 2001, the security services at the United Nations Office in Nairobi responded to 7,212 calls for assistance from UN staff or Offices, and in 2002 to 10,042 calls. Nauludole V. Mataitini, "Security Update from Chief of Security UNON" (Nairobi, 2003).

45. Smith, *Nairobi in the Making*, 141.

46. OHCHR [Office of the High Commissioner for Human Rights], "Protection Against Violence and Discrimination Based on Sexual Orientation and Gender Identity," A/HRC/RES/32/2, Geneva, 2016. Criminalization of LGBTQ sexuality is among the legacies of colonialism. See Enze Han and Joseph O'Mahoney, "British Colonialism and the Criminalization of Homosexuality," *Cambridge Review of International*

Affairs 27, no. 2 (2014): 268–288. For the effects of such criminalization, see Doug Meyer, *Violence against Queer People: Race, Class, Gender, and the Persistence of Anti-LGBT Discrimination* (New Brunswick, NJ: Rutgers University Press, 2015).

47. Danna Harman, "Dark Days for Nairobi—Kenya's Once-Lauded 'Green City in the Sun,'" *Christian Science Monitor*, February 5, 2001, https://www.csmonitor.com/2001/0205/p7s1.html.

48. Arthur Dahl, interview by the author, 2007.

49. Ibrahim Thiaw, interview by the author, 2016.

50. Interviewee 270, interview by the author, 2004.

51. See the 1972 proposal of the Permanent Mission of the Republic of Kenya to the UN with regards to location of UNEP's headquarters.

52. Interviewee 397, interview by the author, 2004.

53. UNEP, "UNEP Biennial Report 1996–1997," 10.

54. ECOSOC, "In-Depth Evaluation of the Programme on Environment—Note by the Secretary-General," 25.

55. UNEP Governing Council, "Decision 17/38 on improvement of facilities at the United Nations Office at Nairobi" (Nairobi, 1993).

56. UNEP, "UNEP Biennial Report 1996–1997," 10.

57. In 2010, UNEP itself published a report on *Sustainable Travel in the United Nations*, offering guidance to UN organizations on how to improve sustainability of travel and reduce the carbon footprint of their travel—how to "travel less and travel more efficiently." Yet, there is limited evidence that this advice has been taken to heart by UNEP or other UN agencies. UNEP, "Sustainable Travel in the United Nations" (Paris, 2010).

58. Christiana Figueres, interview by the author, 2019.

59. See Charlene Mires's account of the dramatic history of the location choice of the United Nations in New York City, *Capital of the World: The Race to Host the United Nations* (New York: New York University Press, 2013).

60. Source notes for box 5.2:

UN Headquarters in New York, https://www.un.org/en/sections/where-we-work/americas/index.html.

NYC Mayor's Office for International Affairs, "United Nations Impact Report" (New York, 2016).

UN Office Geneva, https://www.unog.ch.

UN Headquarters in Geneva, https://careers.un.org/lbw/home.aspx?viewtype=VD&DID=3408.

International Geneva, https://www.geneve-int.ch/facts-figures.

2018 UN Geneva Annual Report, https://www.unog.ch/80256EDD006B8954/(httpAssets)/07818F29E3189146C12583D2005BC330/$file/65409560.pdf.

UN Office Vienna, http://www.unis.unvienna.org/unis/es/unvienna.html.

UN Headquarters in Vienna, https://careers.un.org/lbw/home.aspx?viewtype=VD&DID=2159.

Austrian Embassy, Vienna—Official Seat of International Organisations & Institutions, https://www.austria.org/international-organisations-in-austria.

Federal Ministry Republic of Austria for Europe, Integration and Foreign Affairs, https://www.bmeia.gv.at/en/the-ministry/press/announcements/2014/foreign-minister-kurz-presents-latest-study-about-austria-as-a-centre-of-international-organisations/.

UN Office Nairobi, https://unon.org.

UN Headquarters in Nairobi, https://careers.un.org/lbw/home.aspx?viewtype=VD&DID=2738.

Peter Mwaura, "The Real Value of Having UN Presence in Kenya," *Daily Nation*, December 19, 2004, https://www.nation.co.ke/news/1056-37570-118l5gs/index.html.

61. Henry S. Weber and Mikael Karlström, *Why Community Investment is Good for Nonprofit Anchor Institutions: Understanding Costs, Benefits, and the Range of Strategic Options* (Chicago: Chapin Hall at the University of Chicago, 2009), 176. See also, Dubb, McKinley, and Howard, "The Anchor Dashboard: Aligning Institutional Practice to Meet Low-Income Community Needs"; Donald Kaniaru, interview by the author, 2004 and 2020.

62. Donald Kaniaru, interview by the author, 2020.

63. Kaniaru, interview by the author, 2020.

64. Moses Wetang'ula, "Kenya's Diplomacy Has Come of Age," in *Kenya's Fifty Years of Diplomatic Engagement: From Kenyatta to Kenyatta*, ed. Kipyego Cheluget (Nairobi: Moran Publishers and Worldreader, 2018), 17.

65. Cheluget, *Kenya's Fifty Years of Diplomatic Engagement*, 20.

66. Cheluget, 63.

67. Nasser Ega-Musa, "The United Nations Family Is in Kenya to Stay," *Daily Nation*, June 29, 2014, https://www.nation.co.ke/oped/letters/United-Nations-Nairobi-Office-Kenya/440806-2365524-7ewjuez/index.html.

CHAPTER 6

1. Christiana Figueres, interview by the author, 2020.

2. Warren G. Bennis and Burt Nanus, *Leaders: Strategies for Taking Charge* (New York: HarperCollins, 1985), 213–214.

3. Jessica E. Dinh, Robert G. Lord, William L. Gardner, Jeremy D. Meuser, Robert C. Liden, and Jinyu Hu, "Leadership Theory and Research in the New Millennium: Current Theoretical Trends and Changing Perspectives," *The Leadership Quarterly* 25, no. 1 (2013): 57–58.

4. Devesh Kapur, "Who Gets to Run the World?" *Foreign Policy* 121 (2000): 47; Nina Hall and Ngaire Woods, "Theorizing the role of executive heads in international organizations," 871.

5. Robert Cox, "The Executive Head: An Essay on Leadership in the ILO," *International Organization* 23 (1969): 205.

6. David A. Whetten, "Effective Administrators: Good Management on the College Campus," *Change: The Magazine of Higher Education* 16, no. 8 (1984): 42.

7. The core tasks of the environmental executive were to include (not necessarily listed in order of priority):

1. To consult with regional groups, as well as nations, concerning environmental measures, goals, and standards.
2. To identify and focus attention upon environmental problems and possible solutions.
3. To consult with the international science advisory service.
4. To administer the United Nations Voluntary Fund for the Environment.
5. To encourage the environmental activity of intergovernmental and nongovernmental groups.
6. To develop policy and guidelines with the advice of the United Nations Intergovernmental Body for the Environment.
7. To encourage nations to enter environmentally protective agreements with each other.
8. To provide advisory and good offices for dispute settlement.
9. To call together and/or contract with ad hoc groups of experts.
10. To promote public awareness and education.
11. To promote technical cooperation among nations.
12. To establish a global monitoring system.
13. To provide for the gathering, assessment, and sharing of data.

Source: United States Secretary of State's Advisory Committee on the 1972 UNCHE, "Stockholm and Beyond: Report," 131.

8. United States Secretary of State's Advisory Committee on the 1972 UNCHE, 133.

9. OIOS, Internal Audit Division, "Audit of Official Travel at the United Nations Environment Programme, Report 2018/109," November 16, 2018.

10. Maurice F. Strong, interview by the author, 2008.

11. Strong, interview by the author, 2008.

12. Engfeldt, *From Stockholm to Johannesburg and Beyond*, 72.

13. Interviewee 369, interview by the author, 2007.

14. Mostafa Tolba, interview by the author, 2008.

15. Maurice F. Strong, interview by the author, 2008.

16. John Ralston Saul, "Maurice Strong: Environmental Movement Loses a Founding Father," *The Globe and Mail*, November 30, 2015.

17. Ehsan Masood, "Maurice Strong (1929–2015): Oil Man Who Was First Director of the United Nations Environment Programme," *Nature* 528 (2015): 480–481.

18. Maurice F. Strong, interview by the author, 2008.

19. Strong, interview by the author, 2008.

20. The Cocoyoc Declaration, adopted by the participants in the UNEP/UNCTAD symposium on "Patterns of Resource Use, Environment, and Development Strategies," Cocoyoc, Mexico, October 8–12, 1974.

21. Branislav Gosovic, "Maurice F. Strong, Marc Nerfin, Pope Francis' Laudato Si', SDGs and COP 21," *Other News: Voices Against the Tide,* March 8 2016.

22. Thomas Palme, "Financial Difficulties and Program Review at UNEP Meeting," *Ambio* 5, no. 3 (1976): 144.

23. Palme, "Financial Difficulties and Program Review at UNEP Meeting," 144.

24. Interviewee 369, interview by the author, 2007.

25. Mark Halle, interview by the author, 2008.

26. William R. Moomaw, "Scientist Diplomats or Diplomat Scientists: Who Makes Science Diplomacy Effective?" in *Global Policy* 9, no. 3 (2017): 79.

27. Oran Young argues that regime formation happens in the interplay of these three forms of leadership, and hence studying interactions between leaders is crucial for understanding an institution's creation. See Oran R. Young, "Political leadership and regime formation: on the development of institutions in international society," *International Organization* 45, no. 3 (1991).

28. Mostafa Tolba, interview by the author, 2008.

29. Tolba, interview by the author, 2008.

30. Tolba, *Development without Destruction,* vii.

31. The World Commission on Environment and Development, "Report of the World Commission on Environment and Development: Our Common Future" (Geneva, 1987), 43.

32. Anonymous, "Living History Interview with Dr. Mostafa Kamal Tolba Executive Director United Nations Environment Programme," *Transnational Law and Contemporary Problems* 2, no. 1 (1992): 263.

33. Anonymous, "Living History Interview with Dr. Mostafa Kamal Tolba," 267.

34. Interviewee 295, interview by the author, 2004.

35. Young, "Political Leadership and Regime Formation," 301.

36. Interviewee 924, interview by the author, 2007.

37. Interviewee 532, interview by the author, 2007.

38. Fiona McConnell, quoted in Johnson, *UNEP: The First 40 Years,* 123.

39. Interviewee 934, interview by the author, 2004.

40. Mark Halle, interview by the author, 2017.

41. Interviewee 762, interview by the author, 2004.

42. Interviewee 369, interview by the author, 2007.

43. Mark Halle, interview by the author, 2017.

44. Interviewee 663, interview by the author, 2004.

45. Interviewee 509, interview by the author, 2007.

46. Mark Halle, interview by the author, 2017.

47. Mostafa Tolba, interview by the author, 2008.

48. Sandbrook, "The 'Crisis' in Political Development Theory," 179.

49. Jennifer Clapp and Peter Dauvergne, *Paths to a Green World, the Political Economy of a Global Environment* (Cambridge, MA: MIT Press, 2005), 57.

50. Barbara Ward, "A Decade of Environmental Action," *Environment* 24, no. 4 (1982): 4.

51. Tolba, *Development without Destruction*, 140.

52. David Hughes-Evans, "Dedication to Dr. Mostafa Kamal Tolba," *The Environmentalist* 2, no. 1 (1982): 7.

53. UN General Assembly, "Report on the United Nations Environment Programme's Session of a Special Character," in *Subcommittee Hearings* (New York, 1981).

54. David Struthers, "The United Nations Environment Programme after a Decade: The Nairobi Session of a Special Character, May 1981," *Denver Journal of International Law & Policy* 12, no. 2–3 (1981): 281, note 73.

55. Mohamed El-Ashry, interview by the author, 2017.

56. UN General Assembly, "Process of Preparation of the Environmental Perspective to the Year 2000 and Beyond," A/Res/38/161 (New York, 1983).

57. Mark Halle, interview by the author, 2017.

58. Engfeldt, *From Stockholm to Johannesburg and Beyond*, 153.

59. Interviewee 291, interview by the author, 2017.

60. Mark Halle, interview by the author, 2017.

61. Mostafa Tolba, interview by the author, 2008.

62. Interviewee 950, interview by the author, 2018.

63. Nina Berglund, "Solheim's travel hits UNEP funding," *News in English*, September 24, 2018, https://www.newsinenglish.no/2018/09/24/solheims-travel-hits-UNEP-funding/.

64. Mark Halle, interview by the author, 2017.

65. United Nations Population Information Network (POPIN), "Statement of UNEP, Mrs. Elizabeth Dowdeswell," 1994.

66. Elizabeth Dowdeswell, interview by the author, 2004.

67. Interviewee 369, interview by the author, 2007; Interviewee 336, interview by the author, 2008. In 1994, Dowsdeswell and Kinley published an article on "Constructive Damage to the Status Quo" in *Negotiating Climate Change: The Inside Story of the Rio Convention*, eds. Irving M. Mintzer and J. Amber Leonard (Cambridge: Cambridge University Press: 1994).

68. Fred Boyd, ed., "In Conversation with Elizabeth Dowdeswell," *Canadian Nuclear Society Bulletin* 24, no.1 (2003).

69. Fred Pearce, "Environment Body Goes to Pieces," *New Scientist*, February 15, 1997, https://www.newscientist.com/article/mg15320691-500-environment-body-goes-to-pieces/.

70. Interviewee 393, interview by the author, 2004.

71. Johnson, *UNEP: The First 40 Years*, 147.

72. Interviewee 625, interview by the author, 2005.

73. Interviewee 742, interview by the author, 2004.

74. Interviewee 369, interview by the author, 2007.

75. Elizabeth Dowdeswell quoted in Johnson, *UNEP: The First 40 Years*, 148.

76. Engfeldt, *From Stockholm to Johannesburg and Beyond*, 217.

77. Interviewee 964, interview by the author, 2017.

78. Quoted in Khamisi, *Kenya: Looters and Grabbers*, 34.

79. Idunn Eidheim, interview by the author, 2018.

80. Interviewee 370, interview by the author, 2008.

81. Mark Halle, interview by the author, 2017.

82. Engfeldt, *From Stockholm to Johannesburg and Beyond*, 217.

83. The Republican Revolution, or Gingrich Revolution, refers to the success of the Republican Party in the 1994 US congressional elections, which resulted in a Republican majority in both the House of Representatives and the Senate. The Speaker of the House of Representatives, Newt Gingrich, pursued an ambitious agenda to limit government, including environmental regulation and multilateral engagement.

84. Richard Bernstein, "Why Does the United States Refuse to Pay Its UN Bill?" *New York Times*, August 7, 1988, https://www.nytimes.com/1988/08/07/weekinreview/the-world-why-does-the-united-states-refuse-to-pay-its-un-bill.html

85. John Matuszak, interview by the author, 2018.

86. Engfeldt, *From Stockholm to Johannesburg and Beyond*, 199.

87. The Ågesta Group AB Sweden, "Twenty Years after Stockholm 1972–1992," 27.

88. ECOSOC, "In-Depth Evaluation of the Programme on Environment, E/AC.51/1995/3," 7. The figure for FAO is for 1992–1993, for ILO 1994 and for UNDP 1994–95.

89. Matthew Heimer, "The United Nations Environment Programme: Thinking Globally, Retreating Locally," *Yale Human Rights & Development Law Journal* 1 (1998): 132.

90. Heimer, "The United Nations Environment Programme," 132–133.

91. Engfeldt, *From Stockholm to Johannesburg and Beyond*, 217.

92. UNEP, "Proceedings of the Governing Council at its Nineteenth Session," UNEP. GC/19/34 (Nairobi, 1997).

93. OIOS, "Review of the United Nations Environment Programme (UNEP) and the Administrative Practices of Its Secretariat, Including the United Nations Office in Nairobi (UNON)," 2.

94. Hussein Abaza, head of UNEP's Economics and Trade Branch quoted in Johnson, *UNEP: The First 40 Years*, 165.

95. United Nations, "Review of the United Nations Environment Programme and the Administrative Practices of Its Secretariat, Including the United Nations Office in Nairobi," in *Report of the Secretary-General on the activities of the Office of Internal Oversight Services* (Nairobi, 1997), 8.

96. Engfeldt, *From Stockholm to Johannesburg and Beyond*, 217.

97. UN General Assembly, "Environment and Human Settlements. Report of the Secretary-General."

98. Interviewee 912, interview by the author, 2008.

99. Heimer, "The United Nations Environment Programme," 134.

100. Mostafa Tolba, interview by the author, 2008.

101. Interviewee 729, interview by the author, 2008.

102. Klaus Töpfer, "United Nations Task Force on Environment and Human Settlements," *Linkages Journal* 3, no. 3 (1998).

103. Interviewee 806, interview by the author, 2004.

104. Klaus Töpfer, "Environmental Degradation and Poverty as Inhibitors of Economic Growth," in *5th Annual Conference of the German Council for Sustainable Development* (Berlin, 2005), 3.

105. UNEP, "UNEP Annual Report 1999" (Nairobi, 1999), 15. UNEP comprised six functional divisions: Division of Early Warning and Assessment; Division of Policy Development and Law; Division of Environmental Policy and Implementation; Division of Technology, Industry and Economics; Division of Regional Cooperation and Representation; and Division of Environmental Conventions. See UNEP Annual Report 2000 for the first organizational chart of new structure. UNEP, "Annual Report 2000" (Nairobi, 2000), 36.

106. Dalberg Global Developmnent Advisors, "Review of UNEP's Programme Implementation Mechanisms and Administrative Structures" (New York, 2006), 9.

107. The first suggestion for a target for official aid dates back to 1958 when the World Council of Churches proposed a one-percent target, and all members of the Development Assistance Committee (DAC) of the Organization for Economic Cooperation and Development (OECD) agreed. Because governments cannot control private financial flows, however, efforts emerged to create a target only for official flows. In 1969, the Pearson Commission articulated a 0.7 percent target to be reached no later

than by 1980, and the suggestion was adopted in UN Resolution 2626 on October 24, 1970, which stated that "Each economically advanced country will progressively increase its official development assistance to the developing countries and will exert its best efforts to reach a minimum net amount of 0.7 percent of its gross national product at market prices by the middle of the Decade." In 2018, only five countries contributed in accordance with the target: Sweden, Luxembourg, Norway, Denmark, and the United Kingdom. The United States never committed to this target.

108. Some observers remark that Töpfer's motivation was less a matter of conviction and more a desire to have a more prestigious position such as director general of a specialized agency.

109. Johnson, *UNEP: The First 40 Years*, 200.

110. Interviewee 705, interview by the author, 2017.

111. Interviewee 531, interview by the author, 2017.

112. By comparison, Mostafa Tolba created a total of forty-one new trust funds; Elizabeth Dowdeswell, twenty-three; Achim Steiner, thirty; and Klaus Töpfer, fifty-nine. These accounted for 18 percent, 41 percent, 63 percent, and 61 percent of UNEP's total income, respectively.

113. Tony Brough, interview by the author, 2017.

114. Niko Urho, Maria Ivanova, Anna Dubrova, and Natalia Escobar-Pemberthy, "International Environmental Governance: Accomplishments and Way Forward" (Copenhagen, Denmark: Nordic Council of Ministers, 2019). http://norden.diva-portal.org/smash/get/diva2:1289927/FULLTEXT01.pdf.

115. Johnson, *UNEP: The First 40 Years*, 161.

116. Interviewee 277, interview by the author, 2004.

117. Klaus Töpfer, quoted in Johnson, *UNEP: The First 40 Years*, 159.

118. Interviewee 509, interview by the author, 2007.

119. Interviewee 277 interview by the author, 2004.

120. Interviewee 531, interview by the author, 2017.

121. Interviewee 705, interview by the author, 2017.

122. Interviewee 532, interview by the author, 2007.

123. UNEP, "Annual Report 2000" (Nairobi, 2001), 5.

124. UNEP "Annual Report 2001" (Nairobi, 2002), 7.

125. Interviewee 509, interview by the author, 2007.

126. Engfeldt, *From Stockholm to Johannesburg and Beyond*, 222.

127. Achim Steiner, "Statement of Achim Steiner, Director General of IUCN-the World Conservation Union," in *The High-level Plenary Meeting of the 60th Session of the United Nations General Assembly* (New York, 2005).

128. UNEP, "Time to Make Environment and Economics Team Players" (Nairobi, 2006).

129. Johnson, *UNEP: The First 40 Years*, 208.

130. Julia Pataki, interview by the author, 2017.

131. Ecosystem services refer to how the environment contributes directly to human survival and well-being. We depend on environmental "goods" (water, air, fiber) and "services" (oxygen production, pollination, climate regulation). There are four categories of ecosystem services, as defined by the *Millennium Ecosystem Assessment*:

1. Supporting services (nutrient cycling, oxygen production, soil formation, crop pollination, seed dispersal, pest regulation, waste decomposition)
2. Provisioning services (food, fuel, water, genetic resources, useful natural substances including medicinal plants, fish, game, metals, timber, etc.)
3. Regulating services (climate regulation and stabilisation, storm buffers, water and air purification, flood protection, protection of soils from erosion)
4. Cultural services (recreation, aesthetic and psychological value, knowledge)

132. UNEP, "Time to Make Environment and Economics Team Players," 7.

133. Global Environmental Governance Forum: Reflecting on the Past, Moving into the Future.

134. Ban Ki-moon, interview by the author, 2018.

135. UNEP, "Time to Make Environment and Economics Team Players," 8.

136. UNEP, "Medium-term Strategy 2010–2013" (Nairobi, 2008), 13. In practice, each sub-programme is accompanied with a set of "expected accomplishments" and "indicators of achievement" to help measure progress in terms of outputs, commonly the increase in the number of countries undertaking a specific activity measured against a baseline and a target. UNEP reports on progress in annual programme performance reports and the mid-term and final evaluations of the MTS. In addition, quarterly progress reports from UNEP's executive director inform the regular CPR meetings. Measuring progress of implementation and the display of this information could be improved, specifically by more clearly showing the impact on the ground. Decision UNEP/EA.4/1 (paragraphs 14–15). Available online: https://bit.ly/2Oql6Ki.

137. Interviewee 506, interview by the author, 2017.

138. Interviewee 222, interview by the author, 2018.

139. Interviewee 222, interview by the author, 2018.

140. Idunn Eidheim, interview by the author, 2018.

141. Mark Halle, interview by the author, 2017.

142. Interviewee 531, interview by the author, 2017.

143. UNEP, "Policy Statement by Achim Steiner at the Opening of the Governing Council/Global Ministerial Environment Forum at Its Eleventh Special Session" (Bali, Indonesia, 2010).

144. Johnson, *UNEP: The First 40 Years*, 208.

145. UNEP, "Time to Make Environment and Economics Team Players," 8.

146. Achim Steiner, interview by the author, 2008.

147. A D1 level position is a senior position at the United Nations that requires at least fifteen years of work experience. A D2 level position requires over fifteen years of work experience. The senior appointments then proceed as follows: Assistant Secretary-General (ASG), a head of office appointed by the Secretary-General; Under-Secretary-General (USG), a head of a UN body appointed by the Secretary-General; Deputy Secretary-General, appointed by the Secretary-General following consultations with Member States; Secretary-General, appointed by the General Assembly, on the recommendation of the Security Council.

148. Ban Ki-moon, interview by the author, 2018.

149. Mark Halle, interview by the author, 2017. In 2007, the General Assembly adopted the UN Declaration on the Rights of Indigenous Peoples.

150. UNEP, "Time to Make Environment and Economics Team Players," 11.

151. Catherine Karongo, "Walk through eco-friendly UNEP building," *Capital News FM*, March 7, 2012, https://www.capitalfm.co.ke/news/2012/03/walk-through-eco-friendly-unep-building/; UNEP, "Building for the Future: A United Nations Showcase in Nairobi" (Nairobi, 2011), https://wedocs.unep.org/bitstream/handle/20.500.11822/7859/Building-for-the-Future.pdf.

152. Ed King, "Erik Solheim: Meet the Man Tasked with Protecting Planet Earth," *Climate Home*, May 12, 2016, https://www.climatechangenews.com/2016/05/12/erik-solheim-meet-the-man-tasked-with-protecting-planet-earth/.

153. Interviewee 506, interview by the author, 2017.

154. Nina Berglund, "Ousted Solheim Fires Back at UN," *News in English*, November 28, 2018, https://www.newsinenglish.no/2018/11/28/ousted-solheim-fires-back-at-un/. See also Nina Berglund, "Solheim Resigns as UN Climate Chief," *News in English*, November 20, 2018, https://www.newsinenglish.no/2018/11/20/solheim-resigns-as-un-climate-chief/; Nina Berglund, "Former Minister Scolded at UN," *News in English*, September 13, 2018, https://www.newsinenglish.no/2018/09/13/former-minister-scolded-at-un/; Walter Menya, "Audit Reveals Erik Solheim Wasted Millions in Foreign Travels," *Daily Nation*, September 16, 2018, https://www.nation.co.ke/news/UNEP-boss-Solheim-blew-millions-in-foreign-travels/1056-4761598-bxnp1sz/index.html; Galgallo Fayo, "Embattled UNEP Head Refunds Travel Expenses," *Business Daily Africa*, September 19, 2018, https://www.businessdailyafrica.com/news/Embattled-UNEP-head-refunds-travel-expenses/539546-4766720-s7pshz/index.html; Matt McGrath, "Report Slams 'High Flying' UN Environment Chief," *BBC News*, September 21, 2018, https://www.bbc.com/news/science-environment-45604408.

155. Erik Solheim, interview by the author, 2020.

156. Maria Ivanova, ed., "Champion for Change: Erik Solheim," *Global Leadership Dialogues* 4, no. 1 (Boston: Center for Governance and Sustainability, 2017).

157. Mohamed El-Ashry, interview by the author, 2017.

158. AMCEN, "Draft Decision: Africa's Engagement in the Third Session of the United Nations Environment Assembly of the United Nations Environment Programme,

AMCEN/16/L.5," June 9, 2017. The resolution "urgently request[ed] the Executive Director of the United Nations Environment Programme to refrain from using any nomenclature, titles or designations other than those contained in the General Assembly resolutions establishing the United Nations Environment Programme and the United Nations Environment Assembly, and to reverse any such changes made without due process and reflected on the official communications, stationary, web pages, social media pages or any other related aspects of the United Nations Environment Programme."

159. Mark Halle, interview by the author, 2017.

160. As of June 2019, there are seven divisions at UNEP: Communication Division, Economy Division, Ecosystems Division, Law Division, Science Division, Policy and Programme Division, and Corporate Services Division.

161. Email by Erik Solheim to staff, in the author's possession.

162. Erik Solheim, "Town Hall Meeting" (Nairobi, 2018).

163. In our interview in 2017, published as a Global Leadership Dialogue, Erik Solheim remarked, "The one main change I have done is to make a differently-structured executive office, where I have four special assistants focusing on four different parts of the world. One from Rwanda, one from Norway, one from Japan and one from China with the aim of making it much easier to link up to the ambassadors, to the governments, and to our regional offices and to everyone. For instance, the person working with China, East Asia, she's from China, making communication to everyone there very easy, so I get their input, and they get to hear my views. Of course, then working in a similar way with all the divisions. There is some fear of this, because people are afraid that it will be a filter, but it is exactly the opposite—make it a way for the top leadership to be closer to everyone." Ivanova, "Champion for Change," 5.

164. UNEP, "Internal Communication Survey Report," 19.

165. Nina Berglund, "Ousted Solheim Fires Back at UN."

166. Oli Brown, "Erik Solheim: what he got right, what he got wrong, and what the new UN Environment chief should do next," February 13, 2018, https://olibrown.org/erik-solheim-what-he-got-right-what-he-got-wrong-and-what-the-new-un-environment-chief-should-do-next/.

167. Kristoffer Rønneberg, "Erik Solheim accused of squandering by UN auditors," *Aftenposten*, September 12, 2018, https://www.aftenposten.no/verden/i/L0EjEP/Erik-Solheim-accused-of-squandering-by-UN-auditors.

168. Lisa Abend, "Leaders and Visionaries, Erik Solheim," *Time Magazine*, September 22, 2009.

169. Brown, "Erik Solheim."

170. OIOS, "Evaluation of the United Nations Environment Programme, E/AC.51/2019/7," 22.

171. Franz Perrez, interview by the author, 2018.

172. Robin Hicks and Jessica Cheam, "We Need to Engage Business 'Like Never before', Says New UNEP Head," *Eco-Business*, January 6, 2017, https://www.eco-business.com/news/we-need-to-engage-business-like-never-before-says-new-unep-head/.

173. UNEP, "First Global Multi-Agency Operation Highlights Widespread Marine Pollution Crime" (Nairobi, 2018), 14.

174. Isis Alvarez, "The 3rd United Nations Environment Assembly: A Growing Marketplace for the Private Sector" (Global Forest Coalition, 2017), 2–3.

175. Interviewee 531, interview by the author, 2017.

176. Annabell Waititu, interview by the author, 2017.

177. In his official remarks at the meeting of the Open-ended Committee of Permanent Representatives in November 2017, Erik Solheim stated that many groups fell within the broad civil society category, including terrorist groups such as ISIS. This engendered anger, protests, and requests for an apology.

178. Interviewee 709, interview by the author, 2018.

179. See Lifang, "China Sets Example in Sustainable Development: UN Environment," *Xinhua*, December 10, 2018, http://www.xinhuanet.com//english/2017-12/10/c_136815369.htm; Somini Sengupta, "Why Build Kenya's First Coal Plant? Hint: Think China," *New York Times*, February 27, 2018, https://www.nytimes.com/2018/02/27/climate/coal-kenya-china-power.html.

180. The *Guardian* reported: "Denmark's Ministry of Foreign Affairs (MFA) said it was withholding its 2018 contribution of about $1.6m to UNEP. 'The ministry is familiar with the criticism of Solheim's travel activities,' an MFA spokeswoman told the *Guardian*. 'We take this seriously. We are now awaiting the final audit report and its possible recommendations before we pay additional funds.' Sweden's International Development Agency (SIDA) said they would not approve any new funding until all the issues raised had been resolved. 'SIDA takes all signals of misuse of funds very seriously,' a spokeswoman said." Damian Carrington, "Nations halt funding to UN Environment Programme as outcry over chief grows," *Guardian*, September 25, 2018, https://www.theguardian.com/environment/2018/sep/25/nations-halt-funding-to-un-environment-programme-as-outcry-over-chief-erik-solheim-grows.

181. OIOS, Internal Audit Division, "Audit of Official Travel at the United Nations Environment Programme, Report 2018/109."

182. Nina Berglund, "Ousted Solheim Fires Back at UN."

183. Aicha Afifi, *Review of Air Travel in the United Nations System: Achieving Efficiency Gains and Cost Savings and Enhancing Harmonization, JIU/Rep/2017/3* (Geneva: Joint Inspection Unit, 2017). The report states, "On the basis of data provided by 24 United Nations system organizations, the review found that the overall expenditure on air travel and travel-related expenses—namely airline tickets, daily subsistence allowance (DSA), lump sums, terminal expenses and shipment—totaled approximately $4 billion for the four-year period from 2012 to 2015. This total comprises regular budget and extrabudgetary funding sources and represents air travel and

related expenditures for staff and non-staff, but it excludes air travel and related expenditures incurred by United Nations peacekeeping operations. Air travel and related expenditures, in their totality and as a proportion of each organization's overall expenses, constitute a significant financial element for almost all United Nations system organizations. The total value of air travel and related expenditures would have been higher had all United Nations system organizations provided JIU with the requested information."

184. OIOS, Internal Audit Division, "Audit of Official Travel at the United Nations Environment Programme, Report 2018/109."

185. Erik Solheim, interview by the author, 2018.

186. Brown, "Erik Solheim."

187. Mary Uhl-Bien and Russ Marion, "Complexity Leadership in Bureaucratic Forms of Organizing: A Meso Model," *The Leadership Quarterly* 20, no. 4 (2009): 633.

188. Uhl-Bien and Marion, "Complexity Leadership in Bureaucratif Forms of Organizing," 635.

189. See J. Steven Ott, Sandra J. Parkes, and Richard B. Simpson, eds., *Classic Readings in Organizational Behavior*, 3rd ed. (Belmont, CA: Wadsworth Publishing Company, 2003); Peter M. Senge, *The Fifth Discipline: The Art and Practice of the Learning Organization* (New York: Doubleday, 2010); Philip Selznick, *Leadership in Administration: A Sociological Interpretation* (New Orleans: Quid Pro Books, 1957).

190. James Wilson, *Bureaucracy: What Government Agencies Do and Why They Do It* (Basic Books, 1989), 91–94.

191. Tribute to Mostafa Tolba in Benedick, *Ozone Diplomacy*. Cited in Andersen and Sarma, *Protecting the Ozone Layer*, 139.

CHAPTER 7

1. Barbara Ward, Progress for a Small Planet (Norton, 1979), 265.

2. UN General Assembly, "Report of the Preparatory Committee for the United Nations Conference on the Human Environment on the 3rd Session," A/CONF.48/PC.13 (New York, 1971).

3. Ward, "Only one Earth, Speech at the 1972 Stockholm Conference."

4. Strong, *Where on Earth Are We Going?*, 128; Johan Rockström, et al, "Planetary boundaries: exploring the safe operating space for humanity," *Ecology and society* 14, no. 2 (2009). See also Simon Nicholson and Sikina Jinnah, eds., *New Earth Politics: Essays from the Anthropocene* (Cambridge, MA: MIT Press, 2016).

5. Interviewee 291, interview by the author, 2017; Interviewee 950, interview by the author, 2018; Interviewee 260, interview by the author, 2018.

6. Interviewee 291, interview by the author, 2017.

7. António Guterres, "Vision Statement," April 4, 2016, https://www.un.org/pga/70/wp-content/uploads/sites/10/2016/01/4-April_Secretary-General-Election-Vision-Statement_Portugal-4-April-20161.pdf.

8. UN, "Transcript of Press Conference by Secretary-General Kofi Annan at United Nations Headquarters, SG/SM/10089," quoted in Luisa Blanchfield, "CRS Report for Congress. United Nations Reform: US Policy and International Perspectives" (2007). See also UN Secretary-General, "Strengthening of the United Nations: An Agenda for Further Change," A/57/387 (New York, 2002); "Renewing the United Nations: A Programme for Reform," A/51/950 (New York, 1997); "In Larger Freedom: Towards Development, Security and Human Rights for All," A/59/2005 (New York, 2005).

9. Geoffrey Palmer, "New Ways to Make International Environmental Law," *American Journal of International Law* 96, no. 2 (1992): 259.

10. In 1995, the General Agreement on Tariffs and Trade (GATT)—the international framework, forum, and code of conduct for eight rounds of negotiations over tariff reductions and trade rules dating back to 1947—was succeeded by the World Trade Organization. The primary purpose of the WTO is to ensure that global trade advances smoothly, freely, and predictably. To this end, the organization engages in rulemaking among member nations and offers a system for global trade. WTO rules become a part of a country's domestic legal system and, therefore, apply to local companies and nationals in the conduct of business in the international arena. Theoretically, if a country is a member of the WTO, its local laws cannot contradict WTO rules and regulations. The WTO, therefore, functions as a global authority on trade and has considerably constrained national sovereignty through its right to review countries' domestic trade policies.

11. Kofi Annan, interview by the author, 2017.

12. See UN General Assembly, "Renewing the United Nations: A Programme for Reform."

13. Helmut Kohl, chancellor of the Federal Republic of Germany, "Speech at the Special Session of the General Assembly of the United Nations" (1997), quoted in Frank Biermann, "The Case for a World Environment Organization," *Environment: Science and Policy for Sustainable Development* 42, no. 9 (2000): 24.

14. Similar calls came subsequently from the French Environment Minister Dominique Voynet (2000) and Prime Minister Lionel Jospin (2002); Mikhail Gorbachev of Russia (2001); Ernesto Zedillo of Mexico (2001); the former head of the UN Development Programme and Dean of Yale's Environment School, James Gustave Speth (2005); and WTO directors Renato Ruggiero (1998) and his successor, Supachai Panitchpakdi (2001).

15. The European Union had overtaken the United States as the largest contributor to UNEP's Environment Fund in 1995 and began increasing its financial support significantly and would become UNEP's largest contributor.

16. EU, "Contribution of the European Union and Its Member States to the UN Department of Economic and Social Affairs, Input for the 2012 UNCSD Rio+20 Compilation Document" (2011), quoted in Ivanova, "Institutional Design and UNEP Reform: Historical Insights on Form, Function and Financing."

17. The Task Force comprised the following members:

- Dr. Klaus Töpfer (Chair), Executive Director, UNEP
- Ms. Maria Julia Alsogaray, Minister of Natural Resources and Sustainable Development, Argentina
- Dr. Christina Amoako-Nuama, Minister of Education, Ghana
- Ambassador John Ashe, Ambassador/Deputy Permanent Representative, Permanent Mission of Antigua and Barbuda
- Ms. Julia Carabias Lillo, Minister of Natural Resources and Fisheries, Mexico
- Mr. Nitin Desai, Under-Secretary-General, United Nations Department for Economic and Social Affairs
- Ambassador Lars-Göran Engfeldt, Permanent Representative of Sweden to UNEP and UN-Habitat
- Ms. Guro Fjellanger, Minister of Environment, Norway
- Mr. Jean-Pierre Halbwachs, Assistant Secretary-General, UN Office of Programme Planning, Budget and Accounts
- Sir Martin Holdgate, United Kingdom
- Mr. Ashok Khosla, Development Alternatives, India
- Mr. Martin Khor, Director, Third World Network, Malaysia
- Ambassador Tommy Koh, Ambassador-At-Large, Ministry of Foreign Affairs, Singapore
- Ms. Julia Marton-Lefèvre, LEAD International, New York
- Mr. James Gustave Speth, Administrator, UNDP
- Mr. Maurice Strong (ex-officio), Special Advisor to the Secretary-General
- Dr. Mostafa K. Tolba, President, International Centre for Environment and Development, Cairo, Egypt
- Ambassador Joseph Tomusange, High Commissioner of the Republic of Uganda to India
- Ambassador Makarim Wibisono, Permanent Representative of Indonesia to the United Nations
- Mr. Timothy E. Wirth, President, United Nations Foundation
- Mr. Michael Zammit Cutajar, Executive Secretary, UNFCCC Secretariat

Advisors to the Task Force

- Mr. Peter Thacher
- Hon. Eileen Claussen

18. UN General Assembly, "Report of the Secretary-General on Environment and Human Settlements." Major groups are nine sectors of society recognized at UN for participation in decision-making. These major groups are Women, Children and Youth, Indigenous Peoples, Non-Governmental Organizations, Local Authorities, Workers and Trade Unions, Business and Industry, Scientific and Technological Community, and Farmers.

19. In 2001, in the lead-up to the Johannesburg Summit, Klaus Töpfer came to Yale to meet with my advisor, Professor Daniel Esty, and our team at the Yale Center for Environmental Law and Policy. We had written about the need for a Global Environmental Organization and convened the Global Environmental Governance Dialogues to seek input from a variety of actors across sectors and geographies. Klaus

Töpfer engaged fully and would continue to do so throughout his time as executive director. In 2005, he hosted the team of twenty-eight students and faculty that I led to the UNEP Governing Council in Nairobi to present the results of our independent evaluation to the world's environmental ministers.

20. For discussions of the need for a WEO/GEO and the conditions under which it could be established, see analyses by Frank Biermann, "The Emerging Debate on the Need for a World environment Organization: A Commentary," *Global Environmental Politics* 1, no. 1 (2001): 45–55; Frank Biermann, "Green Global Governance: The Case for a World Environment Organisation," *New Economy* 9, no. 2 (2002): 82–86; Charnovitz, "A World Environment Organization"; Daniel C. Esty and Maria H. Ivanova, "Making International Environmental Efforts Work: the Case for a Global Environmental Organization" (New Haven, CT: Yale Center for Environmental Law and Policy, 2001); Daniel Esty and Maria H. Ivanova, "Toward a Global Environmental Mechanism," in *Worlds Apart: Globalization and the Environment*, ed. J. G. Speth (Washington, DC: Island Press, 2003); Ford C. Runge, "A Global Environmental Organization (GEO) and the World Trading System," *Journal of World Trade* 35, no. 4 (2001): 399–426; Richard G. Tarasofsky, *International Environmental Governance: Strengthening UNEP* (Tokyo: United Nations University, Institute of Advanced Studies, 2002); Joy Hyvarren and Duncan Brack, *Global Environmental Institutions: Analysis and Options for Change* (London: Royal Institute for International Affairs, 2000); Peter Haas, "UN Conferences and Constructivist Governance of the Environment," *Global Governance* 8, no. 1 (2002): 73–91; and Lee Kimball, "The Debate Over a World/Global Environment Organisation," in *Global Environmental institutions*, ed., D. Brack and J. Hyvarinen (London: Royal Institute of International Affairs, 2002). For the case against a Global or World Environment Organization, see Calestous Juma, "The Perils of Centralizing Environmental Governance," *Environment Matters* 6, no. 12 (2000): 13–15; von Moltke, "The Organization of the Impossible"; Sebastian Oberthür, *Clustering of Multilateral Environmental Agreements: Potentials and Limitations* (Tokyo: United Nations University, Institute of Advanced Studies, 2002); and Najam, "The Case Against a New International Environmental Organization," Global Governance 9, No. 3 (July-September 2003), 367–384.

21. Esty and Ivanova, "Making International Environmental Efforts Work," 3.

22. I have continued researching UNEP's creation and performance over the years and have argued that UNEP's institutional design was chosen carefully and that change in its institutional form would not result in improved performance. See Ivanova, "Designing the United Nations Environment Programme: A Story of Compromise and Confrontation, " *International Environmental Agreements: Policy, Law and Economics* 7 (2007); and Ivanova, "Institutional Design and UNEP Reform: Historical Insights on Form, Function and Financing," *International Affairs* 88, no. 3 (2012).

23. UN General Assembly, "2005 World Summit Outcome", A/RES/60/1 (New York, September 2005), para. 169 on "Environmental activities." The main needs highlighted in paragraph 169 of the outcome document include: enhanced coordination; improved policy advice/guidance; strengthened scientific knowledge, assessment,

and cooperation; better treaty compliance; and better integration of environmental activities in the sustainable-development framework at the operational level.

24. See UN General Assembly, "2005 World Summit Outcome"; IEG Co-Chairs Option Paper, "Informal Consultative Process on the Institutional Framework for United Nations' Environmental Activities" (Nairobi, 2008); UNEP "Belgrade Process: Moving Forward with Developing a Set of Options on International Environmental Governance Co-Chairs' Summary. Consultative Group of Ministers or High-level Representatives" (Nairobi, 2009); UNEP, "Nairobi-Helsinki Outcome," Consultative Group of Ministers or High-level Representatives (Nairobi, 2010).

25. The official name of the process was the Informal Consultative Process on the Institutional Framework for the United Nations' Environmental Activities. See Enrique Berruga and Peter Maurer, "Co-Chairmen's Summary of the Informal Consultative Process on the Institutional Framework for the UN's Environmental Activities" (New York, 2006).

26. Keynote address by Marthinus van Schalkwyk, South African Minister of Environmental Affairs and Tourism, at the plenary ministerial consultations on "International Environmental Governance: Help or Hindrance?" United Nations Environment Programme (UNEP) Global Ministerial Environment Forum, February 19, 2009, Nairobi, http://www.info.gov.za/speeches/2009/09022015151004.htm.

27. UNEP, "Nairobi-Helsinki Outcome."

28. Maria Ivanova, "Achim Steiner: Environmental Envoy," *Global Leadership Dialogues* 3, no. 3 (Boston: Center for Governance and Sustainability, 2016).

29. Franz Perrez, interview by the author, 2018.

30. Ibrahim Thiaw, interview by the author, 2016.

31. I. Fazey, N. Schäpke, G. Caniglia, J. Patterson, J. Hultman, B. Van Mierlo, F. Säwe, et al, "Ten Essentials for Action-Oriented and Second Order Energy Transitions, Transformations and Climate Change Research," *Energy Research & Social Science* 40 (2018): 61.

32. Yunae Yi, interview by the author, 2017.

33. In September 2013, following the recommendation of the UN Global Sustainability Panel, UN Secretary-General Ban Ki-moon established the Scientific Advisory Board of the United Nations Secretary-General. It brought together twenty-six leading scientists from around the world in an effort to inform decision-making processes with scientific evidence and knowledge and to promote international and transdisciplinary scientific collaboration. The author served on the Board.

34. For a discussion on environmental goals, see Franz Perrez and Daniel Ziegerer, "A Non-Institutional Proposal to Strengthen International Environmental Governance," *Environmental Policy and Law* 38 (2008): 253–261.

35. Christine Lagarde speaking at the inaugural Paris Peace Forum in 2018, notes in author's possession.

36. Matthias Garschagen, Sylvia Wood, Jennifer Garard, Maria Ivanova, and Amy Luers, "Too Big to Ignore: Global Risk Perception Gaps Between Scientists and Business Leaders," *Earth's Future* 8, https://doi.org/10.1029/2020EF001498.

37. Peter M. Haas, Robert O. Keohane, and Mark A. Levy, *Institutions for the Earth: Sources of Effective International Environmental Protection* (Cambridge, MA: MIT Press, 1993): 17–19; Abram Chayes and Antonia H. Chayes, "On Compliance," *International Organization* 47, no. 2 (1993): 175–176; Harold K. Jacobson and Edith B. Weiss, "Strengthening Compliance with International Environmental Accords: Preliminary Observations from Collaborative Project," *Global Governance* 1, no. 2 (1995): 124.

38. Global Environmental Governance Forum: Reflecting on the Past, Moving into the Future.

39. The Environmental Conventions Index measures the implementation of global environmental conventions and enables self-assessment and comparison with peers. The Index evaluates the implementation of environmental conventions by assessing the actions signatory countries have taken to fulfill their commitments. To date, it includes six conventions in two thematic clusters—biodiversity, and chemicals and waste—and, though still limited in scope, it gives enough information to enable countries to assess where they stand. The Index was developed at the Center for Governance and Sustainability at the University of Massachusetts Boston, supported by the Federal Office for the Environment of Switzerland, the Carnegie Corporation through the Andrew Carnegie Fellows Program, the United Nations Environment Programme, and the McCormack Graduate School of Policy and Global Studies at UMass Boston.

40. See Maria Ivanova, Natalia Escobar-Pemberthy, and Anna Dubrova, *National Implementation of Global Environmental Agreements in Rwanda* (Boston: UMass Boston, 2019).

41. John Scanlon, interview by the author, 2018.

42. Julia Marton-Lefèvre, interview by the author, 2019. See also Julia Marton-Lefèvre in "The Quest for Symphony," dir. Maria Ivanova and Joe Ageyo.

43. The United Nations has implemented issue-based coalitions, broad, multi-partner coalitions led by one or several agencies that coordinate the response to cross-cutting challenges in a particular UN region and develop joint action.

44. John Scanlon, Secretary General of CITES, "Presentation at the 12th special session of GMEF, Plenary Panel on the Institutional Framework for Sustainable Development." February 12, 2012, https://www.cites.org/eng/news/sg/2012/20120221_UNEP-GMEF.php.

45. John Matuszak, interview by the author, 2018.

46. Interviewee 727, interview by the author, 2018.

47. The author, Maria Ivanova, served as a Coordinating Lead Author for the policy chapter in GEO-5 published in 2012 just before the Rio+20 summit. The difficulties in ensuring financing delayed the production process and added uncertainty and unpredictability.

48. UNEP Evaluation and Oversight Unit, "Management Study on Trust Funds and Counterpart Contributions," 32.

49. For the financial figures, see GEF's funding page, https://www.thegef.org/about/funding; United Nations Climate Change, "Achievements of the Clean Development Mechanism: Harnessing Incentive for Climate Action, 2001–2018," 2019, https://unfccc.int/sites/default/files/resource/UNFCCC_CDM_report_2018.pdf; Green Climate Fund, "Initial strategic plan for the GCF," 2016, https://www.greenclimate.fund/documents/20182/761223/Initial_Strategic_Plan_for_the_GCF.pdf/bb18820e-abf0-426f-9d8b-27f5bc6fafeb; UN REDD+, UN REDD Programme Fund, http://mptf.undp.org/factsheet/fund/CCF00; and The World Bank, Environment, https://www.worldbank.org/en/topic/environment/overview#2.

50. "Finance Initiative," http://www.unepfi.org/.

51. John Scanlon, interview by the author, 2018.

52. Interviewee 727, interview by the author, 2018.

53. Youba Sokona, interview by the author, 2018.

54. Manuel Pulgar-Vidal, interview by the author, 2018.

55. "Strategic direction must be clarified at the institutional and programme level plainly articulating the targets UNEP seeks to achieve and the means through which it plans to achieve them," the Dalberg Global Developmnent Advisors study noted. Dalberg Global Developmnent Advisors, "Review of UNEP's Programme Implementation Mechanisms and Administrative Structures," 8.

56. Inger Andersen, executive director of UNEP, "Speech at the 146th Committee of Permanent Representatives" (Nairobi, Kenya, 2019), https://www.unenvironment.org/news-and-stories/speech/146th-committee-permanent-representatives.

57. CCISUA, "UN Global Staff Satisfaction Survey" (in the author's possession, 2017), 38.

58. UNEP Evaluation and Oversight Unit, "1985–1986 Evaluation Report" (Nairobi, 1986); CCISUA, "UN Global Staff Satisfaction Survey," 38; UNEP, "Internal Communication Survey Report," 11; OIOS, "Programme Evaluation of the United Nations Environment Programme," E/AC.51/2013/2, 2013, 3.

59. In figure 7.2, the numbers in the circle represent the number of headquarters at each location.

60. Karen Litfin calls this the "realm of immediacy where meaningful action is possible and most likely to be effective." Karen T. Litfin, "The Gendered Eye in the Sky: A Feminist Perspective on Earth Observation Satellites," *Frontiers: A Journal of Women Studies* 18, no. 2 (1997): 38.

61. Interviewee 165, interview by the author, 2019.

BIBLIOGRAPHY

Abbott, Kenneth W., and Duncan Snidal. "Why States Act through Formal International Organizations." *Journal of Conflict Resolution* 42, no. 1 (1998): 3–32.

Abend, Lisa. "Leaders and Visionaries: Erik Solheim," *Time Magazine*, September 22, 2009. http://content.time.com/time/specials/packages/article/0,28804,1924149_1924152_1924196,00.html.

Achuka, Vincent. "Sh1 Trillion—Shocking Numbers in the Plunder of a Nation," *Standard Digital*, December 9, 2018. https://www.standardmedia.co.ke/business/article/2001305596/the-shame-of-sh1-trillion-queried-yearly-by-auditor.

Afifi, Aicha. *Review of Air Travel in the United Nations System: Achieving Efficiency Gains and Cost Savings and Enhancing Harmonization (JIU/Rep/2017/3)*. Geneva: Joint Inspection Unit, 2017.

The Ågesta Group AB Sweden. *Twenty Years after Stockholm 1972–1992: A Report on the Implementation of the Stockholm Action Plan for the Environment and on Priorities and Institutional Arrangements for the 1980s*. Berlin: Erich Schmidt Verlag, 1992.

Aggarwal, Vinod K. *Institutional Designs for a Complex World: Bargaining, Linkages, and Nesting*. Ithaca, NY: Cornell University Press, 1998.

Akiwumi, Paul, and Terttu Melvasalo. "UNEP's Regional Seas Programme: Approach, Experience and Future Plans." *Marine Policy* 22, no. 3 (1998): 229–234. https://doi.org/10.1016/S0308-597X(98)00009-8.

Algeria, Botswana, Burundi, Cameroon, Central African Republic, Congo, Dahomey, et al. "Draft Resolution Concerning Location of an Environment Secretariat, A/C.2/L.1246 & Rev. 1." 1972.

Allphin Moore Jr., John, and Jerry Pubantz. *The New United Nations: International Organization in the Twenty-First Century*. New York: Routledge, 2017.

Alvarez, Isis. "The 3rd United Nations Environment Assembly: A Growing Marketplace for the Private Sector." Global Forest Coalition, 2017. https://globalforestcoalition.org/es/3rd-united-nations-environment-assembly-growing-marketplace-private-sector (no longer available).

AMCEN. "Draft Decision: Africa's Engagement in the Third Session of the United Nations Environment Assembly of the United Nations Environment Programme, AMCEN/16/L.5." June 9, 2017.

Andersen, Inger. Interview by the author, 2019.

Andersen, Stephen O., and K. Madhava Sarma. *Protecting the Ozone Layer: The United Nations History*. London: Earthscan, 2012.

Andresen, Steinar. "Global Environmental Governance: UN Fragmentation and Co-Ordination." In *Yearbook of International Co-Operation on Environment and Development*, edited by Olav Schram Stokke and Oystein B. Thommessen, 19–26. London: Earthscan, 2001.

Andresen, Steinar. "The Effectiveness of UN Environmental Institutions." *International Environmental Agreements: Politics, Law and Economics* 7, no. 4 (2007): 317–336.

Annan, Kofi. Interview by the author, 2017.

Anonymous. "Living History Interview with Dr. Mostafa Kamal Tolba, Executive Director United Nations Environment Programme." *Transnational Law and Contemporary Problems* 2, no. 1 (1992): 259–271.

Argentina, Brazil, Canada, Iran, Kenya, Jamaica, Malta, et al. "Draft Resolution on Institutional and Financial Arrangements for International Co-Operation, A/C.2/L.1228 & Corr.1 (Russian Only)." 1972.

Arsel, Murat. "Fuelling Misconceptions: UNEP, Natural Resources, the Environment and Conflict." *Development and Change* 42, no. 1 (2011): 448–457.

Åström, Sverker. *Ögonblick: Från Ett Halvsekel I UD-Tjänst [Moment: From Half a Century of Foreign Affairs Duty]*. Stockholm: Lind & Co., 2003.

Bacon, T.C. "Role of the United Nations Environment Program in the Development of International Environmental Law." *Canadian Yearbook of International Law* 12 (1975): 255–266. https://doi.org/10.1017/S0069005800012583.

Ban Ki-moon. Interview by the author, March 2018.

Barnett, Michael N., and Martha Finnemore. "The Politics, Power, and Pathologies of International Organizations." *International Organization* 53, no. 4 (1999): 699–732.

Barnett, Michael N., and Martha Finnemore. *Rules for the World: International Organizations in Global Politics*. Ithaca, NY: Cornell University Press, 2004.

Bauer, Michael W., and Jörn Ege. "Bureaucratic Autonomy of International Organizations' Secretariats." *Journal of European Public Policy* 23, no. 7 (2016): 1019–1037. https://doi.org/10.1080/13501763.2016.1162833.

Bauer, Steffen, Frank Biermann, Klaus Dingwerth, and Bernd Siebenhüner. "Understanding International Bureaucracies: Taking Stock." In *Managers of Global Change: The Influence of International Environmental Bureaucracies*, edited by Frank Biermann and Bernd Siebenhüner, 15–36. Cambridge, MA: MIT Press, 2009.

Bauer, Steffen, and Silke Weinlich. "International Bureaucracies: Organizing World Politics." In *The Ashgate Research Companion to Non-State Actors*, edited by Bob Reinalda, 251–262. Abingdon, UK: Routledge, 2011.

BBC News. "Moi's Legacy to Kenya," August 5, 2002. http://news.bbc.co.uk/2/hi/africa/2161868.stm.

BBC News. "Kenya Election Violence: ICC Names Suspects," December 15, 2010. https://www.bbc.com/news/world-africa-11996652.

Benedick, Richard E. *Ozone Diplomacy: New Directions in Safeguarding the Planet.* Cambridge, MA: Harvard University Press, 1991.

Benedick, Richard E. "US Environmental Policy: Relevance to Europe." *International Environmental Affairs* 1, no. 2 (1989): 91–102.

Bennis, Warren G., and Burt Nanus. *Leaders: Strategies for Taking Charge.* New York: HarperCollins, 1985.

Benz, Arthur, Andreas Corcaci, and Jan Wolfgang Doser. "Unravelling Multilevel Administration. Patterns and Dynamics of Administrative Co-Ordination in European Governance." *Journal of European Public Policy* 23, no. 7 (2016): 999–1018. https://doi.org/10.1080/13501763.2016.1162838.

Berglund, Nina. "Former Minister Scolded at UN." *News in English*, September 13, 2018. https://www.newsinenglish.no/2018/09/13/former-minister-scolded-at-un/.

Berglund, Nina. "Ousted Solheim Fires Back at UN." *News in English*, November 28, 2018. https://www.newsinenglish.no/2018/11/28/ousted-solheim-fires-back-at-un/.

Berglund, Nina. "Solheim Resigns as UN Climate Chief." *News in English*, November 20, 2018. https://www.newsinenglish.no/2018/11/20/solheim-resigns-as-un-climate-chief/.

Berglund, Nina. "Solheim's Travel Hits UNEP Funding." *News in English*, September 24, 2018. https://www.newsinenglish.no/2018/09/24/solheims-travel-hits-UNEP-funding/.

Bernstein, Richard. "Why Does the United States Refuse to Pay Its UN Bill?" *New York Times*, August 7, 1988. https://www.nytimes.com/1988/08/07/weekinreview/the-world-why-does-the-united-states-refuse-to-pay-its-un-bill.html.

Bernstein, Richard. "Green Global Governance: The Case for a World Environment Organization." *New Economy* 9, no. 2 (2002): 82–86.

Bernstein, Richard. "The Emerging Debate on the Need for a World Environment Organization: A Commentary." *Global Environmental Politics* 1, no. 1 (2001): 45–55.

Bernstein, Richard. "The Case for a World Environment Organization" *Environment: Science and Policy for Sustainable Development* 42, no. 9 (2000): 22–31.

Berruga, Enrique, and Peter Maurer. "Co-Chairs' Summary of the Informal Consultative Process on the Institutional Framework for the UN's Environmental Activities." New York: 2006.

Biermann, Frank. "Reforming Global Environmental Governance: The Case for a United Nations Environment Organization (UNEO)." Policy brief published by *Stakeholder Forum*. London, 2011.

Biermann, Frank, and Steffen Bauer. "Managers of Global Governance Assessing and Explaining the Effectiveness of Intergovernmental Organizations." Paper presented at the 44th Annual Convention of the International Studies Association, Portland, Oregon, 2003.

Biermann, Frank, and Steffen Bauer. "Assessing the Effectiveness of Intergovernmental Organisations in International Environmental Politics." *Global Environmental Change* 14, no. 2 (2004): 189–193.

Biermann, Frank, and Steffen Bauer. *A World Environment Organization: Solution or Threat for Effective International Environmental Governance?* Aldershot: Ashgate, 2005.

Biermann, Frank, Michele M. Betsill, Joyeeta Gupta, Norichika Kanie, Louis Lebel, Diana Liverman, Heike Schroeder, Bernd Siebenhüner, and Ruben Zondervan. "Earth System Governance: A Research Framework." *International Environmental Agreements: Politics, Law and Economics* 10, no. 4 (2010): 277–298.

Birch, Eugénie L., David C. Perry, and Henry Louis Taylor Jr. "Universities as Anchor Institutions." *Journal of Higher Education Outreach and Engagement* 17, no. 3 (2013): 9.

Blanchfield, Luisa. "Congressional Research Service CRS Report for Congress. United Nations Reform: US Policy and International Perspectives." 2007.

Boyd, Fred, ed. "In Conversation with Elizabeth Dowdeswell," *Canadian Nuclear Society Bulletin* 24, no.1 (2003).

Branch, Daniel. *Kenya: Between Hope and Despair, 1963–2011*. New Haven, CT: Yale University Press, 2011.

Brough, Tony. Interview by the author, 2017.

Brown, Oli. "Erik Solheim: What He Got Right, What He Got Wrong, and What the New UN Environment Chief Should Do Next," February 13, 2018. https://olibrown.org/erik-solheim-what-he-got-right-what-he-got-wrong-and-what-the-new-un-environment-chief-should-do-next/.

Buck, Stephanie. "In the 1980s, Italy Paid a Nigerian Town $100 a Month to Store Toxic Waste—and It's Happening Again: Toxic Colonialism at Its Worst," *Timeline*, May 26, 2017. https://timeline.com/koko-nigeria-italy-toxic-waste-159a6487b5aa.

Bulkeley, Harriet, Liliana B. Andonova, Michele M. Betsill, Daniel Compagnon, Thomas Hale, Matthew J. Hoffmann, Peter Newell, Matthew Paterson, Stacy D. VanDeveer, and Charles Roger. *Transnational Climate Change Governance*. Cambridge: Cambridge University Press, 2014.

Busch, Per-Olof. "Independent Influence of International Public Administrations: Contours and Future Directions of an Emerging Research Strand." In *Public Administration in the Context of Global Governance*, edited by Soonhee Kim, Shena Ashley and Henry W. Lambright, 45–62. Cheltenham: Edward Elgar, 2014. https://doi.org/10.4337/9781783477807.00017.

Bush, George H. W. "Telegram from the Mission to the United Nations to the Department of State, New York, May 31, 1972." In *Foreign Relations of the United States, 1969–1976*, vol. 5, *United Nations*, edited by Evan M. Duncan, 334–335. Washington, DC: Government Printing Office, 1972.

Bush, George H. W. "Telegram from the Mission to the United Nations to the Department of State, New York, September 15, 1971." In *Foreign Relations of the United States, 1969–1976*, vol. 5, *United Nations*, edited by Evan M. Duncan. Washington, DC: Government Printing Office, 1971.

Camden Higher Education and Health Care Task Force. "A 5 Year Winning Investment: Camden's Anchor Institutions Provide Jobs, Services, and a Bright Future." Camden, NJ, 2008.

Canan, Penelope, and Nancy Reichman. *Ozone Connections: Expert Networks in Global Environmental Governance*. Sheffield, UK: Greenleaf Publishing, 2002.

Carrington, Damian. "Nations Halt Funding to UN Environment Programme as Outcry Over Chief Grows," *Guardian*, September 25, 2018. https://www.theguardian.com/environment/2018/sep/25/nations-halt-funding-to-un-environment-programme-as-outcry-over-chief-erik-solheim-grows.

Cash, David W., William C. Clark, Frank Alcock, Nancy M. Dickson, Noelle Eckley, David H. Guston, Jill Jäger, and Ronald B. Mitchell. "Knowledge Systems for Sustainable Development." *Proceedings of the National Academy of Sciences* 100, no. 14 (2003): 8086–8091.

CCISUA. "UN Global Staff Satisfaction Survey." In the author's possession, 2017.

Charnovitz, Steve. "A World Environment Organization." *Columbia Journal of Environmental Law* 27, no. 2 (2002): 323–362.

Chayes, Abram, and Antonia H. Chayes, "On Compliance." *International Organization* 47, no. 2 (1993): 175–205. https://doi.org/10.1017/S0020818300027910.

Chaytor, Beatrice. *The Development of Global Forest Policy: Overview of Legal and Institutional Frameworks*. London: International Institute for Environment and Development (IIED) and the World Business Council for Sustainable Development (WCBSD), 2001. https://pubs.iied.org/pdfs/G00926.pdf.

Cheluget, Kipyego. *Kenya's Fifty Years of Diplomatic Engagement: From Kenyatta to Kenyatta*. Nairobi: Moran Publishers and Worldreader, 2018.

Chirac, Jacques. "Speech to the Plenary Session of the World Summit on Sustainable Development," Johannesburg, September 2, 2002. http://www.jacqueschirac-asso.fr/archives-elysee.fr/elysee/elysee.fr/anglais/speeches_and_documents/2002-2001/fi005004.html.

Clapp, Jennifer. *Toxic Exports: The Transfer of Hazardous Wastes from Rich to Poor Countries*. Ithaca: Cornell University Press, 2001.

Clapp, Jennifer, and Peter Dauvergne. *Pathways to a Green World, the Political Economy of a Global Environment*. Cambridge, MA: MIT Press, 2005.

Clark, William. "Dedication to Maurice Strong." *The Environmentalist* 4, no. 2 (1984): 89–91.

Collins, Margaret Goud. "International Organizations and Biodiversity." In *Encyclopedia of Biodiversity*, edited by Simon A. Levin, 234–331. Amsterdam: Academic Press, 2013. https://doi.org/10.1016/B978-0-12-384719-5.00395-6.

Conca, Ken. *An Unfinished Foundation: The United Nations and Global Environmental Governance*. New York: Oxford University Press, 2015.

Conca, Ken. "Greening the UN: Environmental Organizations and the UN System." In *NGOs, the UN, and Global Governance*, edited by Thomas Weiss and Leon Gordenker. Boulder, CO: Lynne Riener, 1996.

Conference on the Human Environment. *Development and Environment: Report and Working Papers of Experts Convened by the Secretary-General of the United Nations Conference on the Human Environment (Founex, Switzerland, June 4–12, 1971)*. Environment and Social Sciences, 1. Paris: Mouton, 1972.

Constable, Harriet. "Why Millennials Are Heading for a Wilder Tech City," *BBC Capital*, January 15, 2018. https://www.bbc.com/worklife/article/20180115-why.

Cox, Robert W. "The Executive Head: An Essay on Leadership in the ILO." *International Organization* 23, no. 2 (1969): 205–230. https://doi.org/10.1017/S002081830003157X.

Cox, Robert W., and Harold K. Jacobson. *The Anatomy of Influence: Decision Making in International Organizations*. New Haven, CT: Yale University Press, 1973.

The Cocoyoc Declaration. Adopted by the participants in the UNEP/UNCTAD symposium on "Patterns of Resource Use, Environment, and Development Strategies," Cocoyoc, Mexico, October 8–12, 1974.

Cunningham, Gerard. Interview by the author, 2017.

Cupit, Richard, Rodney Whitlock, and Lynn Williams Whitlock. "The (Im)Morality of International Governmental Organizations." *International Interactions* 21, no. 4 (1996): 389–404.

Dalberg Global Development Advisors. "Review of UNEP's Programme Implementation Mechanisms and Administrative Structures." New York, 2006.

Davenport, Deborah S. "An Alternative Explanation for the Failure of the UNCED Forest Negotiations." *Global Environmental Politics* 5, no. 1 (2005): 105–130. https://doi.org/10.1162/1526380053243549.

de Azevedo Brito, Bernardo. "Statement by the Brazilian Representative, Item 11 of the Agenda." Paper presented at the United Nations Conference on the Human Environment, Stockholm, Sweden, 1972.

Depledge, Joanna. "A Special Relationship: Chairpersons and the Secretariat in the Climate Change Negotiations." *Global Environmental Politics* 7, no. 1 (2007): 45–68.

Desai, Bharat H. "UNEP: A Global Environmental Authority?" *Environmental Policy and Law* 36, no. 3–4 (2006): 137–157.

Desai, Bharat H. *Multilateral Environmental Agreements: Legal Status of the Secretariats*. New York: Cambridge University Press, 2010.

DeSombre, Elizabeth. *Global Environmental Institutions*. 2nd edition. Abingdon, UK: Routledge, 2017.

Dinh, Jessica E., Robert G. Lord, William Gardner, Jeremy D. Meuser, Robert C. Liden, and Jinyu Hu. "Leadership Theory and Research in the New Millennium: Current Theoretical Trends and Changing Perspectives." *The Leadership Quarterly* 25, no. 1 (2013): 36–62.

Dowdeswell, Elizabeth. Interview by the author, 2004.

Dowdeswell, Elizabeth, and Richard J. Kinley. "Constructive Damage to the Status Quo." In *Negotiating Climate Change: The Inside Story of the Rio Convention*, edited by Irving M. Mintzer and J. Amber Leonard, 113–128. Cambridge Energy and Environment Series. Cambridge: Cambridge University Press, 1994. https://doi.org/10.1017/CBO9780511558917.006.

Dubb, Steve, Sarah McKinley, and Ted Howard. *The Anchor Dashboard: Aligning Institutional Practice to Meet Low-Income Community Needs*. Takoma Park, MD: The Democracy Collaborative, 2013.

ECI, "Environmental Conventions Index." http://www.environmentalconventionsindex.org.

Eckhard, Steffen, and Jörn Ege. "International bureaucracies and Their Influence on Policy-Making: A Review of Empirical Evidence." *Journal of European Public Policy* 23, no. 7 (2016): 960–978. https://doi.org/10.1080/13501763.2016.1162837.

ECOSOC. "In-Depth Evaluation of the Programme on Environment, E/AC.51/1995/3." In *Thirty-Fifth Session of the Committee for Programme and Coordination*. New York: United Nations, 1995.

ECOSOC. "Programme Evaluation of the United Nations Environment Programme." E/AC.51/2013/2. New York, 2013.

ECOSOC. "Evaluation of the United Nations Environment Programme" E/AC.51/2019/7. New York, 2019.

Ega-Musa, Nasser. "The United Nations Family is in Kenya to Stay," *Daily Nation*, June 29, 2014. https://www.nation.co.ke/oped/letters/United-Nations-Nairobi-Office-Kenya/440806-2365524-7ewjuez/index.html.

Ege, Jörn, and Michael W. Bauer. "International Bureaucracies from a Public Administration and International Relations Perspective." In *Routledge Handbook of International Organization*, edited by Bob Reinalda, 135–148. London: Routledge, 2013.

Egeberg, Morten. "The Impact of Bureaucratic Structure on Policy Making." *Public Administration* 77, no. 1 (1999): 155–170. https://doi.org/10.1111/1467–9299.00148.

Egypt, Iran, Lebanon, Netherlands, Pakistan, Peru, Philipines, Sudan, Syrian Arab Republic. "Draft Resolution Concerning Development and Environment, A/C.2/L.1236." Paper presented at the United Nations Conference on the Human Environment, Stockholm, Sweden, 1972.

Eidheim, Idunn. Interview by the author, 2018.

El-Ashry, Mohamed. Interview by the author, 2017.

El-Ashry, Mohamed. "Recommendations from the High-Level Panel on System-Wide Coherence on Strengthening International Environmental Governance: Introduction." In *Global Environmental Governance: Perspectives on the Current Debate*, edited by Lydia Swart and Estelle Perry, 7–15. New York: Center for UN Reform Education, 2007.

Ellis, David C. "The Organizational Turn in International Organization Theory." *Journal of International Organization Studies* 1, no. 1 (2010): 11–28.

Engfeldt, Lars-Göran. *From Stockholm to Johannesburg and Beyond: The Evolution of the International System for Sustainable Development Governance and Its Implications*. Stockholm: Utrikesdepartementet (Ministry of Foreign Affairs), 2009.

Environmental Studies Board. *Institutional Arrangements for International Environmental Cooperation: A Report to the Department of State by the Committee for International Environmental Programs*. Washington, DC: National Academies of Sciences, 1972.

Esty, Daniel C., and Maria H. Ivanova. "Making International Environmental Efforts Work: The Case for a Global Environmental Organization." New Haven, CT: Yale Center for Environmental Law and Policy, 2001.

Esty, Daniel C., and Maria H. Ivanova. *Global Environmental Governance: Options and Opportunities*, New Haven, CT: Yale School of Forestry & Environmental Studies, 2002.

Esty, Daniel C., and Maria H. Ivanova. "Towards a Global Environmental Mechanism." In J. Speth, ed., *Worlds Apart: Globalization and the Environment*. Washington, DC: Island Press, 2003.

Ethics and Anti-Corruption Commission, "National Ethics and Corruption Survey, 2016." Kenya: Report #3 of January 2017. http://eacc.go.ke/default/wp-content/uploads/2018/06/Final_EACC_National_Survey_on_Corruption-2016.pdf.

Fayo, Galgallo. "Embattled UNEP Head Refunds Travel Expenses," *Business Daily Africa*, September 19, 2018. https://www.businessdailyafrica.com/news/Embattled-UNEP-head-refunds-travel-expenses/539546-4766720-s7pshz/index.html.

Fazey, I., N. Schäpke, G. Caniglia, J. Patterson, J. Hultman, B. Van Mierlo, F. Säwe, et al. "Ten Essentials for Action-Oriented and Second-Order Energy Transitions, Transformations and Climate Change Research." *Energy Research and Social Science* 40 (2018): 54–70. https://doi.org/10.1016/j.erss.2017.11.026.

Figueres, Christiana, and Tom Rivett-Carnac. *The Future We Choose: Surviving the Climate Crisis*. London: Knopf, 2020.

Fischer, Stephanie. "Holding on to Hope: Q&A with Julia Marton-Lefèvre, Former Director General of the International Union for Conservation of Nature," Stanford Woods Institute for the Environment, May 20, 2019. https://woods.stanford.edu/news/holding-hope-qa-julia-marton-lef-vre-former-director-general-international-union-conservation.

Flanagan, Richard. "Australia is Committing Climate Suicide." *New York Times*, January 3, 2020. https://www.nytimes.com/2020/01/03/opinion/australia-fires-climate-change.html.

FridaysforFuture. Main page. https://www.fridaysforfuture.org/.

Gardner, Richard N. "Toward a World Ecological System," *Washington Post*, April 1, 1970.

Gardner, Richard N. "UN as Policeman." *Saturday Review*, August 7, 1971, 47–50.

Garelick, Glen. "Environment a Breath of Fresh Air: Delegates of 24 Nations Sign a Historic Pact on Ozone." *Time Magazine*, September 28, 1987.

Garschagen, Matthias, Sylvia Wood, Jennifer Garard, Maria Ivanova, and Amy Luers. "Too Big to Ignore: Global Risk Perception Gaps Between Scientists and Business Leaders." *Earth's Future* 8 (2020). https://doi.org/10.1029/2020EF001498.

Geri, Laurance R. "New Public Management and the Reform of International Organizations." *International Review of Administrative Sciences* 67, no. 3 (2001): 445–460. http://doi.org/10.1177/0020852301673004.

GEO. "GEO, Group on Earth Observations." 2017. https://www.earthobservations.org/index.php.

Gimode, Edwin. "An Anatomy of Violent Crime and Insecurity in Kenya: The Case of Nairobi, 1985–1999." *Africa Development Journal* 26, no. 1–2 (2001): 295–335.

Global Environment Facility. "25 Years of GEF." 2016. https://www.thegef.org/sites/default/files/publications/31357FinalWeb.pdf.

Global Environmental Governance Project. Global Environmental Governance Forum: Reflecting on the Past, Moving into the Future, Glion, Switzerland, June 28–July 2, 2009.

Gosovic, Branislav. "Maurice F. Strong, Marc Nerfin, Pope Francis' Laudato Si', SDGs and COP 21," Other News: Voices Against the Tide, March 8, 2016.

Gray, Julia. "Life, Death, or Zombie? The Vitality of International Organizations." *International Studies Quarterly* 63, no. 1 (March 2018): 1–13. http://doi.org/10.1093/isq/sqx086.

Gray, Mark Allan. "The United Nations Environment Programme: An Assessment." *Environmental Law* 20, no. 2 (1990): 291–311.

Green, Fitzhugh. "Remarks by US Delegate Fitzhugh Green to the Stockholm Human Environment Preparatory Committee." In *World's People Must be Informed, Persuaded to Back Environment Correction Measures*, edited by US Information Service. Geneva, 1972.

Gupta, Joyeeta. "A History of International Climate Change Policy." *Wiley Interdisciplinary Reviews: Climate Change* 1, no. 5 (2010): 636–653.

Gupta, Sanjay. "Jan Egeland," *Time Magazine*, May 8, 2006. http://content.time.com/time/specials/packages/article/0,28804,1975813_1975847_1976579,00.html.

Guterres, Antònio. "Vision Statement," April 4, 2016. https://www.un.org/pga/70/wp-content/uploads/sites/10/2016/01/4-April_Secretary-General-Election-Vision-Statement_Portugal-4-April-20161.pdf.

Haas, Ernst. *When Knowledge Is Power: Three Models of Change in International Organizations*. Berkeley: University of California Press, 1990.

Haas, Peter M. "Banning chlorofluorocarbons: epistemic community efforts to protect stratospheric ozone." *International Organization* 46, no. 1 (1992): 187–224. http://doi.org/10.1017/S002081830000148X.

Haas, Peter M. "Institutions: United Nations Environment Programme." *Environment* 36, no. 7 (1994): 43–45.

Haas, Peter M. "UN Conferences and Constructivist Governance of the Environment." *Global Governance* 8, no. 1 (2002): 73–91.

Haas, Peter M., Robert O. Keohane, and Mark A. Levy. *Institutions for the Earth: Sources of Effective International Environmental Protection*. Cambridge, MA: MIT Press, 1993.

Habermas, Jürgen. *The Theory of Communicative Action*. Boston: Beacon Press, 1984.

Haftel, Yoram Z., and Alexander Thompson. "The Independence of International Organizations: Concept and Applications." *Journal of Conflict Resolution* 50, no. 2 (2006): 253–275. http://doi.org/10.1177/0022002705285288.

Hamer, Mick. "The Filthy Rich." *New Scientist* 173, no. 2324 (January 5, 2002): 77.

Hall, Nina, and Ngaire Woods. "Theorizing the Role of Executive Heads in International Organizations." *European Journal of International Relations* 24, no. 4 (2018): 865–886. http://doi.org/10.1177/1354066117741676.

Hall, Peter A., and Rosemary C. R. Taylor. "Political Science and the Three New Institutionalisms." *Political Studies* 44, no. 5 (1996): 936–957. https://doi.org/10.1111/j.1467-9248.1996.tb00343.x.

Halle, Mark. "The UNEP that We Want: Reflections on UNEP's Future Challenges," *International Institute for Sustainable Development Commentary*. Prangins, Switzerland, 2007. https://www.iisd.org/sites/default/files/publications/unep_we_want.pdf.

Halle, Mark. Interview by the author, 2008.

Halle, Mark. Interview by the author, 2017.

Halle, Mark. Interview by the author, 2018.

Hammond, Thomas H. "Agenda Control, Organizational Structure, and Bureaucratic Politics." *American Journal of Political Science* 30, no. 2 (1986): 379–420. http://doi.org/10.2307/2111102.

Han, Enze, and Joseph O'Mahoney. "British Colonialism and the Criminalization of Homosexuality." *Cambridge Review of International Affairs* 27, no. 2 (2014): 268–288. http://doi.org/10.1080/09557571.2013.867298.

Hardy, Michael. "The United Nations Environment Problem." *Natural Resources Journal* 13, no. 2 (April 1973): 235–255.

Harman, Danna. "Dark Days for Nairobi—Kenya's Once-Lauded 'Green City in the Sun.'" *Christian Science Monitor*, February 5, 2001. https://www.csmonitor.com/2001/0205/p7s1.html.

Harrison, Gordon. "Is there a United Nations Environment Programme? Special Investigation at the Request of the Ford Foundation." In the author's possession, 1977.

Hawkins, Darren G., David A. Lake, Daniel L. Nielson, and Michael J. Tierney, eds. *Delegation and Agency in International Organizations*. Cambridge: Cambridge University Press, 2006.

Head, John W. "The Challenge of International Environmental Management: A Critique of the United Nations Environment Programme." *Virginia Journal of International Law* 18, no. 2 (1977–1978): 269–288.

Heimer, Matthew. "The United Nations Environment Programme: Thinking Globally, Retreating Locally." *Yale Human Rights & Development Law Journal* 1, no. 1 (1998): 129–135.

Herrmann, Stefanie M., and Charles F. Hutchinson. "The Changing Contexts of the Desertification Debate." *Journal of Arid Environments* 63, no. 3 (2005): 538–555.

Herter Jr., Christian A. "Letter to Maurice Strong, Secretary-General of UNCHE Commenting on 'A Framework for Environmental Action'." Unpublished letter, in the author's possession, 1972.

Hicks, Robin, and Jessica Cheam. "We Need to Engage Business 'Like Never Before', Says New UNEP Head," *Eco-Business*, January 6, 2017. https://www.eco-business.com/news/we-need-to-engage-business-like-never-before-says-new-unep-head/.

Hierlmeier, Jodie. "UNEP: Retrospect and Prospect-Options for Reforming the Global Environmental Governance Regime." *Georgetown Environmental Law Review* 14, no. 4 (2001): 767–805.

Holdgate, Martin W. *The Green Web: A Union for World Conservation*. London: Earthscan, 1999.

Holdgate, Martin W., Mohammed Kassas, and Gilbert F. White. *The World Environment, 1972–1982: A Report by the United Nations Environment Programme*. Nairobi: United Nations Environment Programme, 1982.

Hooghe, Lisbet, and Marks, Gary. "Delegation and Pooling in International Organizations." *The Review of International Organizations* 10 (2015): 305–328. https://doi.org/10.1007/s11558-014-9194-4.

Hughes-Evans, David. "Dedication to Dr. Mostafa Kamal Tolba." *The Environmentalist* 2, no. 1 (1982): 5–12.

Hulm, Peter. "The Regional Seas Program; What Fate for United Nations Environment Programme's Crown Jewels?" *Ambio* 12, no. 1 (1983): 2–13.

Hyvarren, Joy, and Duncan Brack. "Global Environmental Institutions: Analysis and Options for Change." London: Royal Institute for International Affairs, 2000.

IEG Co-Chairs Option Paper. "Informal Consultative Process on the Institutional Framework for United Nations' Environmental Activities," Nairobi, 2008.

Imber, Mark F. *Environment, Security, and UN Reform* (New York: Springer, 1994).

Inomata, Tadanori. *Management Review of Environmental Governance within the United Nations System (JIU/REP/2008/3)*. Geneva: Joint Inspection Unit, 2008.

IUCN. "About us." https://www.iucn.org/about.

IUCN. *The Impact of IUCN Resolutions on International Conservation Efforts: An Overview*. Gland, Switzerland: IUCN, 2018. https://portals.iucn.org/library/node/47226.

IUCN General Assembly. "Resolution 15/10. Genetic Resources." 1981.

Ivanova, Maria. *Can the Anchor Hold? Rethinking the UN Environment Programme for the 21st Century*. New Haven, CT: Yale School of Forestry & Environmental Studies, 2005.

Ivanova, Maria. "Designing the United Nations Environment Programme: A Story of Compromise and Confrontation." *International Environmental Agreements: Politics, Law and Economics* 7, no. 3 (2007): 337–361.

Ivanova, Maria. "UNEP in Global Environmental Governance: Design, Leadership, Location." *Global Environmental Politics* 10, no. 1 (2010): 30–59.

Ivanova, Maria. "A New Global Architecture for Sustainability Governance." In *State of the World 2012: Moving Toward Sustainable Prosperity*, 104–117. Washington, DC: Worldwatch Institute, 2012.

Ivanova, Maria. "Institutional Design and UNEP Reform: Historical Insights on Form, Function and Financing." *International Affairs* 88, no. 3 (2012): 565–584.

Ivanova, Maria. *Environmental Envoy: Achim Steiner*, Global Leadership Dialogues 3, no. 3. Boston: Center for Governance and Sustainability, 2016.

Ivanova, Maria. *Champion for Change: Erik Solheim*, Global Leadership Dialogues 4, no. 1. Boston: Center for Governance and Sustainability, 2017.

Ivanova, Maria. "Coloring the UN Environmental: The Catalytic Role of the UN Environment Programme," *Global Governance* 26, no. 2 (2020): 307–324. https://doi.org/10.1163/19426720-02602007.

Ivanova, Maria, and Melissa Goodall. "Global Environmental Outlook (GEO): An Integrated Environmental Assessment." In *The Encyclopedia of Sustainability: Measurements, Indicators, and Research Methods for Sustainability*, edited by Ian Spellerberg, 160–164. Great Barrington, MA: Berkshire Publishing Group, 2012.

Ivanova, Maria, and Natalia Escobar-Pemberthy. "The UN, Global Governance and the SDGs." In *Routledge Handbook of the Resource Nexus*, edited by Raimund Bleischwitz, Holger Hoff, Catalina Spataru, Ester van der Voet and Stacy D. VanDeveer, 486–503. London and New York: Routledge, 2017.

Ivanova, Maria, Natalia Escobar-Pemberthy, and Anna Dubrova, *National Implementation of Global Environmental Agreements in Rwanda*, Boston, MA: UMass Boston, 2019.

Iwama, Toru. "Multilateral Environmental Institutions and Coordinating Mechanisms." In *Emerging Forces in Environmental Governance*, edited by N. Kanie and P. M. Haas. United Nations University Press, 2004.

Jacobson, Harold K., and Edith B. Weiss. "Strengthening Compliance with International Environmental Accords: Preliminary Observations from Collaborative Project." *Global Governance* 1, no. 2 (1995): 119–148.

Jinnah, Sikina, and Simon Nicholson, eds. *New Earth Politics: Essays from the Anthropocene*. Cambridge, MA: MIT Press, 2016.

Joachim, Jutta, Bob Reinalda, and Bertjan Verbeek. *International Organizations and Implementation: Enforcers, Managers, Authorities?* London: Routledge, 2008.

Johnson, Stanley. *UNEP: The First 40 Years: A Narrative*. Nairobi, Kenya: UNEP, 2012.

Johnson, Tana. "Institutional Design and Bureaucrats' Impact on Political Control." In *The Journal of Politics* 75, no. 1 (2013): 183–197. http://doi.org/10.1017/S0022381612000953.

Johnson, Tana. *Organizational Progeny: Why Governments are Losing Control Over the Proliferating Structures of Global Governance*. Oxford: Oxford University Press, 2014.

Johnson, Tana, and Johannes Urpelainen. "International Bureaucrats and the Formation of Intergovernmental Organizations: Institutional Design Discretion Sweetens the Pot." *International Organization* 68, no. 1 (2014): 177–209. http://doi.org/10.1017/S0020818313000349.

Jörgens, Helge, Nina Kolleck, and Barbara Saerbeck. "Exploring the Hidden Influence of International Treaty Secretariats: Using Social Network Analysis to Analyse the Twitter Debate on the 'Lima Work Programme on Gender.'"*Journal of European Public Policy* 23, no. 7 (2016): 979–998. http://doi.org/10.1080/13501763.2016.1162836.

Juma, Calestous. Interview by the author, 2017.

Juma, Calestous. "The Perils of Centralizing Environmental Governance." *Environment Matters* 6, no. 12 (2000): 13–15.

Kaniaru, Donald. "Kenya: A Special Honor to Have the UNEP Here," *The Nation*, December 19, 2004.

Kaniaru, Donald. Interview by the author, 2004.

Kaniaru, Donald. Interview by the author, 2018.

Kapur, Devesh. "Who Gets to Run the World?" *Foreign Policy* 121 (2000): 44–50. http://doi.org/10.2307/1149618.

Karimi, Joseph. "Efforts To End Corruption In Harambees," *Standard Digital*, August 28, 2013. https://www.standardmedia.co.ke/article/2000092053/efforts-to-end-corruption-in-harambees.

Karongo, Catherine. "Walk Through Eco-Friendly UNEP Building," *Capital News FM*, March 7, 2012. https://www.capitalfm.co.ke/news/2012/03/walk-through-eco-friendly-unep-building/.

Kassas, Mohammed. "Desertification: A General Review." *Journal of Arid Environments* 30, no. 2 (1995): 115–128. https://doi.org/10.1016/S0140-1963(05)80063-1.

Katz Cogan, Jacob, Ian Hurd, and Ian Johnstone. *The Oxford Handbook of International Organizations*. Oxford: Oxford University Press, 2017.

Kaufman, Herbert. *The Forest Ranger: A Study in Administrative Behavior*. Baltimore: Johns Hopkins University Press, 1960.

Khamisi, Joe. *Kenya: Looters and Grabbers: 54 Years of Corruption and Plunder by the Elite, 1963–2017*. Zionsville, IN: Jodey Book Publishers, 2018.

Kim, Soonhee, Shena Ashley, and Henry W. Lambright. *Public Administration in the Context of Global Governance*. Cheltenham, UK: Edward Elgar, 2014.

Kimball, Lee. "The Debate Over a World/Global Environment Organisation." In *Global Environmental Institutions*, edited by D. Brack and J. Hyvarinen, 19–31. London: The Royal Institute of International Affairs, 2002.

Kimenyi, Mwangi S., and Josephine Kibe. "Africa's Powerhouse," Brookings Institution, January 6, 2014. https://www.brookings.edu/opinions/africas-powerhouse/.

King, Ed. "Erik Solheim: Meet the Man Tasked With Protecting Planet Earth," *Climate Home News*, May 12, 2016. https://www.climatechangenews.com/2016/05/12/erik-solheim-meet-the-man-tasked-with-protecting-planet-earth/.

Knill, Christoph, Steffen Eckhard, and Stephan Grohs. "Administrative Styles in the 'European Commission and the OSCE-Secretariat: Striking Similarities Despite Different Organizational Settings.'" *Journal of European Public Policy* 23, no. 7 (2016): 1057–1076. http://doi.org/10.1080/13501763.2016.1162832.

Kohler, Pia M. *Science Advice and Global Environmental Governance: Expert Institutions and the Implementation of International Environmental Treaties*. London: Anthem Press, 2020.

Kopylov, Mikhail Nikolaevich. "UNEP-35. Сколько Еще? (UNEP-35. How Much More Ahead?)" *Московский журнал международного права (Moskovsky zhurnal mezhduranodnogo prava)* 66, no. 2 (2007): 17–23.

Kopylov, Mikhail Nikolaevich, and Aleksandr Solntsev. "Международное Экологическое Право на Пороге Реформ (The International Law on the Eve of Reforms)." *Московский журнал международного права (Moskovsky zhurnal mezhduranodnogo prava)* 1, no. 77 (2014): 110–131.

Koremenos, Barbara, Charles Lipson, and Duncan Snidal. "The Rational Design of International Institutions." *International Organization* 55, no. 4 (2001): 761–799.

Kramarz, Teresa, and Susan Park. "Accountability in Global Environmental Governance: A Meaningful Tool For Action?" *Global Environmental Politics* 16, no. 2 (2016): 1–21.

Larigauderie, Anne, and Harold A. Mooney. "The Intergovernmental Science-Policy Platform on Biodiversity and Ecosystem Services: Moving a Step Closer to an IPCC-Like Mechanism for Biodiversity." *Current Opinion in Environmental Sustainability* 2, no. 1–2 (2010): 9–14. http://doi.org/10.1016/j.cosust.2010.02.006.

Larres, Klaus, and Ruth Wittlinger. *Understanding Global Politics: Actors and Themes in International Affairs*. London: Routledge, 2019.

Le Prestre, Philippe G., John D. Reid, and E. Thomas Morehouse, eds. *Protecting the Ozone Layer: Lessons, Models, and Prospects*. Boston, MA: Kluwer, 1998.

Litfin, Karen. *Ozone Discourses: Science and Politics in Global Environmental Cooperation*. New York: Columbia University Press, 1994.

Litfin, Karen. "The Gendered Eye in the Sky: A Feminist Perspective on Earth Observation Satellites." *Frontiers: A Journal of Women Studies* 18, no. 2 (1997): 26–47.

Lonergan, Steve. "The Role of UNEP in Desertification Research and Mitigation." *Journal of Arid Environments* 63, no. 3 (2005): 533–534. http://doi.org/10.1016/j.jaridenv.2005.03.001.

Lovejoy, Thomas. "Eden No More." *Science Advances* 5, no. 5 (2019). http://doi.org/10.1126/sciadv.aax7492.

Lynch, Gabrielle. *Performances of Injustice: The Politics of Truth, Justice and Reconciliation in Kenya*. Cambridge: Cambridge University Press, 2018.

Maathai, Wangari. *Unbowed: A Memoir*. New York: Alfred A. Knopf, 2006.

MacDonald, Gordon J. "International Institutions for Environmental Management." *International Organization* 26, no. 2 (1972): 372–400. https://doi.org/10.1017/S0020818300003374.

MacNeill, James. Interview by the author, 2009.

MacNeill, James. "The Forgotten Imperative of Sustainable Development." *Environmental Policy and Law* 36, no. 3–4 (2006): 167–170.

Magraw, Dan. Interview by the author, 2018.

Mansfield, Bill. Interview by the author, 2008.

March, James G., and Johan P. Olsen. "The New Institutionalism: Organizational Factors in Political Life." *American Political Science Review* 78, no. 3 (1983): 734–749. https://doi.org/10.2307/1961840.

Martin, Lisa L., and Beth A. Simmons. "Theories and Empirical Studies of International Institutions." *International Organization* 52, no. 4 (1998): 729–757. https://doi.org/10.1162/002081898550734.

Marton-Lefèvre, Julia "The Role of the Scientific Community in the Preparation of and Follow-up to UNCED." In *Negotiating International Regimes: Lessons Learned from the United Nations Conference on Environment and Development*, edited by Bertram I. Spector, Gunnar Sjöstedt and I. William Zartman, 171–180. London: Graham & Trotman/M. Nijhoff, 1994.

Masood, Ehsan. "Maurice Strong (1929–2015): Oil Man Who Was First Director of the United Nations Environment Programme." *Nature* 528 (2015): 480–481.

Masood, Ehsan. "The Battle for the Soul of Biodiversity," *Nature* 560 (2018): 423–425. https://doi.org/10.1038/d41586-018-05984-3.

Masood, Ehsan. "The Globe's Green Avenger," *Nature* 460 (2009): 454-455.

Mathai, Wanjira. "3 Ways to Uproot a Culture of Corruption," TED talk, 2019. https://www.ted.com/talks/wanjira_mathai_3_ways_to_uproot_a_culture_of_corruption?language=en.

Matuszak, John. Interview by the author, 2018.

McConnell, Fiona. *The Biodiversity Convention: A Negotiating History*. London: Kluwer Law International, 1996.

McCormick, Erin, et al. "Where Does Your Plastic Go? Global Investigation Reveals America's Dirty Secret," *Guardian*, June 17, 2019. https://www.theguardian.com/us-news/2019/jun/17/recycled-plastic-america-global-crisis.

McCormick, John. *Reclaiming Paradise: The Global Environmental Movement*. Bloomington: Indiana University Press, 1989.

McCrummen, Stephanie. "Incumbent Declared Winner in Kenya's Disputed Election," *Washington Post*, December 31, 2007. https://www.washingtonpost.com/wp-dyn/content/article/2007/12/30/AR2007123002506_pf.html.

McDermott, Constance L., Aran O'Carroll, and Peter Wood. "International Forest Policy—the Instruments, Agreements and Processes That Shape It." Department of Economic and Social Affairs United Nations Forum on Forests Secretariat, 2007. https://www.un.org/esa/forests/wp-content/uploads/2015/06/Intl_Forest_Policy_instruments_agreements.pdf.

McDonald, John W., and Noa Zanolli. *The Shifting Grounds of Conflict and Peacebuilding: Stories and Lessons*. Lanham, MD: Rowman and Littlefield, 2009.

McGrath, Matt. "Report Slams 'High Flying' UN Environment Chief," *BBC News*, September 21, 2018. https://www.bbc.com/news/science-environment-45604408.

McGraw, Désirée. "The CBD—Key Characteristics and Implications for Implementation." *Review of European, Comparative & International Environmental Law* 11, no. 1 (2002): 17–28. https://doi.org/10.1111/1467-9388.00299.

McInerney, Thomas. "UNEP, International Environmental Governance, and the 2030 Sustainable Development Agenda." Working Paper, UNEP, 2017. https://wedocs.unep.org/bitstream/handle/20.500.11822/21247/UNEP_IEG_2030SDA.pdf.

Mee, Laurence D. "The Role of United Nations Environment Programme and United Nations Development Programme in Multilateral Environmental Agreements." *International Environmental Agreements: Politics, Law and Economics* 5, no. 3 (2005): 227–263.

Menya, Walter. "Audit Reveals Erik Solheim Wasted Millions In Foreign Travels," *The Daily Nation*, September 16, 2018. https://www.nation.co.ke/news/UNEP-boss-Solheim-blew-millions-in-foreign-travels/1056-4761598-bxnp1sz/index.html.

Meyer, Doug. *Violence Against Queer People: Race, Class, Gender, and the Persistence of Anti-LGBT Discrimination*. New Brunswick, NJ: Rutgers University Press, 2015.

Miller, Norman N. "The United Nations Environment Programme." American Universities Field Staff Reports 17: 1–36. Hanover, NH: American Universities Field Staff, 1979.

Mingst, Karen A., Margaret P. Karns, and Alynna J. Lyon. *The United Nations in the 21st Century: Dilemmas in World Politics*. 3rd ed. Boulder: Westview Press, 2016.

Mires, Charlene. *Capital of the World: The Race to Host the United Nations*. New York: New York University Press, 2013.

Mitchell, Ronald. "Evaluating the Performance of Environmental Institutions: What to Evaluate and How to Evaluate It?" In *Institutions and Environmental Change: Principal Findings, Applications, and Research Frontiers*, edited by Oran Young, Leslie King, and Heike Schroeder. Cambridge, MA: MIT Press, 2008.

Mohammed, Amina. Interview by the author, 2018.

Moomaw, William R. "Scientist Diplomats or Diplomat Scientists: Who Makes Science Diplomacy Effective?" *Global Policy* 9, no. 3 (2018): 78–80. https://doi.org/10.1111/1758-5899.12520.

Mudallali, Amal. "The Global Pact for the Environment and the Sustainable Development Agenda." Conference at Columbia University, September 24, 2019.

Mwaura, Peter. "The Real Value of Having UN Presence in Kenya," *Daily Nation*, December 19, 2004. https://www.nation.co.ke/news/1056-37570-118l5gs/index.html.

Najam, Adil. "The Case Against a New International Environmental Organization." *Global Governance* 9, no. 3 (2003): 367–385.

Najam, Adil. "The Case against GEO, WEO, or Whatever-Else-EO." In *Global Environmental Institutions: Perspectives on Reform*, edited by D. Brack and J. Hyvarinen. London: Royal Institute of International Affairs, 2002.

Najam, Adil. "Why We Don't Need a New International Environmental Organization." Working Paper Series no. 64. Islamabad, Pakistan: Sustainable Development Policy Institute, 2001.

Najam, Adil, Loli Christopoulou, and William R. Moomaw. "The Emergent 'System' of Global Environmental Governance." *Global Environmental Politics* 4, no. 4 (2004): 23–35.

Najam, Adil, Mihaela Papa, and Nadaa Taiyab. *Global Environmental Governance: A Reform Agenda*. Winnipeg: International Institute for Sustainable Development (IISD), 2006.

Ndii, David, and Anne Waiguru. *Harambee: Pooling Together or Pulling Apart?* Nairobi, Kenya: Transparency International Kenya and the Friedrich Ebert Stiftung, 2001.

Nicholson, Simon, and Sikina Jinnah, eds. *New Earth Politics: Essays from the Anthropocene*. Cambridge, MA: MIT Press, 2016.

Nielson, Daniel L., and Michael J. Tierney. "Delegation to International Organizations: Agency Theory and World Bank Environmental Reform." *International Organization* 57, no. 2 (2003): 241–276. http://doi.org/10.1017/S0020818303572010.

NYC Mayor's Office for International Affairs. "United Nations Impact Report 2016." New York, 2016. https://www1.nyc.gov/site/international/programs/un-impact-report-2016.page.

O'Donnell, Jefcoate. "Kenya's Bid for LGBT Equality Hits a Wall," *Foreign Policy*, May 24, 2019. https://foreignpolicy.com/2019/05/24/kenyas-bid-for-lgbt-equality-hits-a-wall-section-162-section-165-court-decision-law/.

O'Neill, Kate. *Waste Trading Among Rich Nations: Building a New Theory of Environmental Regulation*. Cambridge, MA: MIT Press, 2000.

O'Sullivan, Dermot. "UN Environment Program Targets Issue of Hazardous Waste Exports." *Chemical & Engineering News* 66, no. 39 (1988): 24–29. http://doi.org/10.1021/cen-v066n039.p024.

Oberthür, Sebastian. "Clustering of Multilateral Environmental Agreements: Potentials and Limitations." *International Environmental Agreements: Politics, Law and Economics* 2 (2002): 317–340. http://doi.org/10.1023/A:1021364902607.

Office of Policy Development and Inter-Agency Affairs. "Review and Analysis of the Environment Coordination Board and ACC Reports and of the Process and Modalities of the Preparation of SWMTEP." In the author's possession, 1993.

OHCHR [Office of the High Commissioner for Human Rights]. "Protection Against Violence and Discrimination Based on Sexual Orientation and Gender Identity." A/HRC/RES/32/2. Geneva, 2016.

OIOS [Office of Internal Oversight Services at the United Nations]. "Review of the United Nations Environment Programme (UNEP) and the Administrative Practices of its Secretariat, Including the United Nations Office in Nairobi (UNON)." A/51/810. New York, 1997.

OIOS Internal Audit Division. "Audit of Official Travel at the United Nations Environment Programme, Report 2018/109," November 16, 2018.

Omondi, Dominic. "Survey: Kenya Ranked Third Most Corrupt Country in the World," *Standard Digital*, February 26, 2016. https://www.standardmedia.co.ke/article/2000193065/survey-kenya-ranked-third-most-corrupt-country-in-the-world.

Ott, J. Steven, Sandra J. Parkes, and Richard B. Simpson, eds. *Classic Readings in Organizational Behavior*. 3rd ed. Belmont, CA: Wadsworth Publishing Company, 2003.

Padma, T. V. "African Nations Push UN to Improve Drought Research." *Nature News*, September 13, 2019. https://www.nature.com/articles/d41586-019-02760-9.

Palme, Thomas. "Financial Difficulties and Program Review at UNEP Meeting." *Ambio* 5, no. 3 (1976): 143–147.

Palmer, Geoffrey. "New Ways to Make International Environmental Law." *American Journal of International Law* 96, no. 2 (1992): 259–283. https://doi.org/10.2307/2203234.

Park, Susan. "Theorizing Norm Diffusion Within International Organizations." *International Politics* 43, no. 3 (2006): 342–361.

Parson, Edward A. *Protecting the Ozone Layer: Science and Strategy*. Oxford: Oxford University Press, 2003.

Pasztor, Janos. Interview by the author, 2017.

Pataki, Julia. Interview by the author, 2017.

Payet, Rolph. Interview by the author, 2018.

Pearce, Fred. "Environment Body Goes to Pieces." *New Scientist*, February 15, 1997. https://www.newscientist.com/article/mg15320691-500-environment-body-goes-to-pieces/.

Pease, Kelly-Kate S. *International Organizations: Perspectives on Global Governance*. New York: Routledge, 2018.

Perrez, Franz Xaver. Interview by the author, 2018.

Perrez, Franz Xaver, and Daniel Ziegerer. "A Non-Institutional Proposal to Strengthen International Environmental Governance." *Environmental Policy and Law* 38, no. 5 (2008): 253–261.

Petsonk, Carol Annette. "The Role of the United Nations Environment Programme in the Development of International Environmental Law." *American University Journal of International Law & Policy* 5, no. 2 (1989): 351–391.

Pevehouse, Jon, and Inken von Borzyskowski. "International Organizations in World Politics." In *The Oxford Handbook of International Organizations*, edited by Jacob Katz Cogan, Ian Hurd, and Ian Johnstone. Oxford: Oxford University Press, 2016.

Pfeffer, Jeffrey, and Gerald R. Salancik. *The External Control of Organizations: A Resource Dependence Perspective*. Stanford, CA: Stanford University Press, 2003.

Phombeah, Grey. "Moi's Legacy to Kenya," *BBC News*, August 5, 2002. http://news.bbc.co.uk/2/hi/africa/2161868.stm.

Prial, Frank. "Program to Clean Up Mediterranian Sea is Approved." *New York Times*, March 11, 1981. https://www.nytimes.com/1981/03/11/world/program-to-clean-up-mediterranean-sea-is-approved.html.

Psirmoi, Daniel. "Petition Over Word "Harambee" Splits Senators." *Standard Digital*, February 15, 2018. https://www.standardmedia.co.ke/article/2001269763/petition-over-word-harambee-splits-senators.

Pulgar-Vidal, Manuel. Interview by the author, 2018.

Ralston Saul, John. "Maurice Strong: Environmental Movement Loses a Founding Father." *The Globe and Mail*, November 30, 2015. https://www.theglobeandmail.com

/news/world/maurice-strong-environmental-movement-loses-a-founding-father/article 27524715/.

Reilly, Bill. Interview by the author, 2007.

Reinalda, Bob, and Bertjan Verbeek. *Autonomous Policy Making by International Organizations*. London: Routledge, 1998.

Reinalda, Bob, and Bertjan Verbeek. *Decision Making within International Organizations*. London: Routledge, 2004.

Reinalda, Bob, and Bertjan Verbeek. *Routledge History of International Organizations: From 1815 to the Present Day*. London: Routledge, 2009.

Rice, Xan. "The Looting of Kenya." *Guardian*, August 31, 2007. https://www.theguardian.com/world/2007/aug/31/kenya.topstories3.

Rockström, Johan, et al. "Planetary Boundaries: Exploring the Safe Operating Space for Humanity." *Ecology and Society* 14, no. 2, article 32 (2009). https://www.ecologyandsociety.org/vol14/iss2/art32/.

Rønneberg, Kristoffer. "Erik Solheim Accused of Squandering by UN Auditors." *Aftenposten*, September 12, 2018. https://www.aftenposten.no/verden/i/L0EjEP/Erik-Solheim-accused-of-squandering-by-UN-auditors.

Rosendal, Kristin G. "Impacts of Overlapping International Regimes: The Case of Biodiversity." *Global Governance* 7, no. 1 (2001): 95–117.

Rowland, Wade. *The Plot to Save the World: The Life and Times of the Stockholm Conference on the Human Environment*. Toronto: Clarke, Irwin & Co, 1973.

RS. "Halt 'Garbage Imperialism.'" *Christian Science Monitor*, November 15, 1988. https://www.csmonitor.com/1988/1115/etoxic.html.

Ruckelshaus, William. Interview by the author, 2009.

Rydbeck, Olof. "Statement by Ambassador Olof Rydbeck in the Preparatory Committee for the United Nations Conference on the Human Environment at Its Fourth Session in New York on Monday, 6 March 1972." Delivered at the Fourth Session of the Preparatory Committee for the United Nations Conference on the Human Environment, New York, March 6, 1972.

Sand, Peter. "The Concept of Public Trusteeship in the Transboundary Governance of Biodiversity." In *Transboundary Governance of Biodiversity*, edited by Louis J. Kotzé and Thilo Marauhn. Leiden, The Netherlands: Brill Nijhoff Publishers, 2014.

Sandbrook, Richard. "The 'Crisis' in Political Development Theory." *The Journal of Development Studies* 12, no. 2 (1976): 165–185.

Scanlon, John. "Presentation at the 12th Special Session of GMEF, Plenary Panel on the Institutional Framework for Sustainable Development." February 12, 2012. https://www.cites.org/eng/news/sg/2012/20120221_UNEP-GMEF.php.

Scanlon, John. Interview by the author, 2018.

Scarborough, Rowan. "'Peace Dividend' Apparently Paying Off." *Washington Times*, March 9, 1998.

Scharpf, Fritz W. "Does Organization Matter? Task Structure and Interaction in the Ministerial Bureaucracy." *Organization and Administrative Sciences* 8, no. 1 (1977): 149–168.

Schmidt, Falk, and Nick Nuttal. *Contributions Towards a Sustainable World in Dialogue with Klaus Töpfer*. München: Oekom Verlag, 2014.

Schwab, Klaus. *The Global Competitiveness Report 2019*, World Economic Forum (2019). http://www3.weforum.org/docs/WEF_TheGlobalCompetitivenessReport2019.pdf.

Scott, Karen N. "International Environmental Governance: Managing Fragmentation through Institutional Connection." *Melbourne Journal of International Law* 12, no. 1 (2011): 178–215.

Scott, W. Richard. *Organizations: Rational, Natural, and Open Systems*. Upper Saddle River, NJ: Prentice-Hall, 2003.

Selznick, Philip. *Leadership in Administration: A Sociological Interpretation*. New Orleans: Quid Pro Books, 1957.

Sending, Ole Jacob. "The International Civil Servant." *International Political Sociology* 8, no. 3 (2014): 338–340. https://doi.org/10.1111/ips.12065.

Senge, Peter M. *The Fifth Discipline: The Art and Practice of the Learning Organization*. New York: Doubleday, 2010.

Sengupta, Somini. "Why Build Kenya's First Coal Plant? Hint: Think China." *New York Times*, February 27, 2018. https://www.nytimes.com/2018/02/27/climate/coal-kenya-china-power.html.

Sengupta, Somini. "'Bleak' U.N. Report on a Planet in Peril Looms Over New Climate Talks." *New York Times*, November 26, 2019. https://www.nytimes.com/2019/11/26/climate/greenhouse-gas-emissions-carbon.html.

Smith, Constance. *Nairobi in the Making: Landscapes of Time and Urban Belonging*. Oxford: James Currey, 2019.

Smouts, Marie-Claude. *Tropical Forests, International Jungle: The Underside of Global Ecopolitics*. New York: Palgrave Macmillan, 2003.

Sokona, Youba. Interview by the author, 2018.

Solheim, Erik. Interview by the author, 2018.

Solheim, Erik. Interview by the author, 2020.

Solheim, Erik. "UNEP Town Hall Meeting." Nairobi, 2018.

Speth, James Gustave. *The Bridge at the Edge of the World: Capitalism, the Environment, and Crossing from Crisis to Sustainability*. New Haven, CT: Yale University Press, 2009.

Speth, James Gustave. Interview by the author, 2009.

Speth, James Gustave. "A Memorandum in Favor of a World Environment Organization." In *United Nations Environment Organization—Towards an International Environment Organization*, edited by Andreas Rechkemmer. Baden-Baden: Nomos Verlagsgesellschaft, 2005.

Speth, James Gustave. *Red Sky at Morning: America and the Crisis of the Global Environment*. New Haven, CT: Yale University Press, 2005.

Sprinz, Detlef, and Tapani Vaahtoranta. "The Interest-Based Explanation of International Environmental Policy." *International Organization* 48, no. 1 (1994): 77–105. http://doi.org/10.1017/S0020818300000825.

Steiner, Achim. Interview by the author, 2008.

Steiner, Achim. "Statement of Achim Steiner, Director General of IUCN—the World Conservation Union." In *The High-level Plenary Meeting of the 60th Session of the United Nations General Assembly*. New York, 2005.

Steiner, Achim, Lee A. Kimball, and John Scanlon. "Global Governance for the Environment and the Role of Multilateral Environmental Agreements in Conservation." *Oryx* 37, no. 2 (2003): 227–237. https://doi.org/10.1017/S0030605303000401.

Stone, Diane. "Global Public Policy, Transnational Policy Communities, and Their Networks." *Policy Studies Journal* 36, no. 1 (2008): 19–38. https://doi.org/10.1111/j.1541-0072.2007.00251.x.

Stone, Peter. *Did We Save the Earth at Stockholm?* London: Earth Island, 1973.

Strahan, Susan E. "Decline in Antarctic Ozone Depletion and Lower Stratospheric Chlorine Determined from Aura Microwave Limb Sounder Observations." *Geophysical Research Letters* 45, no. 1 (2018): 383–390. https://doi.org/10.1002/2017GL074830.

Stringer, Lindsay C. "Reviewing the International Year of Deserts and Desertification 2006: What Contribution Towards Combating Global Desertification and Implementing the United Nations Convention to Combat Desertification?" *Journal of Arid Environments* 72, no. 11 (2008): 2065–2074.

Strong, Maurice. "Closing Statement." Speech, United Nations Conference on the Human Environment, Stockholm, Sweden, 1972.

Strong, Maurice. Interview by the author, 2008.

Strong, Maurice. "Opening Remarks by Maurice F. Strong, Secretary-General Designate." Paper presented at the Informal Meeting of Preparatory Committee for the United Nations Conference on Human Environment, November 9, 1970.

Strong, Maurice. *Where on Earth Are We Going?* Toronto: Alfred A. Knopf Canada, 2000.

Struthers, David. "The United Nations Environment Programme after a Decade: The Nairobi Session of a Special Character, May 1981." *Denver Journal of International Law & Policy* 12, no. 2–3 (1981): 269–284.

Sullivan, Walter. "A UN Role is Envisioned in Global Pollution Drive." *New York Times*, May 24, 1971.

Swanson, Timothy. *Global Action for Biodiversity: An International Framework for Implementing the Convention on Biological Diversity*. London: Routledge, 1997.

"Sweden's Environment—Problems and Protection, 1960–2010." Swedish Environmental Protection Agency, 2011. https://www.naturvardsverket.se/Documents/publikationer6400/978-91-620-8501-8.pdf?pid=4183.

Tarasofsky, Richard G. *Assessing the International Forest Regime*. Gland, Switzerland: IUCN Environmental Law Centre, 1999.

Tarasofsky, Richard G. "UN Intergovernmental Forum on Forests Ends—UN Forum on Forests to Begin." *Environmental Policy and Law* 30, no. 1–2 (2000): 32–33.

Thacher, Peter S. "Multilateral Cooperation and Global Change." *Journal of International Affairs* 44, no. 2 (1991): 433–455.

Thomas, David S.G., and Nicholas J. Middleton. *Desertification: Exploding the Myth*. Chichester, UK: John Wiley & Sons, 1994.

Thunberg, Greta. "Our House Is on Fire." *Guardian*, January 25, 2019. https://www.theguardian.com/environment/2019/jan/25/our-house-is-on-fire-greta-thunberg16-urges-leaders-to-act-on-climate.

Tolba, Mostafa K. *Development without Destruction: Evolving Environmental Perceptions*. Dublin: Tycooley International, 1982.

Tolba, Mostafa K. *Earth Matters: Environmental Challenges for the 1980s*. Nairobi: United Nations Environment Program, 1983.

Tolba, Mostafa K. Interview by the author, 2008.

Töpfer, Klaus. "Environmental Degradation and Poverty as Inhibitors of Economic Growth." In *5th Annual Conference of the German Council for Sustainable Development*. Berlin, 2005.

Töpfer, Klaus. "United Nations Task Force on Environment and Human Settlements." *Linkages Journal* 3, no. 3 (1998).

Trondal, Jarle. "The Public Administration Turn in Integration Research." *Journal of European Public Policy* 14, no. 6 (2007): 960–972. https://doi.org/10.1080/13501760701498061.

Uhl-Bien, Mary, and Russ Marion. "Complexity Leadership in Bureaucratic Forms of Organizing: A Meso Model." *The Leadership Quarterly* 20, no. 4 (2009): 631–650.

Union of International Associations. "The Yearbook of International Organizations Online." 2013. http://www.uia.org/yearbook.

United Nations. "International Organizational Implications of Action Proposals." In *United Nations Conference on the Human Environment*. Stockholm, 1972.

United Nations. "Report of the Secretary-General on Environment and Human Settlements." New York, 1999.

United Nations. "Report of the United Nations Conference on the Human Environment, Stockholm, 5–16 June 1972." New York, 1973.

United Nations. "Review of the United Nations Environment Programme and the Administrative Practices of Its Secretariat, Including the United Nations Office in Nairobi." In *Report of the Secretary-General on the activities of the Office of Internal Oversight Services*. Nairobi, 1997.

United Nations. Transcript of Press Conference by Secretary-General Kofi Annan at United Nations Headquarters. SG/SM/10089. 2005.

United Nations. "UN Careers Facebook Page." 2012, https://www.facebook.com/UN.Careers/posts/the-un-headquarters-in-nairobi-kenya-is-a-great-place-to-work-to-learn-about-job/349028025115362/.

United Nations. *World Economic Situation and Prospects*, New York, 2019.

UN General Assembly. "2005 World Summit Outcome." A/RES/60/1. New York, 2005.

UN General Assembly. "Agenda Item 30: Environment and Human Settlements—Report of the Secretary-General." A/53/463. New York, 1998.

UN General Assembly. "Declaration of the United Nations Conference on the Human Environment (Stockholm Declaration)." A/CONF.48/14. In *United Nations Conference on the Human Environment*. Stockholm, 1972.

UN General Assembly. "Economic and Social Council Resolution 1346 (X.L.V.)." 1968.

UN General Assembly. "Environment and Human Settlements. Report of the Secretary-General." A/53/463. New York, 1998.

UN General Assembly. "Fund of the United Nations Environment Programme: Financial Report and Audited Financial Statements for the Biennum Ended 31 December 2013 and Report of the Board of Auditors." A/69/5/Add.7. New York, 2014.

UN General Assembly. "Fund of the United Nations Environment Programme: Financial Report and Audited Financial Statements for the Year Ended 31 December 2014 and Report of the Board of Auditors." A/70/5/Add.7. New York, 2015.

UN General Assembly. "Fund of the United Nations Environment Programme: Financial Report and Audited Financial Statements for the Year Ended 31 December 2015 and Report of the Board of Auditors." A/71/5/Add.7. New York, 2016.

UN General Assembly. "Fund of the United Nations Environment Programme: Financial Report and Audited Financial Statements for the Year Ended 31 December 2016 and Report of the Board of Auditors." A/72/5/Add.7. New York, 2017.

UN General Assembly. "Gaps in International Environmental Law and Environment-Related Instruments: Towards a Global Pact for the Environment." A/73/419. New York, 2018.

UN General Assembly. "In Larger Freedom: Towards Development, Security and Human Rights for All." A/59/2005. New York, 2005.

UN General Assembly. "Official Records: 1466th–1488th Meeting of the Second Committee," edited by Second Committee. New York, 1972.

UN General Assembly. "Process of Preparation of the Environmental Perspective to the Year 2000 and Beyond." A/Res/38/161. New York, 1983.

UN General Assembly. "Renewing the United Nations: A Programme for Reform." A/51/950. New York, 1997.

UN General Assembly. "Report of the Preparatory Committee for the United Nations Conference on the Human Environment on the 3rd Session." A/CONF.48/PC.13. New York, 1971.

UN General Assembly. "Report of the Secretary General on United Nations Committee of the Human Environment." A/CONF.48/PC.11. New York, 1971.

UN General Assembly. "Report on the United Nations Environment Programme's Session of a Special Character." In *Subcommittee Hearings*, New York, 1981.

UN General Assembly. "Resolution 2997 (XXVII) Institutional and Financial Arrangements for International Cooperation." New York, 1972.

UN General Assembly. "Resolution 3129 (XXVIII) On the Establishment of International Standards on Shared Resources." New York, 1973.

UN General Assembly. "Resolution 72/277 Towards a Global Pact for the Environment," A/72/L.51 & Add.1(as amended by A/72/L.53), New York, 2018.

UN General Assembly. "Restructuring of the Economic and Social Sectors of the United Nations System." A/Res/32/197." New York, 1977.

UN General Assembly. "Strengthening of the United Nations Environment Programme." A/Res/48/174. New York, 1993.

UN General Assembly. "Strengthening of the United Nations: An Agenda for Further Change." A/57/387. New York, 2002.

UN General Assembly. "Summary Record of the 1466th Meeting." Second Committee of the United Nations General Assembly. New York, 1972.

UN General Assembly. "Summary Record of the 1474th Meeting." Second Committee of the United Nations General Assembly. New York, 1972.

UN General Assembly. "Summary Record of the 1478th Meeting." Second Committee of the United Nations General Assembly. New York, 1972.

UN General Assembly. "Summary Record of the 1482nd Meeting." Second Committee of the United Nations General Assembly. New York, 1972.

UN General Assembly. "Summary Record of the 1483rd Meeting." Second Committee of the United Nations General Assembly. New York, 1972.

UN General Assembly. "Summary Record of the 1487th Meeting." Second Committee of the United Nations General Assembly. New York, 1972.

UN General Assembly. "Summary Record of the 1488th Meeting." Second Committee of the United Nations General Assembly. New York, 1972.

UN General Assembly. "United Nations Conference on the Human Environment: Report of the Second Committee." New York, 1972.

UN Information Service. "Preparatory Committee for Conference on Human Environment Completes General Debate." Geneva, 1971.

UN Information Service. "President Proposes Voluntary UN Environment Fund." Geneva, 1972.

UN Information Service. "Success of the Stockholm Conference: Statement by Russell E. Train, Chairman United States Delegation to the United Nations Conference on the Human Environment." Stockholm, 1972.

UNEP. "Annual Report 1998." Nairobi, 1998.

UNEP. "Annual Report 1999." Nairobi, 1999.

UNEP. "Annual Report 2000." Nairobi, 2000.

UNEP. "Annual Report 2001." Nairobi, 2001.

UNEP. "Annual Review." Nairobi, 1979.

UNEP. "Belgrade Process: Moving Forward with Developing a Set of Options on International Environmental Governance, Co-Chairs' Summary. Consultative Group of Ministers or High-level Representatives." Nairobi, 2009.

UNEP. "Biennial Report 1996–1997: UNEP's 25 for Life on Earth." Nairobi, 1997.

UNEP. "Building for the Future: A United Nations Showcase in Nairobi." Nairobi, 2011. https://wedocs.unep.org/bitstream/handle/20.500.11822/7859/Building-for-the-Future.pdf?sequence=3&%3BisAllowed=.

UNEP. "Emissions Gap Report." 2018.

UNEP. "First Global Multi-Agency Operation Highlights Widespread Marine Pollution Crime." Nairobi, 2018.

UNEP. Global Ministerial Environment Forum of UNEP, 26th session. UNEP/GC/26/1. Nairobi, 2010.

UNEP. "Governing Council Decision 6/1 Programme Policy and Implementation." Nairobi, 1978.

UNEP. "Governing Council Decision 17/38 on Improvement of Facilities at the United Nations Office at Nairobi." Nairobi, 1993.

UNEP. "Governing Council Decision 20/15. Assessment of the Functioning of the Secretariat of the United Nations Environment Programme." Nairobi, 1999.

UNEP. "Governing Council Decision 27/2 Implementation of Paragraph 88 of the Outcome Document of the United Nations Conference on Sustainable Development." Nairobi, 2013.

UNEP. "Human Resources Management Report." 2019. In the author's possession.

UNEP. "Internal Communication Survey Report." 2016. In the author's possession.

UNEP. "Medium-Term Strategy 2010–2013." Nairobi, 2008.

UNEP. "Medium-Term Strategy 2014–2017." Nairobi, 2015.

UNEP. "Nairobi-Helsinki Outcome." Consultative Group of Ministers or High-level Representatives. Nairobi, 2010.

UNEP. "Nairobi Declaration on the Role and Mandate of United Nations Environment Prorgamme." UNEP/GC19/1/1997. Paper presented at the Nineteenth Session of the United Nations Governing Council, New York, 1997.

UNEP. "Policy Statement by Achim Steiner at the Opening of the Governing Council/Global Ministerial Environment Forum at its Eleventh Special Session." Bali, Indonesia, 2010.

UNEP. "Proceedings of the Governing Council at its Nineteenth Session." UNEP. GC/19/34. Nairobi, 1997.

UNEP. "Review of Major Achievements in the Implementation of the Stockholm Action Plan." UNEP/GC.10/6/Add.1. Nairobi, 1982.

UNEP. "Sustainable Travel in the United Nations." UNEP DTIE, Sustainable Production and Consumption Branch. Paris, 2010.

UNEP. "UN Reform. Implications for the Environment Pillar." UNEP/Ded/040506. Nairobi, 2006.

UNEP. "Understanding Synergies and Mainstreaming Among the Biodiversity Related Conventions: A Special Contributory Volume by Key Biodiversity Convention Secretariats and Scientific Bodies." Nairobi, 2016.

UNEP. United Nations Environment Programme: Highlights of the Biennium, 1994–1995. UNEP/GC/19/INF.16. Nairobi, 1995.

UNEP. *World Atlas of Desertification*. Baltimore: Edward Arnold, 1992.

UNEP Evaluation and Oversight Unit. "1985–1986 Evaluation Report." Nairobi, 1986.

UNEP Evaluation and Oversight Unit. "Formative Evaluation of the UNEP Medium-Term Strategy 2014–2017: A Review of UNEP Programming Processes and Documents." Nairobi, 2015.

UNEP Evaluation and Oversight Unit. "Management Study on Trust Funds and Counterpart Contributions." Nairobi, 1999.

UNEP Evaluation and Oversight Unit. "Mid-Term Evaluation of UNEP's Medium-Term Strategy 2010–2013." Nairobi, 2013.

UNEP and WMO. *Integrated Assessment of Black Carbon and Tropospheric Ozone*. Nairobi: 2011.

UNEP and CCAC. *Time to Act to Reduce Short-Lived Climate Pollutants*. Paris: 2014.

UN Information Service. "Preparatory Committee for Conference on Human Environment Completes General Debate." Geneva, 1971.

UN Population Information Network (POPIN). "Statement of UNEP, Mrs. Elizabeth Dowdeswell." 1994.

US Congress. "After the Cold War: Living with Lower Defense Spending," OTA-ITE-524, Washington, DC: US Government Printing Office, 1992.

US Congress, House Committee on Foreign Affairs, Subcommittee on International Organizations and Movements. "Participation by the United States in the United Nations Environment Program: Hearings Before the Subcommittee on International Organizations and Movements of the Committee on Foreign Affairs, House of Representatives, Ninety-third Congress, first session, on H.R. 5696," April 5 and 10, 1973. Washington, DC: U.S. Govt. Print. Off., 1973.

US Mission to the UN. "Statement by Christian A. Herter, Jr., United States Representative, in the Preparatory Committee for the United Nations Conference on the Human Environment, on Item 4, International Organizational Implications." New York, NY, 1972.

US Secretary of State's Advisory Committee on the 1972 United Nations Conference on the Human Environment. "Stockholm and Beyond: Report." Washington, DC, 1972.

Urho, Niko. Interview by the author, 2019.

Urho, Niko, Maria Ivanova, Anna Dubrova, and Natalia Escobar-Pemberthy. *International Environmental Governance: Accomplishments and Way Forward*. Copenhagen: Nordic Council of Ministers, 2019. http://norden.diva-portal.org/smash/get/diva2:1289927/FULLTEXT01.pdf.

van der Hel, Sandra, and Frank Biermann. "The Authority of Science in Sustainability Governance: A Structured Comparison of Six Science Institutions Engaged with the Sustainable Development Goals." *Environmental Science and Policy* 77 (2017): 211–220. https://doi.org/10.1016/j.envsci.2017.03.008.

VanDeveer, Stacy D. "Protecting Europe's Seas: Lessons from the Last 25 Years." *Environment: Science and Policy for Sustainable Development* 42, no. 6 (2000): 10–26.

VanDeveer, Stacy D., and Geoffrey D. Dabelko. "It's Capacity, Stupid: International Assistance and National Implementation." *Global Environmental Politics* 1, no. 2 (2001): 18–29.

Venzke, Ingo. "International Bureaucracies from a Political Science Perspective—Agency, Authority and International Institutional Law." In *The Exercise of Public Authority by International Institutions: Advancing International Institutional Law*, edited by Armin von Bogdandy, Rüdiger Wolfrum, Jochen von Bernstorff, Philipp Dann, and Matthias Goldmann, 67–98. Berlin: Springer, 2010.

Verón, Santiago R., Jose M. Paruelo, and Martín Oesterheld. "Assessing Desertification." *Journal of Arid Environments* 66, no. 4 (2006): 751–763. https://doi.org/10.1016/j.jaridenv.2006.01.021.

von Moltke, Konrad. "Why UNEP Matters." In *Green Globe Yearbook*, edited by Helge Ole Bergesen and Georg Parmann, 55–64. Oxford: Oxford University Press, 1996.

von Moltke, Konrad. "The Organization of the Impossible." *Global Environmental Politics* 1, no. 1 (2001): 23–28.

Waiguru, Anne. "Corruption and patronage politics: The case of 'Harambee' in Kenya." *Transparency International*, 2002.

Ward, Barbara. "A Decade of Environmental Action." *Environment* 24, no. 4 (1982): 4–5.

Ward, Barbara. "Only One Earth, Stockholm 1972." Reprinted in *Evidence for Hope: The Search for Sustainable Development: The Story of the International Institute for Environment and Development, 1972–2002*, edited by Nigel Cross. Earthscan, 2003.

Ward, Barbara. *Progress for a Small Planet.* New York, London: W. W. Norton: 1982.

Waugh, David. *Geography: An Integrated Approach*. Oxford: Oxford University Press, 2014.

Weber, Henry S., and Mikael Karlström. *Why Community Investment is Good for Nonprofit Anchor Institutions: Understanding Costs, Benefits, and the Range of Strategic Options*. Chicago: Chapin Hall at the University of Chicago, 2009.

Weinlich, Silke. *The UN Secretariat's Influence on the Evolution of Peacekeeping*. Basingstoke, UK: Palgrave Macmillan, 2014.

Weiss, Thomas G. *What's Wrong with the United Nations and How to Fix It.* Oxford: Polity Press, 2016.

Weiss, Thomas G. *Would the World Be Better Without the UN?* Oxford: Polity Press, 2018.

Weiss, Thomas G., and Danielle A. Zach. "Virtual issue: 70 years of the United Nations in *International Affairs*." Oxford University Press, 2018. https://doi.org/10.1093/ia/iiy040.

Weiss, Thomas G., and Pallavi Roy. *The UN and the Global South, 1945 and 2015*. London: Routledge, 2017.

Weiss, Thomas G., and Rorden Wilkinson. *International Organization and Global Governance*. London: Routledge, 2018.

Weiss, Thomas G., and Rorden Wilkinson. *Rethinking Global Governance*. Oxford: Polity Press, 2019.

Wendt, Alexander E. "The Agent-Structure Problem in International Relations Theory." *International Organization* 41, no. 3 (1987): 335–370. https://doi.org/10.1017/S002081830002751X.

Wetang'ula, Moses. "Kenya's Diplomacy Has Come of Age." In *Kenya's Fifty Years of Diplomatic Engagement: From Kenyatta to Kenyatta*, edited by Kipyego Cheluget. Nairobi: Moran Publishers and Worldreader, 2018.

Whetten, David A. "Effective Administrators: Good Management on the College Campus." *Change: The Magazine of Higher Education* 16, no. 8 (1984): 38–43.

White, Robert M. "The World Climate Conference: Report by the Conference Chairman." *WMO Bulletin* 28, no. 3 (1979).

Wightman, David. "United Nations Conference on the Human Environment: The International Organisational Implications of Action Proposals: Second Draft." In the author's possession, n.d.

Wilson, James. *Bureaucracy: What Government Agencies Do and Why They Do It*. New York: Basic Books, 1989.

WMO. "The Changing Atmosphere. Implications for Global Security No. 710." Geneva, 1989.

WMO. *Report of the International Conference on the Assessment of the Role of Carbon Dioxide and of Other Greenhouse Gases in Climate Variations and Associated Impacts, No. 661*. Geneva, 1986.

WMO. "World Climate Programme." http://www.wmo.int/pages/prog/wcp/wcp.html.

World Bank. "Violence in the City: Understanding and Supporting Community Responses to Urban Violence." Washington, DC, 2011.

World Bank. "World Bank Data: Kenya." https://data.worldbank.org/country/kenya.

World Commission on Environment and Development. *Report of the World Commission on Environment and Development: Our Common Future*. Geneva, 1987.

XinhuaNet. "China Sets Example in Sustainable Development: UN Environment." *Xinhua*, December 10, 2018. http://www.xinhuanet.com//english/2017-12/10/c_136815369.htm.

Yi, Yunae. Interview by the author, 2017.

Young, Oran R. "Political Leadership and Regime Formation: On the Development of Institutions in International Society." *International Organization* 45, no. 3 (1991): 281–308.

Zammit Cutajar, Michael. Interview by the author, 2017.

Zegart, Amy B. *Flawed by Design: The Evolution of the CIA, JCS, and NSC*. Stanford, CA: Stanford University Press, 1999.

Zillman, John. "A History of Climate Activities." *WMO Bulletin* 58, no. 3 (2009): 141–150.

INDEX